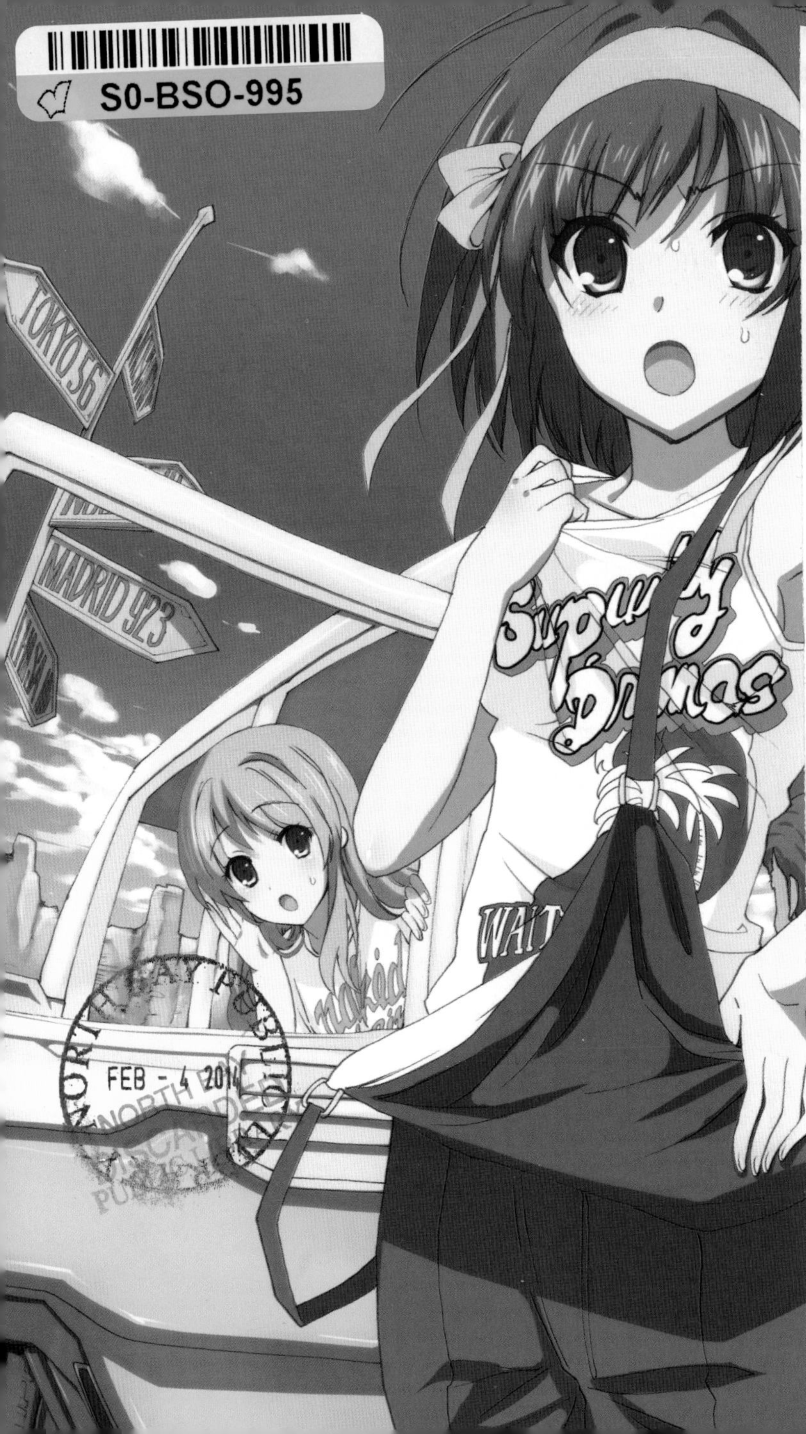
TOKYO 56
MADRID 923

CONTENTS

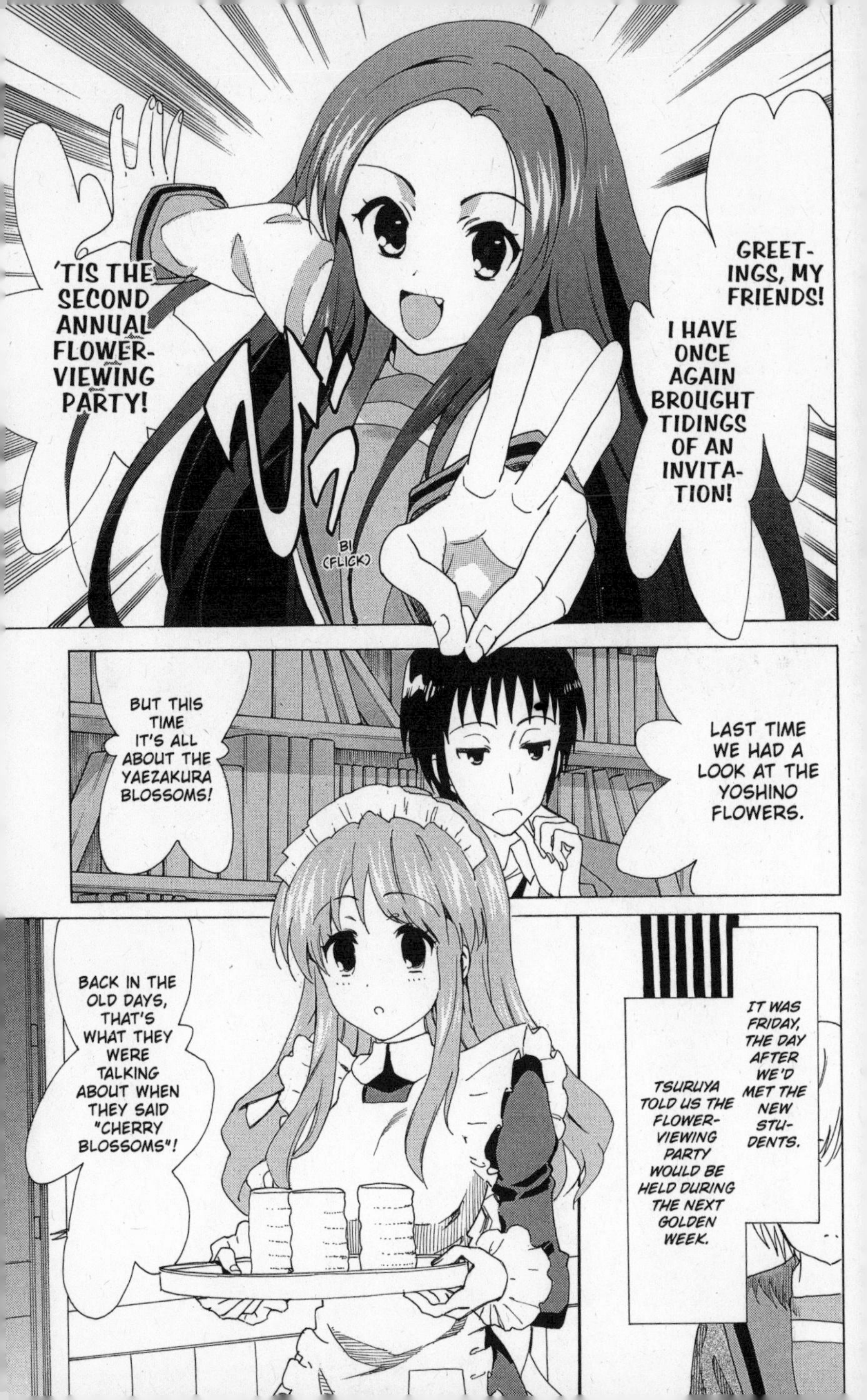

GREETINGS, MY FRIENDS!
I HAVE ONCE AGAIN BROUGHT TIDINGS OF AN INVITATION!
'TIS THE SECOND ANNUAL FLOWER-VIEWING PARTY!
BI (FLICK)
LAST TIME WE HAD A LOOK AT THE YOSHINO FLOWERS.
BUT THIS TIME IT'S ALL ABOUT THE YAEZAKURA BLOSSOMS!
IT WAS FRIDAY, THE DAY AFTER WE'D MET THE NEW STUDENTS.
TSURUYA TOLD US THE FLOWER-VIEWING PARTY WOULD BE HELD DURING THE NEXT GOLDEN WEEK.
BACK IN THE OLD DAYS, THAT'S WHAT THEY WERE TALKING ABOUT WHEN THEY SAID "CHERRY BLOSSOMS"!

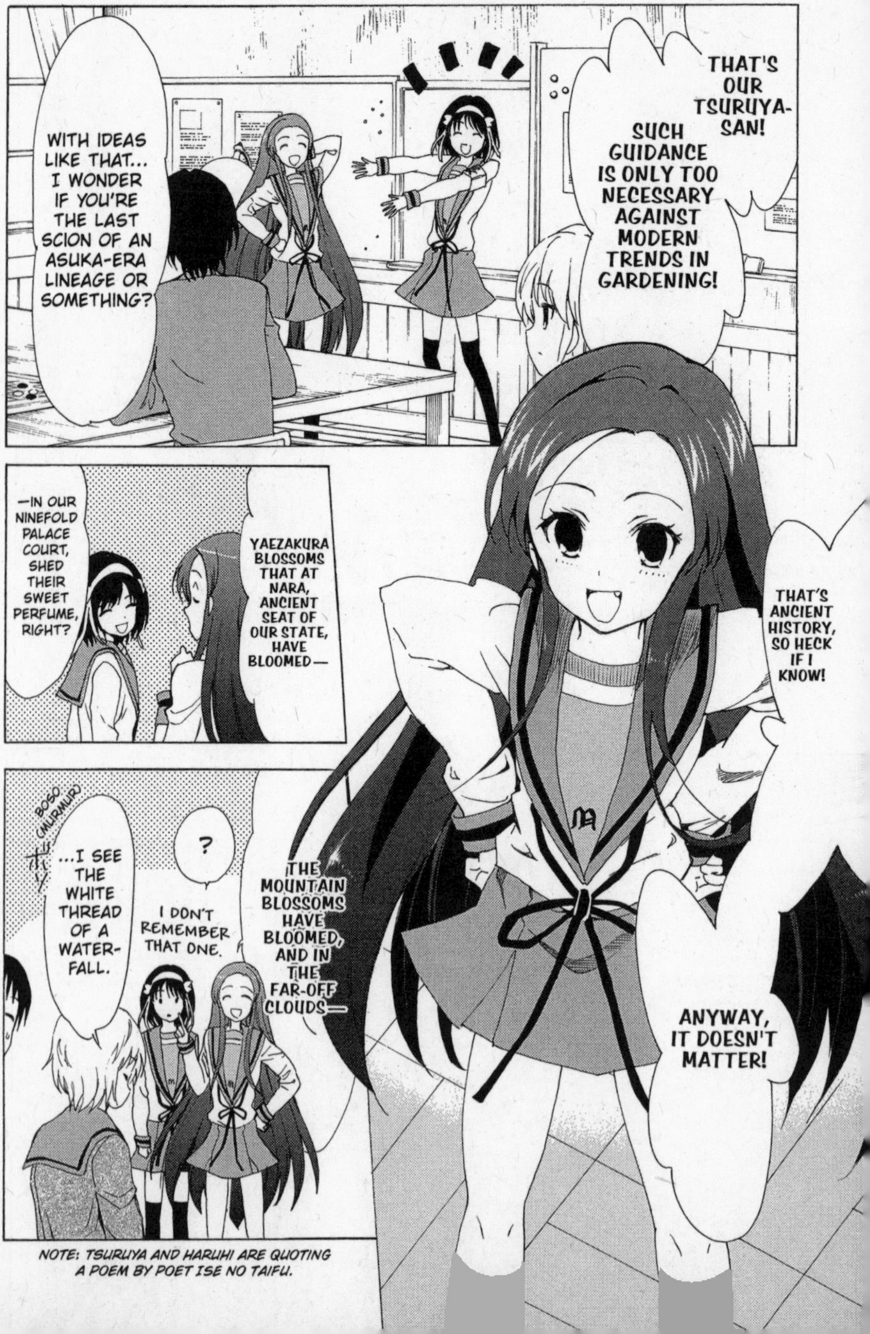
THAT'S OUR TSURUYA-SAN!
SUCH GUIDANCE IS ONLY TOO NECESSARY AGAINST MODERN TRENDS IN GARDENING!
WITH IDEAS LIKE THAT... I WONDER IF YOU'RE THE LAST SCION OF AN ASUKA-ERA LINEAGE OR SOMETHING?
THAT'S ANCIENT HISTORY, SO HECK IF I KNOW!
ANYWAY, IT DOESN'T MATTER!
YAEZAKURA BLOSSOMS THAT AT NARA, ANCIENT SEAT OF OUR STATE, HAVE BLOOMED—
—IN OUR NINEFOLD PALACE COURT, SHED THEIR SWEET PERFUME, RIGHT?
THE MOUNTAIN BLOSSOMS HAVE BLOOMED, AND IN THE FAR-OFF CLOUDS—
?
I DON'T REMEMBER THAT ONE.
...I SEE THE WHITE THREAD OF A WATER-FALL.
BOSO (MURMUR)

NOTE: TSURUYA AND HARUHI ARE QUOTING A POEM BY POET ISE NO TAIFU.

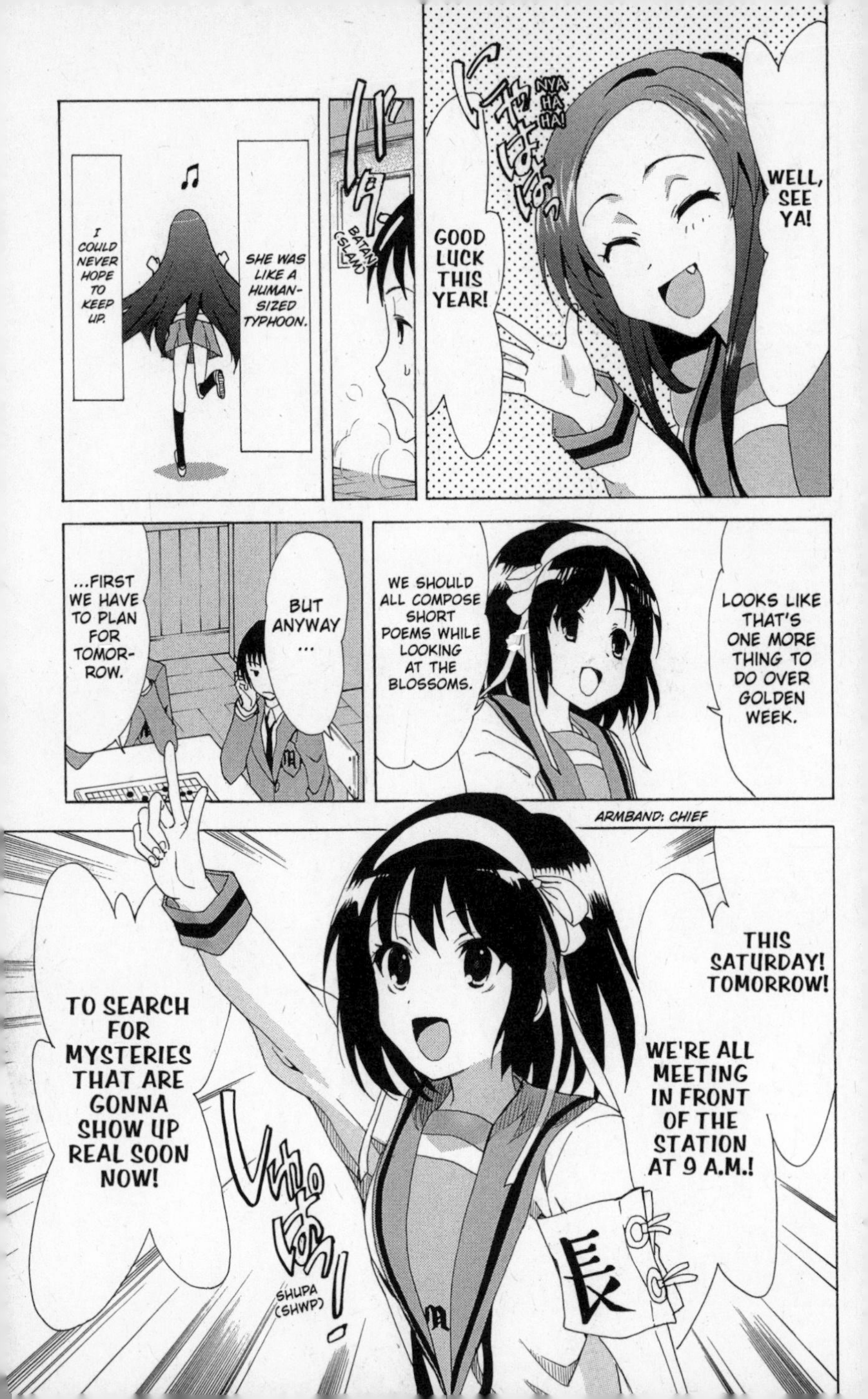
WELL, SEE YA!
NYA HA HA!
GOOD LUCK THIS YEAR!
BATAN (SLAM)
SHE WAS LIKE A HUMAN-SIZED TYPHOON.
I COULD NEVER HOPE TO KEEP UP.
LOOKS LIKE THAT'S ONE MORE THING TO DO OVER GOLDEN WEEK.
WE SHOULD ALL COMPOSE SHORT POEMS WHILE LOOKING AT THE BLOSSOMS.
BUT ANYWAY...
...FIRST WE HAVE TO PLAN FOR TOMORROW.
ARMBAND: CHIEF
THIS SATURDAY! TOMORROW!
WE'RE ALL MEETING IN FRONT OF THE STATION AT 9 A.M.!
TO SEARCH FOR MYSTERIES THAT ARE GONNA SHOW UP REAL SOON NOW!
SHUPA (SHWP)

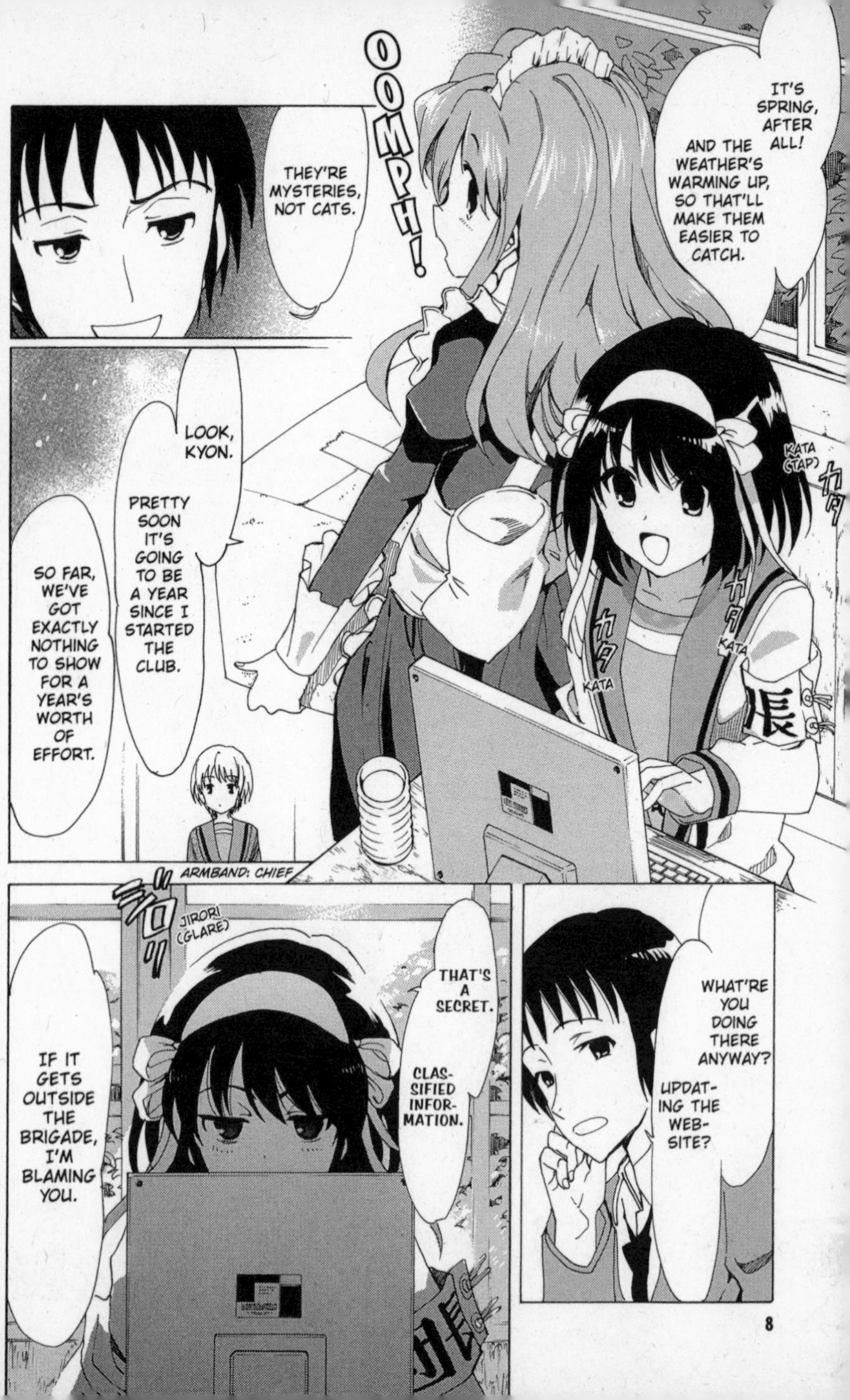
IT'S SPRING, AFTER ALL!
AND THE WEATHER'S WARMING UP, SO THAT'LL MAKE THEM EASIER TO CATCH.
OOMPH!
KATA (TAP)
KATA
KATA
ARMBAND: CHIEF
THEY'RE MYSTERIES, NOT CATS.
LOOK, KYON.
PRETTY SOON IT'S GOING TO BE A YEAR SINCE I STARTED THE CLUB.
SO FAR, WE'VE GOT EXACTLY NOTHING TO SHOW FOR A YEAR'S WORTH OF EFFORT.
WHAT'RE YOU DOING THERE ANYWAY?
UPDATING THE WEBSITE?
JIRORI (GLARE)
THAT'S A SECRET.
CLASSIFIED INFORMATION.
IF IT GETS OUTSIDE THE BRIGADE, I'M BLAMING YOU.

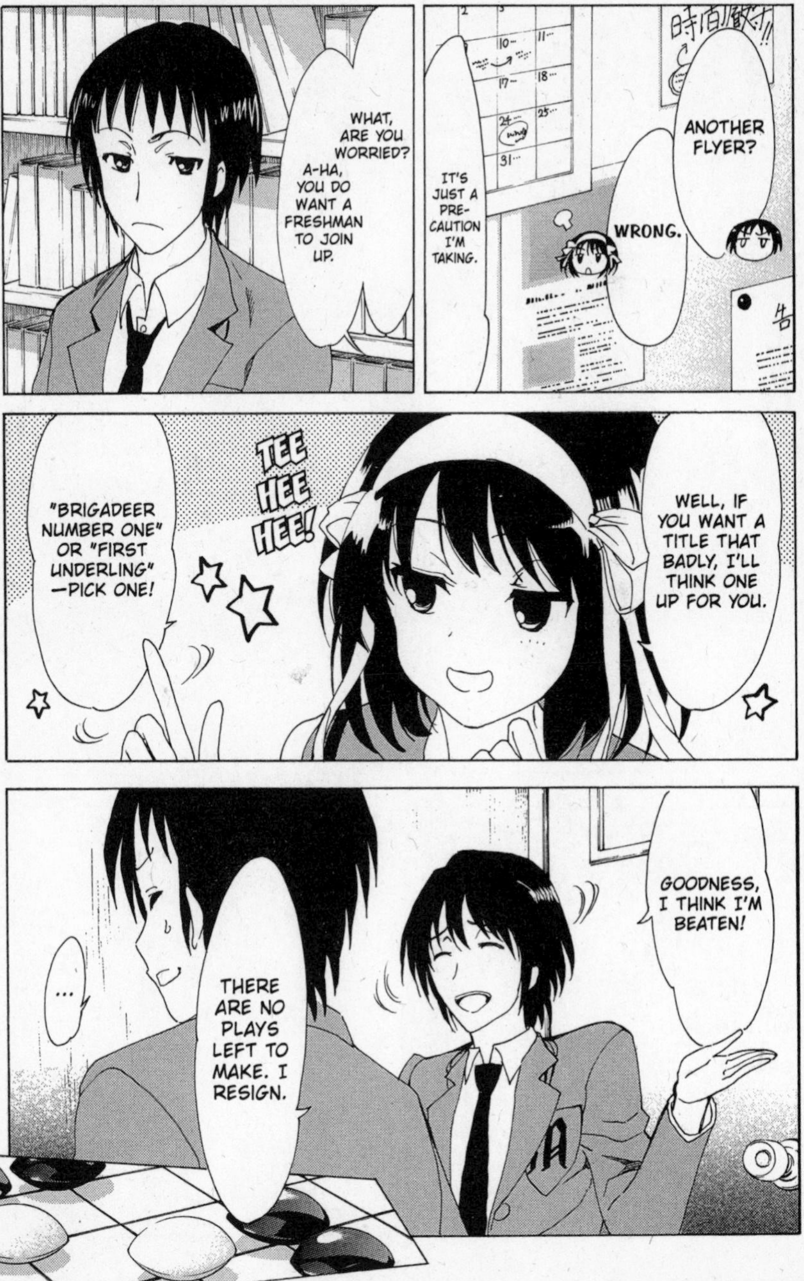
ANOTHER FLYER?
WRONG.
IT'S JUST A PRE-CAUTION I'M TAKING.
WHAT, ARE YOU WORRIED? A-HA, YOU DO WANT A FRESHMAN TO JOIN UP.
WELL, IF YOU WANT A TITLE THAT BADLY, I'LL THINK ONE UP FOR YOU.
TEE HEE HEE!
"BRIGADEER NUMBER ONE" OR "FIRST UNDERLING" —PICK ONE!
GOODNESS, I THINK I'M BEATEN!
THERE ARE NO PLAYS LEFT TO MAKE. I RESIGN.
...

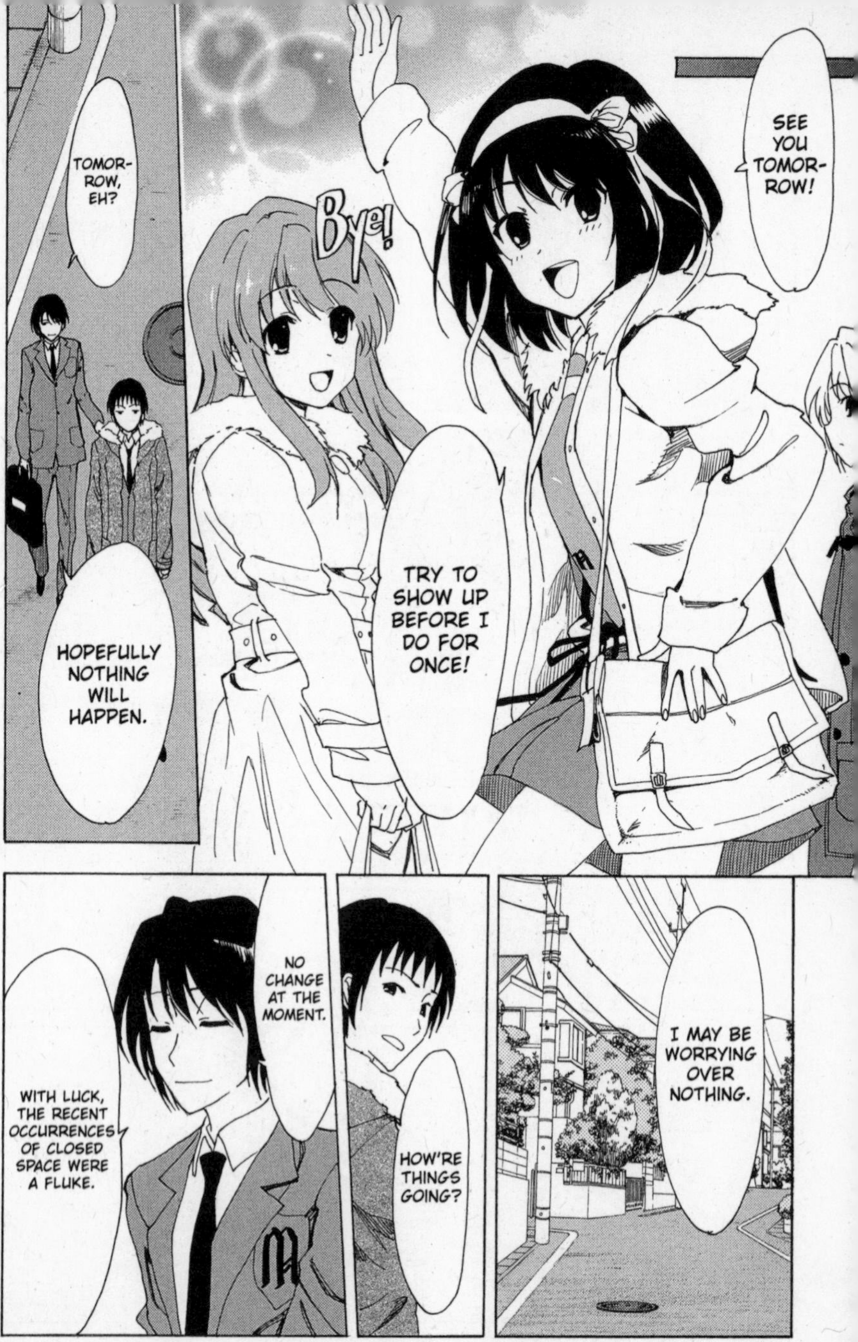
SEE YOU TOMORROW!
Bye!
TRY TO SHOW UP BEFORE I DO FOR ONCE!
TOMORROW, EH?
HOPEFULLY NOTHING WILL HAPPEN.
I MAY BE WORRYING OVER NOTHING.
HOW'RE THINGS GOING?
NO CHANGE AT THE MOMENT.
WITH LUCK, THE RECENT OCCURRENCES OF CLOSED SPACE WERE A FLUKE.

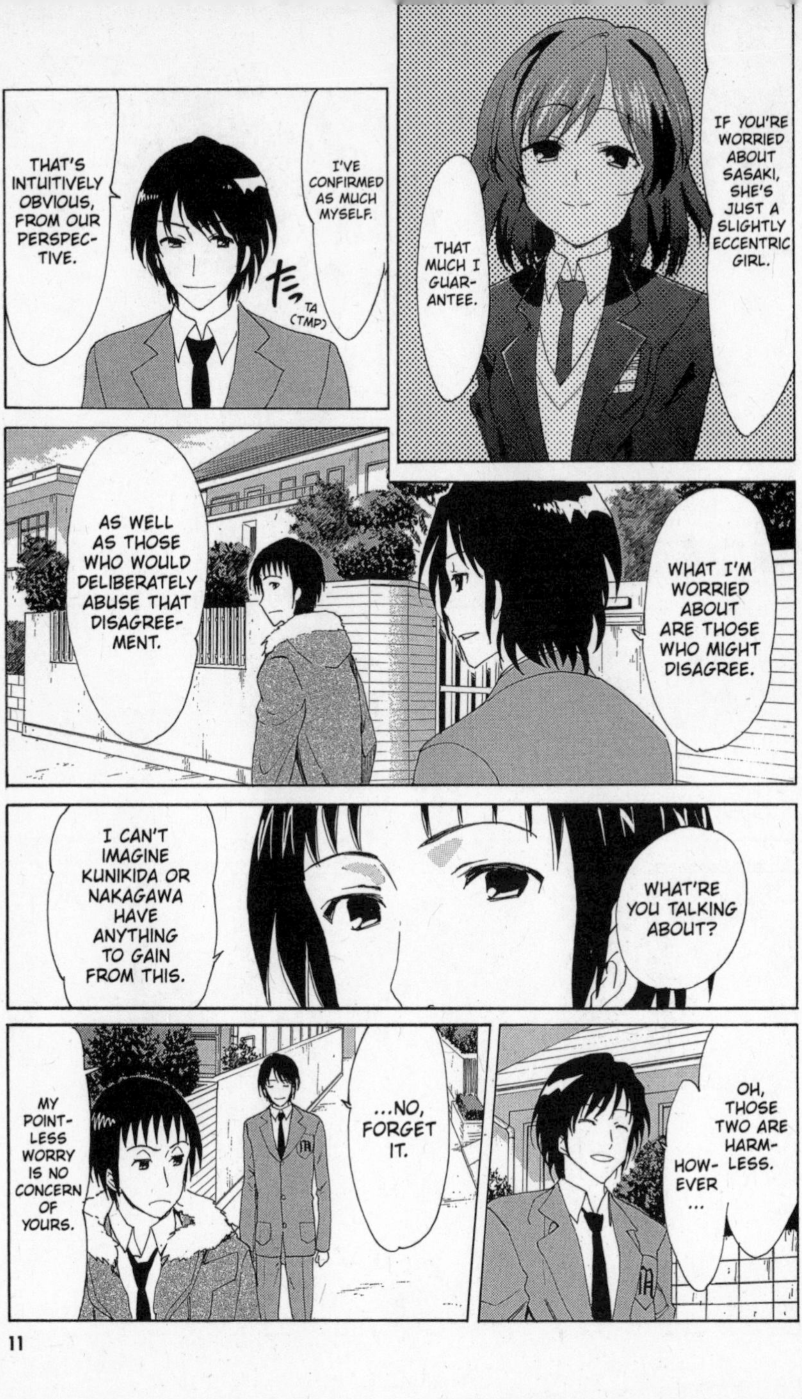
IF YOU'RE WORRIED ABOUT SASAKI, SHE'S JUST A SLIGHTLY ECCENTRIC GIRL.
THAT MUCH I GUAR-ANTEE.
I'VE CONFIRMED AS MUCH MYSELF.
TA (TMP)
THAT'S INTUITIVELY OBVIOUS, FROM OUR PERSPEC-TIVE.
WHAT I'M WORRIED ABOUT ARE THOSE WHO MIGHT DISAGREE.
AS WELL AS THOSE WHO WOULD DELIBERATELY ABUSE THAT DISAGREE-MENT.
WHAT'RE YOU TALKING ABOUT?
I CAN'T IMAGINE KUNIKIDA OR NAKAGAWA HAVE ANYTHING TO GAIN FROM THIS.
OH, THOSE TWO ARE HARM-LESS.
HOW-EVER ...
...NO, FORGET IT.
MY POINT-LESS WORRY IS NO CONCERN OF YOURS.

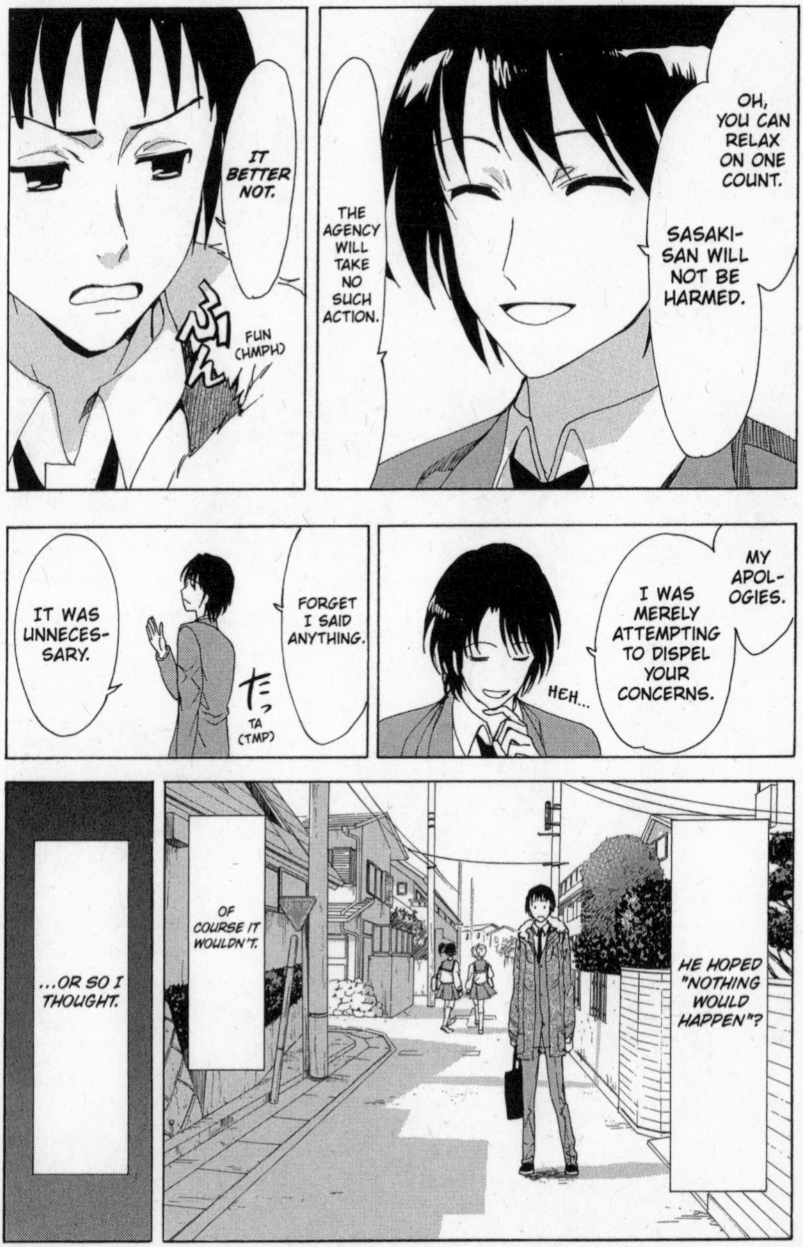
OH, YOU CAN RELAX ON ONE COUNT.
SASAKI-SAN WILL NOT BE HARMED.
THE AGENCY WILL TAKE NO SUCH ACTION.
IT BETTER NOT.
ふん
FUN (HMPH)
MY APOLOGIES.
I WAS MERELY ATTEMPTING TO DISPEL YOUR CONCERNS.
HEH...
FORGET I SAID ANYTHING.
IT WAS UNNECESSARY.
たっ
TA (TMP)
HE HOPED "NOTHING WOULD HAPPEN"?
OF COURSE IT WOULDN'T.
...OR SO I THOUGHT.

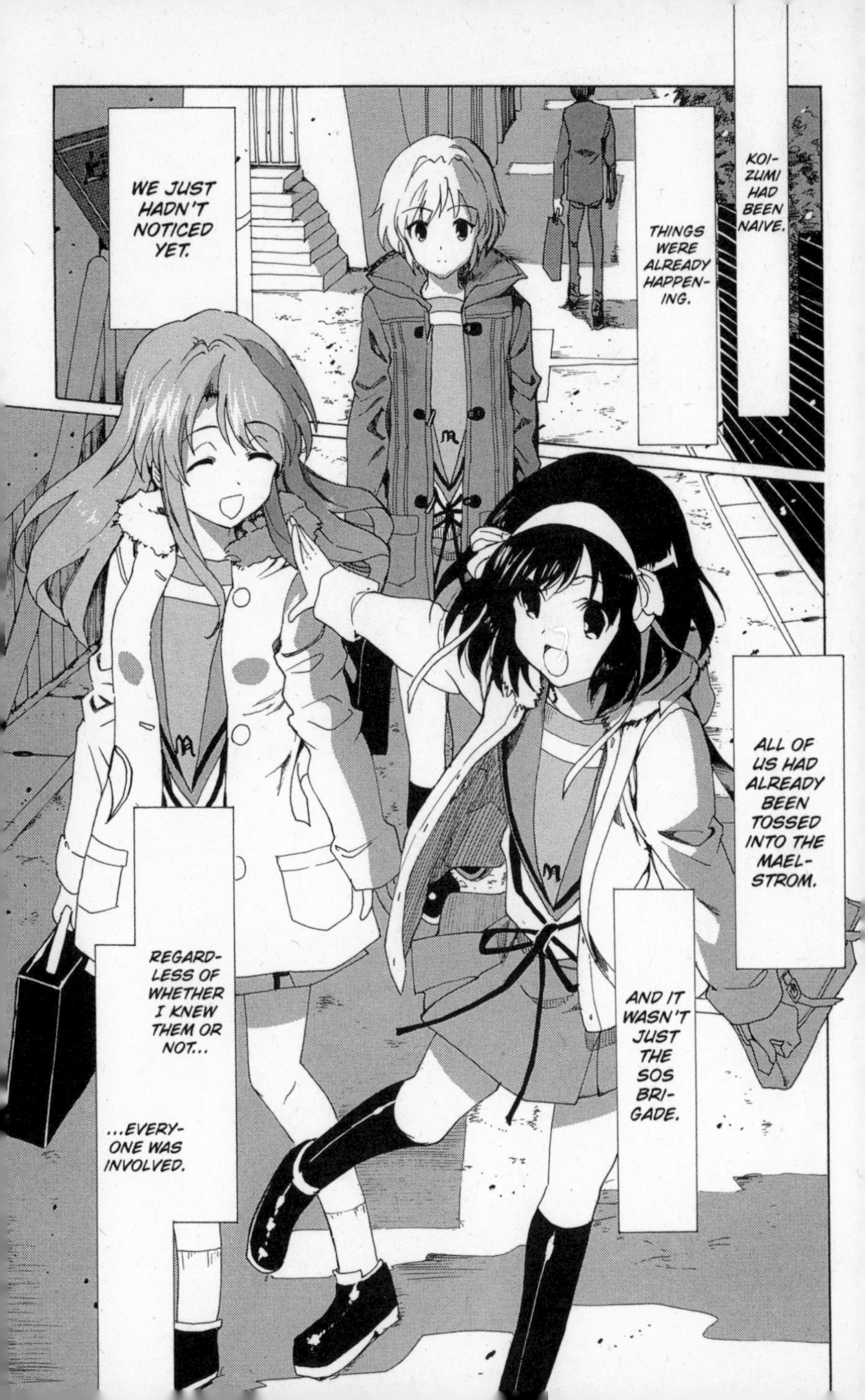
KOIZUMI HAD BEEN NAIVE.
THINGS WERE ALREADY HAPPENING.
WE JUST HADN'T NOTICED YET.
ALL OF US HAD ALREADY BEEN TOSSED INTO THE MAELSTROM.
AND IT WASN'T JUST THE SOS BRIGADE.
REGARDLESS OF WHETHER I KNEW THEM OR NOT...
...EVERYONE WAS INVOLVED.

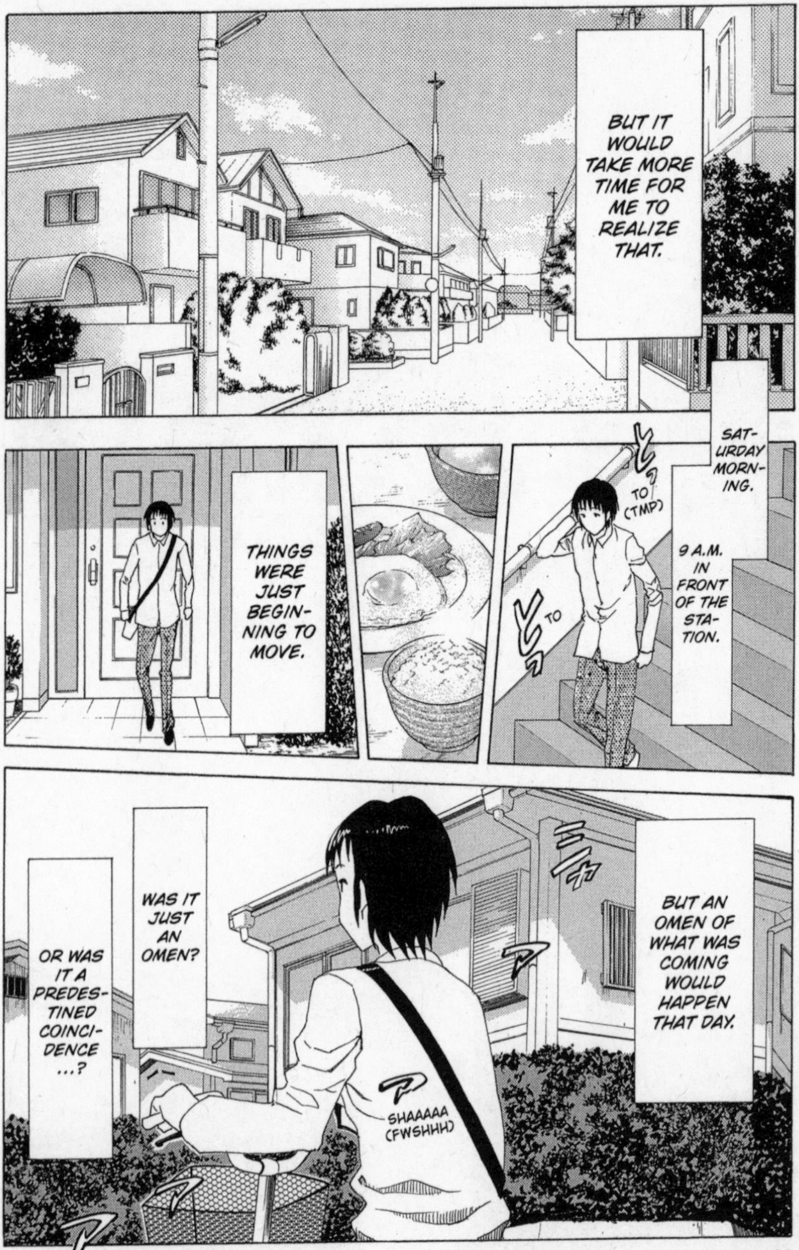
BUT IT WOULD TAKE MORE TIME FOR ME TO REALIZE THAT.
SATURDAY MORNING.
9 A.M. IN FRONT OF THE STATION.
TO (TMP)
TO
THINGS WERE JUST BEGINNING TO MOVE.
BUT AN OMEN OF WHAT WAS COMING WOULD HAPPEN THAT DAY.
SHAAAAA (FWSHHH)
WAS IT JUST AN OMEN?
OR WAS IT A PREDESTINED COINCIDENCE ...?

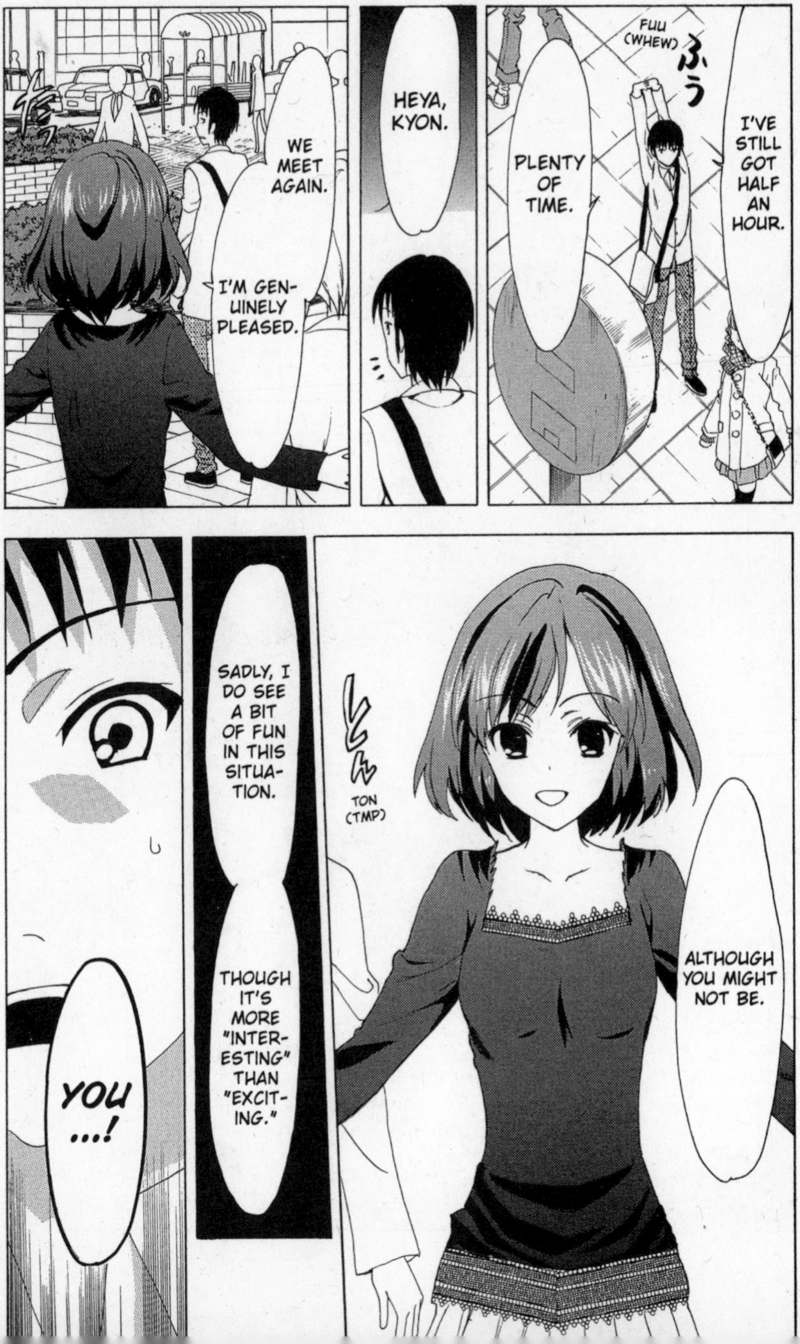
ふう
FUU (WHEW)
I'VE STILL GOT HALF AN HOUR.
PLENTY OF TIME.
HEYA, KYON.
WE MEET AGAIN.
I'M GENUINELY PLEASED.
ALTHOUGH YOU MIGHT NOT BE.
とん
TON (TMP)
SADLY, I DO SEE A BIT OF FUN IN THIS SITUATION.
THOUGH IT'S MORE "INTERESTING" THAN "EXCITING."
YOU ...!

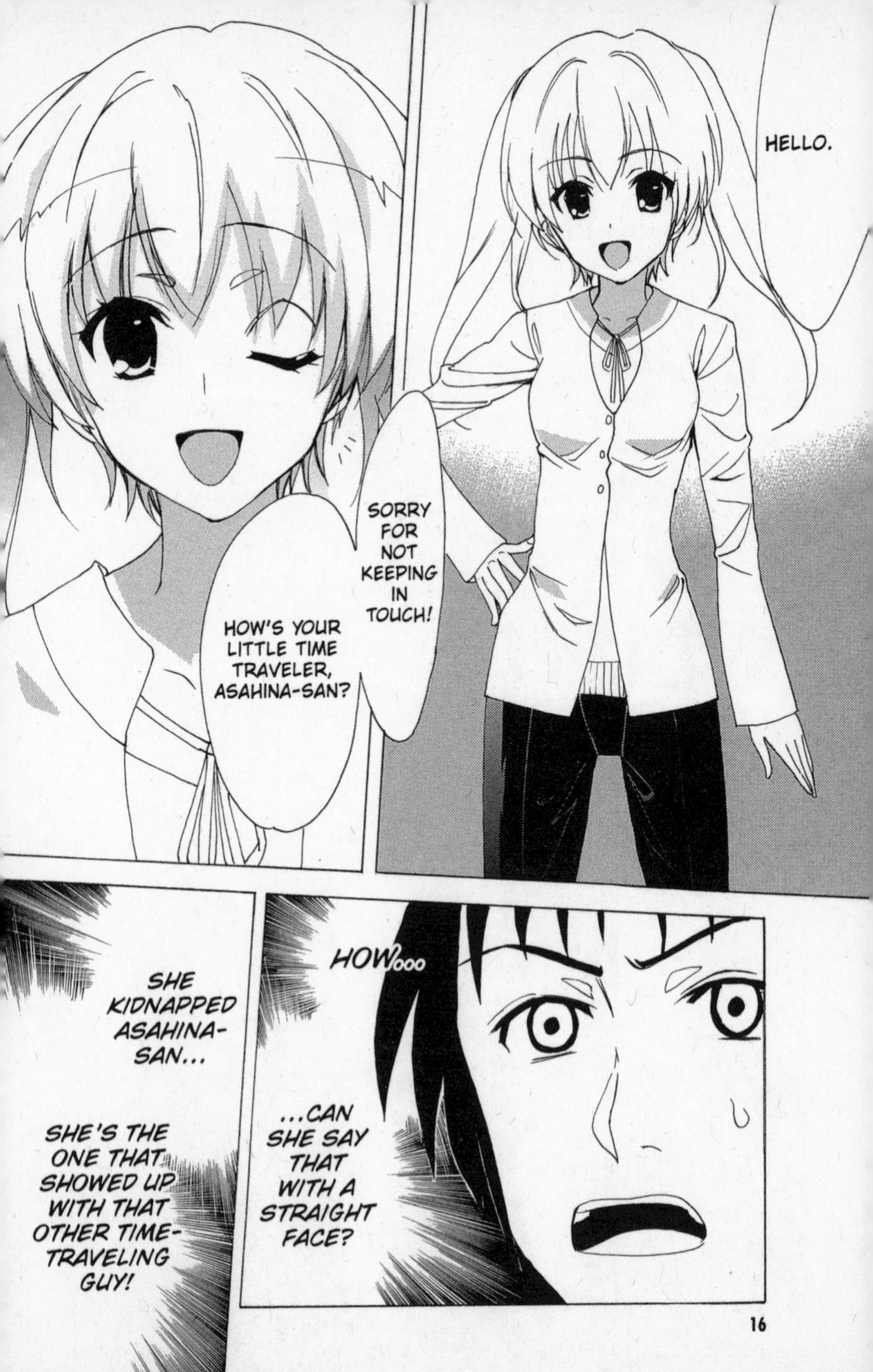
HELLO.
SORRY FOR NOT KEEPING IN TOUCH!
HOW'S YOUR LITTLE TIME TRAVELER, ASAHINA-SAN?
HOW...
...CAN SHE SAY THAT WITH A STRAIGHT FACE?
SHE KIDNAPPED ASAHINA-SAN...
SHE'S THE ONE THAT SHOWED UP WITH THAT OTHER TIME-TRAVELING GUY!

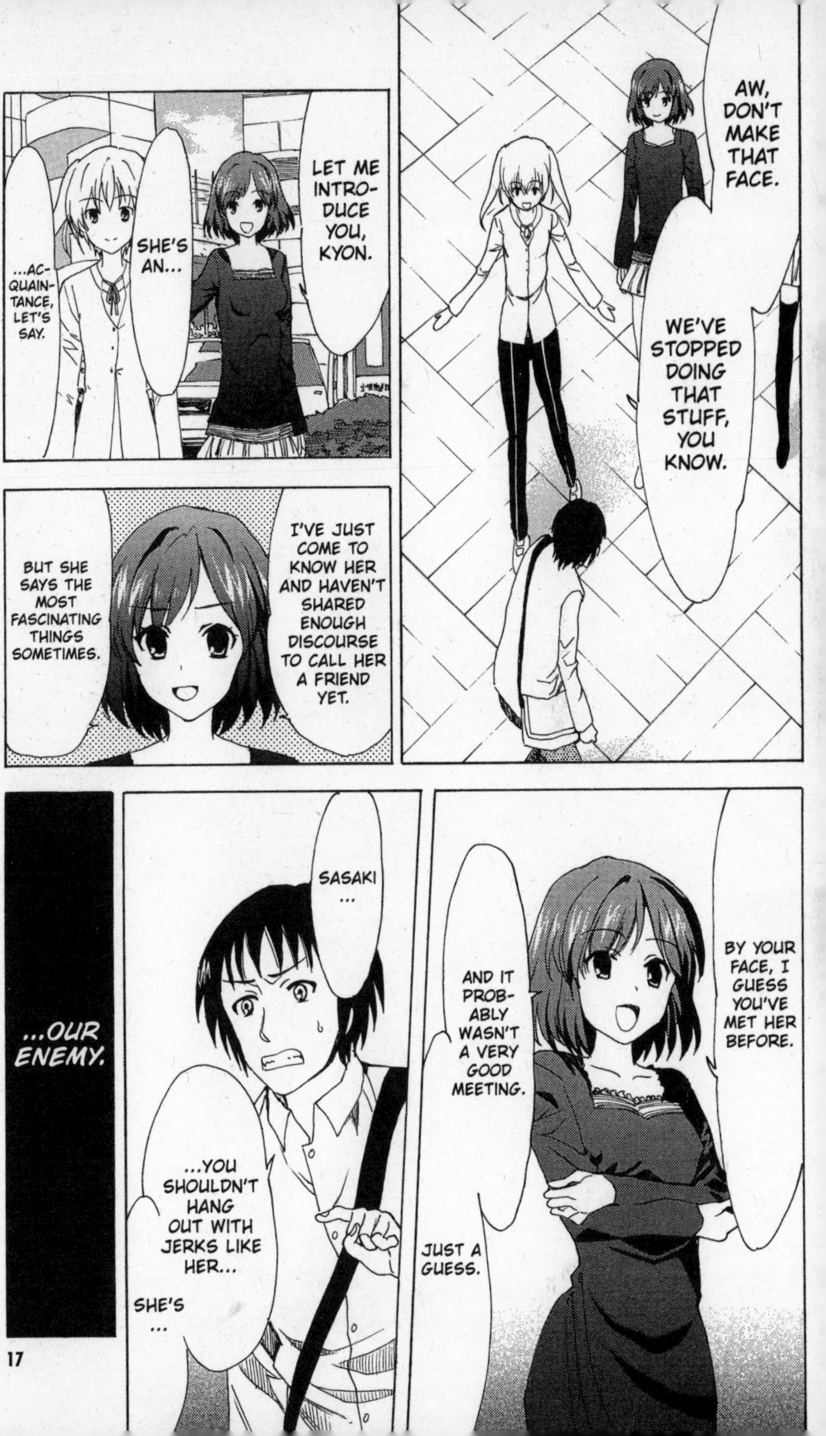

AW, DON'T MAKE THAT FACE.
WE'VE STOPPED DOING THAT STUFF, YOU KNOW.
LET ME INTRO-DUCE YOU, KYON.
SHE'S AN...
...AC-QUAIN-TANCE, LET'S SAY.
I'VE JUST COME TO KNOW HER AND HAVEN'T SHARED ENOUGH DISCOURSE TO CALL HER A FRIEND YET.
BUT SHE SAYS THE MOST FASCINATING THINGS SOMETIMES.
BY YOUR FACE, I GUESS YOU'VE MET HER BEFORE.
AND IT PROB-ABLY WASN'T A VERY GOOD MEETING.
JUST A GUESS.
SASAKI ...
...YOU SHOULDN'T HANG OUT WITH JERKS LIKE HER...
SHE'S ...
...OUR ENEMY.

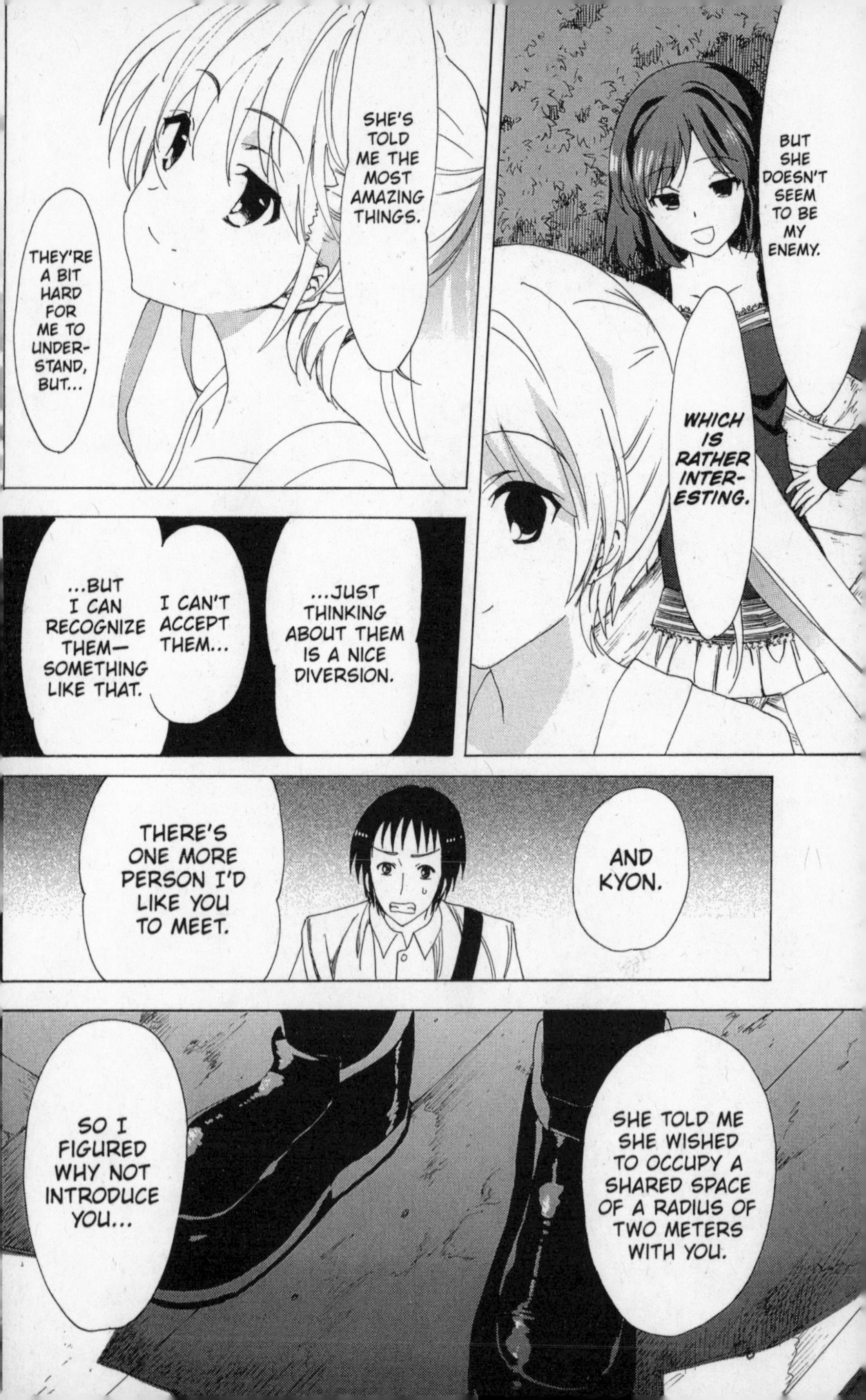
BUT SHE DOESN'T SEEM TO BE MY ENEMY.
WHICH IS RATHER INTER-ESTING.
SHE'S TOLD ME THE MOST AMAZING THINGS.
THEY'RE A BIT HARD FOR ME TO UNDER-STAND, BUT...
...JUST THINKING ABOUT THEM IS A NICE DIVERSION.
I CAN'T ACCEPT THEM...
...BUT I CAN RECOGNIZE THEM— SOMETHING LIKE THAT.
AND KYON.
THERE'S ONE MORE PERSON I'D LIKE YOU TO MEET.
SHE TOLD ME SHE WISHED TO OCCUPY A SHARED SPACE OF A RADIUS OF TWO METERS WITH YOU.
SO I FIGURED WHY NOT INTRODUCE YOU...

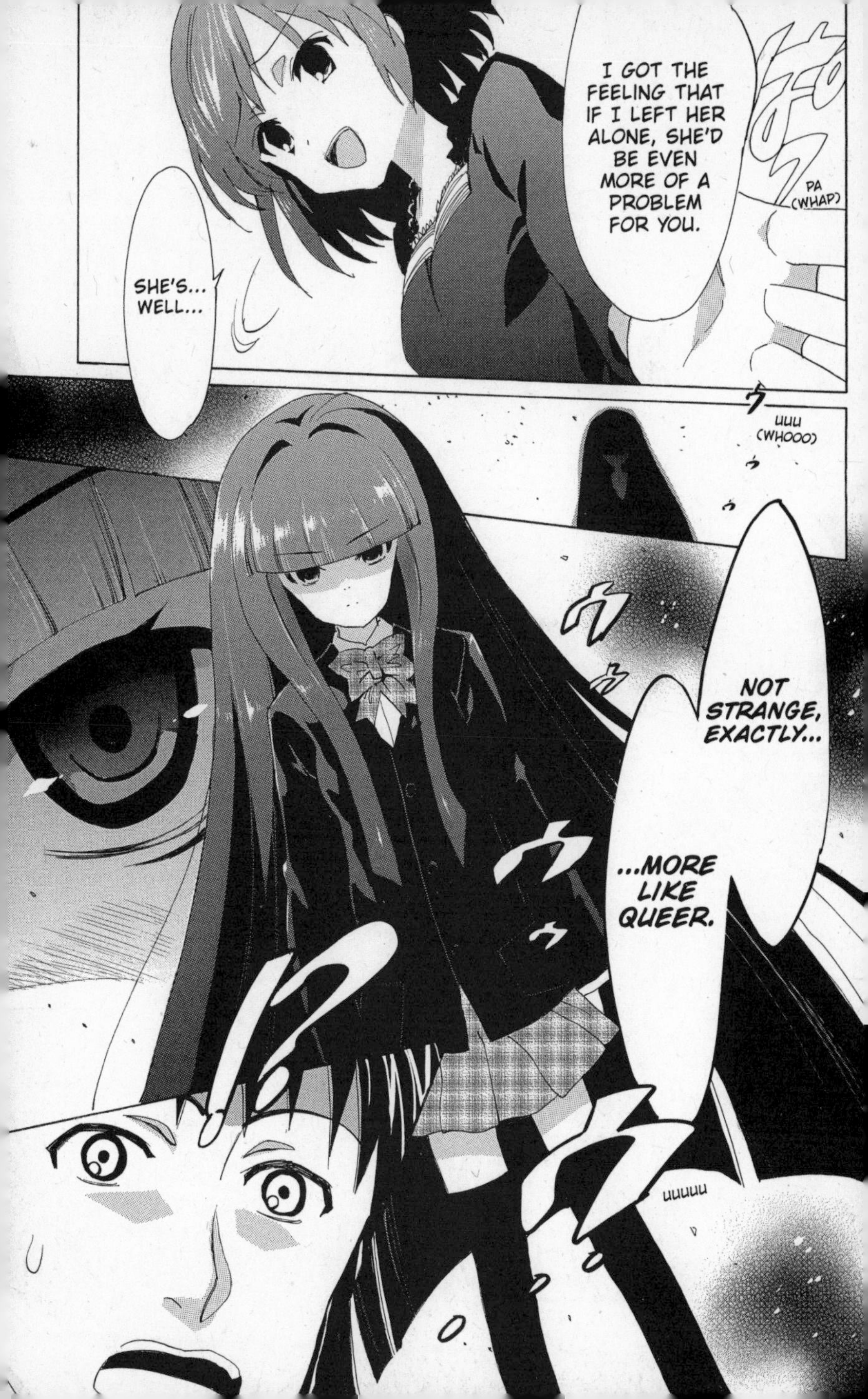
PA (WHAP)
I GOT THE FEELING THAT IF I LEFT HER ALONE, SHE'D BE EVEN MORE OF A PROBLEM FOR YOU.
SHE'S... WELL...
uuu (WHOOO)
NOT STRANGE, EXACTLY...
...MORE LIKE QUEER.
uuuuu

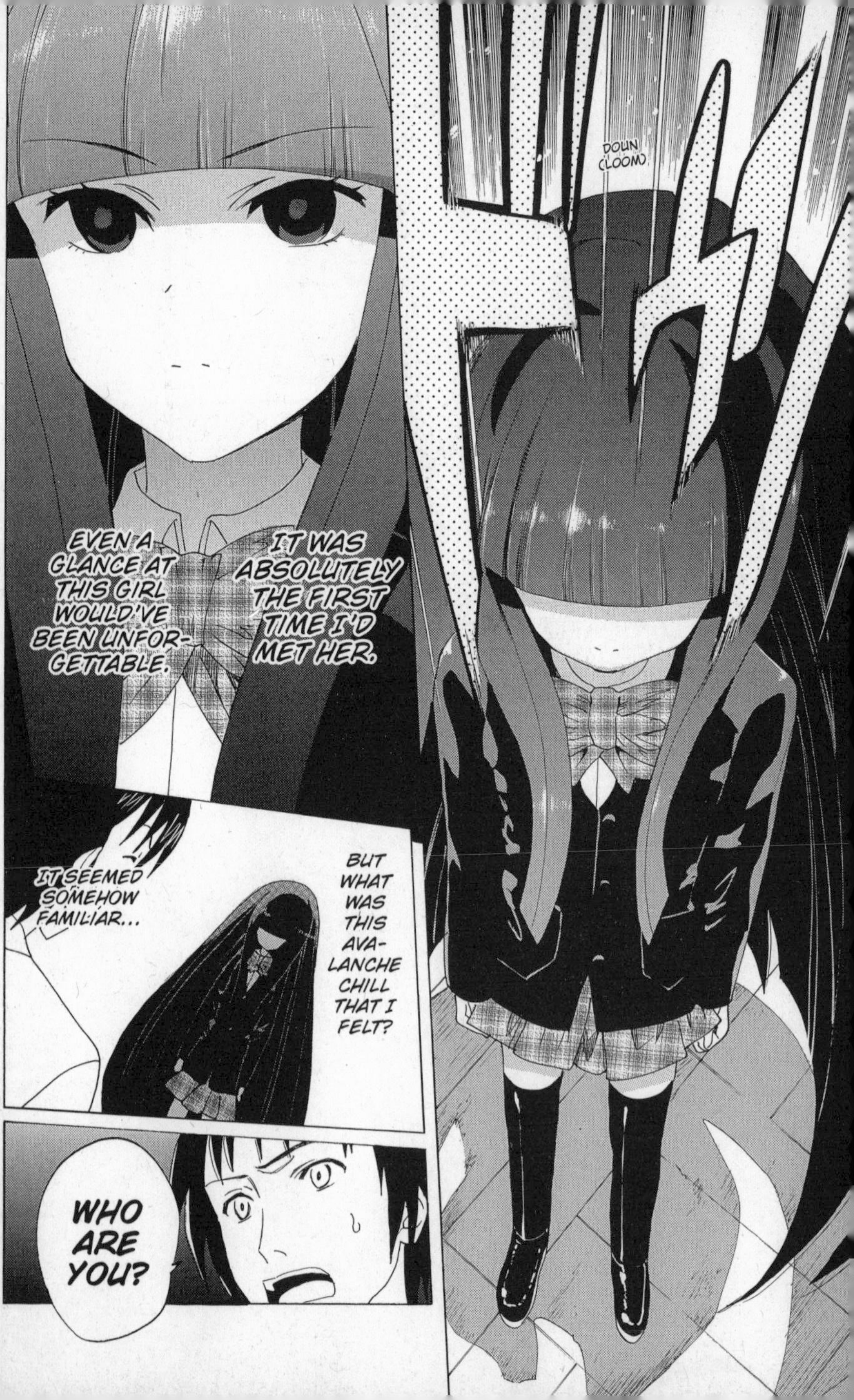
DOUN (LOOM)
IT WAS ABSOLUTELY THE FIRST TIME I'D MET HER.
EVEN A GLANCE AT THIS GIRL WOULD'VE BEEN UNFOR-GETTABLE.
BUT WHAT WAS THIS AVA-LANCHE CHILL THAT I FELT?
IT SEEMED SOMEHOW FAMILIAR...
WHO ARE YOU?

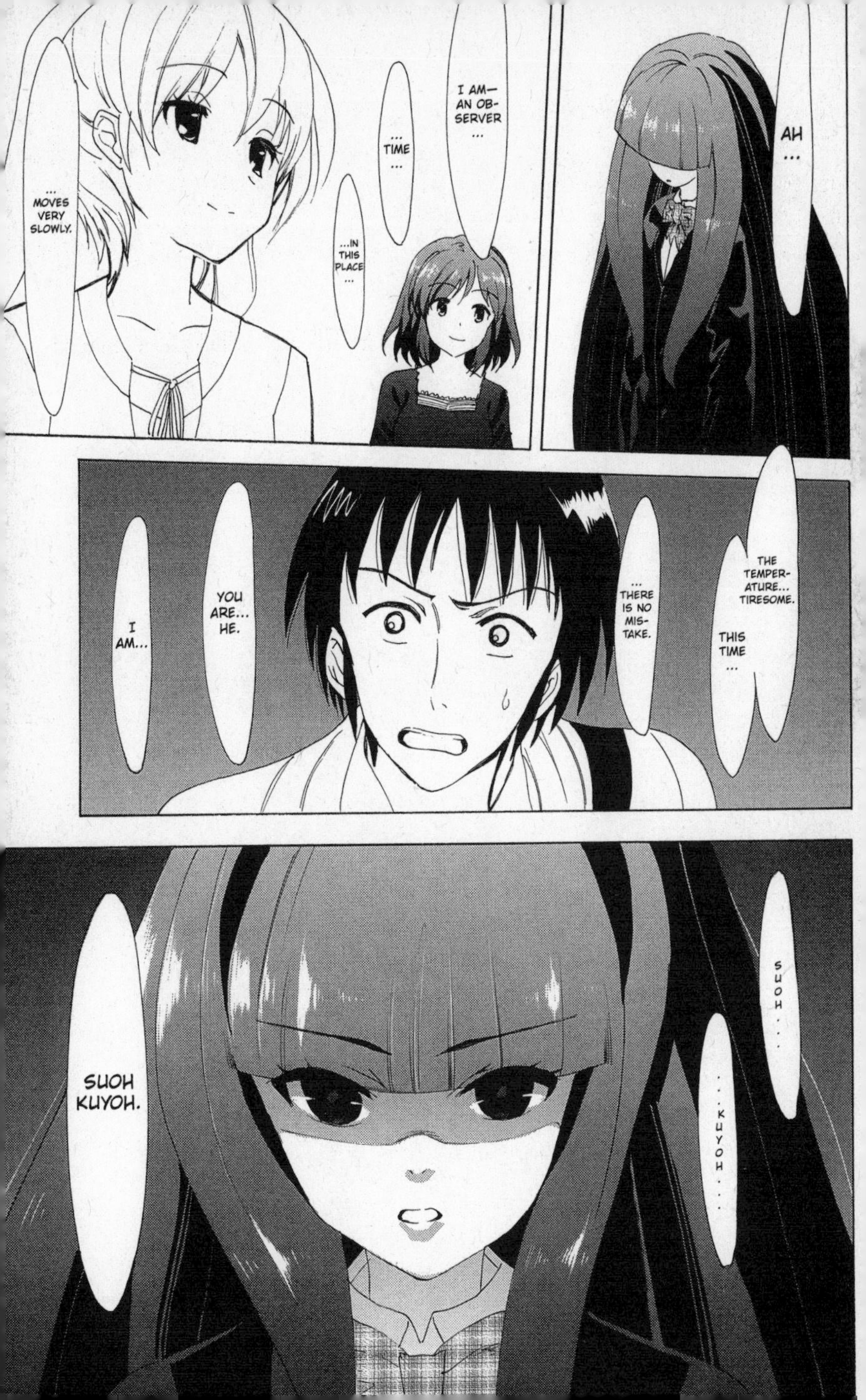
AH ...
I AM— AN OB- SERVER ...
... TIME ...
...IN THIS PLACE ...
... MOVES VERY SLOWLY.
THE TEMPER- ATURE... TIRESOME.
THIS TIME ...
... THERE IS NO MIS- TAKE.
YOU ARE... HE.
I AM...
SUOH . . .
. . . KUYOH . . .
SUOH KUYOH.

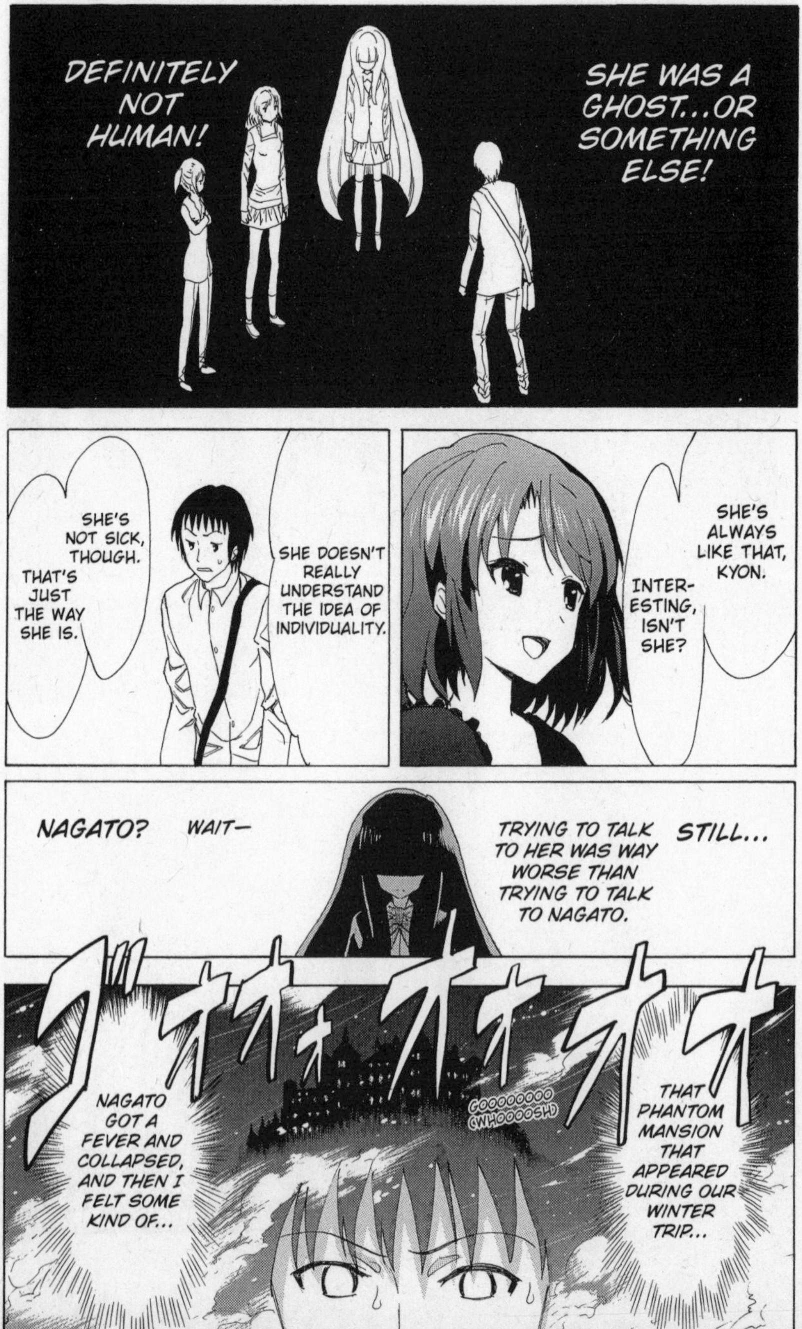
SHE WAS A GHOST...OR SOMETHING ELSE!
DEFINITELY NOT HUMAN!
SHE'S ALWAYS LIKE THAT, KYON.
INTERESTING, ISN'T SHE?
SHE DOESN'T REALLY UNDERSTAND THE IDEA OF INDIVIDUALITY.
SHE'S NOT SICK, THOUGH.
THAT'S JUST THE WAY SHE IS.
STILL...
TRYING TO TALK TO HER WAS WAY WORSE THAN TRYING TO TALK TO NAGATO.
WAIT—
NAGATO?
THAT PHANTOM MANSION THAT APPEARED DURING OUR WINTER TRIP...
GOOOOOOOO (WHOOOOSH)
NAGATO GOT A FEVER AND COLLAPSED, AND THEN I FELT SOME KIND OF...

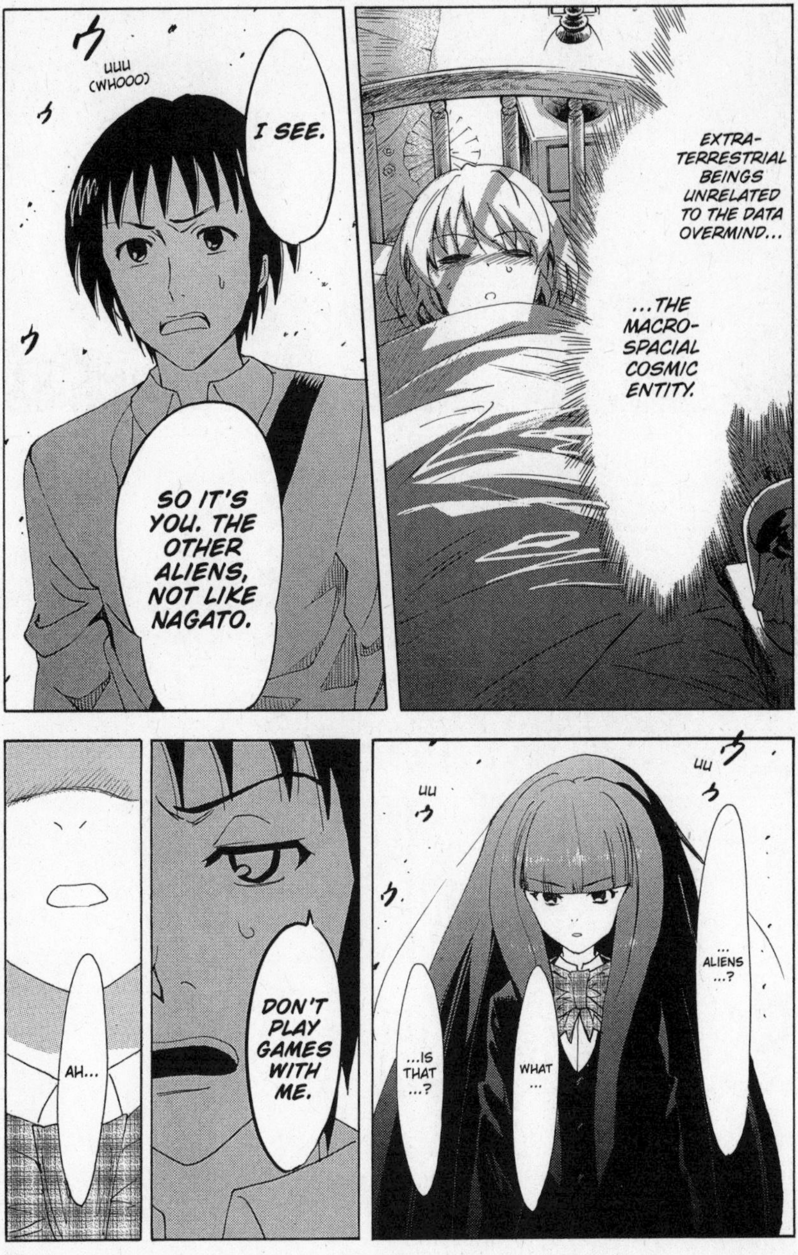
EXTRA-TERRESTRIAL BEINGS UNRELATED TO THE DATA OVERMIND...
...THE MACRO-SPACIAL COSMIC ENTITY.
I SEE.
UUU (WHOOO)
SO IT'S YOU. THE OTHER ALIENS, NOT LIKE NAGATO.
UU
UU
...ALIENS...?
WHAT...
...IS THAT...?
DON'T PLAY GAMES WITH ME.
AH...

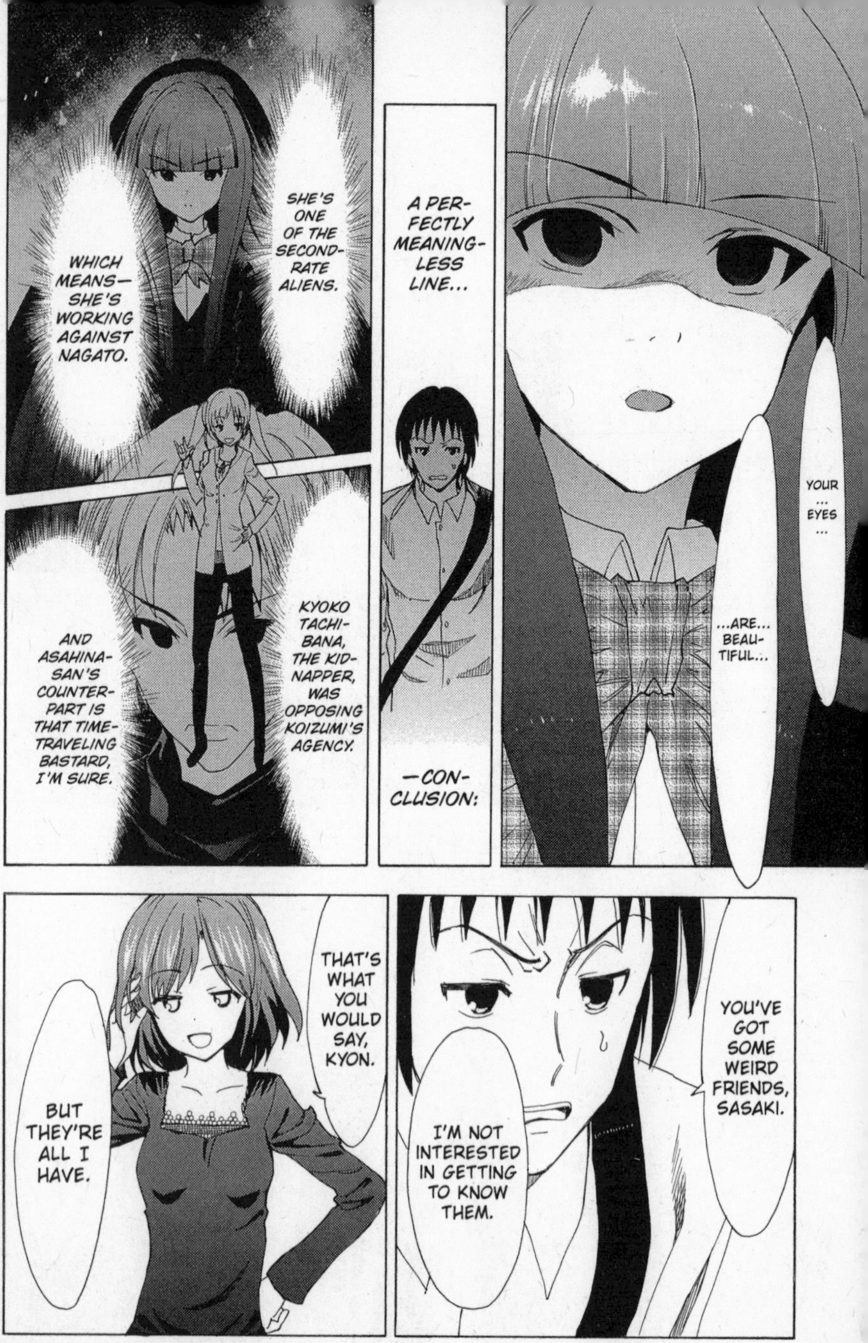
YOUR... EYES...
...ARE... BEAUTIFUL...
A PERFECTLY MEANINGLESS LINE...
—CONCLUSION:
SHE'S ONE OF THE SECOND-RATE ALIENS.
WHICH MEANS—SHE'S WORKING AGAINST NAGATO.
KYOKO TACHIBANA, THE KIDNAPPER, WAS OPPOSING KOIZUMI'S AGENCY.
AND ASAHINA-SAN'S COUNTERPART IS THAT TIME-TRAVELING BASTARD, I'M SURE.
YOU'VE GOT SOME WEIRD FRIENDS, SASAKI.
I'M NOT INTERESTED IN GETTING TO KNOW THEM.
THAT'S WHAT YOU WOULD SAY, KYON.
BUT THEY'RE ALL I HAVE.

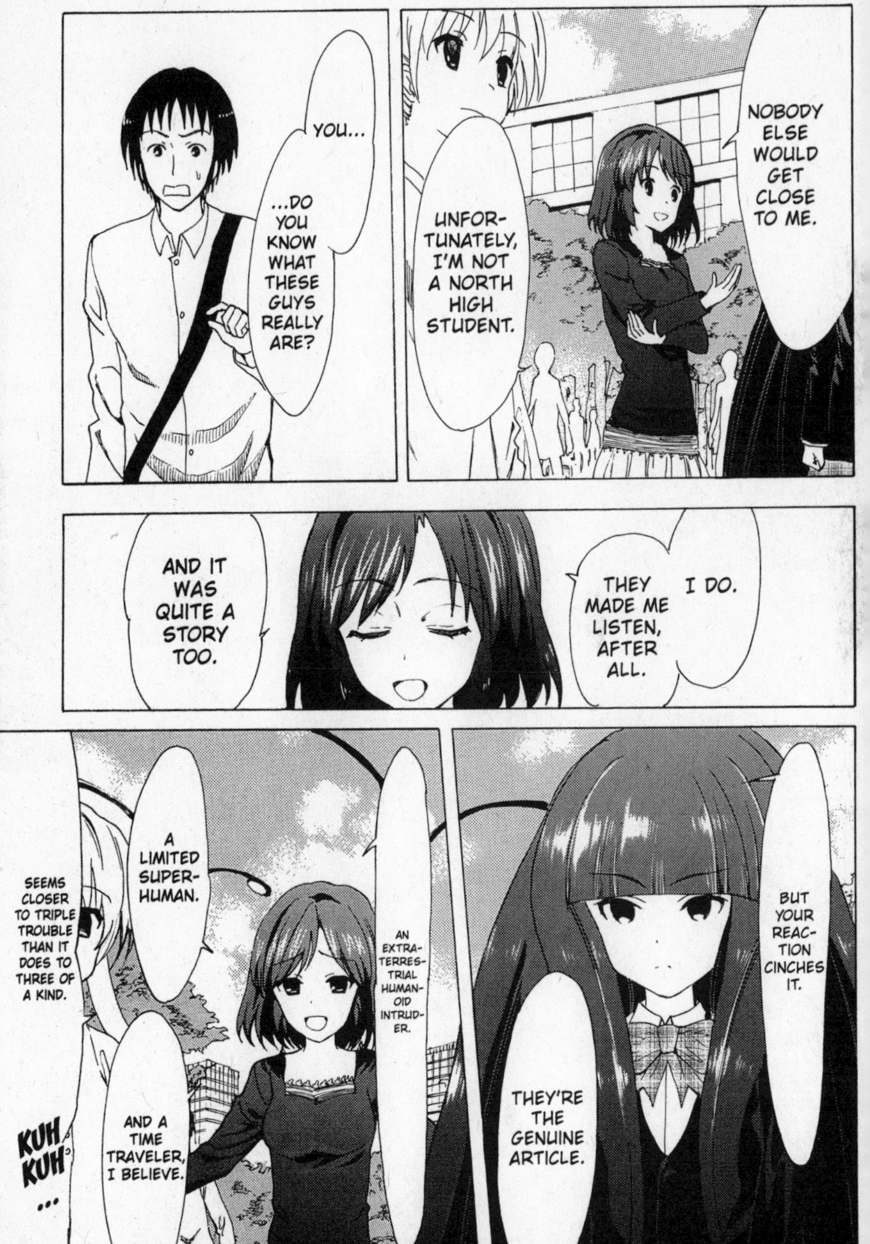
NOBODY ELSE WOULD GET CLOSE TO ME.
UNFORTUNATELY, I'M NOT A NORTH HIGH STUDENT.
YOU...
...DO YOU KNOW WHAT THESE GUYS REALLY ARE?
I DO.
THEY MADE ME LISTEN, AFTER ALL.
AND IT WAS QUITE A STORY TOO.
BUT YOUR REACTION CINCHES IT.
THEY'RE THE GENUINE ARTICLE.
AN EXTRATERRESTRIAL HUMANOID INTRUDER.
A LIMITED SUPERHUMAN.
AND A TIME TRAVELER, I BELIEVE.
SEEMS CLOSER TO TRIPLE TROUBLE THAN IT DOES TO THREE OF A KIND.
KUH KUH...

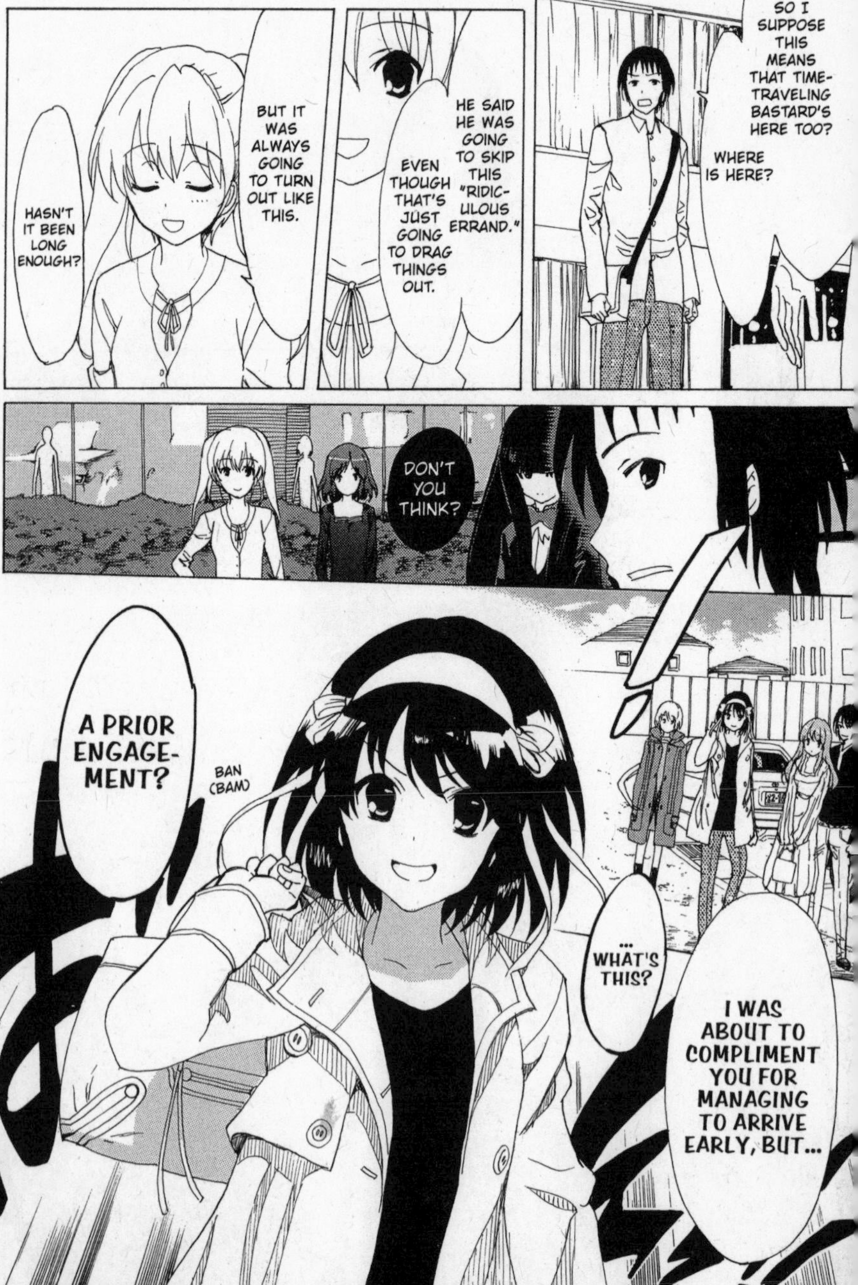
SO I SUPPOSE THIS MEANS THAT TIME-TRAVELING BASTARD'S HERE TOO?
WHERE IS HERE?
HE SAID HE WAS GOING TO SKIP THIS "RIDICULOUS ERRAND."
EVEN THOUGH THAT'S JUST GOING TO DRAG THINGS OUT.
BUT IT WAS ALWAYS GOING TO TURN OUT LIKE THIS.
HASN'T IT BEEN LONG ENOUGH?
DON'T YOU THINK?
I WAS ABOUT TO COMPLIMENT YOU FOR MANAGING TO ARRIVE EARLY, BUT...
... WHAT'S THIS?
A PRIOR ENGAGEMENT?
BAN (BAM)

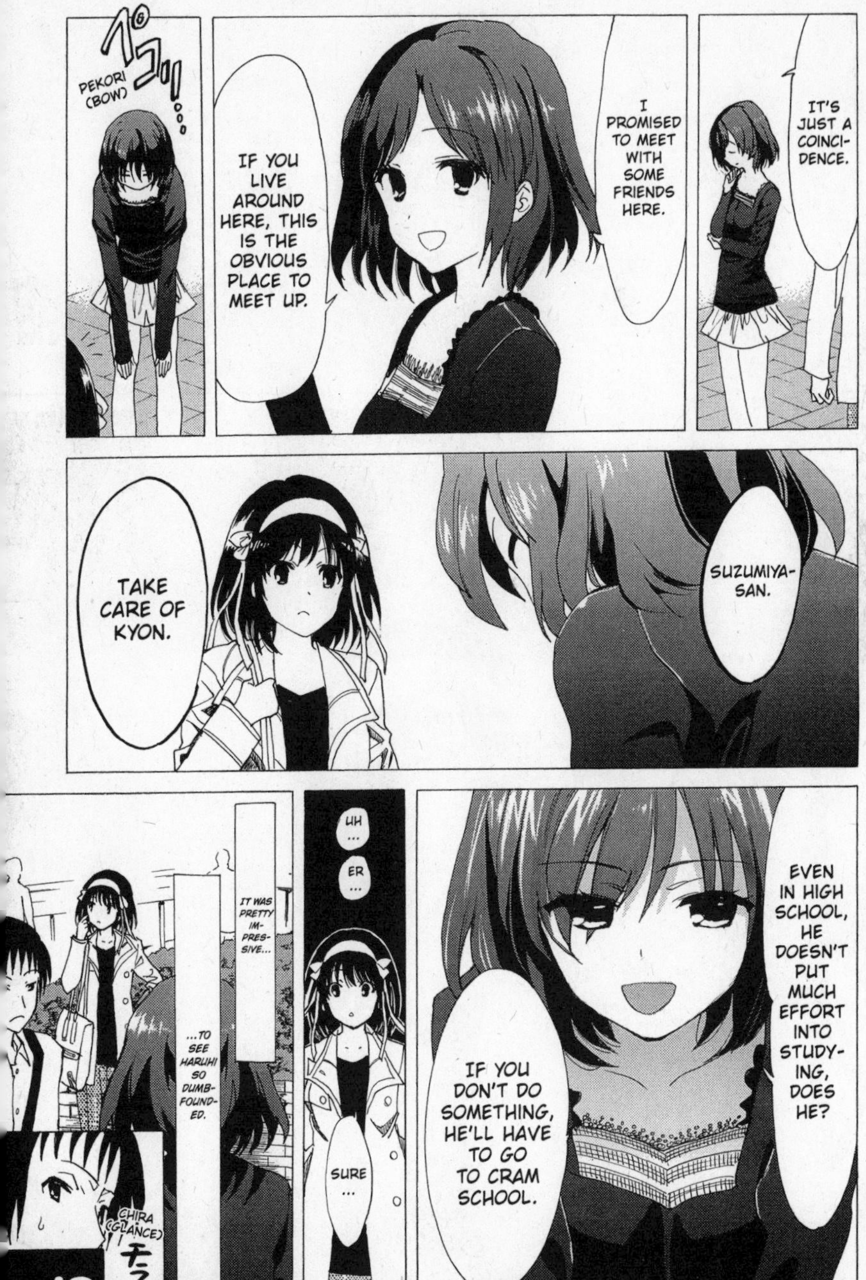
IT'S JUST A COINCIDENCE.
I PROMISED TO MEET WITH SOME FRIENDS HERE.
IF YOU LIVE AROUND HERE, THIS IS THE OBVIOUS PLACE TO MEET UP.
PEKORI (BOW)
SUZUMIYA-SAN.
TAKE CARE OF KYON.
EVEN IN HIGH SCHOOL, HE DOESN'T PUT MUCH EFFORT INTO STUDYING, DOES HE?
IF YOU DON'T DO SOMETHING, HE'LL HAVE TO GO TO CRAM SCHOOL.
UH...
ER...
SURE...
IT WAS PRETTY IMPRESSIVE...
...TO SEE HARUHI SO DUMBFOUNDED.
CHIRA (GLANCE)
!?

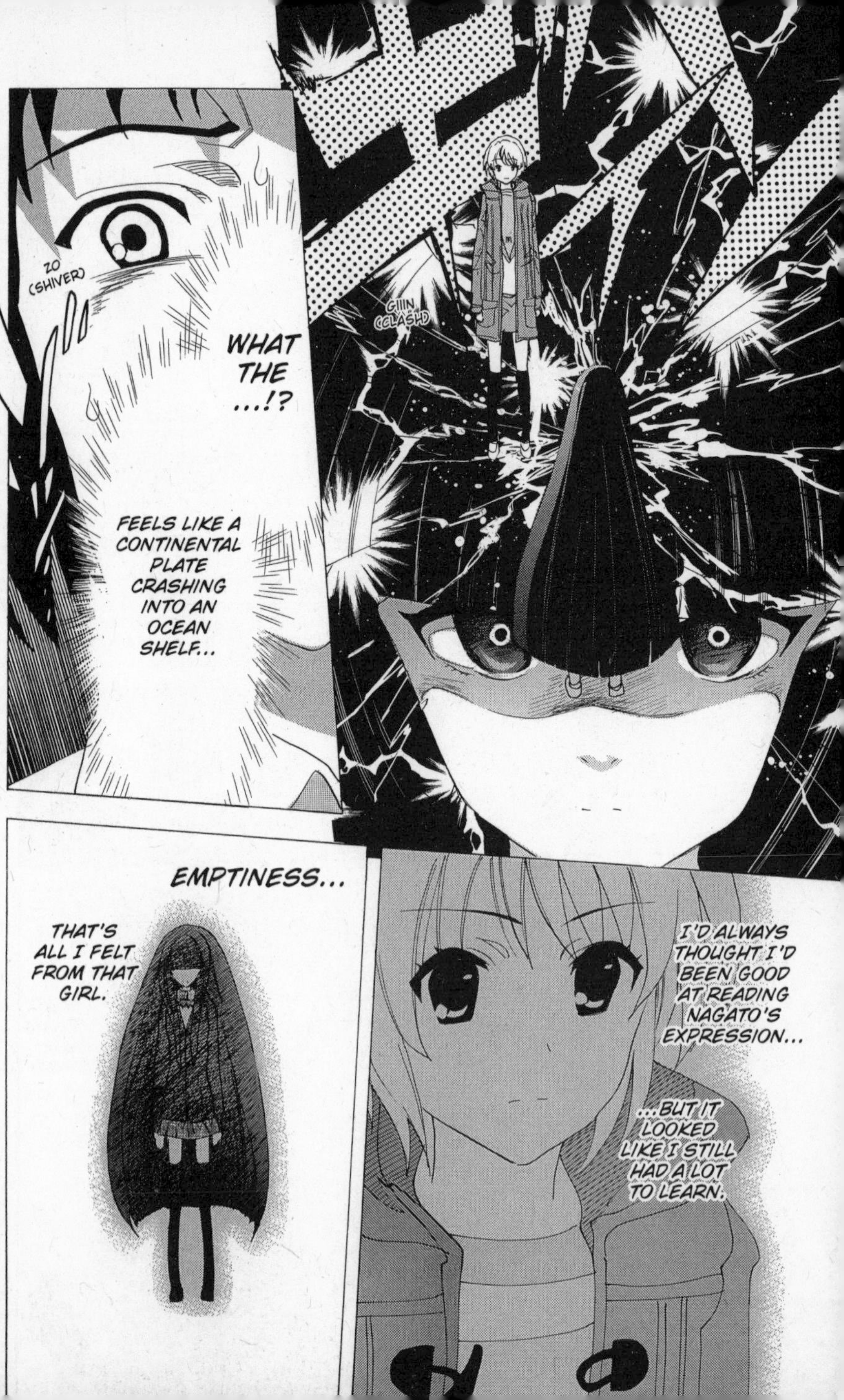
GIIIN (CLASH)
ZO (SHIVER)
WHAT THE ...!?
FEELS LIKE A CONTINENTAL PLATE CRASHING INTO AN OCEAN SHELF...
I'D ALWAYS THOUGHT I'D BEEN GOOD AT READING NAGATO'S EXPRESSION...
...BUT IT LOOKED LIKE I STILL HAD A LOT TO LEARN.
EMPTINESS...
THAT'S ALL I FELT FROM THAT GIRL.

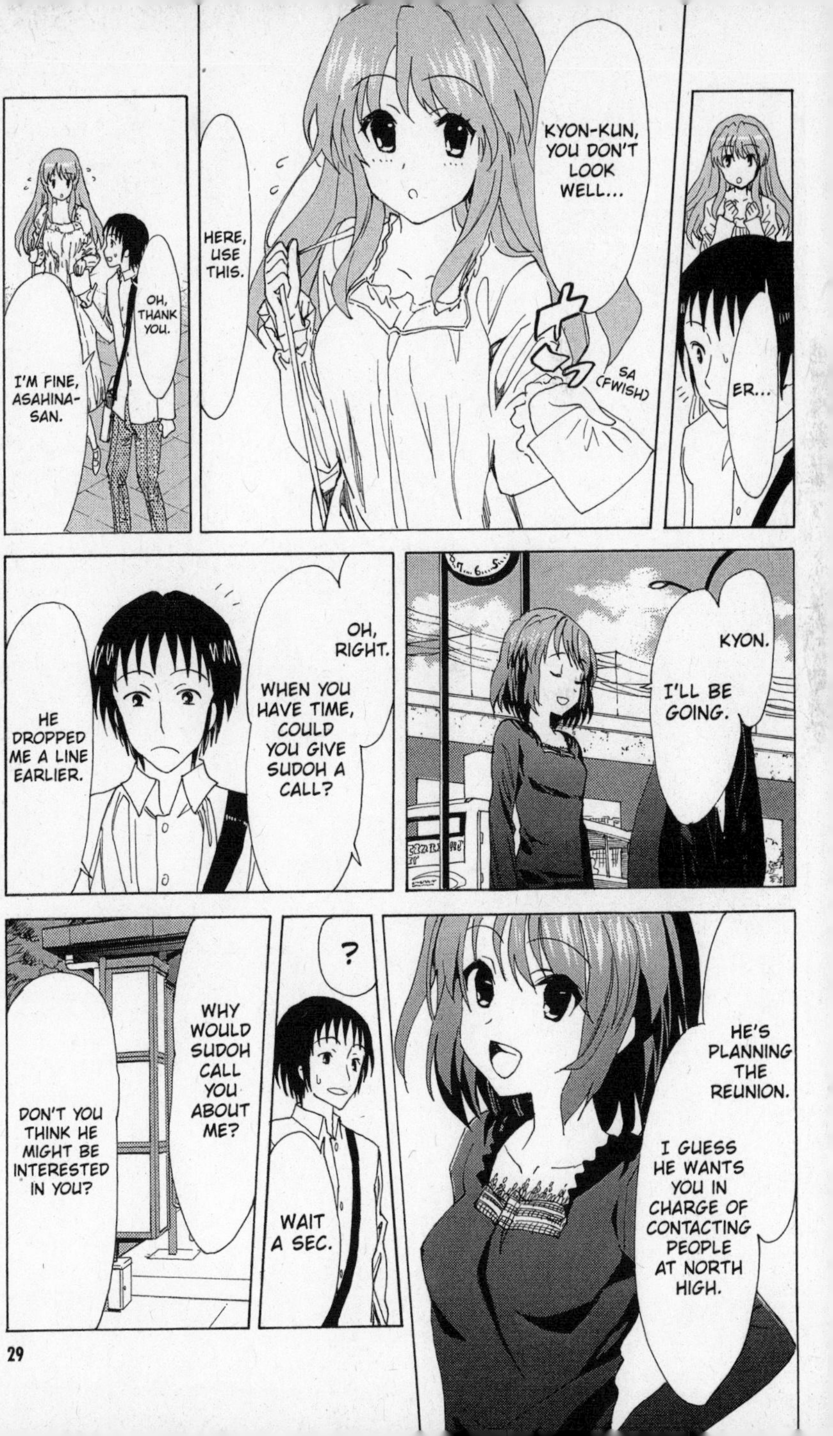
ER...
KYON-KUN, YOU DON'T LOOK WELL...
SA (FWISH)
HERE, USE THIS.
OH, THANK YOU.
I'M FINE, ASAHINA-SAN.
KYON.
I'LL BE GOING.
OH, RIGHT.
WHEN YOU HAVE TIME, COULD YOU GIVE SUDOH A CALL?
HE DROPPED ME A LINE EARLIER.
HE'S PLANNING THE REUNION.
I GUESS HE WANTS YOU IN CHARGE OF CONTACTING PEOPLE AT NORTH HIGH.
?
WAIT A SEC.
WHY WOULD SUDOH CALL YOU ABOUT ME?
DON'T YOU THINK HE MIGHT BE INTERESTED IN YOU?

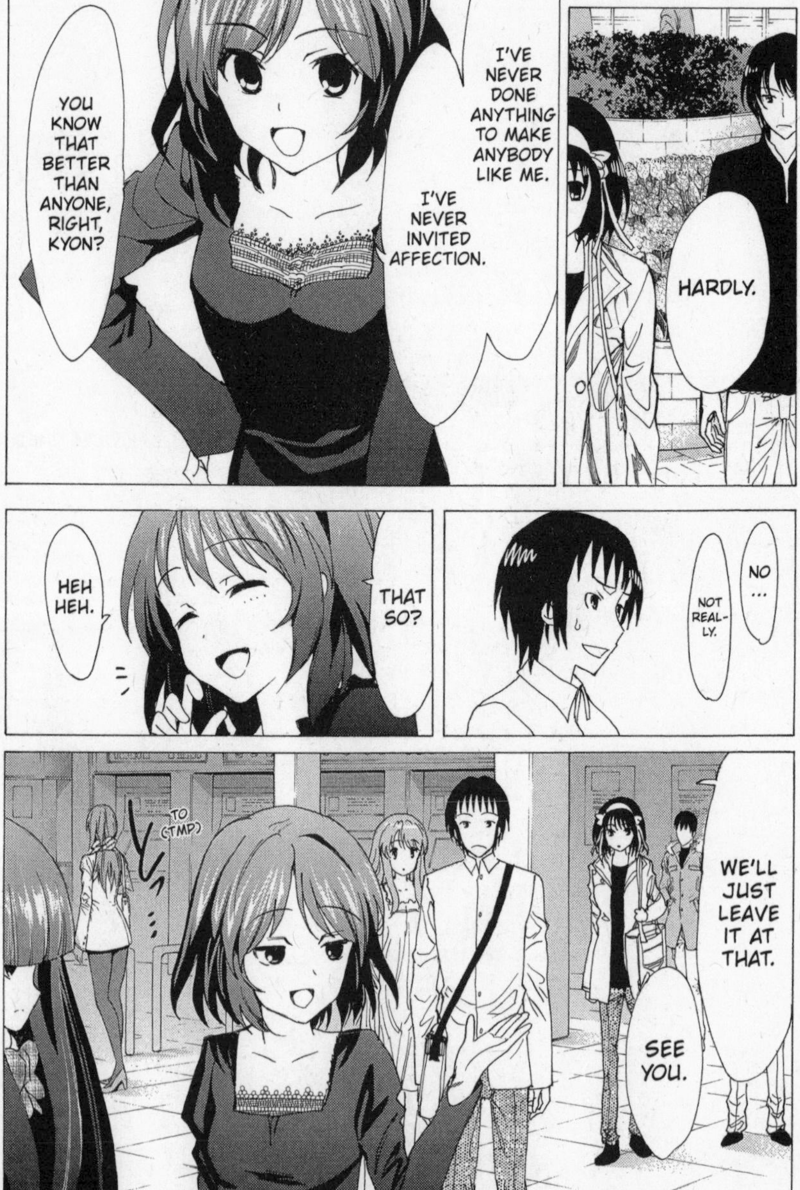
HARDLY.
I'VE NEVER DONE ANYTHING TO MAKE ANYBODY LIKE ME.
I'VE NEVER INVITED AFFECTION.
YOU KNOW THAT BETTER THAN ANYONE, RIGHT, KYON?
NO ...
NOT REALLY.
THAT SO?
HEH HEH.
WE'LL JUST LEAVE IT AT THAT.
SEE YOU.
TO (TMP)

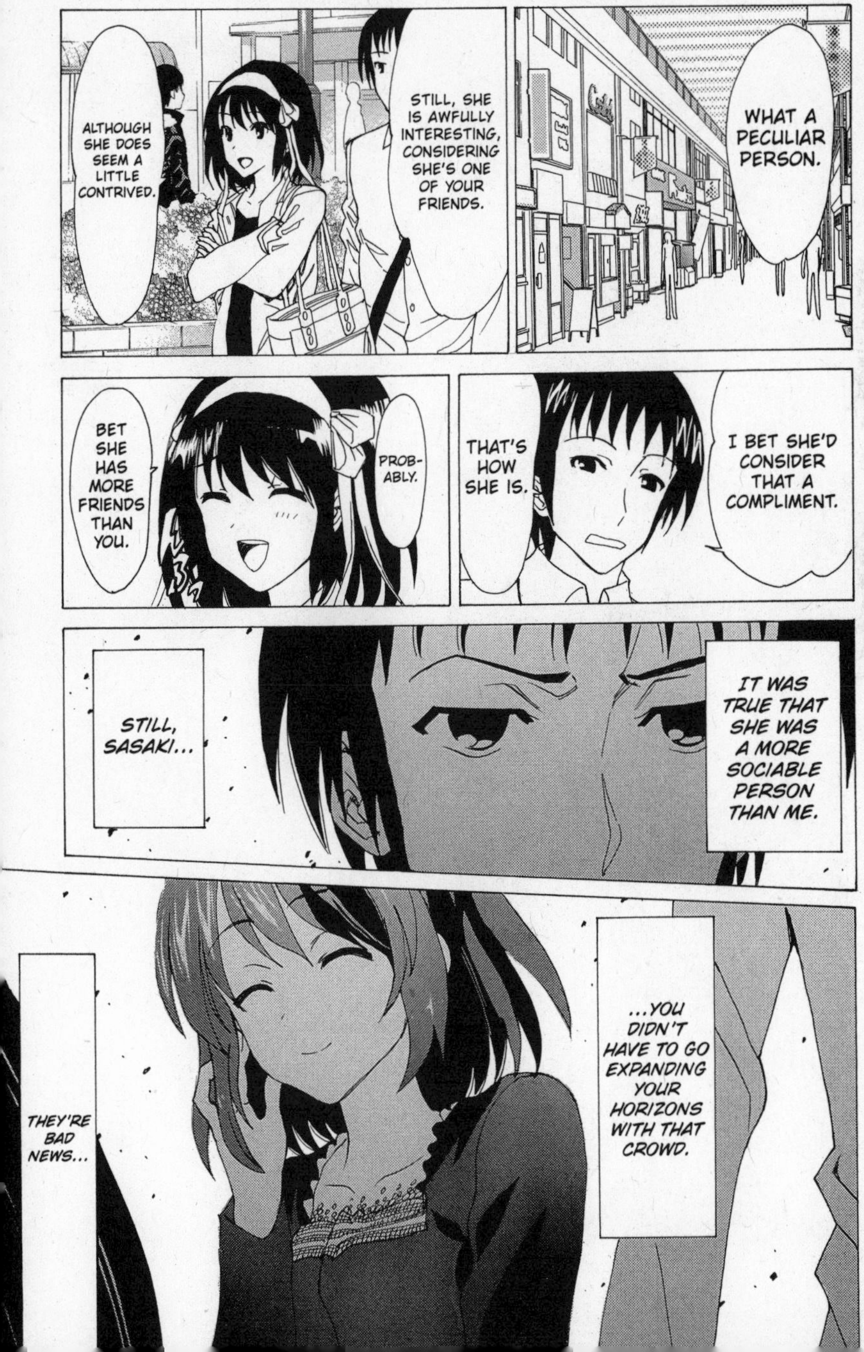
WHAT A PECULIAR PERSON.
STILL, SHE IS AWFULLY INTERESTING, CONSIDERING SHE'S ONE OF YOUR FRIENDS.
ALTHOUGH SHE DOES SEEM A LITTLE CONTRIVED.
I BET SHE'D CONSIDER THAT A COMPLIMENT.
THAT'S HOW SHE IS.
PROB-ABLY.
BET SHE HAS MORE FRIENDS THAN YOU.
IT WAS TRUE THAT SHE WAS A MORE SOCIABLE PERSON THAN ME.
STILL, SASAKI...
...YOU DIDN'T HAVE TO GO EXPANDING YOUR HORIZONS WITH THAT CROWD.
THEY'RE BAD NEWS...

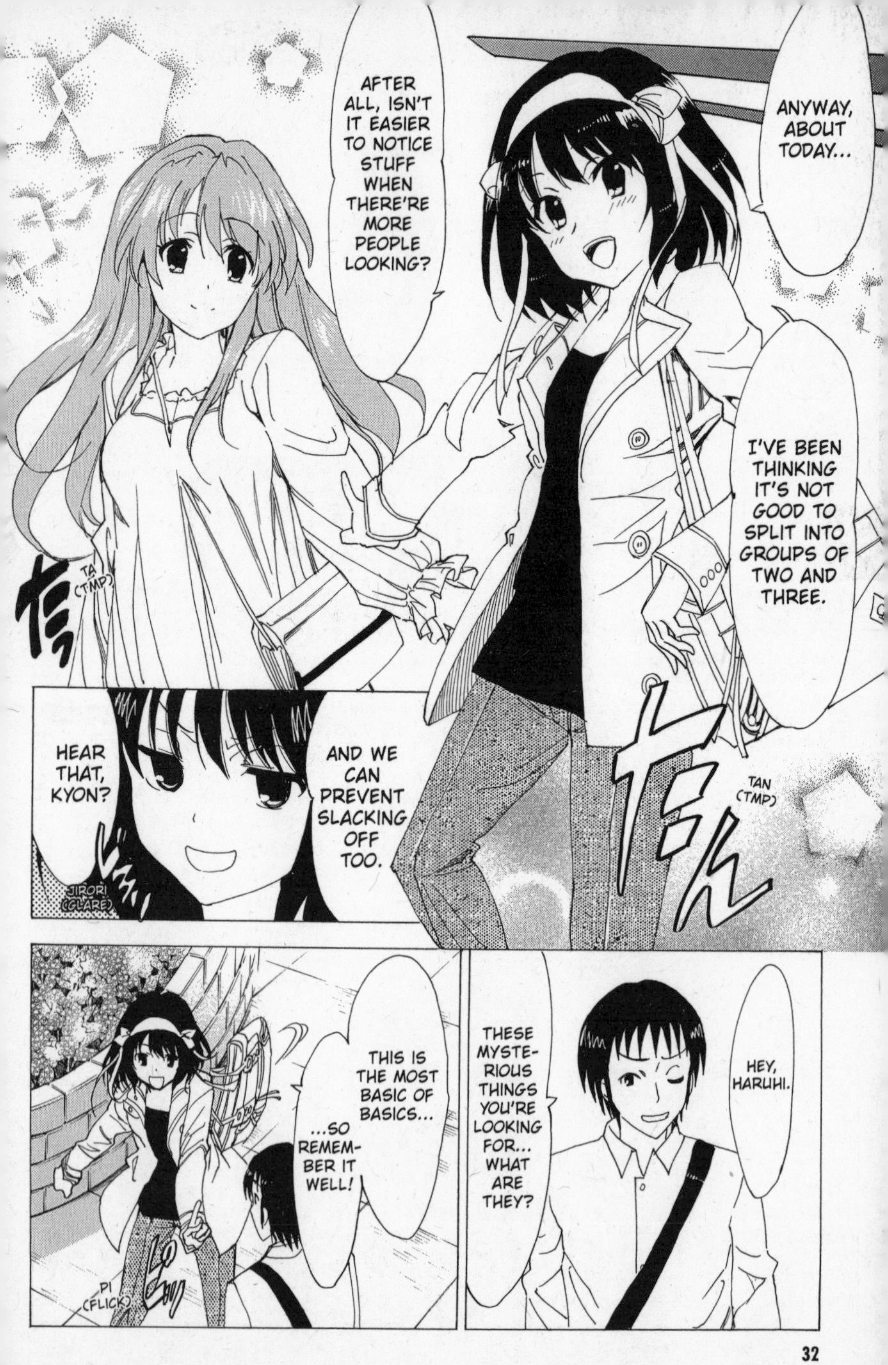

ANYWAY, ABOUT TODAY...
I'VE BEEN THINKING IT'S NOT GOOD TO SPLIT INTO GROUPS OF TWO AND THREE.
AFTER ALL, ISN'T IT EASIER TO NOTICE STUFF WHEN THERE'RE MORE PEOPLE LOOKING?
TAN (TMP)
TA (TMP)
AND WE CAN PREVENT SLACKING OFF TOO.
HEAR THAT, KYON?
JIRORI (GLARE)
HEY, HARUHI.
THESE MYSTERIOUS THINGS YOU'RE LOOKING FOR... WHAT ARE THEY?
THIS IS THE MOST BASIC OF BASICS...
...SO REMEMBER IT WELL!
PI (FLICK)

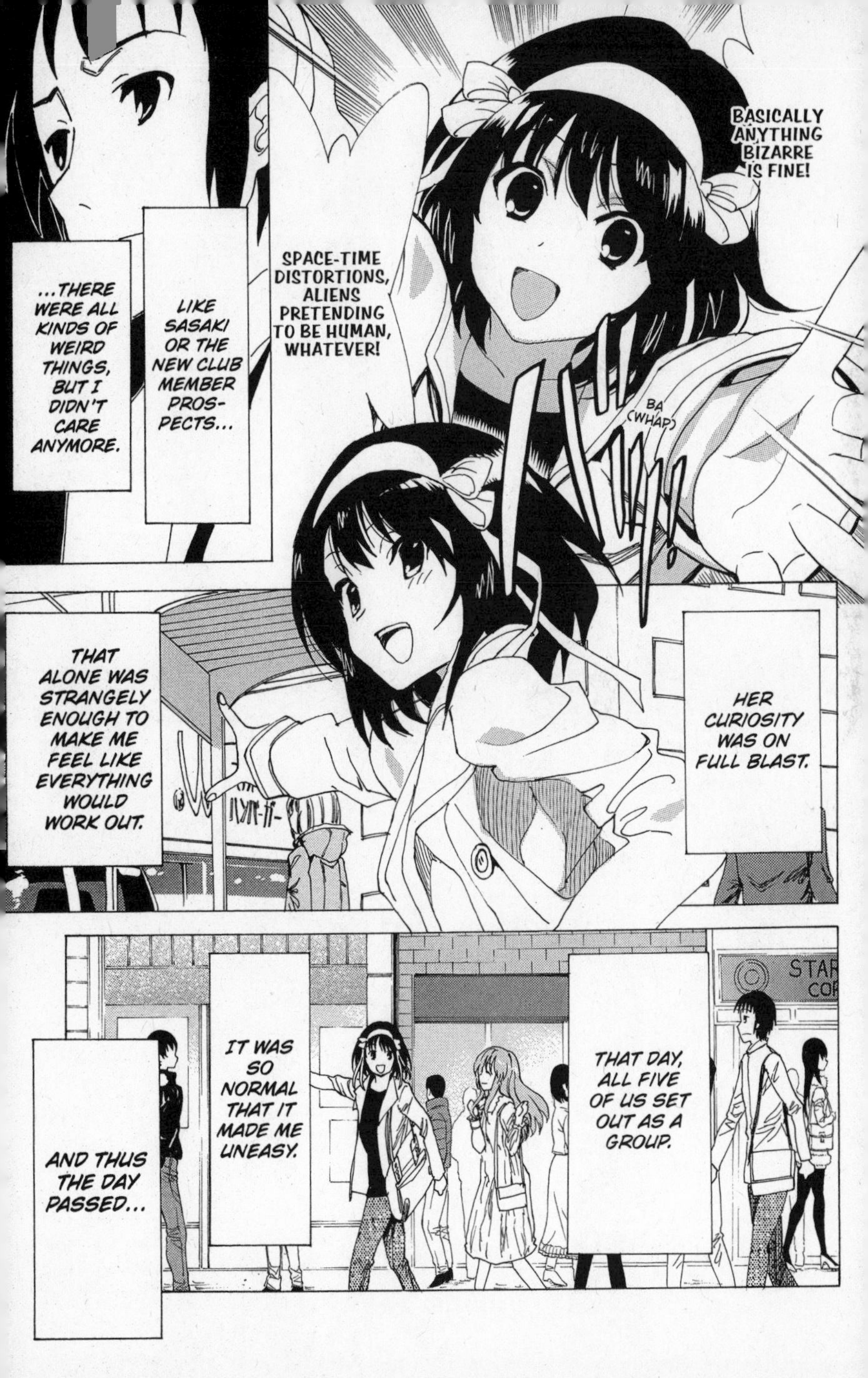
BASICALLY ANYTHING BIZARRE IS FINE!
SPACE-TIME DISTORTIONS, ALIENS PRETENDING TO BE HUMAN, WHATEVER!
BA (WHAP)
LIKE SASAKI OR THE NEW CLUB MEMBER PROSPECTS...
...THERE WERE ALL KINDS OF WEIRD THINGS, BUT I DIDN'T CARE ANYMORE.
HER CURIOSITY WAS ON FULL BLAST.
THAT ALONE WAS STRANGELY ENOUGH TO MAKE ME FEEL LIKE EVERYTHING WOULD WORK OUT.
THAT DAY, ALL FIVE OF US SET OUT AS A GROUP.
IT WAS SO NORMAL THAT IT MADE ME UNEASY.
AND THUS THE DAY PASSED...

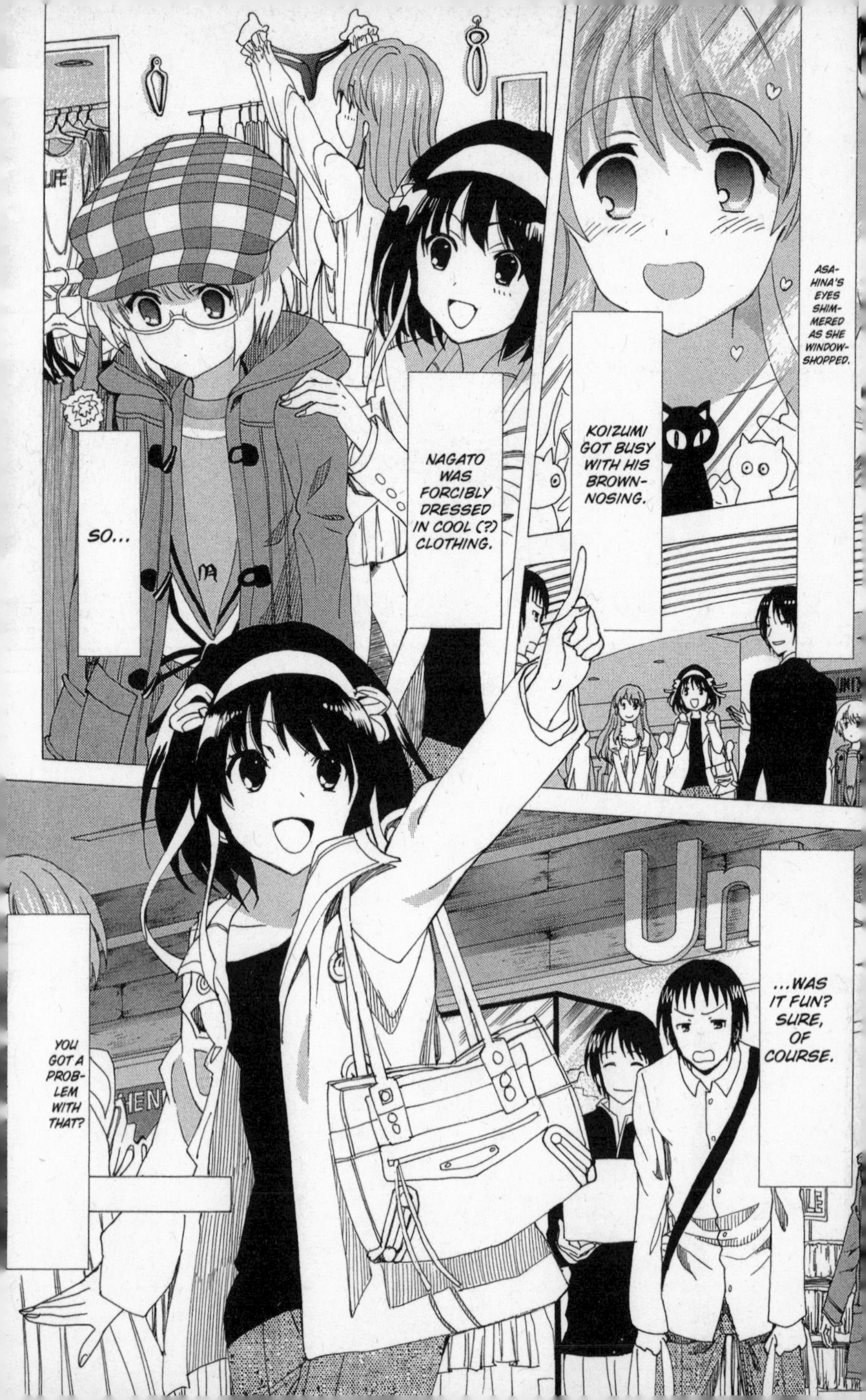
ASA-HINA'S EYES SHIM-MERED AS SHE WINDOW-SHOPPED.
KOIZUMI GOT BUSY WITH HIS BROWN-NOSING.
NAGATO WAS FORCIBLY DRESSED IN COOL (?) CLOTHING.
SO...
...WAS IT FUN? SURE, OF COURSE.
YOU GOT A PROB-LEM WITH THAT?

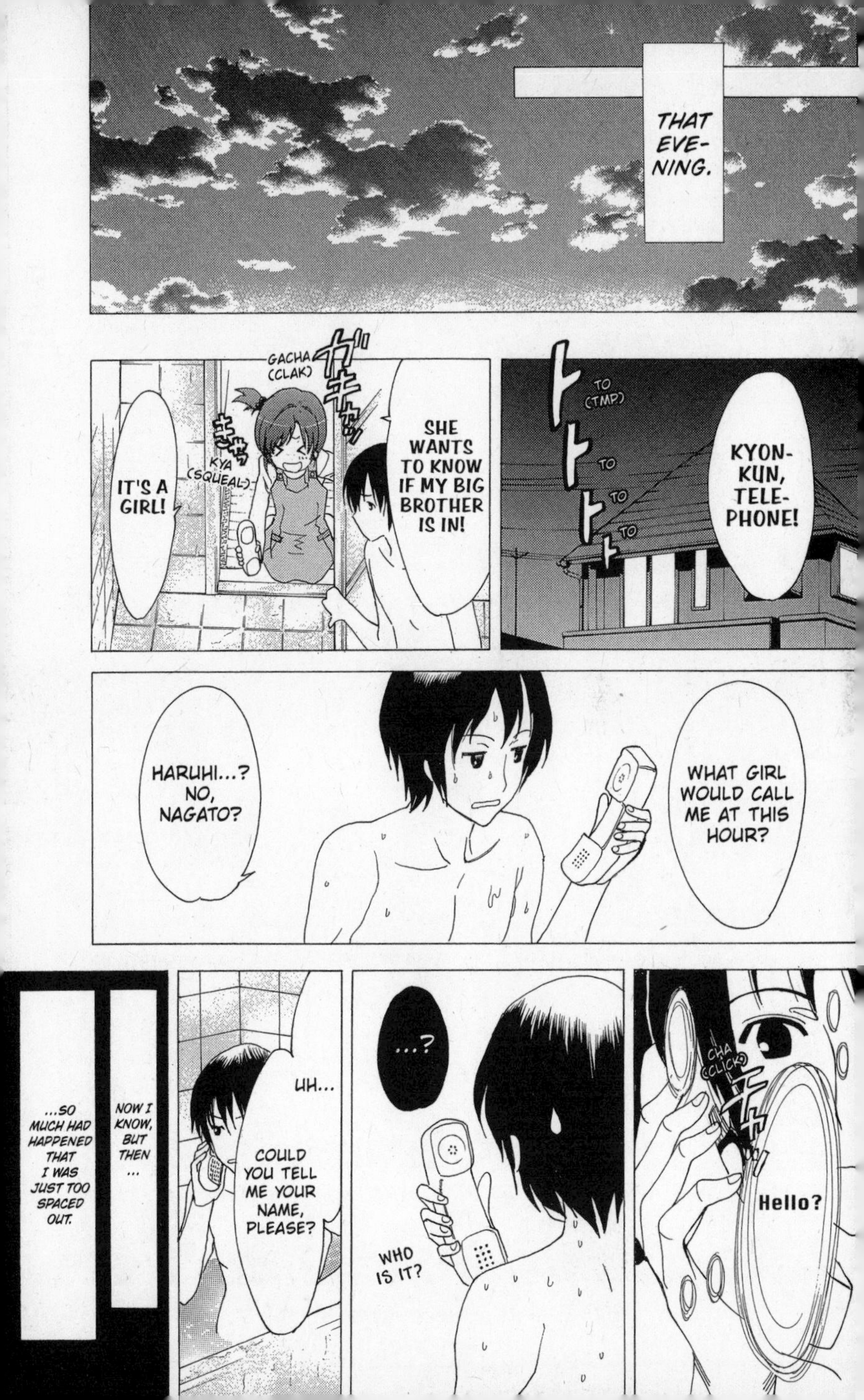
THAT EVENING.
TO (TMP)
TO
TO
TO
KYON-KUN, TELEPHONE!
SHE WANTS TO KNOW IF MY BIG BROTHER IS IN!
GACHA (CLAK)
KYA (SQUEAL)
IT'S A GIRL!
WHAT GIRL WOULD CALL ME AT THIS HOUR?
HARUHI...? NO, NAGATO?
CHA (CLICK)
Hello?
...?
WHO IS IT?
UH...
COULD YOU TELL ME YOUR NAME, PLEASE?
NOW I KNOW, BUT THEN ...
...SO MUCH HAD HAPPENED THAT I WAS JUST TOO SPACED OUT.

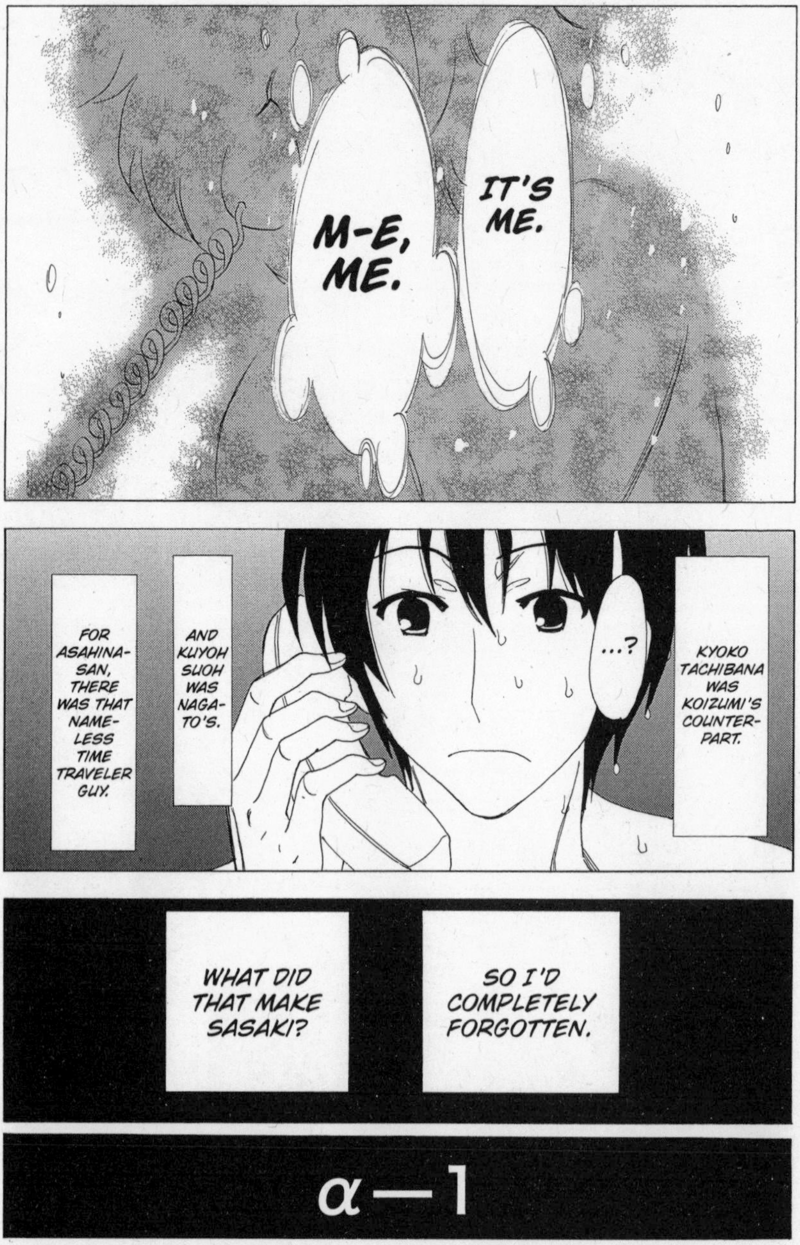
IT'S ME.
M-E, ME.
KYOKO TACHIBANA WAS KOIZUMI'S COUNTERPART.
...?
AND KUYOH SUOH WAS NAGATO'S.
FOR ASAHINA-SAN, THERE WAS THAT NAMELESS TIME TRAVELER GUY.
SO I'D COMPLETELY FORGOTTEN.
WHAT DID THAT MAKE SASAKI?
α—1

THE DISSOCIATION OF HARUHI SUZUMIYA III : END

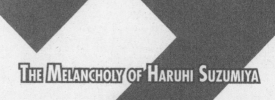
THE MELANCHOLY OF HARUHI SUZUMIYA

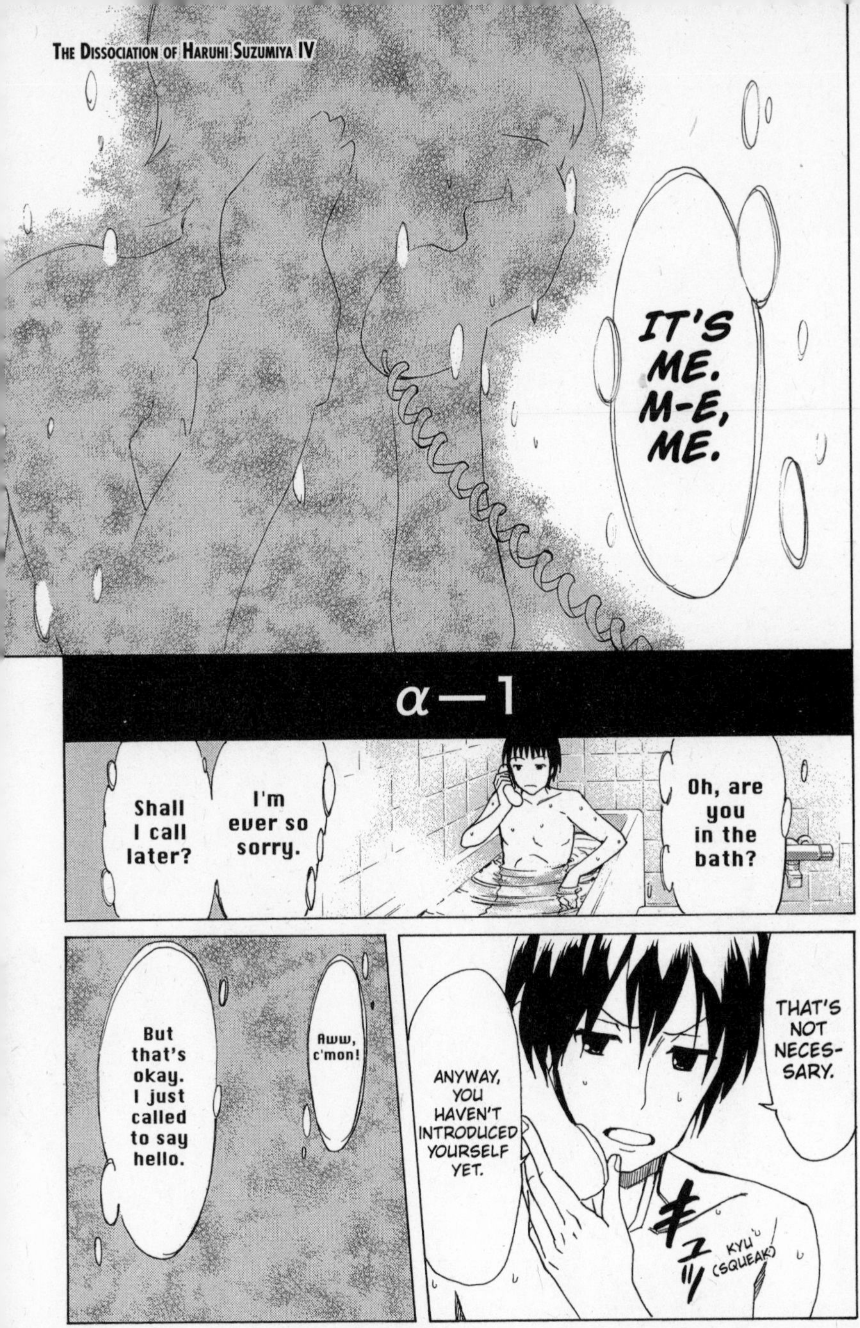
IT'S ME. M-E, ME.
α—1
Oh, are you in the bath?
I'm ever so sorry.
Shall I call later?
THAT'S NOT NECES-SARY.
ANYWAY, YOU HAVEN'T INTRODUCED YOURSELF YET.
KYU (SQUEAK)
Aww, c'mon!
But that's okay. I just called to say hello.

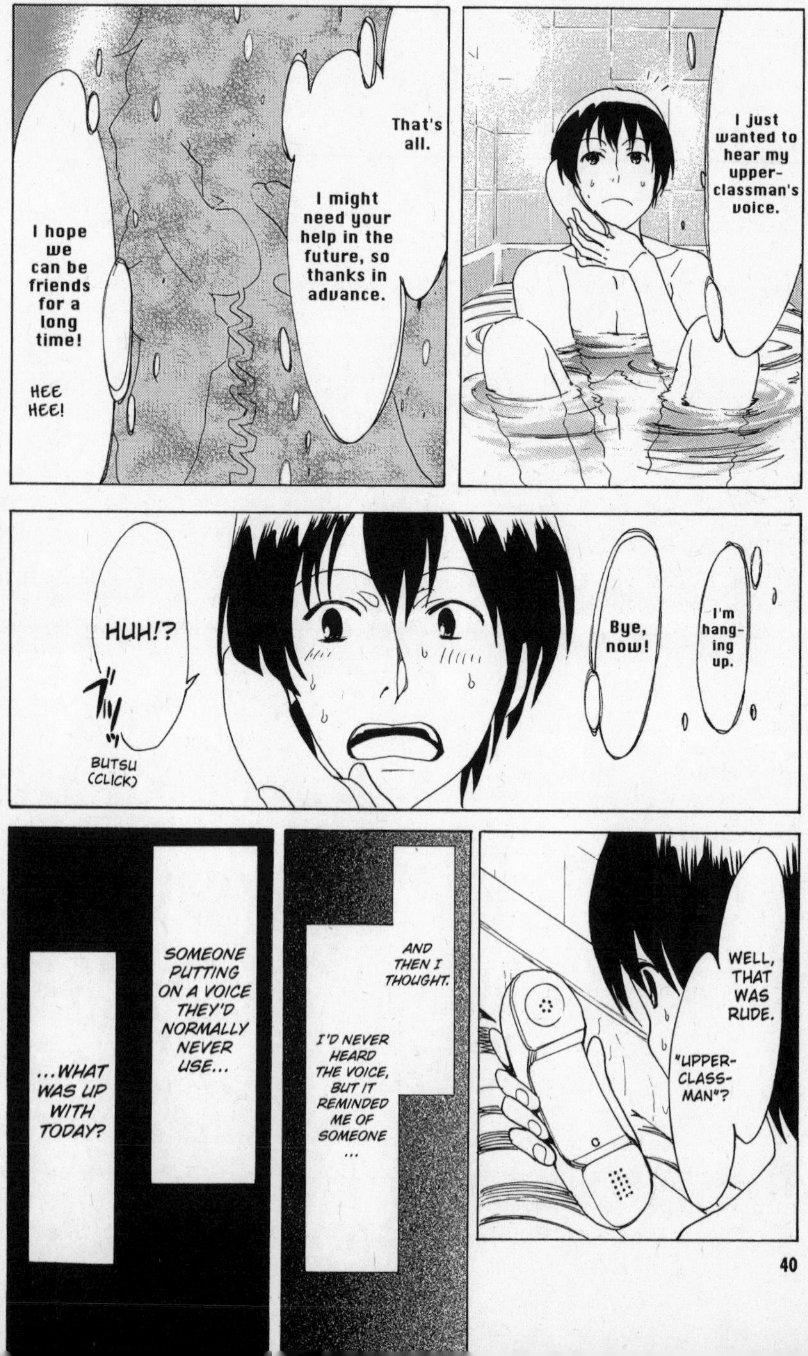
I just wanted to hear my upperclassman's voice.
That's all.
I might need your help in the future, so thanks in advance.
I hope we can be friends for a long time!
HEE HEE!
I'm hanging up.
Bye, now!
HUH!?
BUTSU (CLICK)
WELL, THAT WAS RUDE.
"UPPERCLASSMAN"?
AND THEN I THOUGHT.
I'D NEVER HEARD THE VOICE, BUT IT REMINDED ME OF SOMEONE ...
SOMEONE PUTTING ON A VOICE THEY'D NORMALLY NEVER USE...
...WHAT WAS UP WITH TODAY?

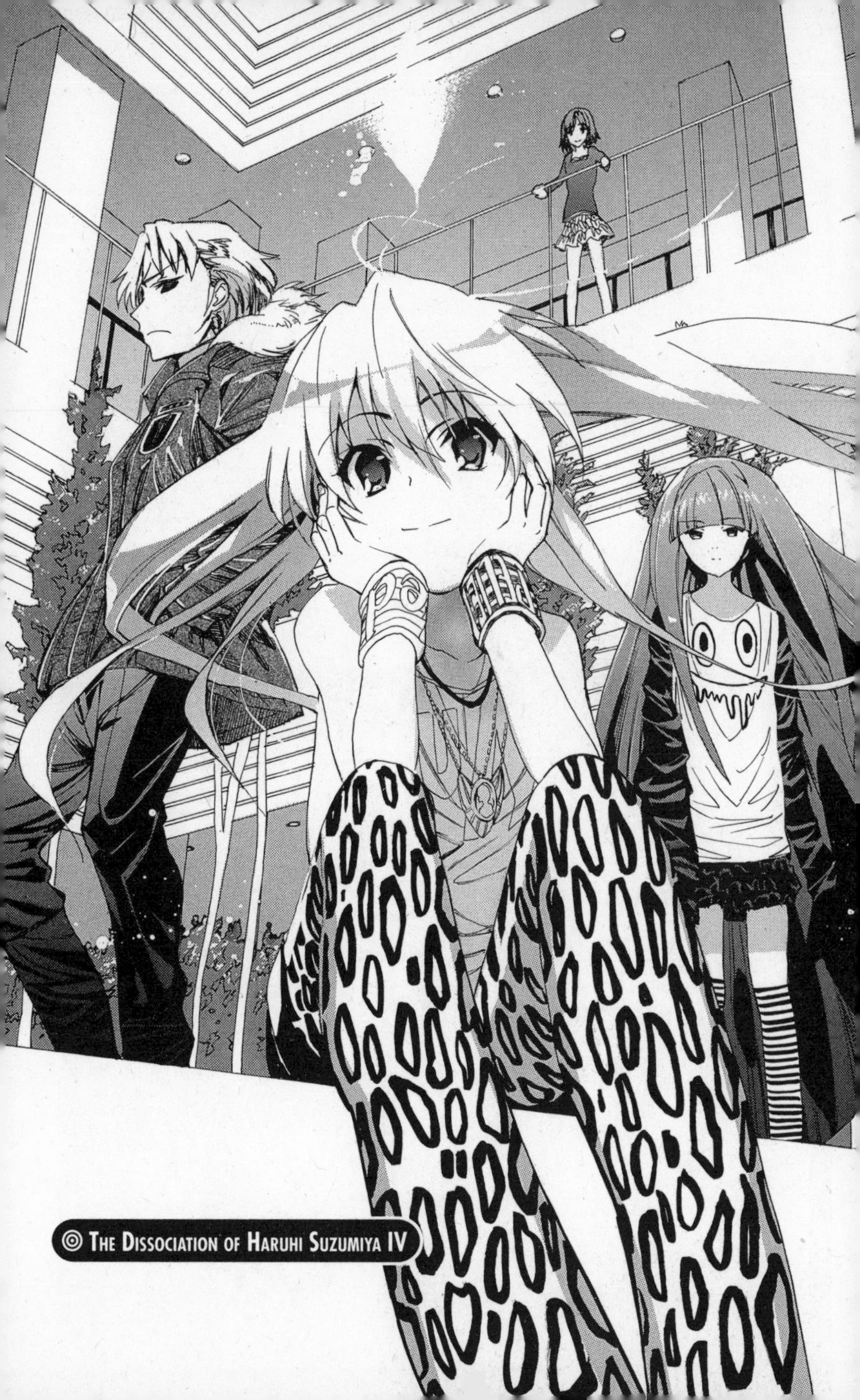
◎ The Dissociation of Haruhi Suzumiya IV

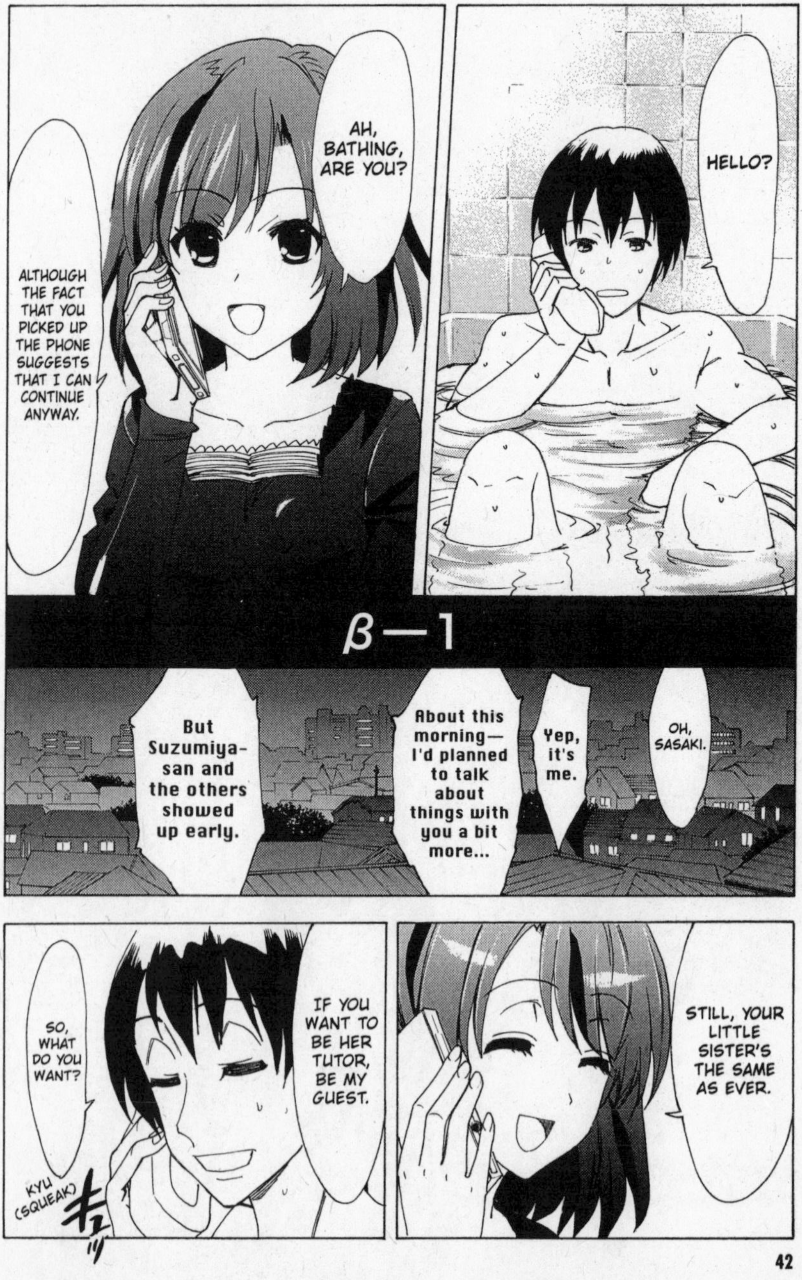
HELLO?
AH, BATHING, ARE YOU?
ALTHOUGH THE FACT THAT YOU PICKED UP THE PHONE SUGGESTS THAT I CAN CONTINUE ANYWAY.
β—1
OH, SASAKI.
Yep, it's me.
About this morning—I'd planned to talk about things with you a bit more...
But Suzumiya-san and the others showed up early.
STILL, YOUR LITTLE SISTER'S THE SAME AS EVER.
IF YOU WANT TO BE HER TUTOR, BE MY GUEST.
SO, WHAT DO YOU WANT?
KYU (SQUEAK)

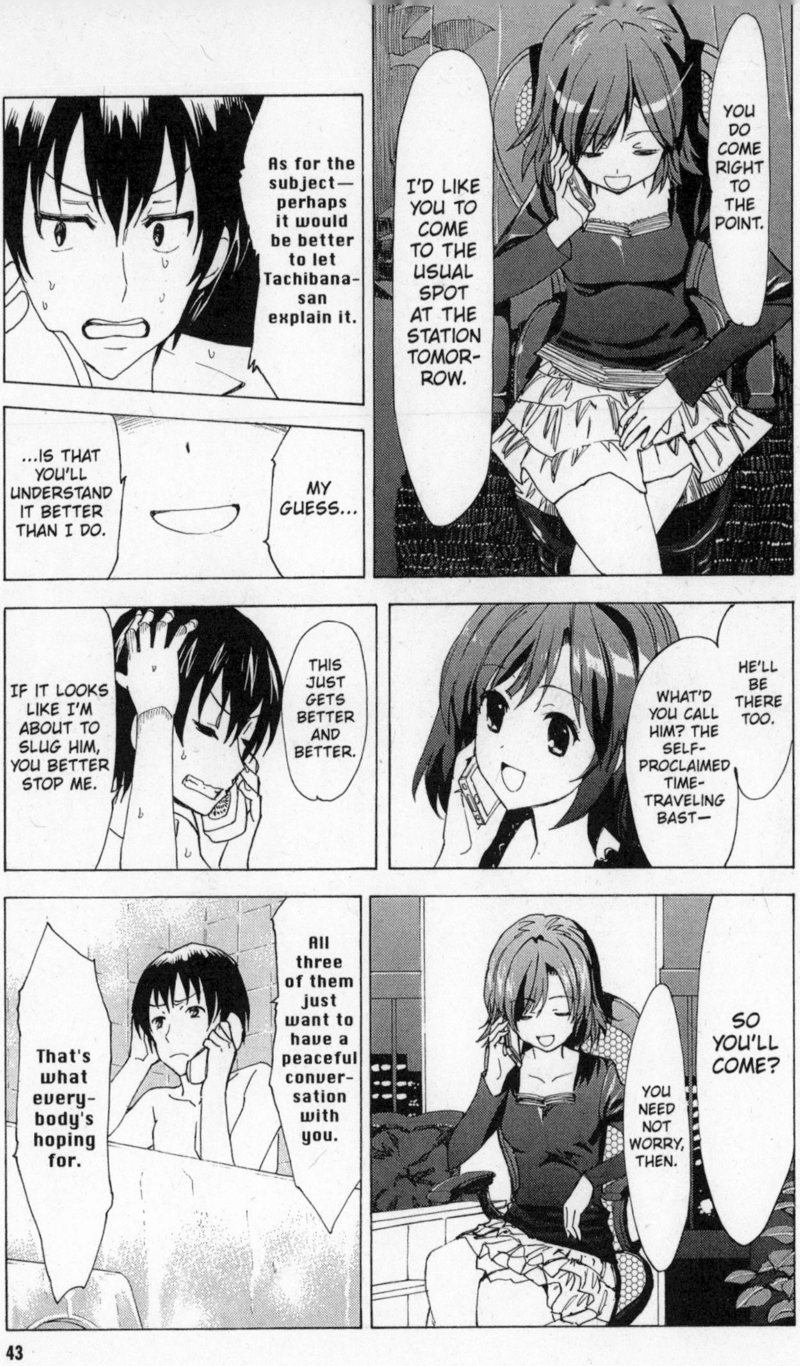
YOU DO COME RIGHT TO THE POINT.
I'D LIKE YOU TO COME TO THE USUAL SPOT AT THE STATION TOMORROW.
As for the subject—perhaps it would be better to let Tachibana-san explain it.
MY GUESS...
...IS THAT YOU'LL UNDERSTAND IT BETTER THAN I DO.
HE'LL BE THERE TOO.
WHAT'D YOU CALL HIM? THE SELF-PROCLAIMED TIME-TRAVELING BAST—
THIS JUST GETS BETTER AND BETTER.
IF IT LOOKS LIKE I'M ABOUT TO SLUG HIM, YOU BETTER STOP ME.
SO YOU'LL COME?
YOU NEED NOT WORRY, THEN.
All three of them just want to have a peaceful conversation with you.
That's what everybody's hoping for.

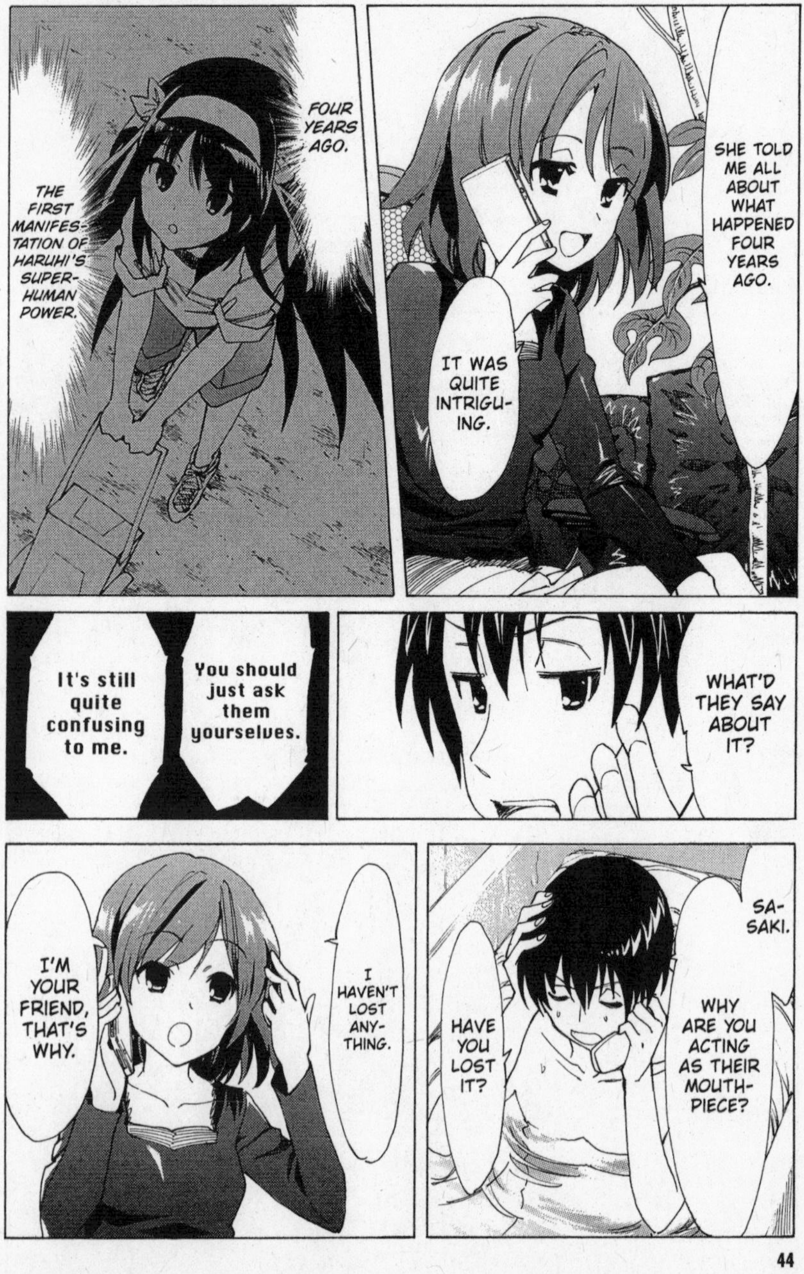
SHE TOLD ME ALL ABOUT WHAT HAPPENED FOUR YEARS AGO.
IT WAS QUITE INTRIGUING.
FOUR YEARS AGO.
THE FIRST MANIFESTATION OF HARUHI'S SUPERHUMAN POWER.
WHAT'D THEY SAY ABOUT IT?
You should just ask them yourselves.
It's still quite confusing to me.
SASAKI.
WHY ARE YOU ACTING AS THEIR MOUTHPIECE?
HAVE YOU LOST IT?
I HAVEN'T LOST ANYTHING.
I'M YOUR FRIEND, THAT'S WHY.

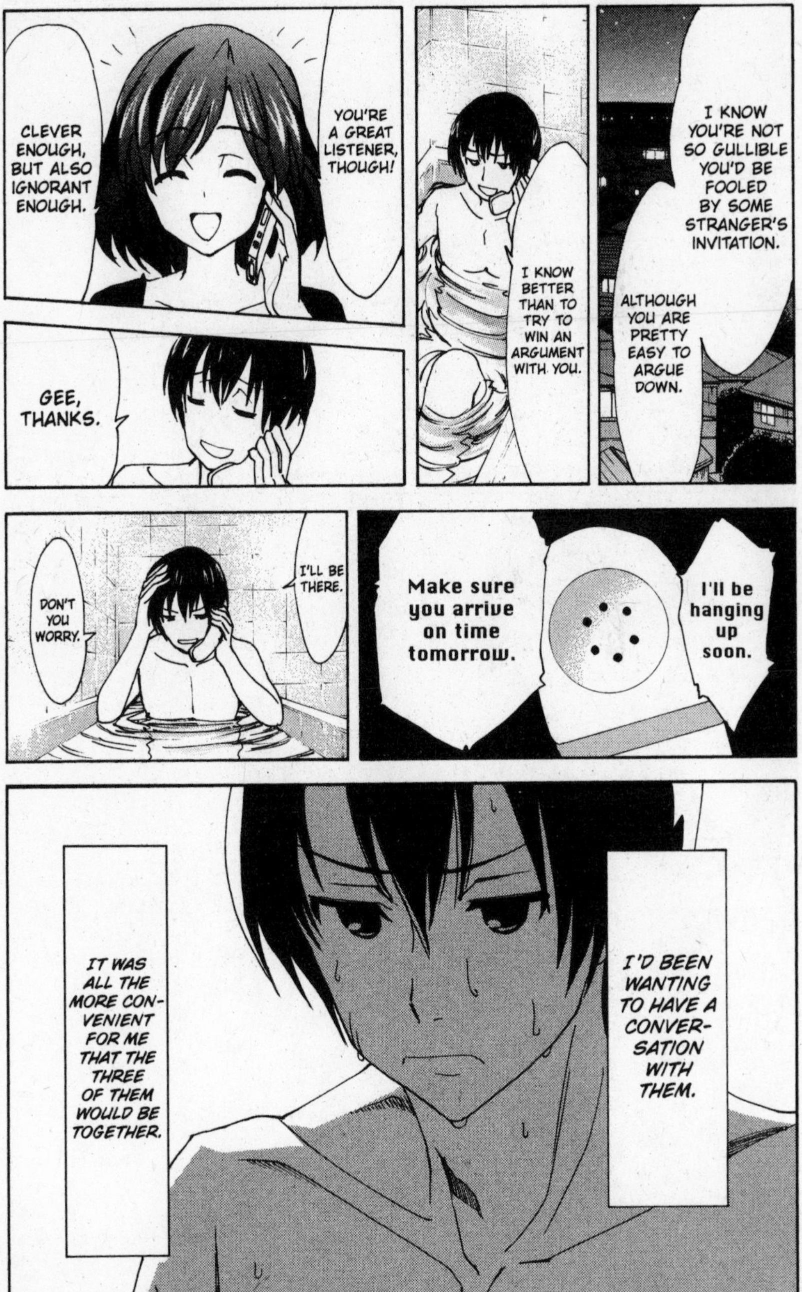
I KNOW YOU'RE NOT SO GULLIBLE YOU'D BE FOOLED BY SOME STRANGER'S INVITATION.
ALTHOUGH YOU ARE PRETTY EASY TO ARGUE DOWN.
I KNOW BETTER THAN TO TRY TO WIN AN ARGUMENT WITH YOU.
YOU'RE A GREAT LISTENER, THOUGH!
CLEVER ENOUGH, BUT ALSO IGNORANT ENOUGH.
GEE, THANKS.
I'll be hanging up soon.
Make sure you arrive on time tomorrow.
I'LL BE THERE.
DON'T YOU WORRY.
I'D BEEN WANTING TO HAVE A CONVER-SATION WITH THEM.
IT WAS ALL THE MORE CON-VENIENT FOR ME THAT THE THREE OF THEM WOULD BE TOGETHER.

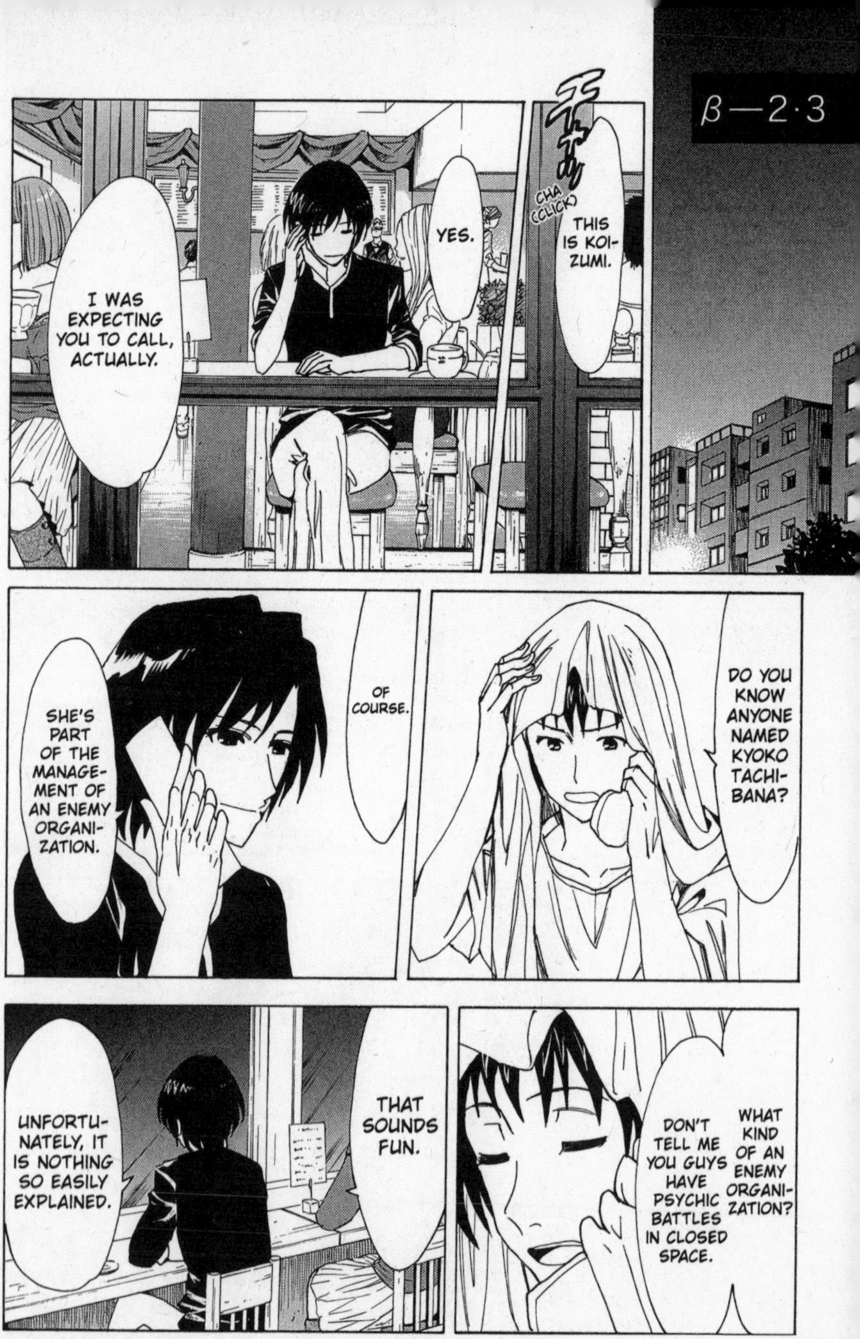
β—2·3
CHA (CLICK)
THIS IS KOI-ZUMI.
YES.
I WAS EXPECTING YOU TO CALL, ACTUALLY.
DO YOU KNOW ANYONE NAMED KYOKO TACHI-BANA?
OF COURSE.
SHE'S PART OF THE MANAGE-MENT OF AN ENEMY ORGANI-ZATION.
WHAT KIND OF AN ENEMY ORGANI-ZATION?
DON'T TELL ME YOU GUYS HAVE PSYCHIC BATTLES IN CLOSED SPACE.
THAT SOUNDS FUN.
UNFORTU-NATELY, IT IS NOTHING SO EASILY EXPLAINED.

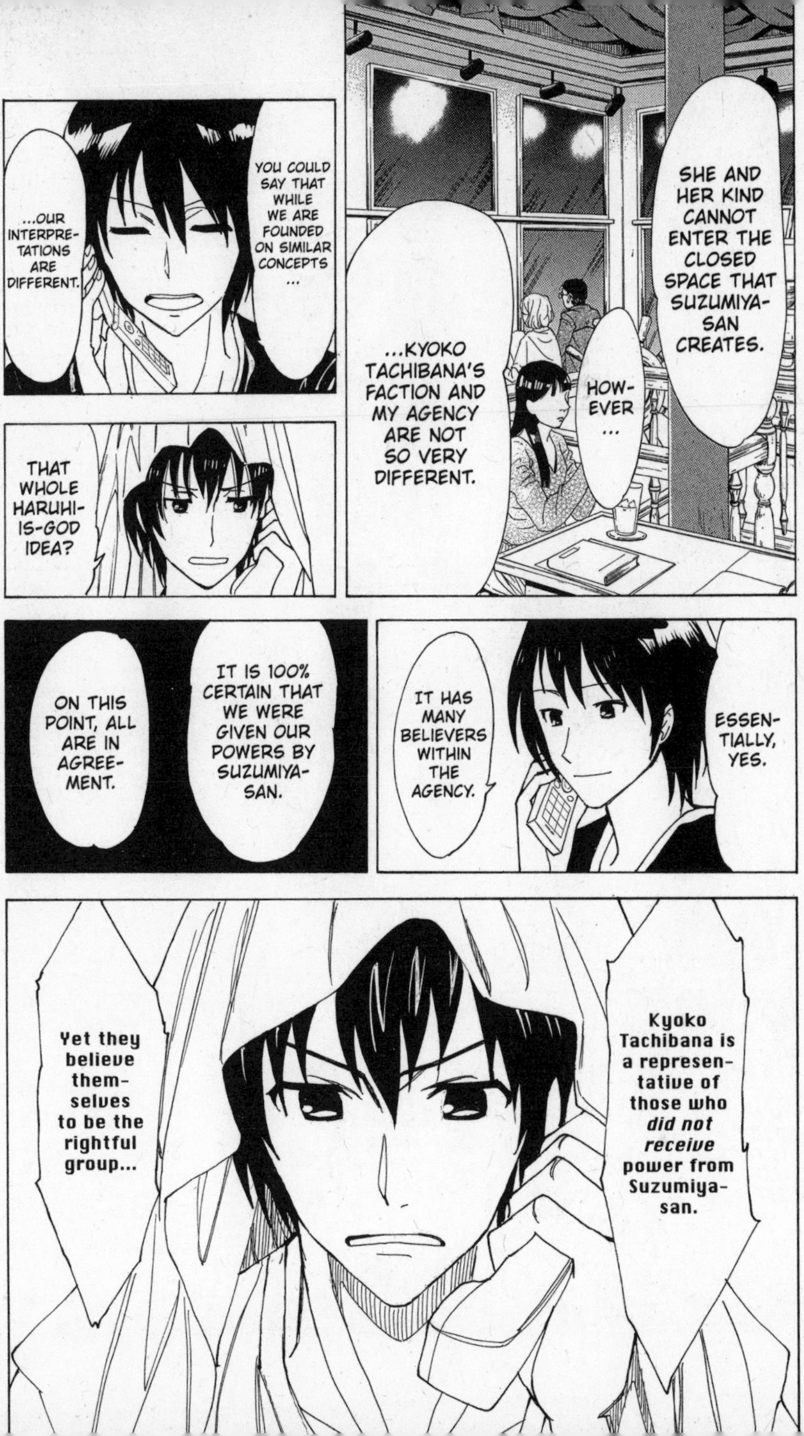
SHE AND HER KIND CANNOT ENTER THE CLOSED SPACE THAT SUZUMIYA-SAN CREATES.
HOWEVER...
...KYOKO TACHIBANA'S FACTION AND MY AGENCY ARE NOT SO VERY DIFFERENT.
YOU COULD SAY THAT WHILE WE ARE FOUNDED ON SIMILAR CONCEPTS...
...OUR INTERPRETATIONS ARE DIFFERENT.
THAT WHOLE HARUHI-IS-GOD IDEA?
ESSENTIALLY, YES.
IT HAS MANY BELIEVERS WITHIN THE AGENCY.
IT IS 100% CERTAIN THAT WE WERE GIVEN OUR POWERS BY SUZUMIYA-SAN.
ON THIS POINT, ALL ARE IN AGREEMENT.
Kyoko Tachibana is a representative of those who *did not receive* power from Suzumiya-san.
Yet they believe themselves to be the rightful group...

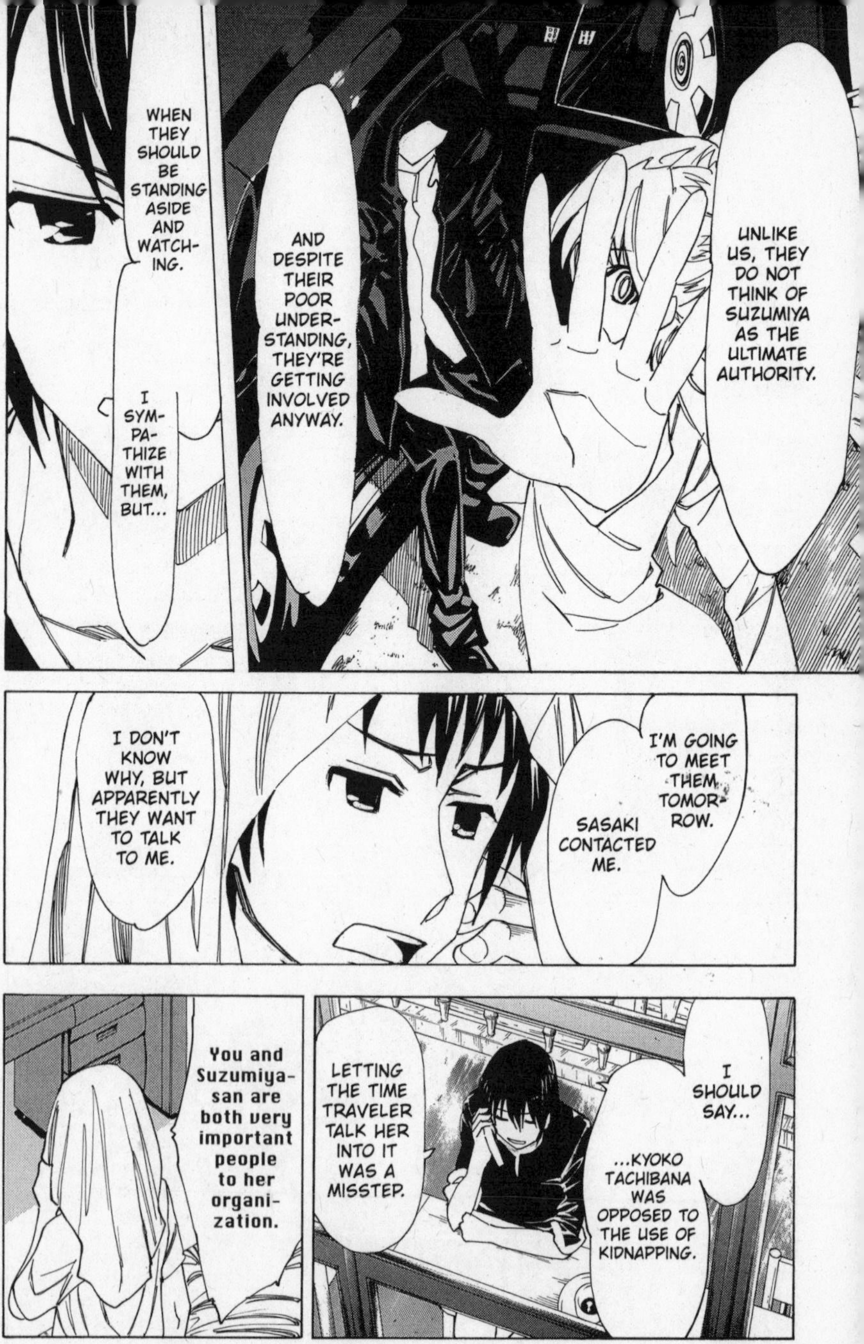
UNLIKE US, THEY DO NOT THINK OF SUZUMIYA AS THE ULTIMATE AUTHORITY.
AND DESPITE THEIR POOR UNDER-STANDING, THEY'RE GETTING INVOLVED ANYWAY.
WHEN THEY SHOULD BE STANDING ASIDE AND WATCH-ING.
I SYM-PA-THIZE WITH THEM, BUT...
I'M GOING TO MEET THEM TOMOR-ROW.
SASAKI CONTACTED ME.
I DON'T KNOW WHY, BUT APPARENTLY THEY WANT TO TALK TO ME.
I SHOULD SAY...
...KYOKO TACHIBANA WAS OPPOSED TO THE USE OF KIDNAPPING.
LETTING THE TIME TRAVELER TALK HER INTO IT WAS A MISSTEP.
You and Suzumiya-san are both very important people to her organi-zation.

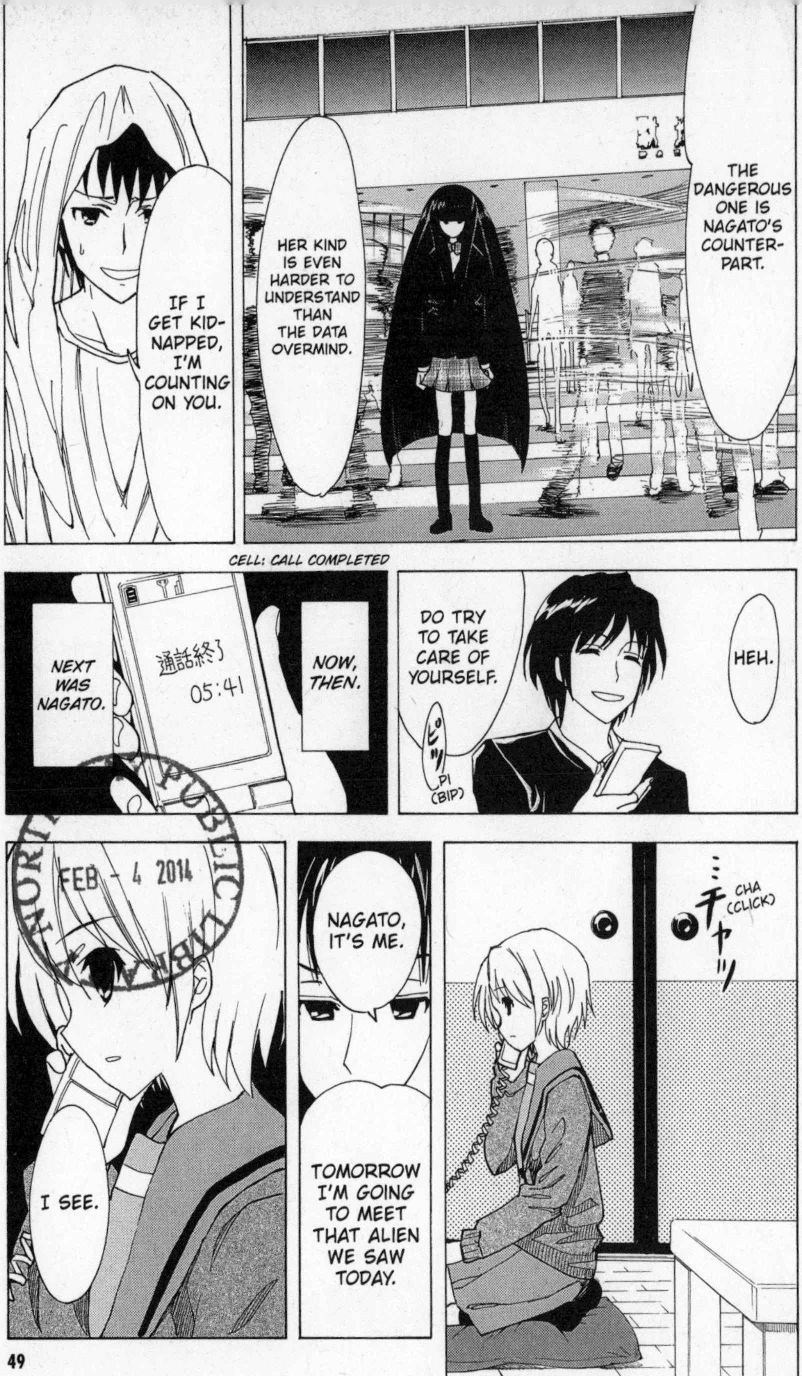
THE DANGEROUS ONE IS NAGATO'S COUNTER-PART.
HER KIND IS EVEN HARDER TO UNDERSTAND THAN THE DATA OVERMIND.
IF I GET KID-NAPPED, I'M COUNTING ON YOU.
HEH.
DO TRY TO TAKE CARE OF YOURSELF.
ピッ
PI (BIP)
NOW, THEN.
通話終了
05:41
CELL: CALL COMPLETED
NEXT WAS NAGATO.
チャッ
CHA (CLICK)
NAGATO, IT'S ME.
TOMORROW I'M GOING TO MEET THAT ALIEN WE SAW TODAY.
I SEE.

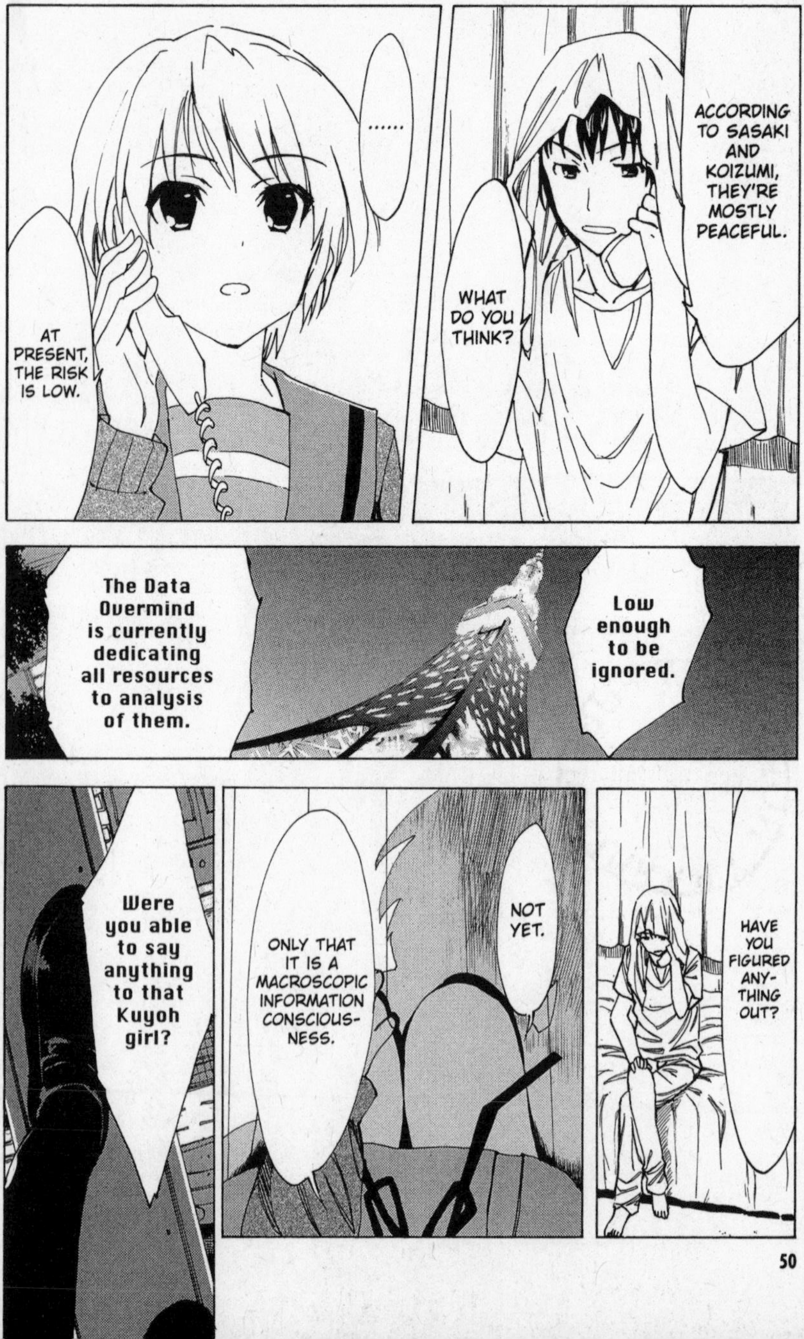
ACCORDING TO SASAKI AND KOIZUMI, THEY'RE MOSTLY PEACEFUL.
WHAT DO YOU THINK?
......
AT PRESENT, THE RISK IS LOW.
Low enough to be ignored.
The Data Overmind is currently dedicating all resources to analysis of them.
HAVE YOU FIGURED ANY-THING OUT?
NOT YET.
ONLY THAT IT IS A MACROSCOPIC INFORMATION CONSCIOUS-NESS.
Were you able to say anything to that Kuyoh girl?

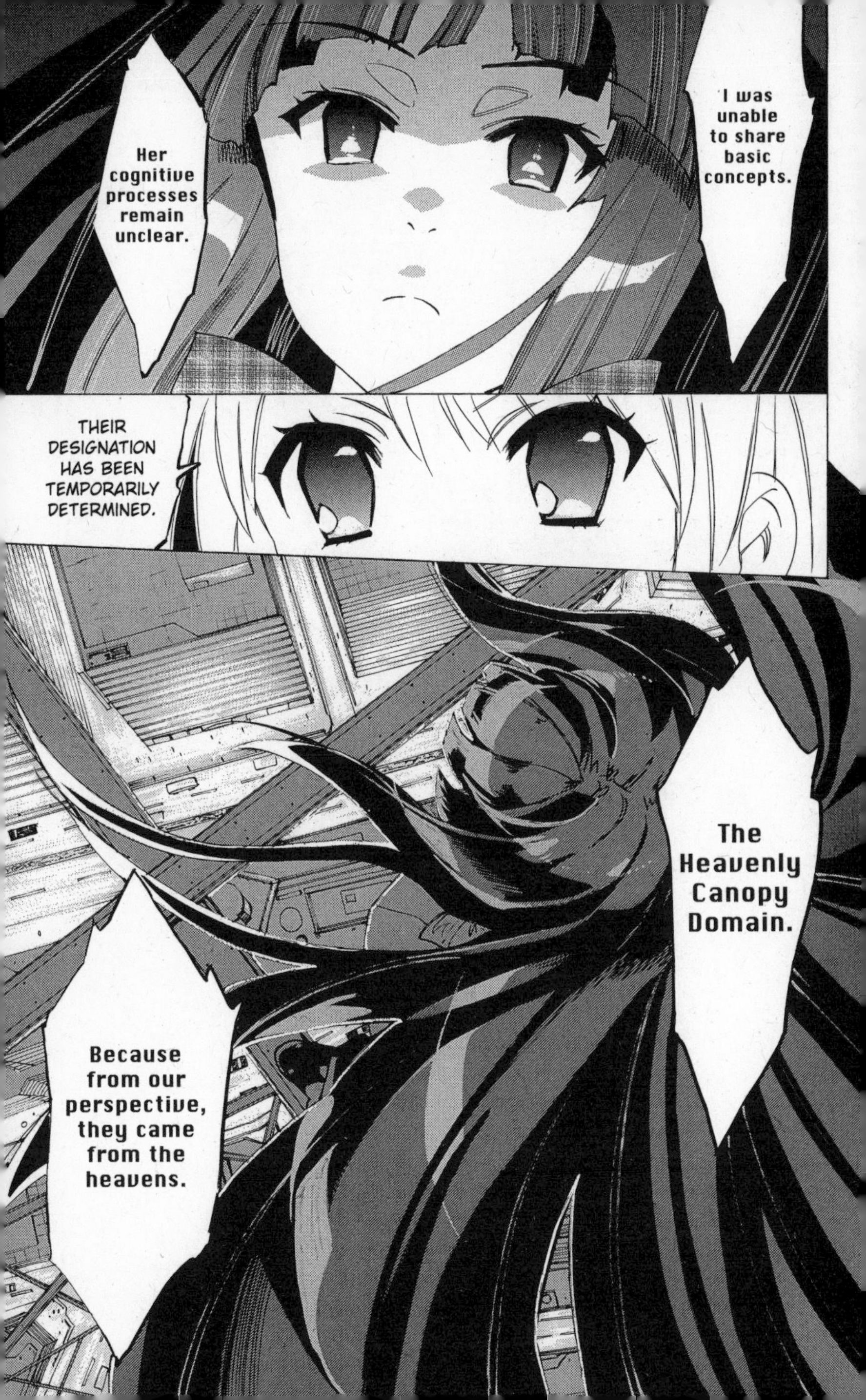
I was unable to share basic concepts.
Her cognitive processes remain unclear.
THEIR DESIGNATION HAS BEEN TEMPORARILY DETERMINED.
The Heavenly Canopy Domain.
Because from our perspective, they came from the heavens.

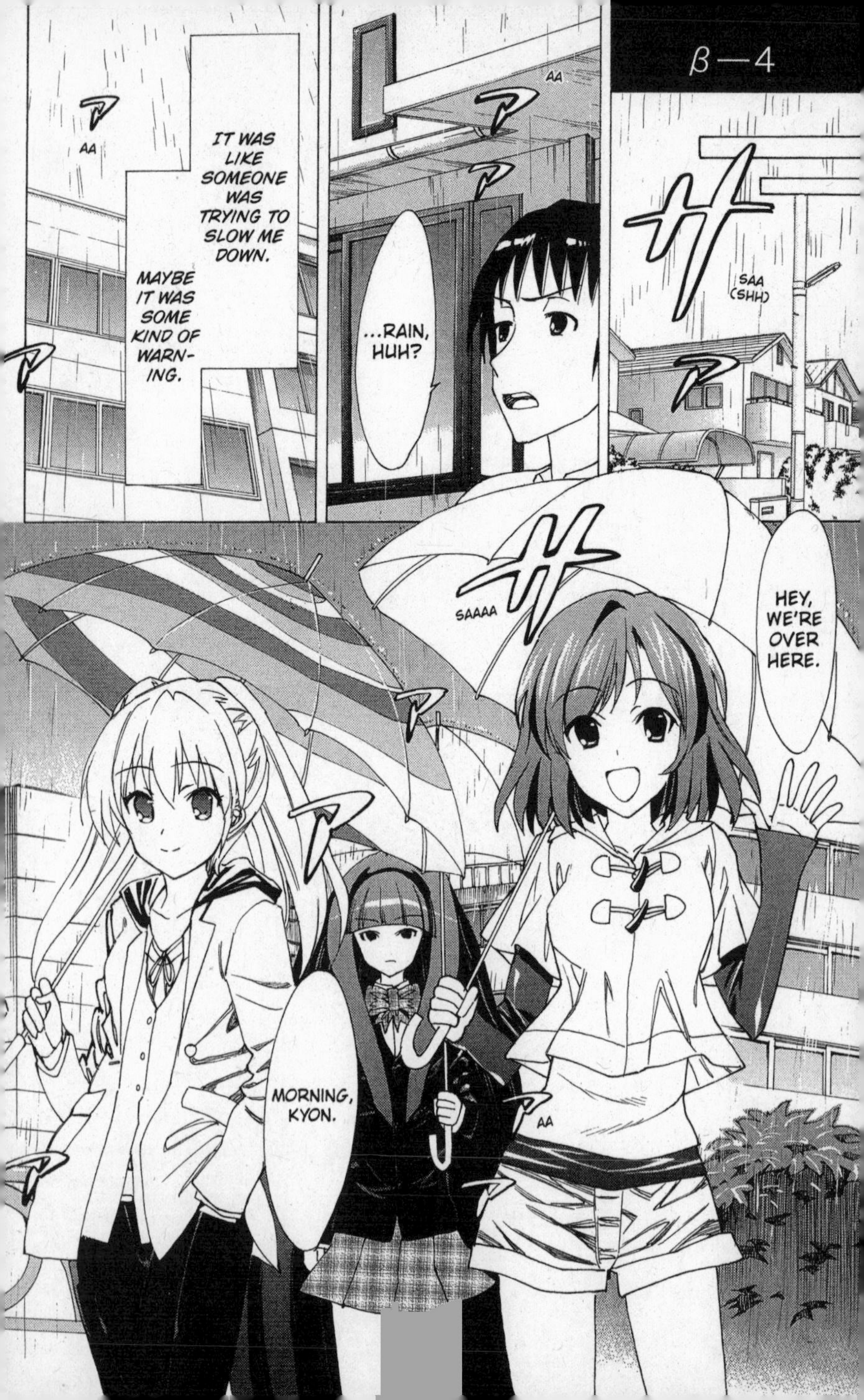
β—4
SAA (SHH)
AA
...RAIN, HUH?
IT WAS LIKE SOMEONE WAS TRYING TO SLOW ME DOWN.
MAYBE IT WAS SOME KIND OF WARN-ING.
AA
HEY, WE'RE OVER HERE.
SAAAA
MORNING, KYON.
AA

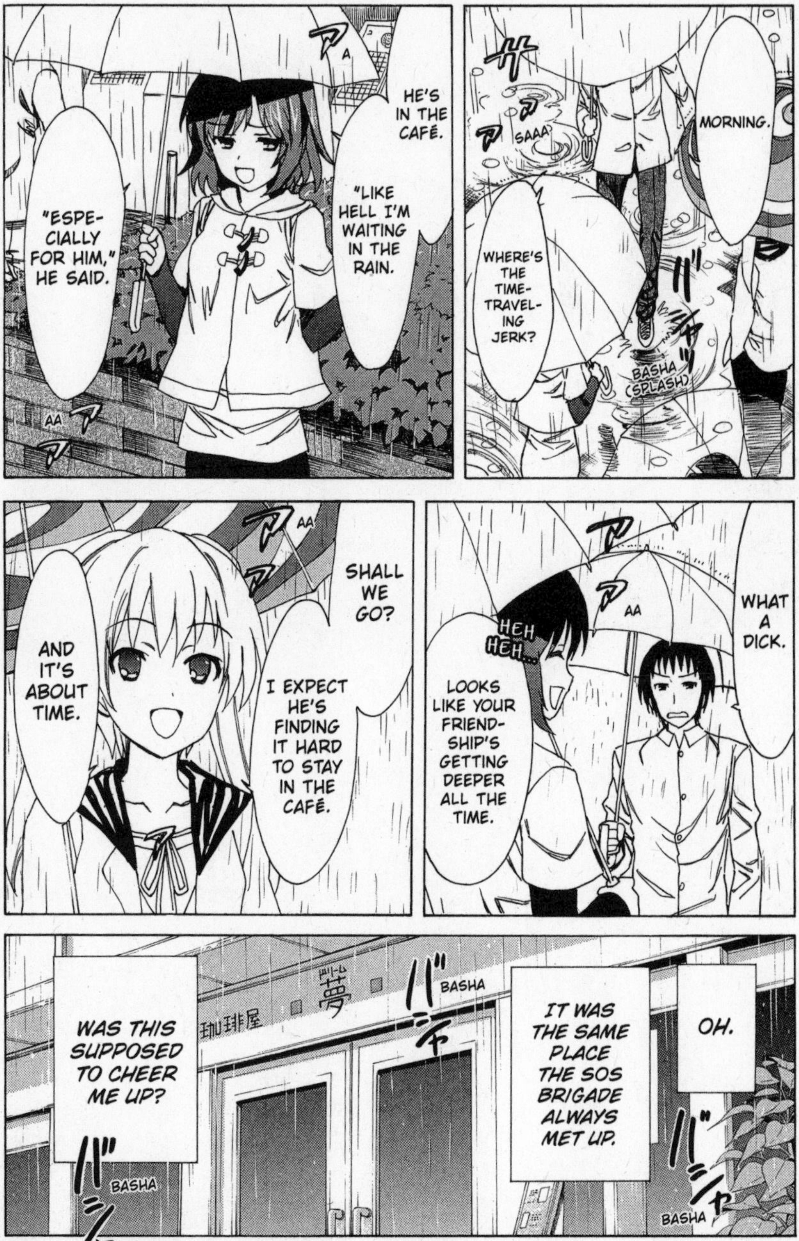
SAAA
MORNING.
WHERE'S THE TIME-TRAVEL-ING JERK?
BASHA (SPLASH)
A
HE'S IN THE CAFÉ.
"LIKE HELL I'M WAITING IN THE RAIN.
"ESPE-CIALLY FOR HIM," HE SAID.
AA
AA
WHAT A DICK.
HEH HEH...
LOOKS LIKE YOUR FRIEND-SHIP'S GETTING DEEPER ALL THE TIME.
AA
SHALL WE GO?
I EXPECT HE'S FINDING IT HARD TO STAY IN THE CAFÉ.
AND IT'S ABOUT TIME.
OH.
IT WAS THE SAME PLACE THE SOS BRIGADE ALWAYS MET UP.
BASHA
夢
珈琲屋
WAS THIS SUPPOSED TO CHEER ME UP?
BASHA
BASHA

SIGN: DREAM COFFEE SHOP

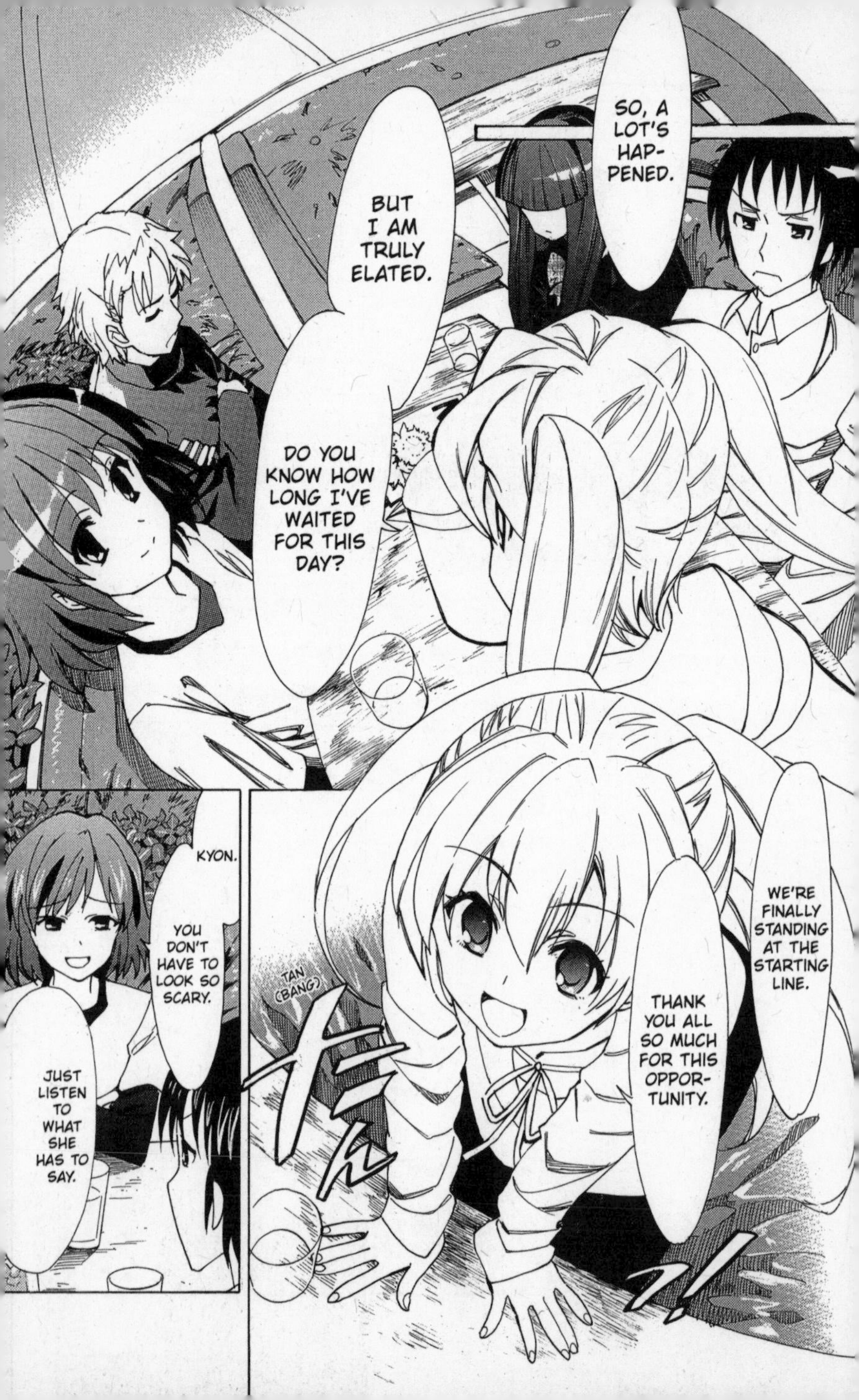
SO, A LOT'S HAP-PENED.
BUT I AM TRULY ELATED.
DO YOU KNOW HOW LONG I'VE WAITED FOR THIS DAY?
WE'RE FINALLY STANDING AT THE STARTING LINE.
THANK YOU ALL SO MUCH FOR THIS OPPOR-TUNITY.
TAN (BANG)
KYON.
YOU DON'T HAVE TO LOOK SO SCARY.
JUST LISTEN TO WHAT SHE HAS TO SAY.

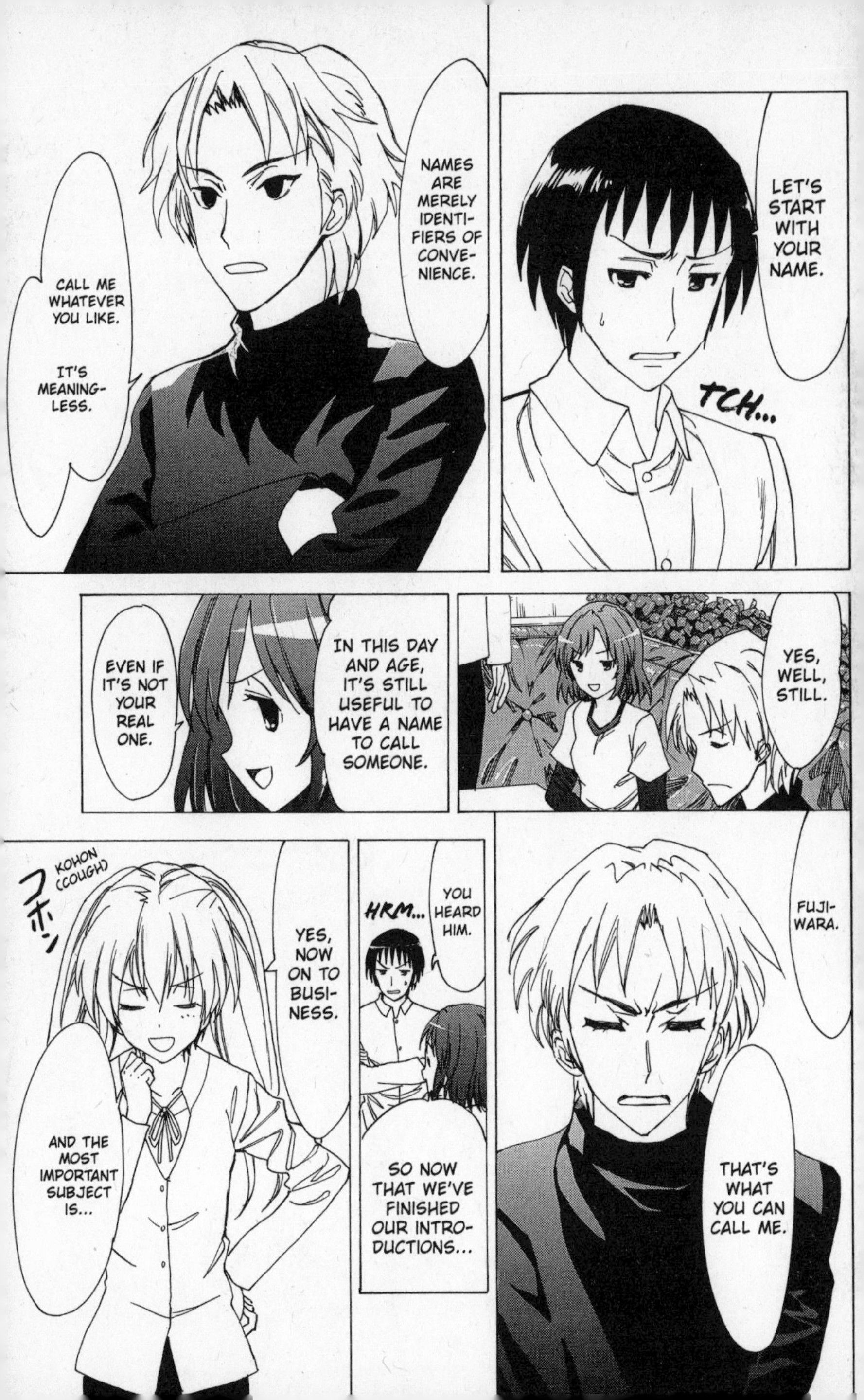
LET'S START WITH YOUR NAME.
TCH...
NAMES ARE MERELY IDENTIFIERS OF CONVENIENCE.
CALL ME WHATEVER YOU LIKE.
IT'S MEANINGLESS.
YES, WELL, STILL.
IN THIS DAY AND AGE, IT'S STILL USEFUL TO HAVE A NAME TO CALL SOMEONE.
EVEN IF IT'S NOT YOUR REAL ONE.
FUJIWARA.
THAT'S WHAT YOU CAN CALL ME.
YOU HEARD HIM.
HRM...
SO NOW THAT WE'VE FINISHED OUR INTRODUCTIONS...
YES, NOW ON TO BUSINESS.
KOHON (COUGH)
AND THE MOST IMPORTANT SUBJECT IS...

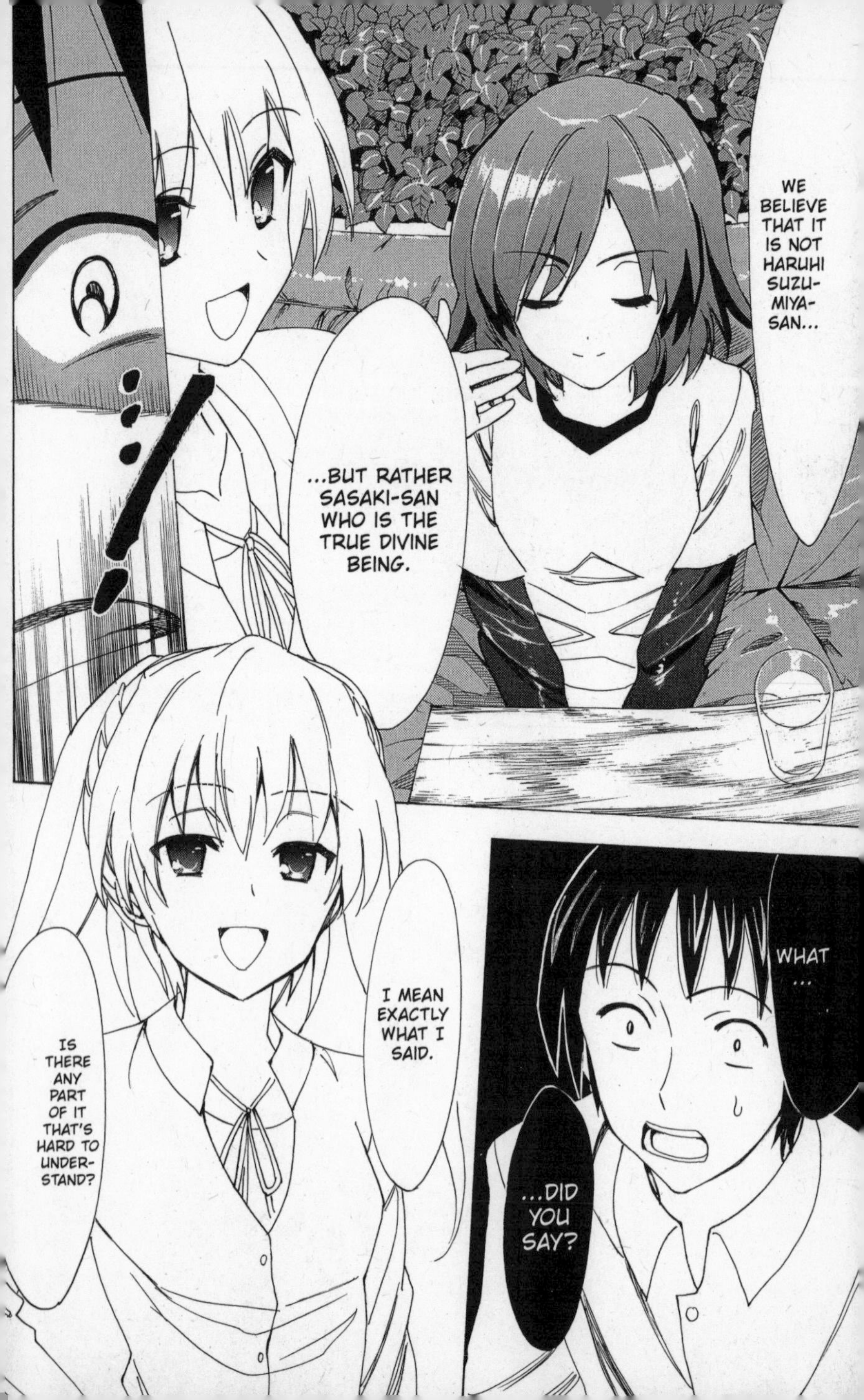
WE BELIEVE THAT IT IS NOT HARUHI SUZUMIYA-SAN...
...BUT RATHER SASAKI-SAN WHO IS THE TRUE DIVINE BEING.
...!
WHAT ...
...DID YOU SAY?
I MEAN EXACTLY WHAT I SAID.
IS THERE ANY PART OF IT THAT'S HARD TO UNDERSTAND?

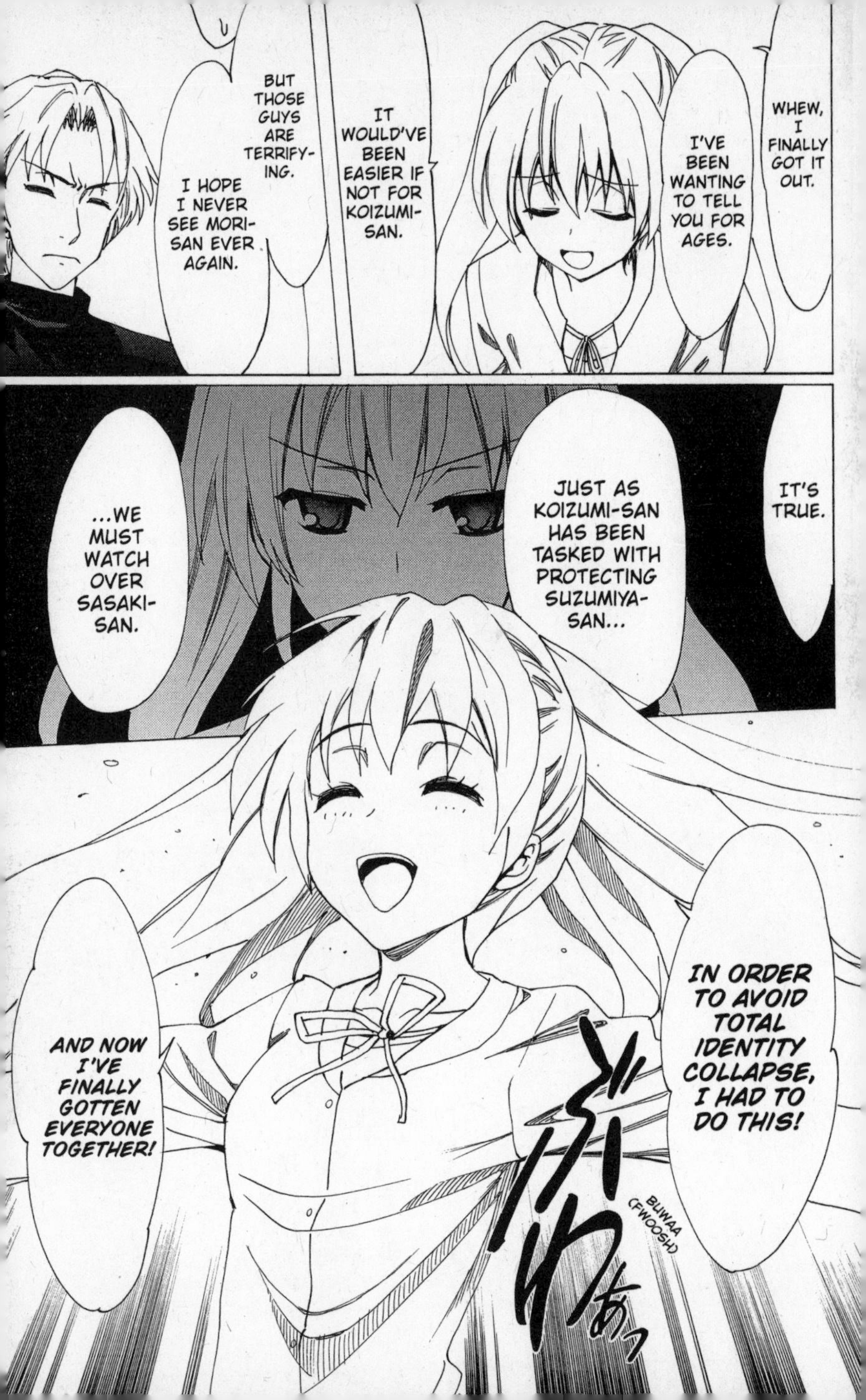
WHEW, I FINALLY GOT IT OUT.
I'VE BEEN WANTING TO TELL YOU FOR AGES.
IT WOULD'VE BEEN EASIER IF NOT FOR KOIZUMI-SAN.
BUT THOSE GUYS ARE TERRIFY-ING.
I HOPE I NEVER SEE MORI-SAN EVER AGAIN.
IT'S TRUE.
JUST AS KOIZUMI-SAN HAS BEEN TASKED WITH PROTECTING SUZUMIYA-SAN...
...WE MUST WATCH OVER SASAKI-SAN.
IN ORDER TO AVOID TOTAL IDENTITY COLLAPSE, I HAD TO DO THIS!
BUWAA (FWOOSH)
AND NOW I'VE FINALLY GOTTEN EVERYONE TOGETHER!

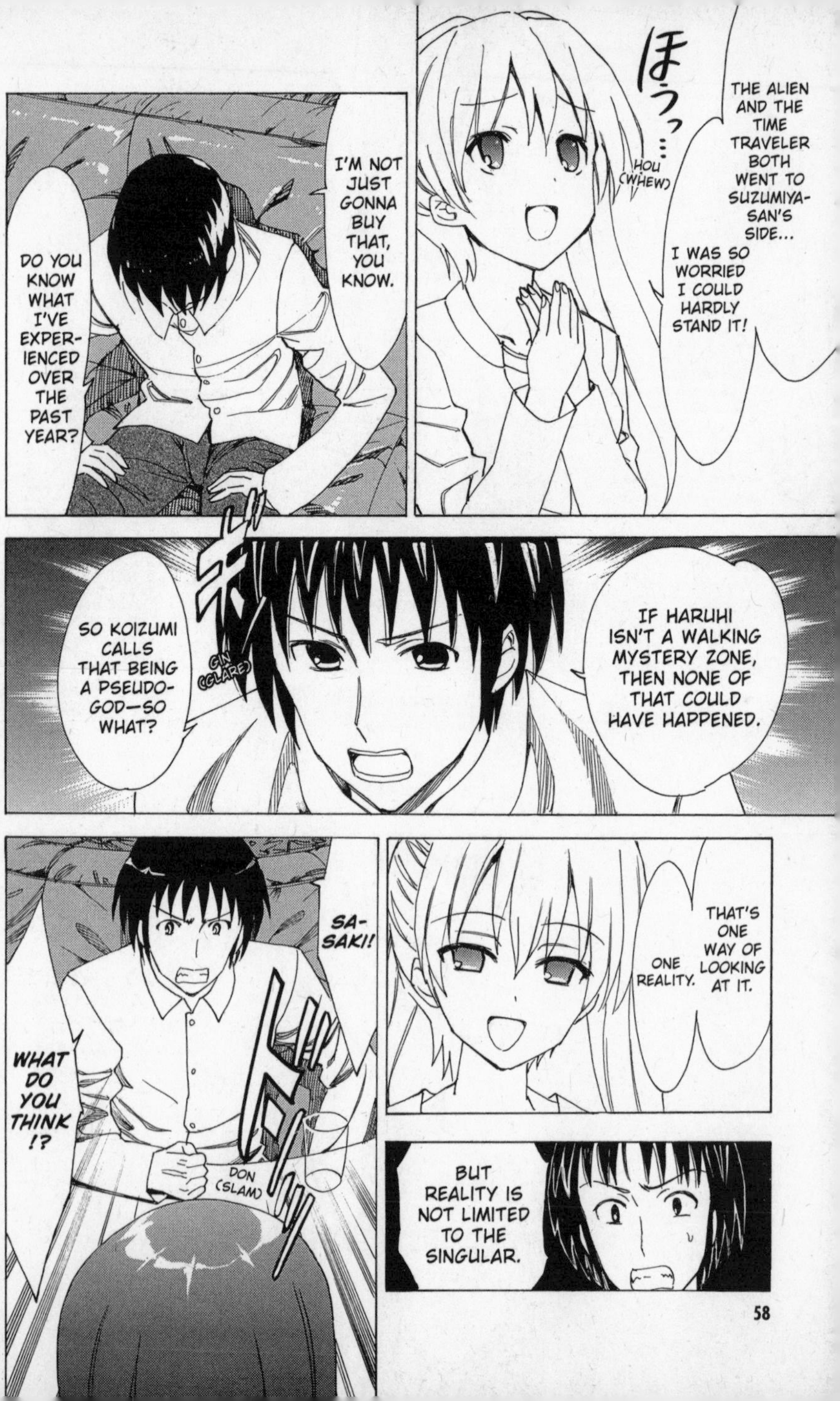
ほうっ…
HOU (WHEW)
THE ALIEN AND THE TIME TRAVELER BOTH WENT TO SUZUMIYA-SAN'S SIDE…
I WAS SO WORRIED I COULD HARDLY STAND IT!
I'M NOT JUST GONNA BUY THAT, YOU KNOW.
DO YOU KNOW WHAT I'VE EXPERIENCED OVER THE PAST YEAR?
IF HARUHI ISN'T A WALKING MYSTERY ZONE, THEN NONE OF THAT COULD HAVE HAPPENED.
GIN (GLARE)
SO KOIZUMI CALLS THAT BEING A PSEUDO-GOD—SO WHAT?
THAT'S ONE WAY OF LOOKING AT IT.
ONE REALITY.
BUT REALITY IS NOT LIMITED TO THE SINGULAR.
SA-SAKI!
WHAT DO YOU THINK!?
DON (SLAM)

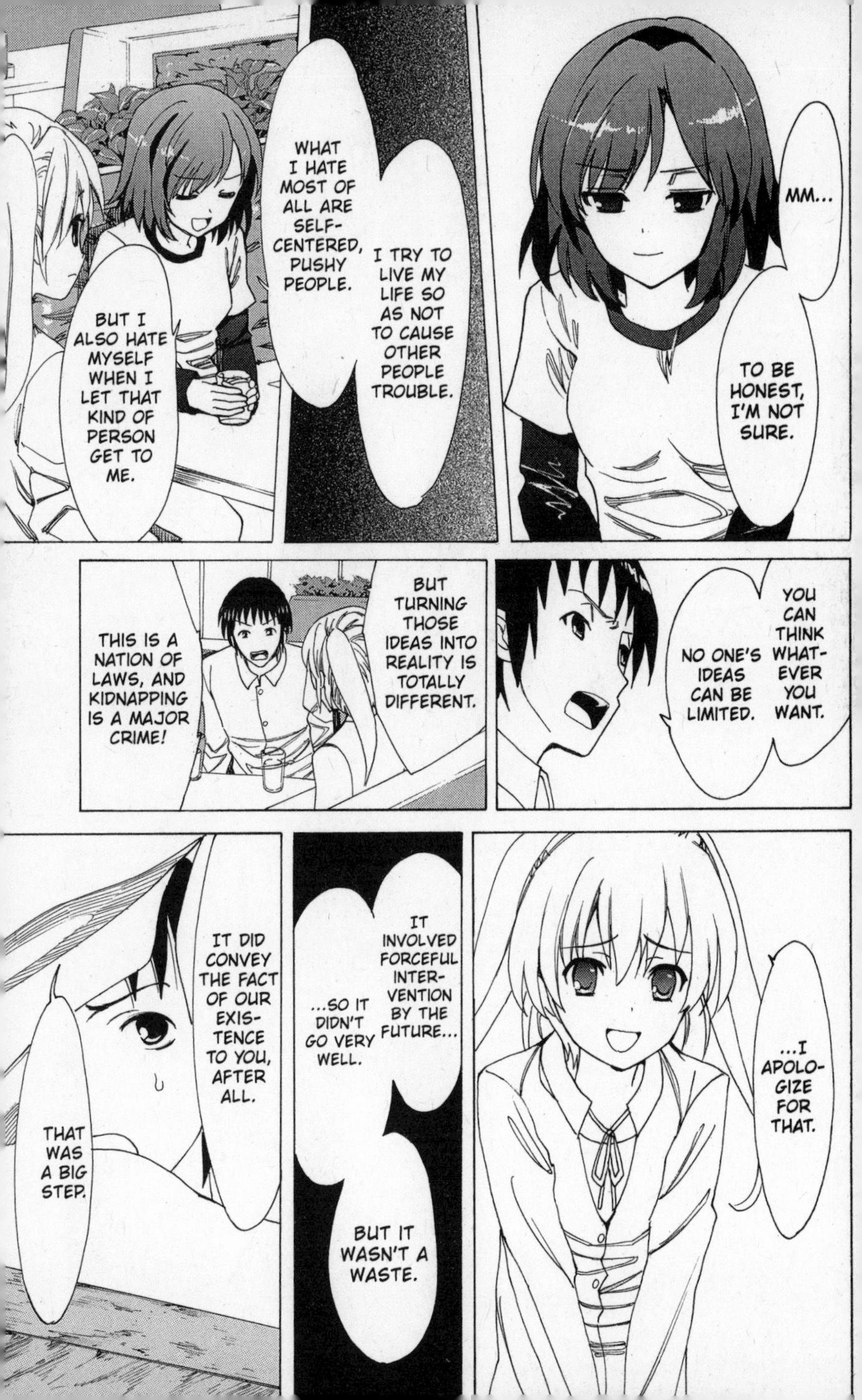
MM...
TO BE HONEST, I'M NOT SURE.
I TRY TO LIVE MY LIFE SO AS NOT TO CAUSE OTHER PEOPLE TROUBLE.
WHAT I HATE MOST OF ALL ARE SELF-CENTERED, PUSHY PEOPLE.
BUT I ALSO HATE MYSELF WHEN I LET THAT KIND OF PERSON GET TO ME.
YOU CAN THINK WHATEVER YOU WANT.
NO ONE'S IDEAS CAN BE LIMITED.
BUT TURNING THOSE IDEAS INTO REALITY IS TOTALLY DIFFERENT.
THIS IS A NATION OF LAWS, AND KIDNAPPING IS A MAJOR CRIME!
...I APOLOGIZE FOR THAT.
IT INVOLVED FORCEFUL INTERVENTION BY THE FUTURE...
...SO IT DIDN'T GO VERY WELL.
BUT IT WASN'T A WASTE.
IT DID CONVEY THE FACT OF OUR EXISTENCE TO YOU, AFTER ALL.
THAT WAS A BIG STEP.

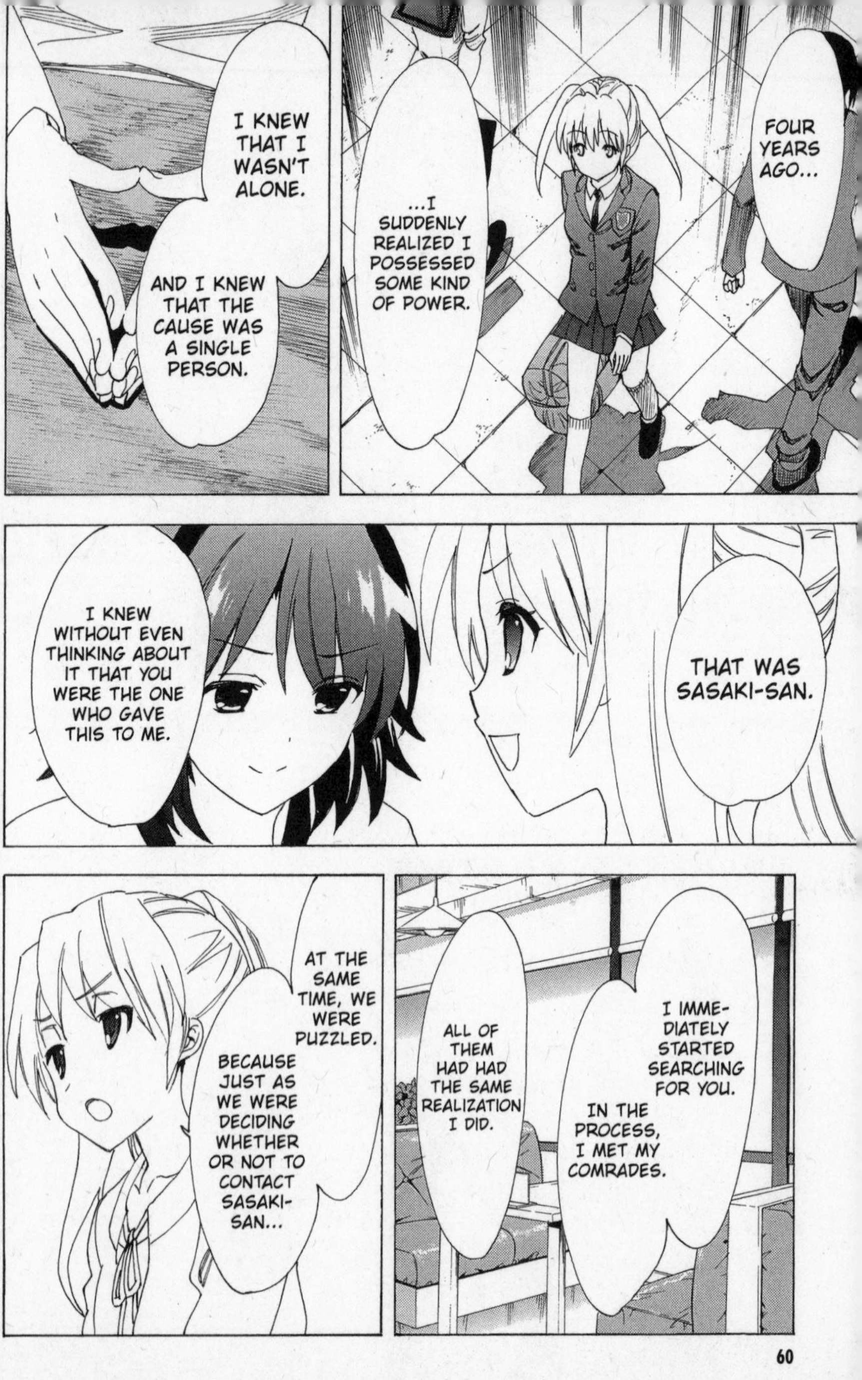
FOUR YEARS AGO...
...I SUDDENLY REALIZED I POSSESSED SOME KIND OF POWER.
I KNEW THAT I WASN'T ALONE.
AND I KNEW THAT THE CAUSE WAS A SINGLE PERSON.
THAT WAS SASAKI-SAN.
I KNEW WITHOUT EVEN THINKING ABOUT IT THAT YOU WERE THE ONE WHO GAVE THIS TO ME.
I IMME-DIATELY STARTED SEARCHING FOR YOU.
IN THE PROCESS, I MET MY COMRADES.
ALL OF THEM HAD HAD THE SAME REALIZATION I DID.
AT THE SAME TIME, WE WERE PUZZLED.
BECAUSE JUST AS WE WERE DECIDING WHETHER OR NOT TO CONTACT SASAKI-SAN...

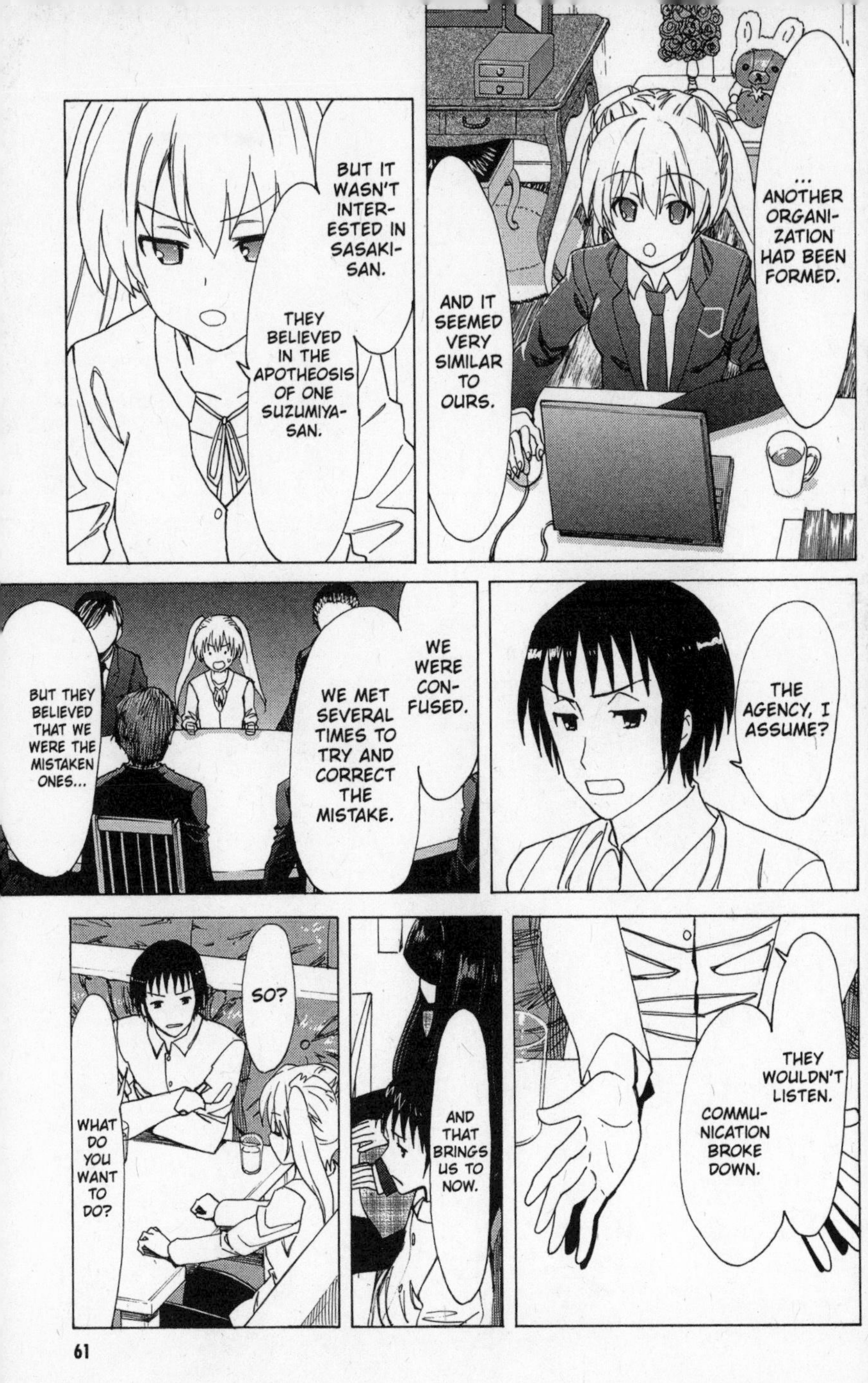
... ANOTHER ORGANIZATION HAD BEEN FORMED.
AND IT SEEMED VERY SIMILAR TO OURS.
BUT IT WASN'T INTERESTED IN SASAKI-SAN.
THEY BELIEVED IN THE APOTHEOSIS OF ONE SUZUMIYA-SAN.
THE AGENCY, I ASSUME?
WE WERE CONFUSED.
WE MET SEVERAL TIMES TO TRY AND CORRECT THE MISTAKE.
BUT THEY BELIEVED THAT WE WERE THE MISTAKEN ONES...
THEY WOULDN'T LISTEN.
COMMUNICATION BROKE DOWN.
AND THAT BRINGS US TO NOW.
SO?
WHAT DO YOU WANT TO DO?

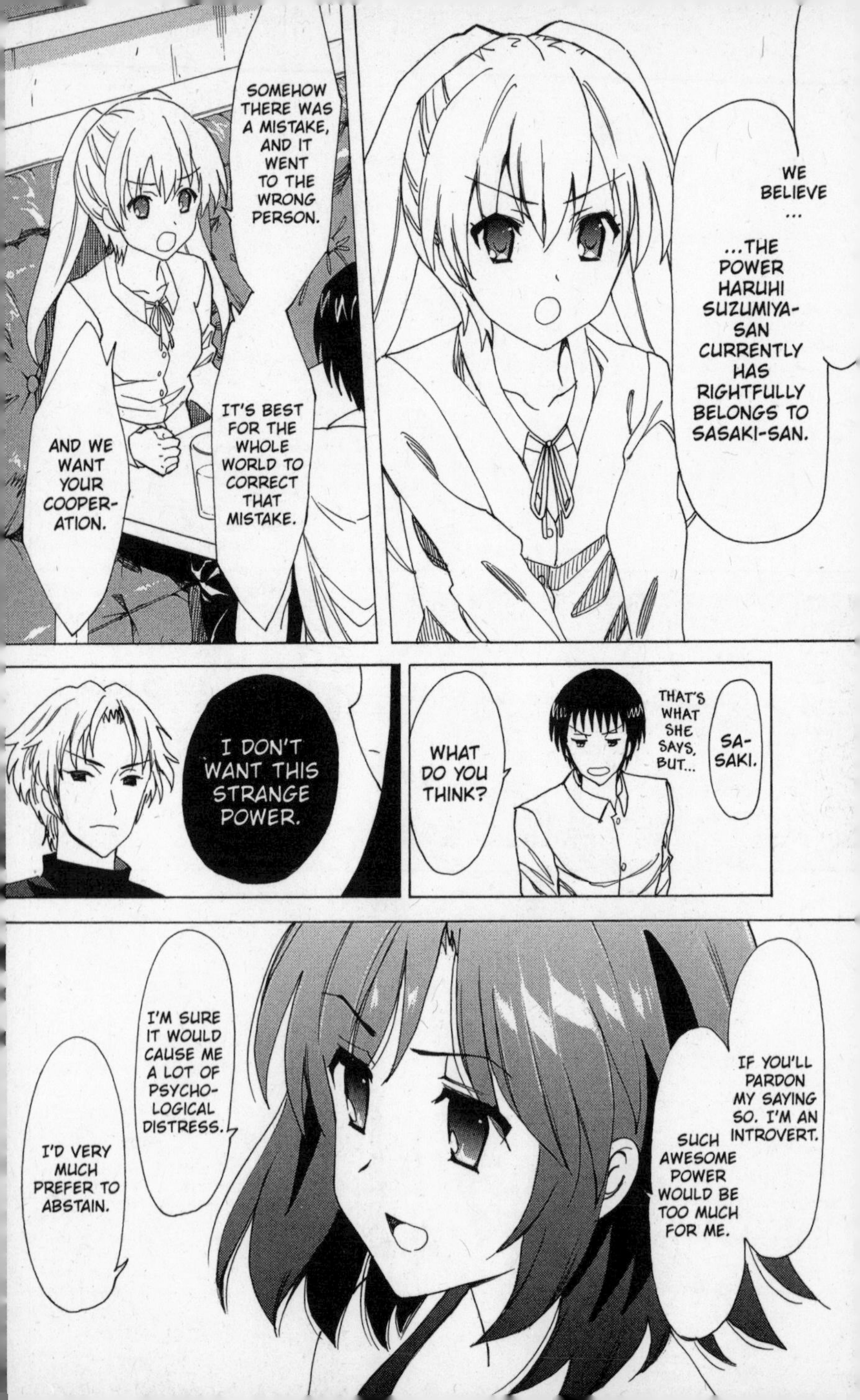
WE BELIEVE ...
...THE POWER HARUHI SUZUMIYA-SAN CURRENTLY HAS RIGHTFULLY BELONGS TO SASAKI-SAN.
SOMEHOW THERE WAS A MISTAKE, AND IT WENT TO THE WRONG PERSON.
IT'S BEST FOR THE WHOLE WORLD TO CORRECT THAT MISTAKE.
AND WE WANT YOUR COOPERATION.
SA-SAKI.
THAT'S WHAT SHE SAYS, BUT...
WHAT DO YOU THINK?
I DON'T WANT THIS STRANGE POWER.
IF YOU'LL PARDON MY SAYING SO. I'M AN INTROVERT.
SUCH AWESOME POWER WOULD BE TOO MUCH FOR ME.
I'M SURE IT WOULD CAUSE ME A LOT OF PSYCHOLOGICAL DISTRESS.
I'D VERY MUCH PREFER TO ABSTAIN.

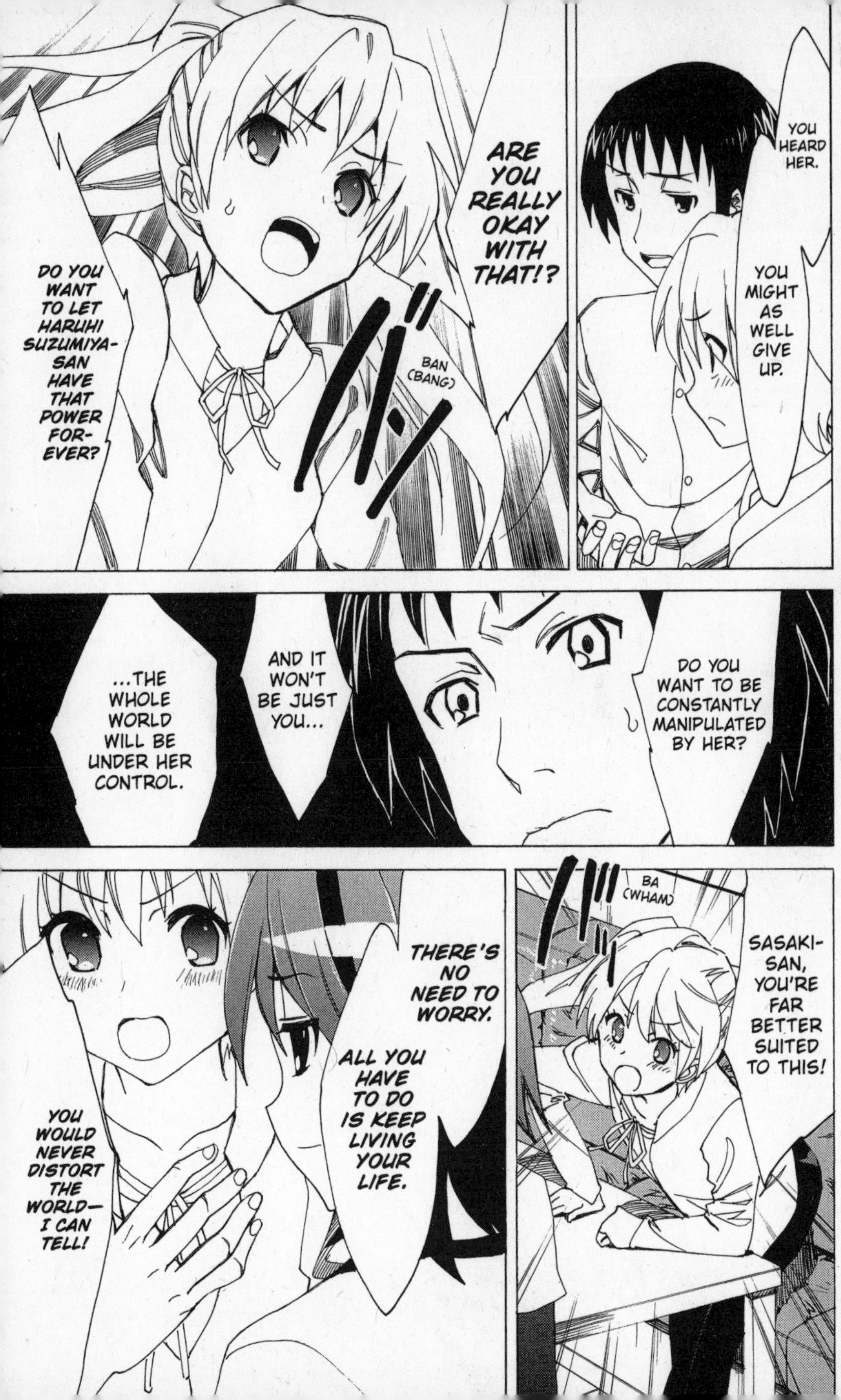
YOU HEARD HER.
YOU MIGHT AS WELL GIVE UP.
ARE YOU REALLY OKAY WITH THAT!?
BAN (BANG)
DO YOU WANT TO LET HARUHI SUZUMIYA-SAN HAVE THAT POWER FOREVER?
DO YOU WANT TO BE CONSTANTLY MANIPULATED BY HER?
AND IT WON'T BE JUST YOU...
...THE WHOLE WORLD WILL BE UNDER HER CONTROL.
BA (WHAM)
SASAKI-SAN, YOU'RE FAR BETTER SUITED TO THIS!
THERE'S NO NEED TO WORRY.
ALL YOU HAVE TO DO IS KEEP LIVING YOUR LIFE.
YOU WOULD NEVER DISTORT THE WORLD—I CAN TELL!

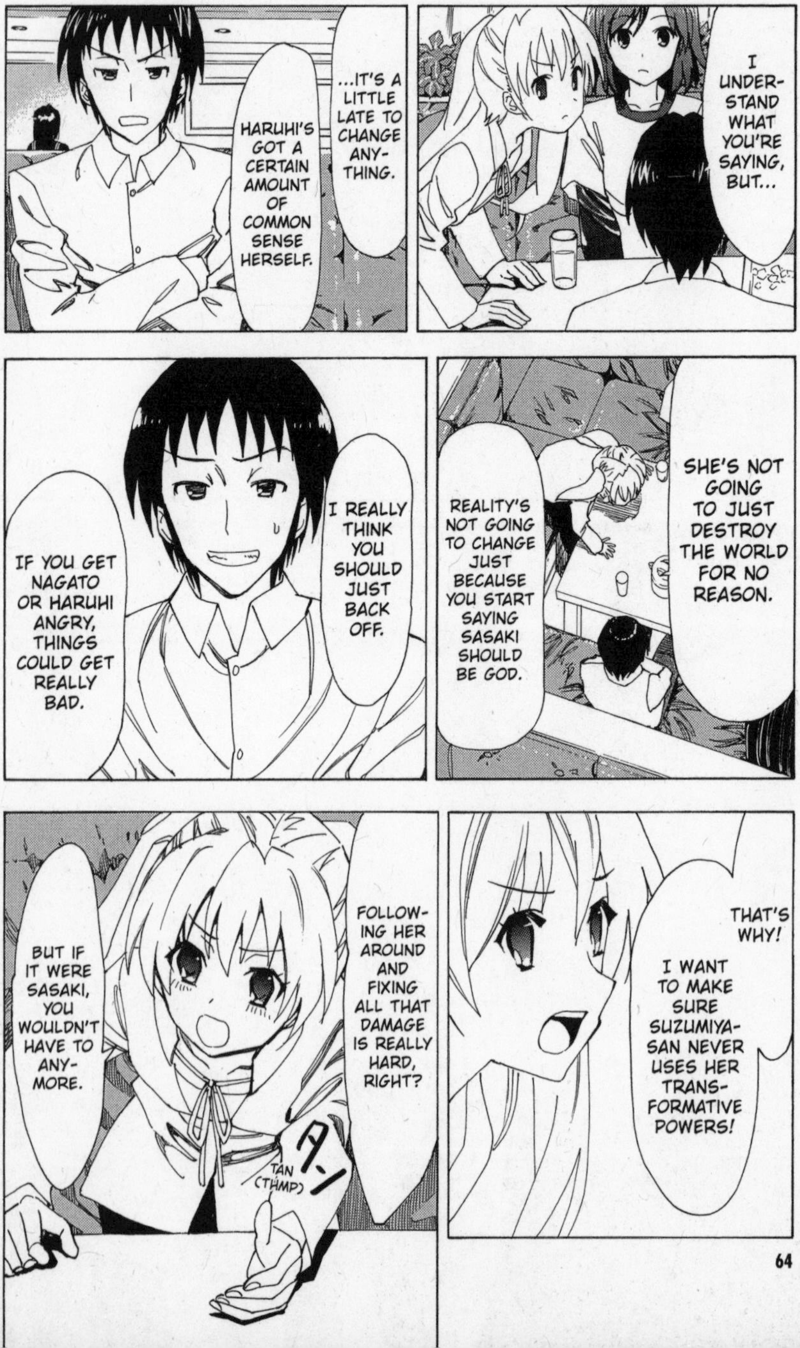
I UNDERSTAND WHAT YOU'RE SAYING, BUT...
...IT'S A LITTLE LATE TO CHANGE ANYTHING.
HARUHI'S GOT A CERTAIN AMOUNT OF COMMON SENSE HERSELF.
SHE'S NOT GOING TO JUST DESTROY THE WORLD FOR NO REASON.
REALITY'S NOT GOING TO CHANGE JUST BECAUSE YOU START SAYING SASAKI SHOULD BE GOD.
I REALLY THINK YOU SHOULD JUST BACK OFF.
IF YOU GET NAGATO OR HARUHI ANGRY, THINGS COULD GET REALLY BAD.
THAT'S WHY!
I WANT TO MAKE SURE SUZUMIYA-SAN NEVER USES HER TRANSFORMATIVE POWERS!
FOLLOWING HER AROUND AND FIXING ALL THAT DAMAGE IS REALLY HARD, RIGHT?
BUT IF IT WERE SASAKI, YOU WOULDN'T HAVE TO ANYMORE.
TAN (THMP)

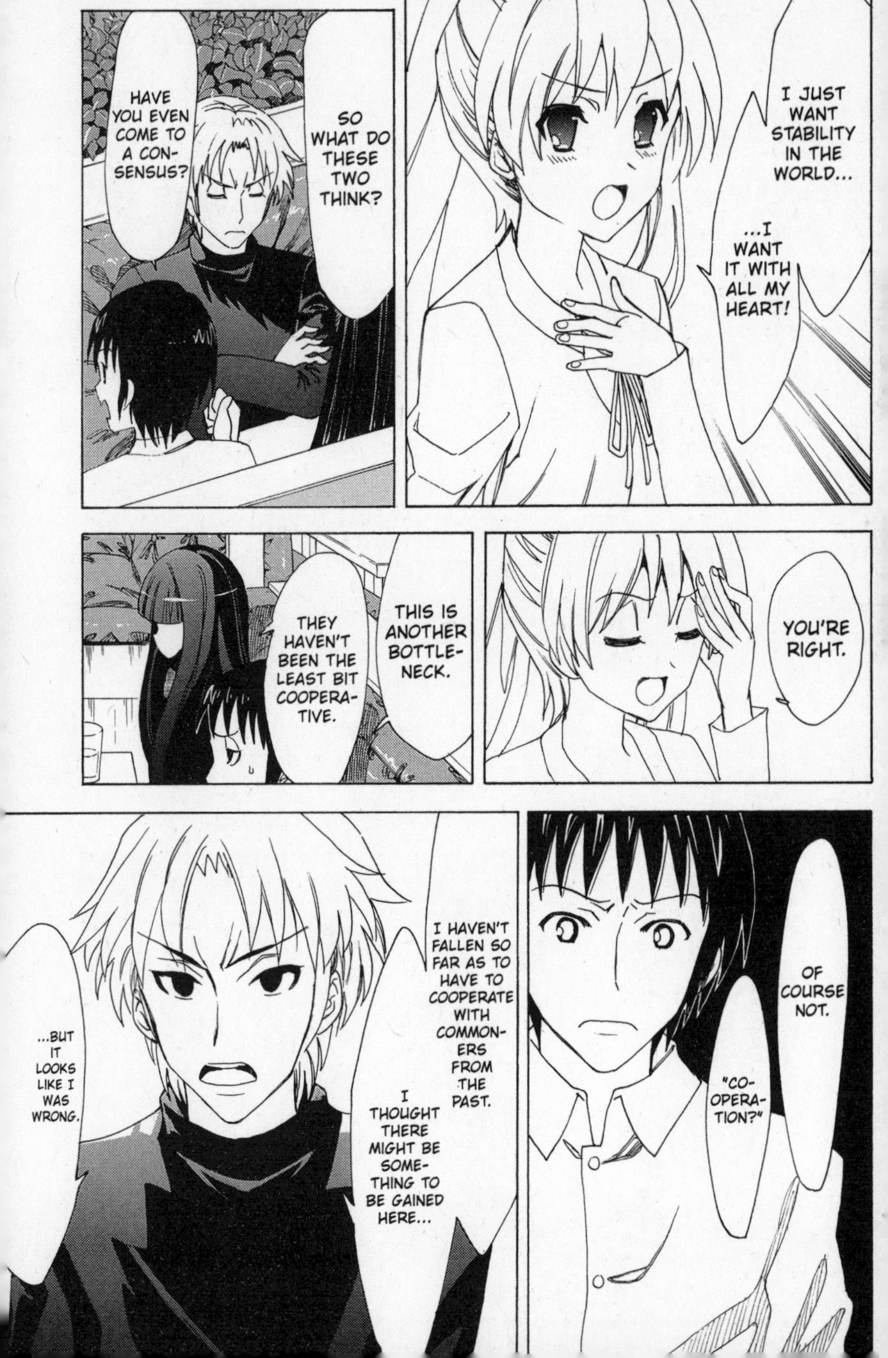
I JUST WANT STABILITY IN THE WORLD...
...I WANT IT WITH ALL MY HEART!
SO WHAT DO THESE TWO THINK?
HAVE YOU EVEN COME TO A CONSENSUS?
YOU'RE RIGHT.
THIS IS ANOTHER BOTTLENECK.
THEY HAVEN'T BEEN THE LEAST BIT COOPERATIVE.
OF COURSE NOT.
"COOPERATION?"
I HAVEN'T FALLEN SO FAR AS TO HAVE TO COOPERATE WITH COMMONERS FROM THE PAST.
I THOUGHT THERE MIGHT BE SOMETHING TO BE GAINED HERE...
...BUT IT LOOKS LIKE I WAS WRONG.

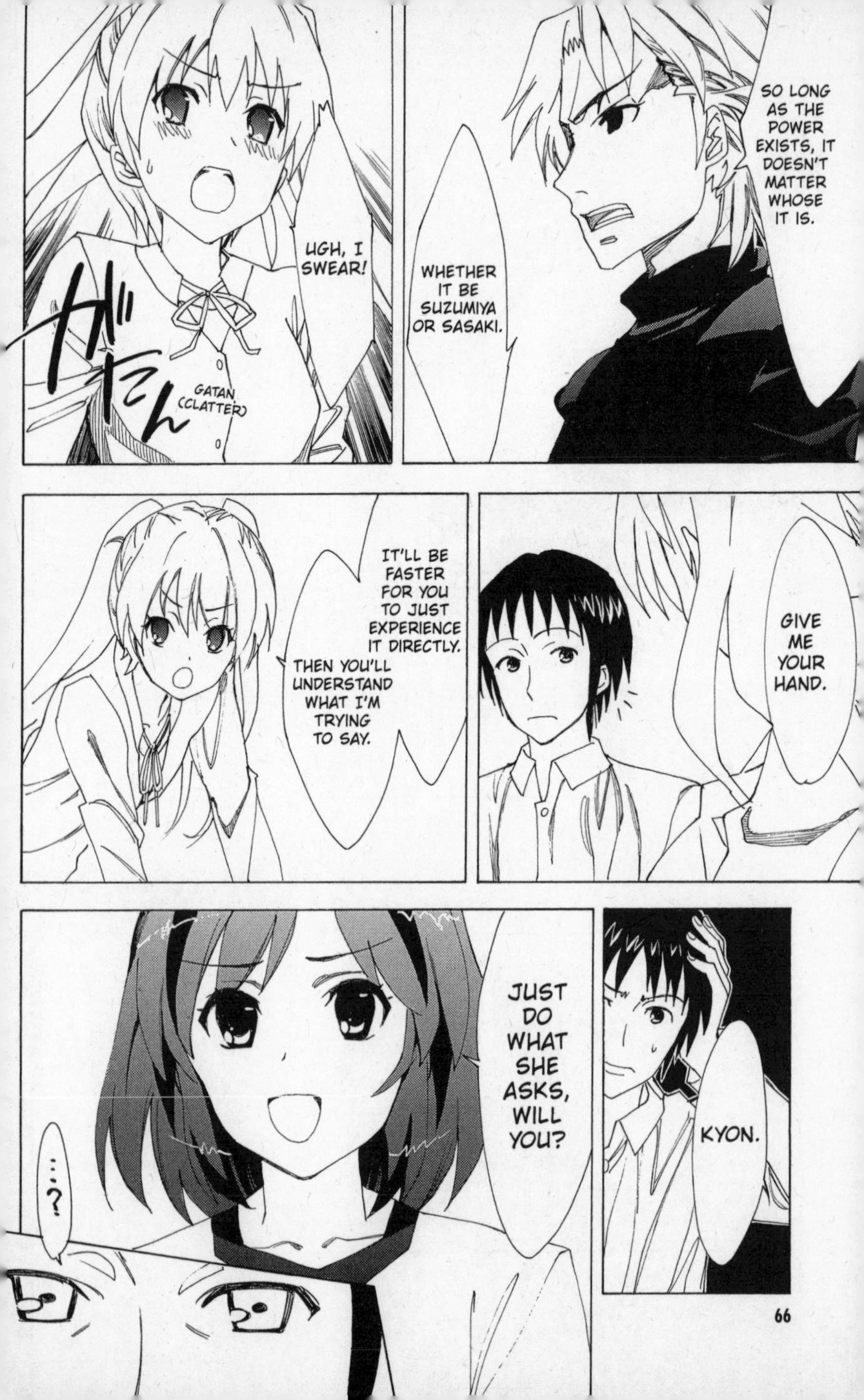
SO LONG AS THE POWER EXISTS, IT DOESN'T MATTER WHOSE IT IS.
WHETHER IT BE SUZUMIYA OR SASAKI.
UGH, I SWEAR!
GATAN (CLATTER)
GIVE ME YOUR HAND.
IT'LL BE FASTER FOR YOU TO JUST EXPERIENCE IT DIRECTLY.
THEN YOU'LL UNDERSTAND WHAT I'M TRYING TO SAY.
KYON.
JUST DO WHAT SHE ASKS, WILL YOU?
...?

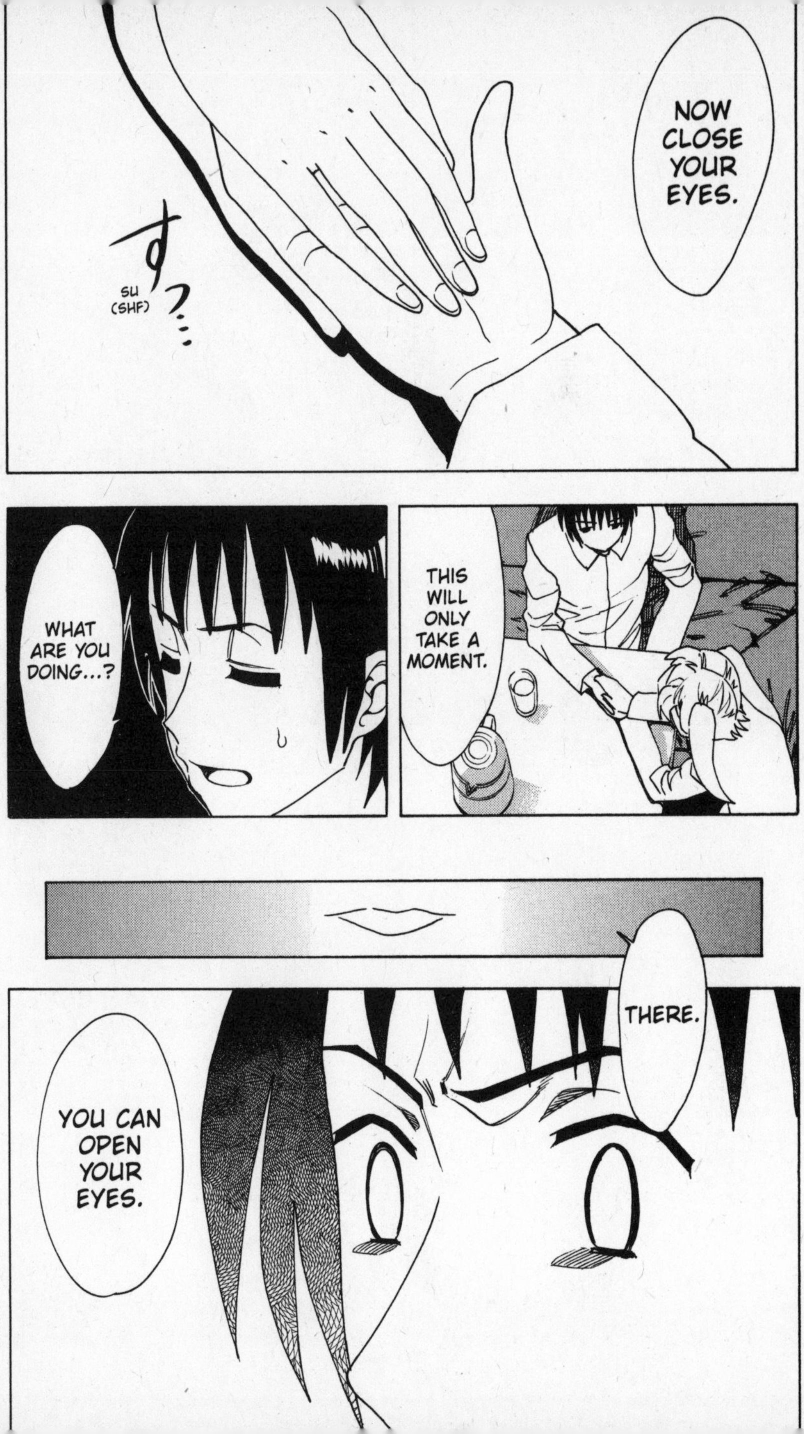
NOW CLOSE YOUR EYES.
すっ…
SU (SHF)
THIS WILL ONLY TAKE A MOMENT.
WHAT ARE YOU DOING...?
THERE.
YOU CAN OPEN YOUR EYES.

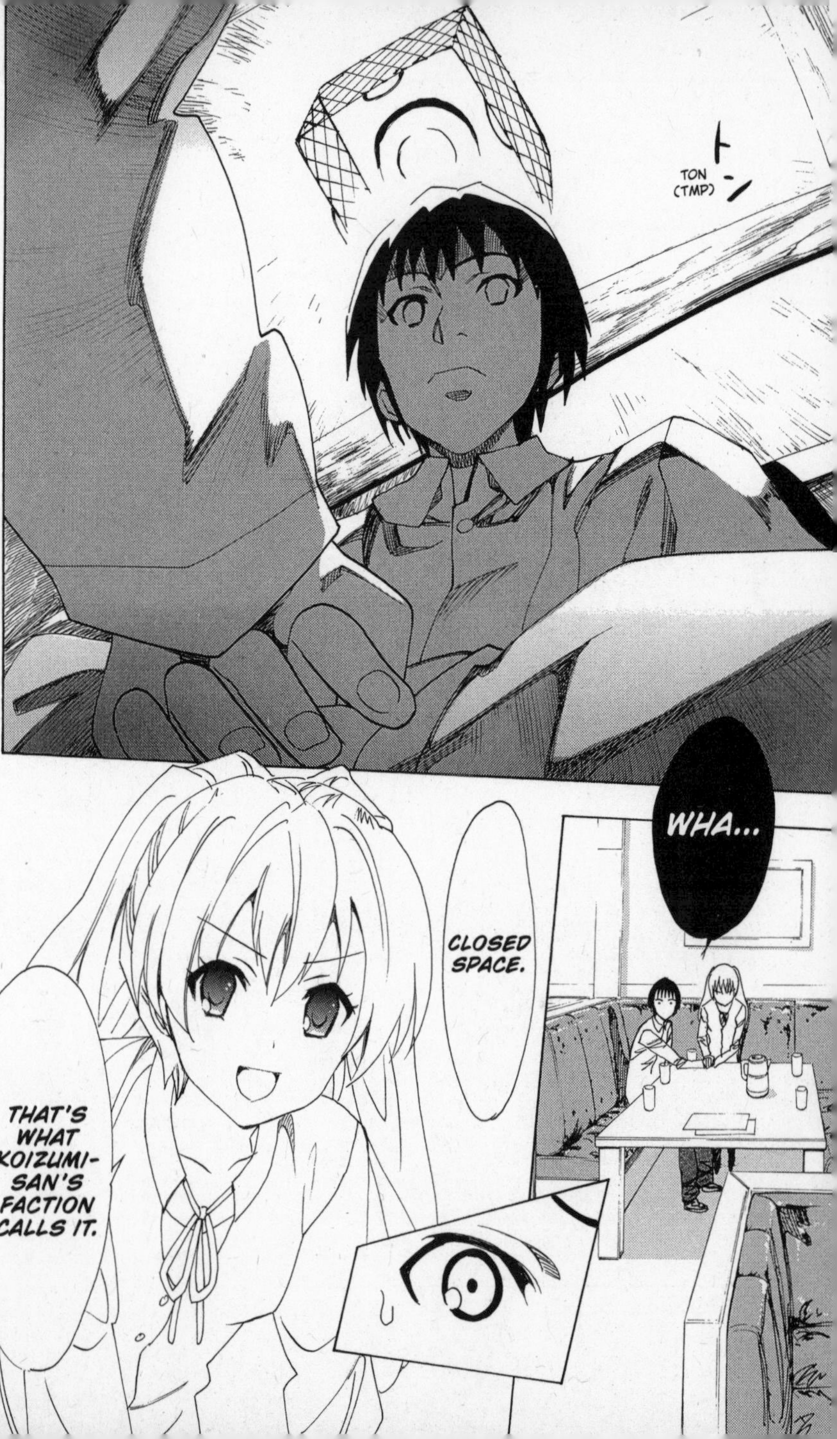
TON (TMP)
WHA...
CLOSED SPACE.
THAT'S WHAT KOIZUMI-SAN'S FACTION CALLS IT.

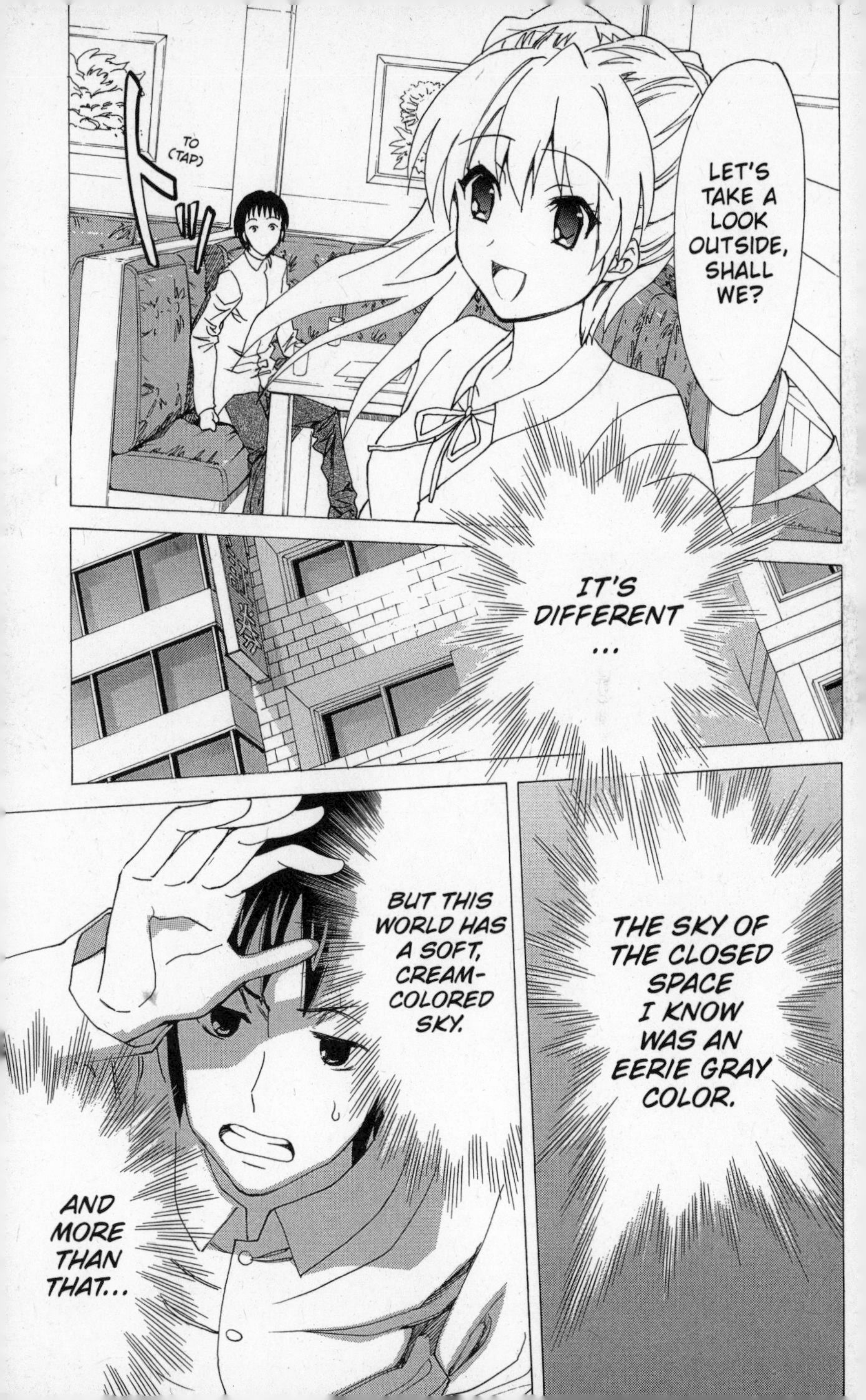
LET'S TAKE A LOOK OUTSIDE, SHALL WE?
TO (TAP)
IT'S DIFFERENT ...
THE SKY OF THE CLOSED SPACE I KNOW WAS AN EERIE GRAY COLOR.
BUT THIS WORLD HAS A SOFT, CREAM-COLORED SKY.
AND MORE THAN THAT...

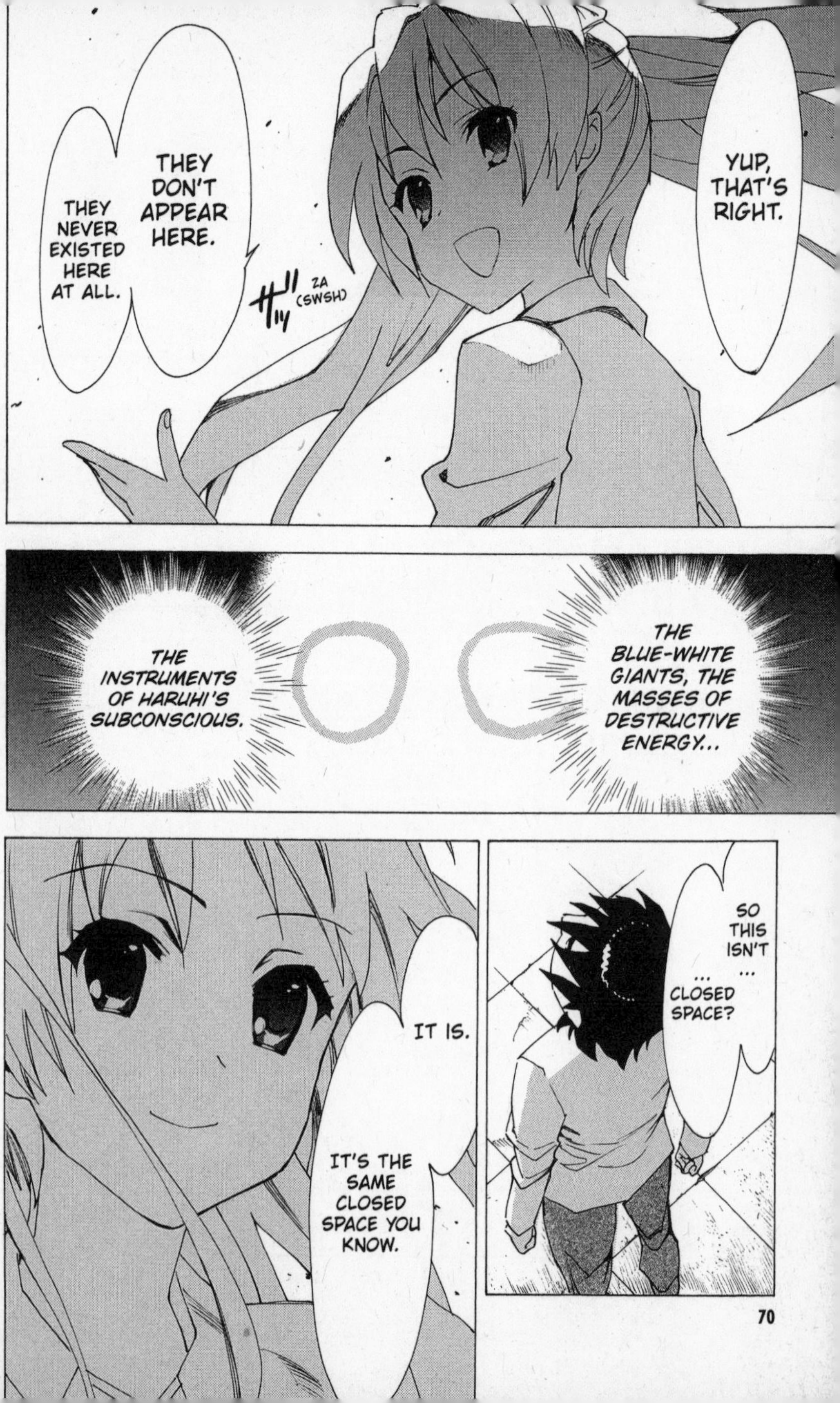
YUP, THAT'S RIGHT.
THEY DON'T APPEAR HERE.
THEY NEVER EXISTED HERE AT ALL.
ZA (SWSH)
THE BLUE-WHITE GIANTS, THE MASSES OF DESTRUCTIVE ENERGY...
THE INSTRUMENTS OF HARUHI'S SUBCONSCIOUS.
SO THIS ISN'T ... ... CLOSED SPACE?
IT IS.
IT'S THE SAME CLOSED SPACE YOU KNOW.

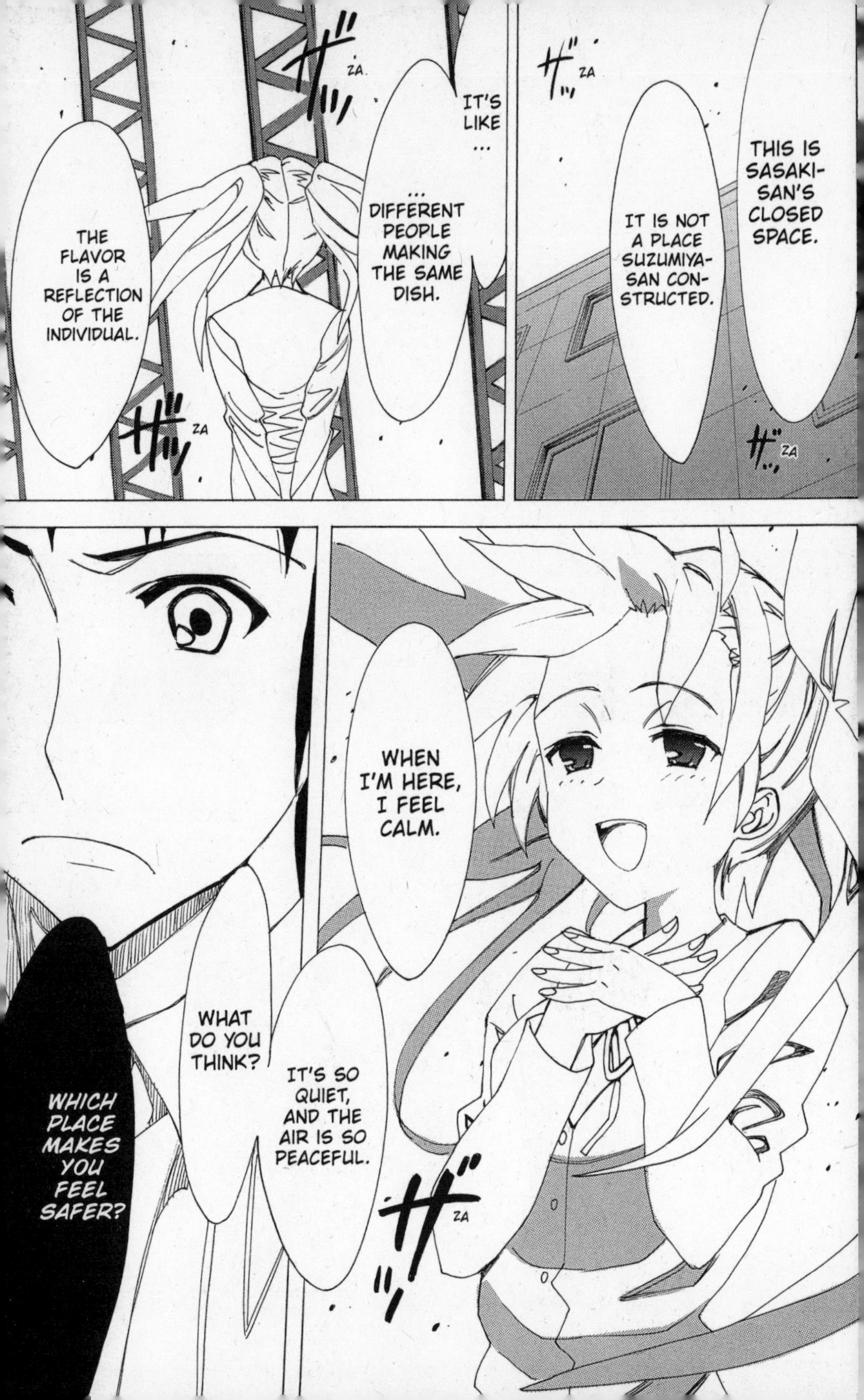
ZA
THIS IS SASAKI-SAN'S CLOSED SPACE.
IT IS NOT A PLACE SUZUMIYA-SAN CONSTRUCTED.
ZA
ZA.
IT'S LIKE ...
... DIFFERENT PEOPLE MAKING THE SAME DISH.
THE FLAVOR IS A REFLECTION OF THE INDIVIDUAL.
ZA
WHEN I'M HERE, I FEEL CALM.
IT'S SO QUIET, AND THE AIR IS SO PEACEFUL.
ZA
WHAT DO YOU THINK?
WHICH PLACE MAKES YOU FEEL SAFER?

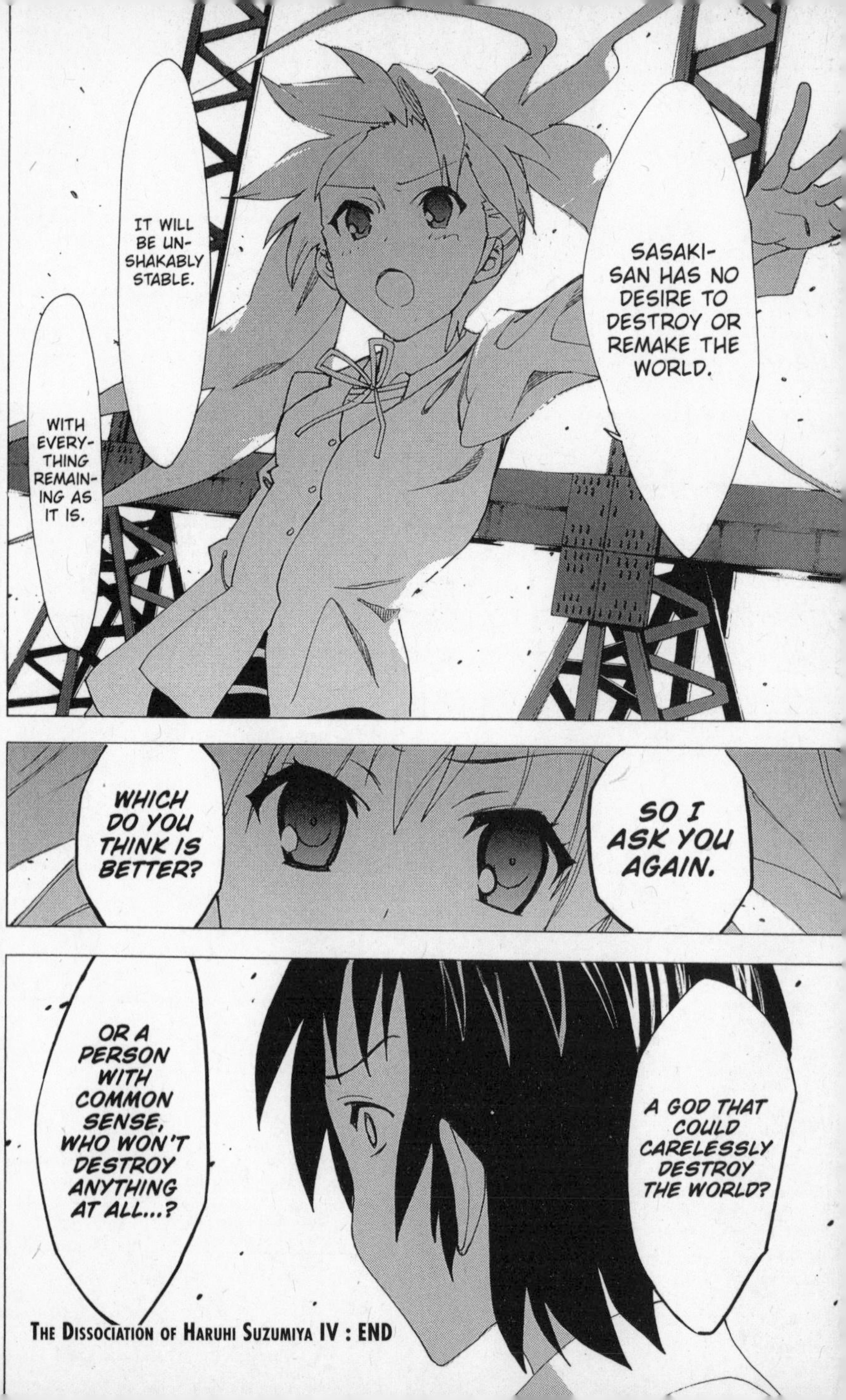
SASAKI-SAN HAS NO DESIRE TO DESTROY OR REMAKE THE WORLD.
IT WILL BE UNSHAKABLY STABLE.
WITH EVERYTHING REMAINING AS IT IS.
SO I ASK YOU AGAIN.
WHICH DO YOU THINK IS BETTER?
A GOD THAT COULD CARELESSLY DESTROY THE WORLD?
OR A PERSON WITH COMMON SENSE, WHO WON'T DESTROY ANYTHING AT ALL...?
THE DISSOCIATION OF HARUHI SUZUMIYA IV : END

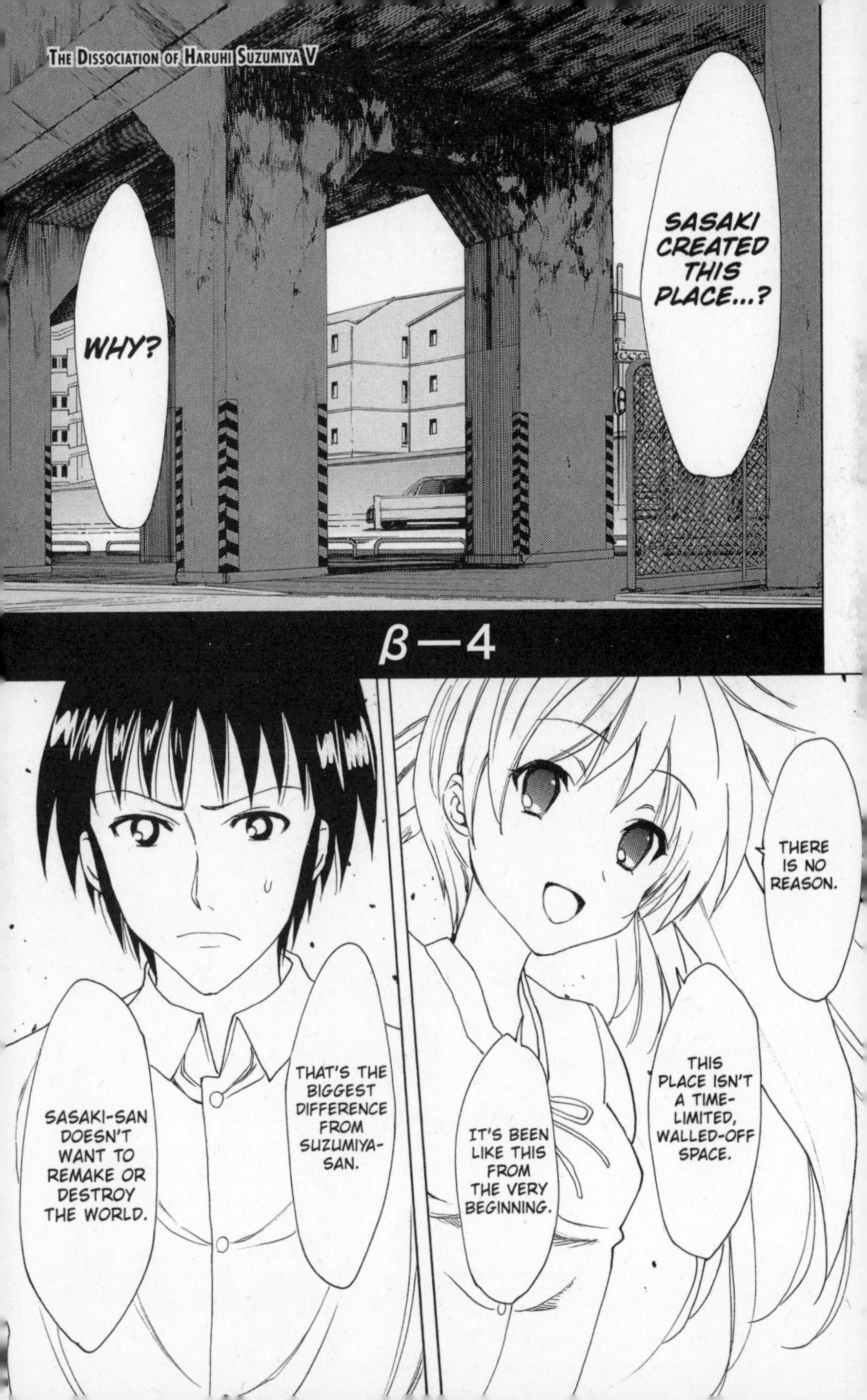
SASAKI CREATED THIS PLACE...?
WHY?
β—4
THERE IS NO REASON.
THIS PLACE ISN'T A TIME-LIMITED, WALLED-OFF SPACE.
IT'S BEEN LIKE THIS FROM THE VERY BEGINNING.
THAT'S THE BIGGEST DIFFERENCE FROM SUZUMIYA-SAN.
SASAKI-SAN DOESN'T WANT TO REMAKE OR DESTROY THE WORLD.

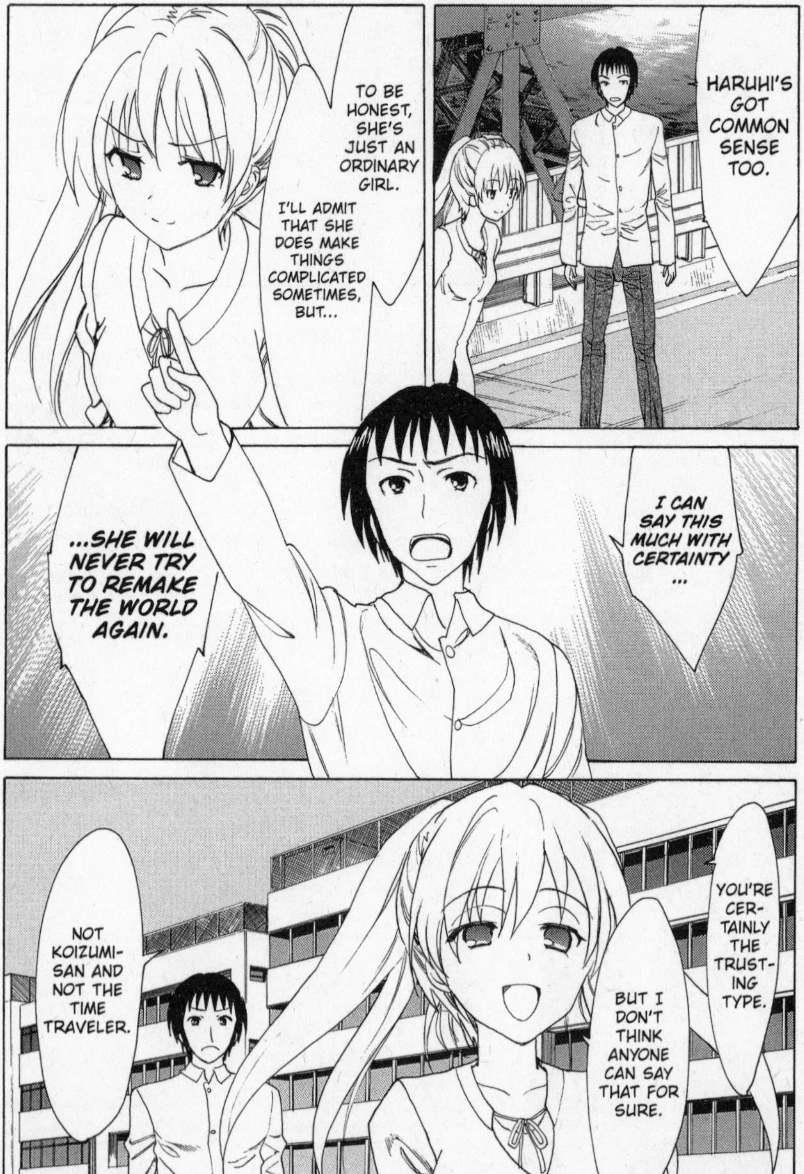
HARUHI'S GOT COMMON SENSE TOO.
TO BE HONEST, SHE'S JUST AN ORDINARY GIRL.
I'LL ADMIT THAT SHE DOES MAKE THINGS COMPLICATED SOMETIMES, BUT...
I CAN SAY THIS MUCH WITH CERTAINTY...
...SHE WILL NEVER TRY TO REMAKE THE WORLD AGAIN.
YOU'RE CER-TAINLY THE TRUST-ING TYPE.
BUT I DON'T THINK ANYONE CAN SAY THAT FOR SURE.
NOT KOIZUMI-SAN AND NOT THE TIME TRAVELER.

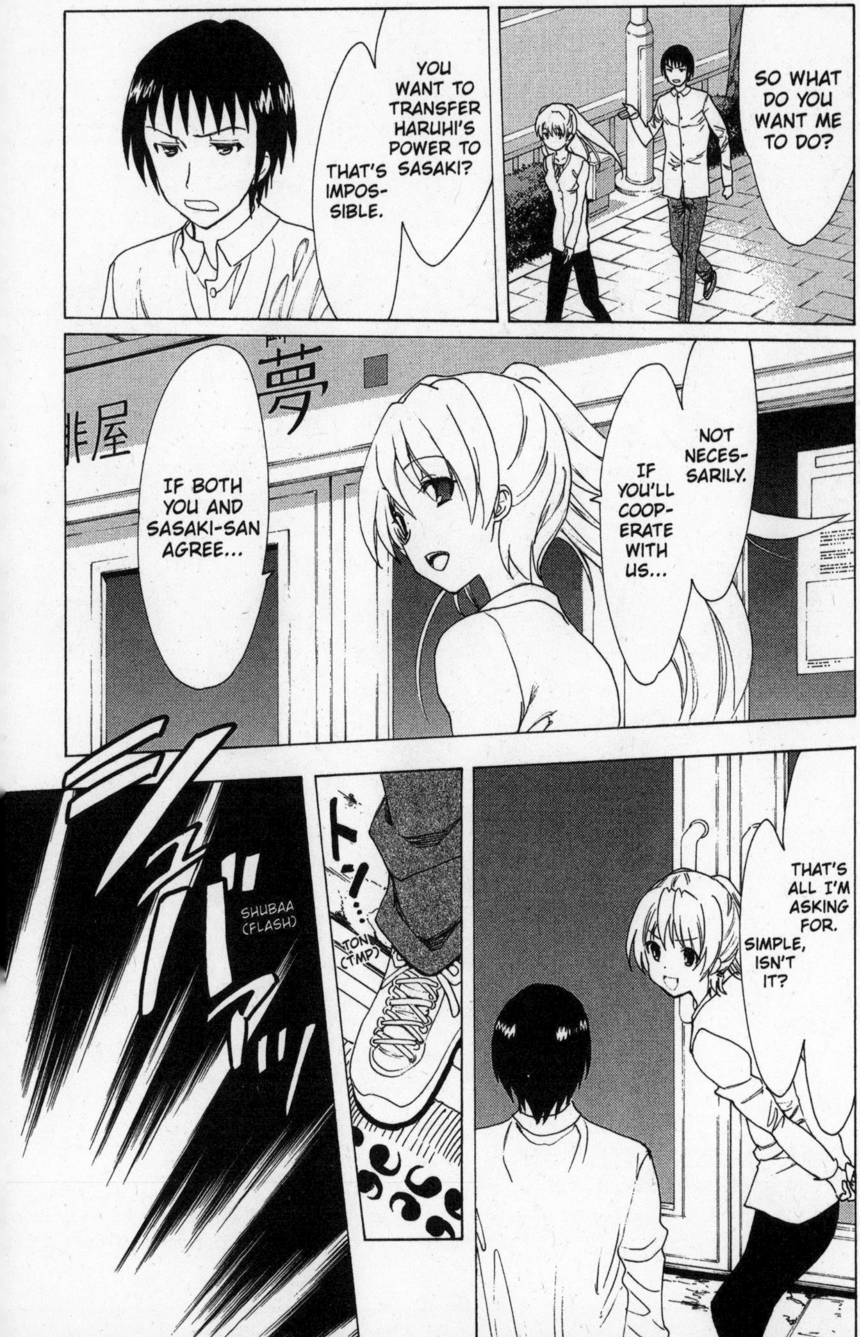
SO WHAT DO YOU WANT ME TO DO?
YOU WANT TO TRANSFER HARUHI'S POWER TO SASAKI?
THAT'S IMPOS-SIBLE.
NOT NECES-SARILY.
IF YOU'LL COOP-ERATE WITH US...
IF BOTH YOU AND SASAKI-SAN AGREE...
THAT'S ALL I'M ASKING FOR.
SIMPLE, ISN'T IT?
TON (TMP)
SHUBAA (FLASH)

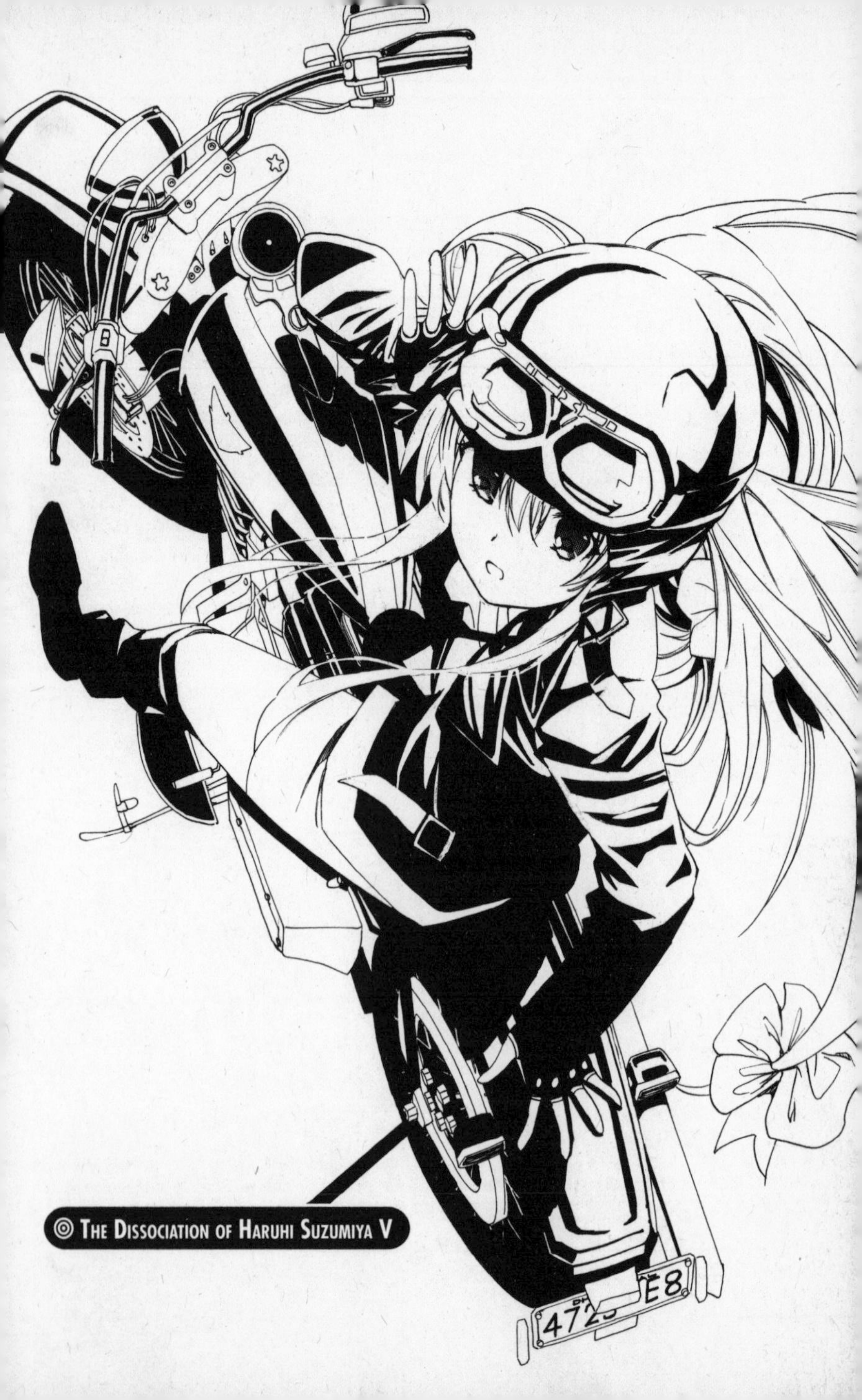

◎ The Dissociation of Haruhi Suzumiya V

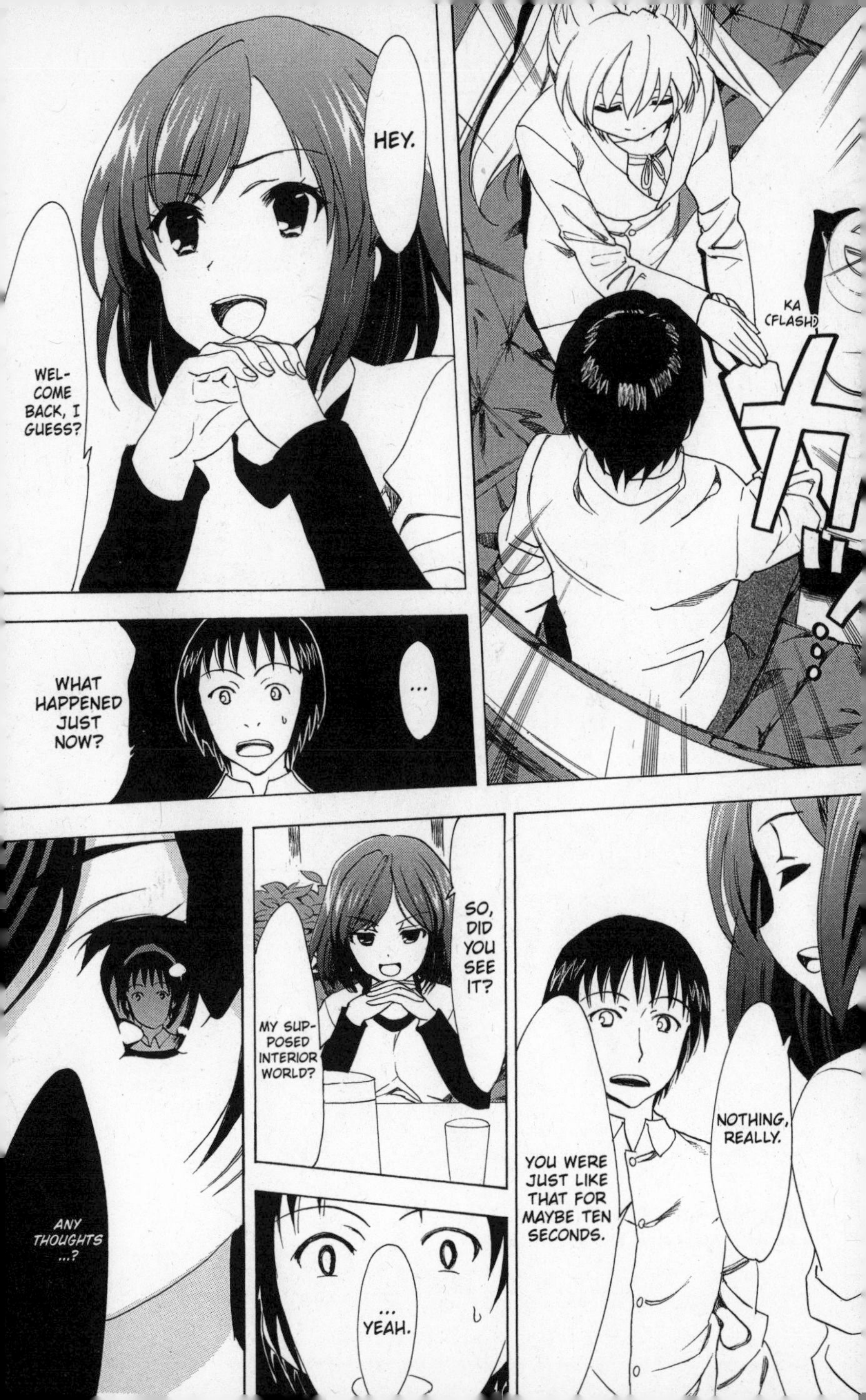
KA (FLASH)
HEY.
WEL-COME BACK, I GUESS?
...
WHAT HAPPENED JUST NOW?
NOTHING, REALLY.
YOU WERE JUST LIKE THAT FOR MAYBE TEN SECONDS.
SO, DID YOU SEE IT?
MY SUP-POSED INTERIOR WORLD?
... YEAH.
ANY THOUGHTS ...?

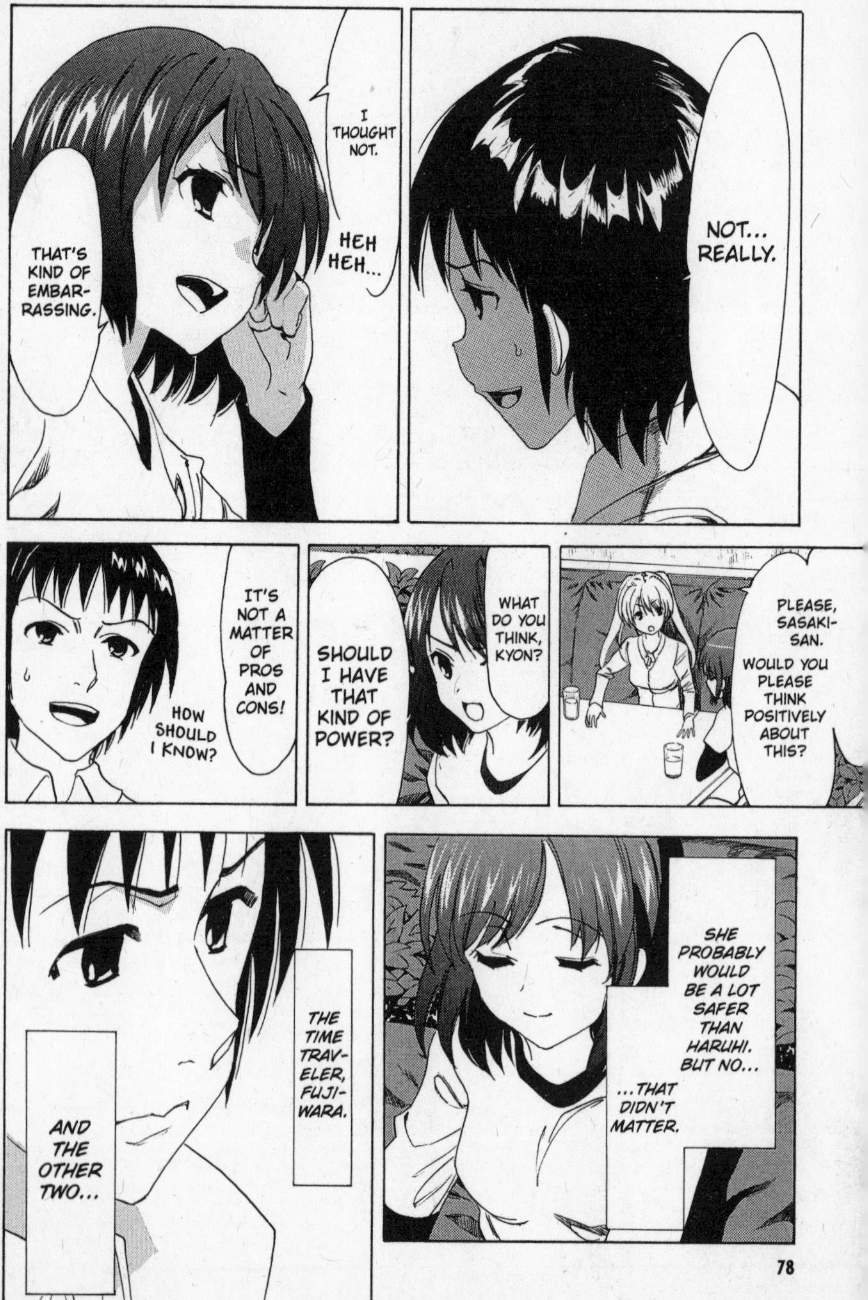
NOT... REALLY.
I THOUGHT NOT.
HEH HEH...
THAT'S KIND OF EMBARRASSING.
PLEASE, SASAKI-SAN.
WOULD YOU PLEASE THINK POSITIVELY ABOUT THIS?
WHAT DO YOU THINK, KYON?
SHOULD I HAVE THAT KIND OF POWER?
IT'S NOT A MATTER OF PROS AND CONS!
HOW SHOULD I KNOW?
SHE PROBABLY WOULD BE A LOT SAFER THAN HARUHI. BUT NO...
...THAT DIDN'T MATTER.
THE TIME TRAVELER, FUJIWARA.
AND THE OTHER TWO...

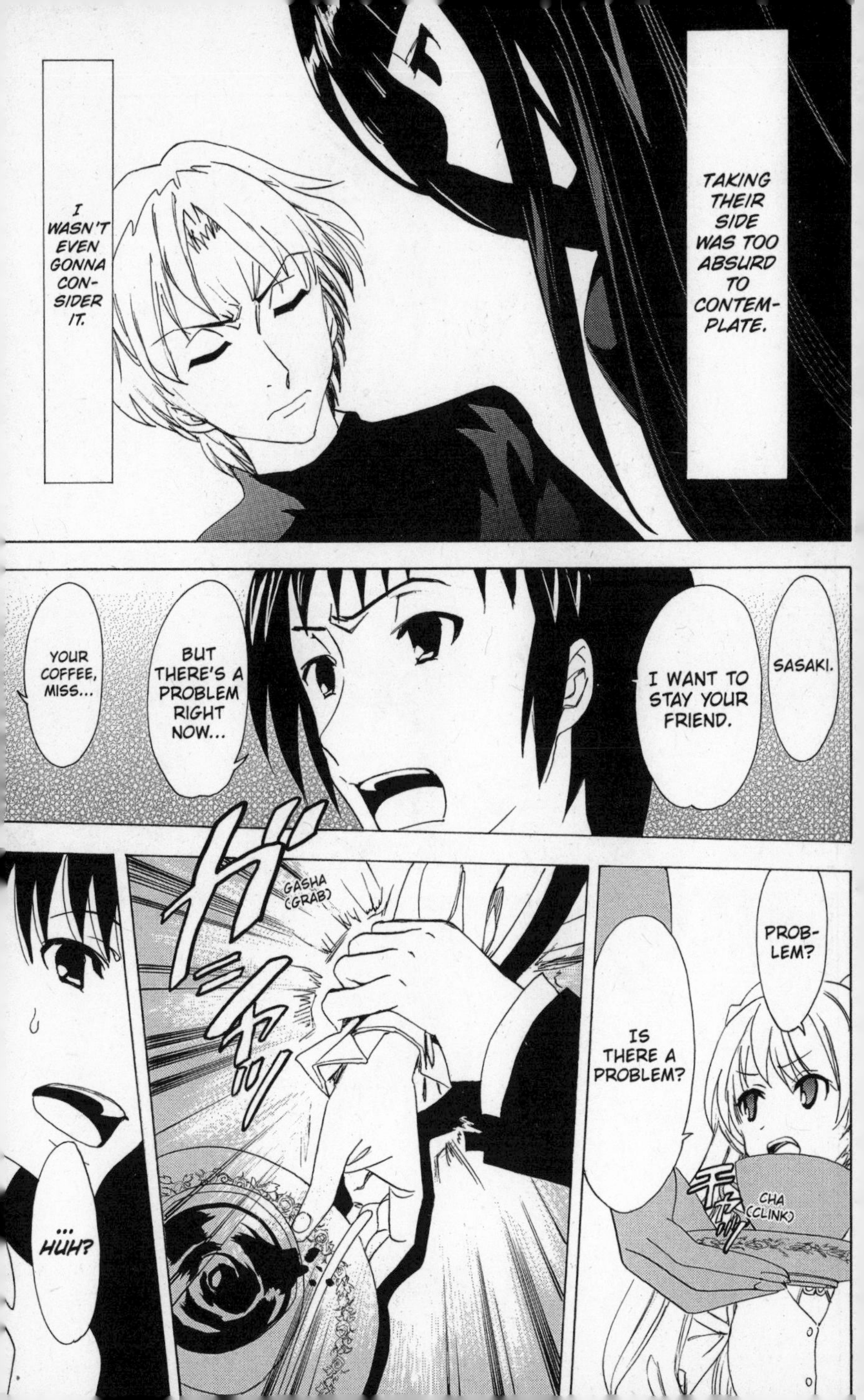
TAKING THEIR SIDE WAS TOO ABSURD TO CONTEM-PLATE.
I WASN'T EVEN GONNA CON-SIDER IT.
SASAKI.
I WANT TO STAY YOUR FRIEND.
BUT THERE'S A PROBLEM RIGHT NOW...
YOUR COFFEE, MISS...
PROB-LEM?
IS THERE A PROBLEM?
CHA (CLINK)
GASHA (GRAB)
... HUH?

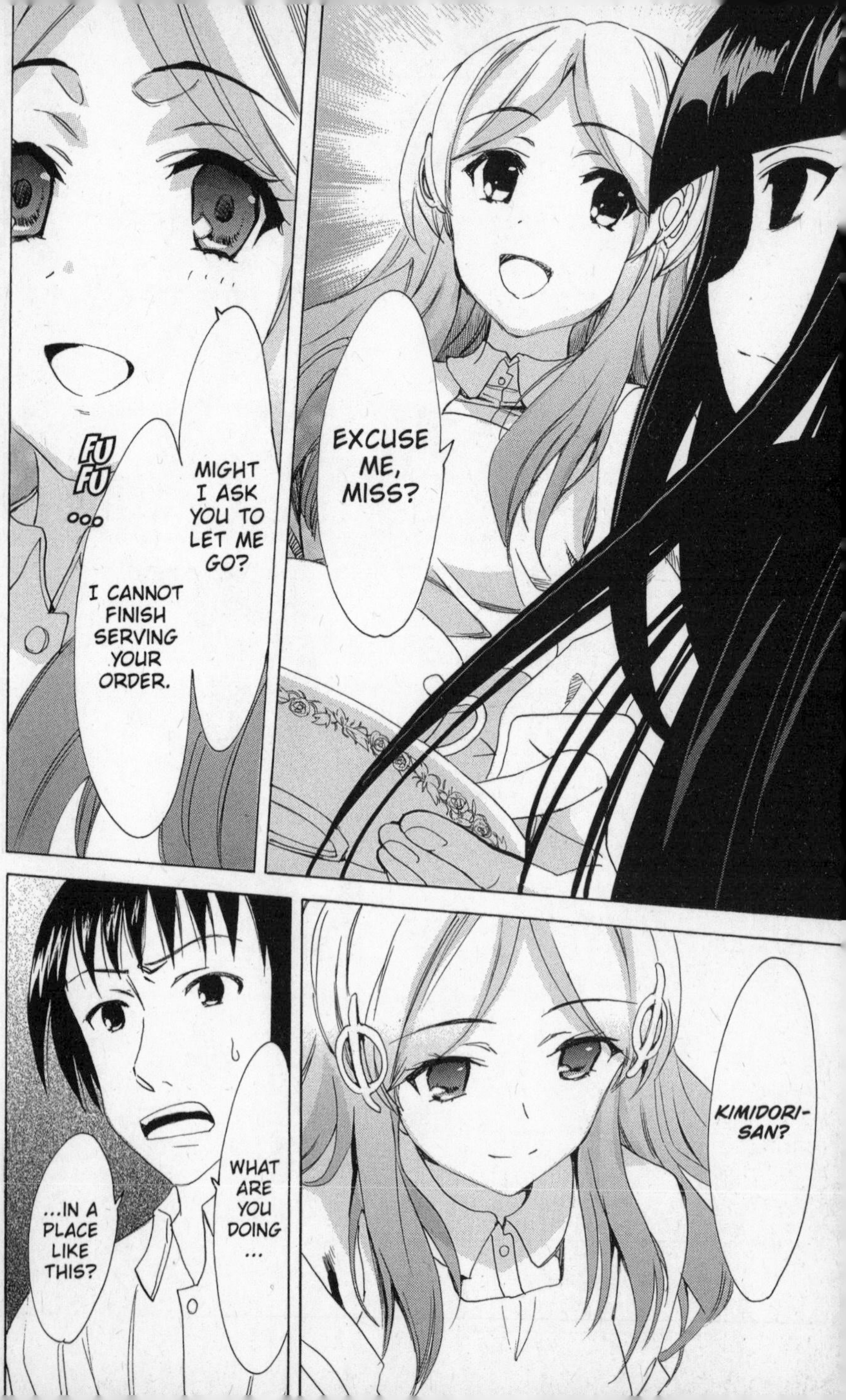
EXCUSE ME, MISS?
MIGHT I ASK YOU TO LET ME GO?
I CANNOT FINISH SERVING YOUR ORDER.
FUFU ooo
KIMIDORI-SAN?
WHAT ARE YOU DOING ...
...IN A PLACE LIKE THIS?

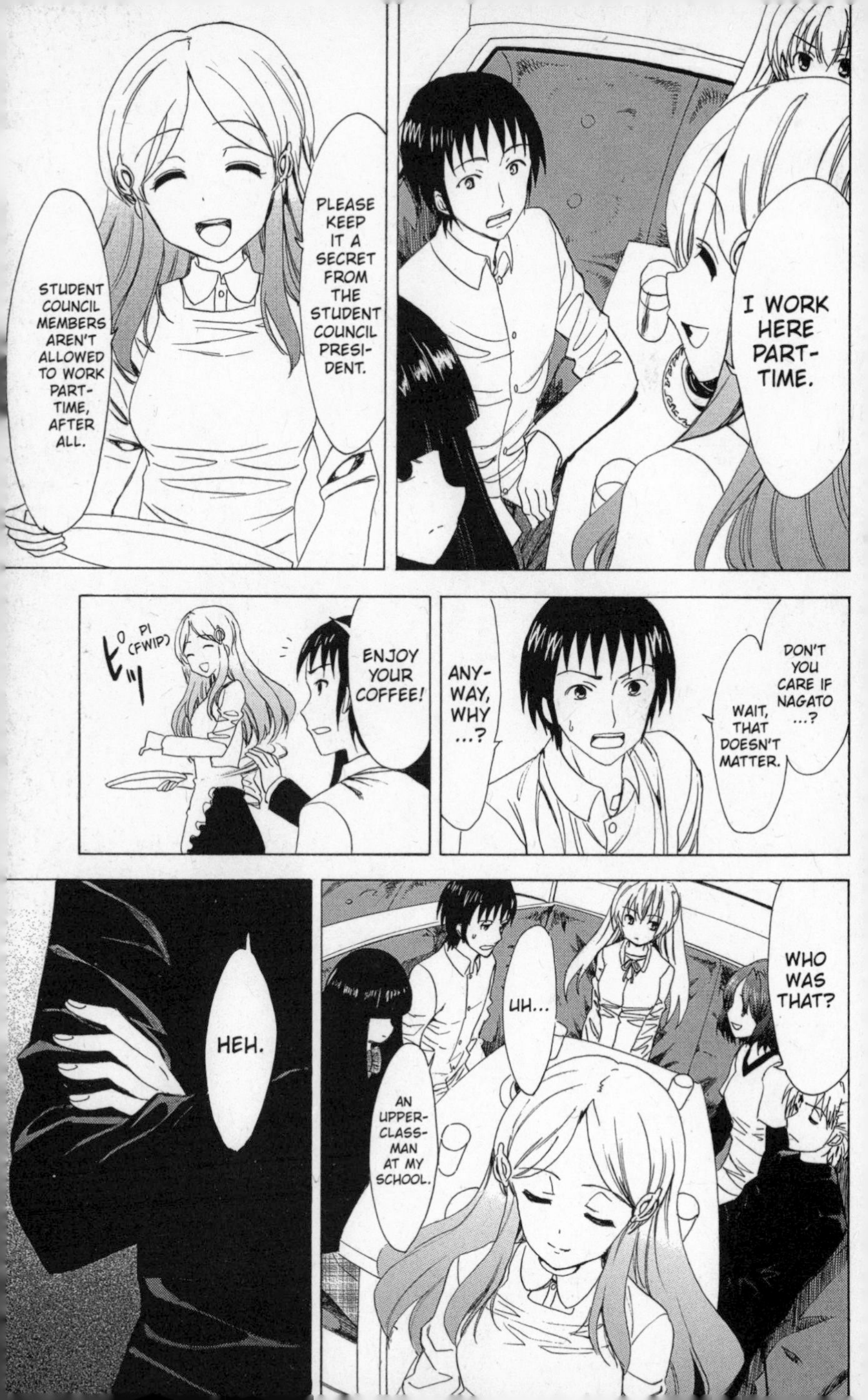
I WORK HERE PART-TIME.
PLEASE KEEP IT A SECRET FROM THE STUDENT COUNCIL PRESIDENT.
STUDENT COUNCIL MEMBERS AREN'T ALLOWED TO WORK PART-TIME, AFTER ALL.
DON'T YOU CARE IF NAGATO ...?
WAIT, THAT DOESN'T MATTER.
ANY-WAY, WHY ...?
ENJOY YOUR COFFEE!
PI (FWIP)
WHO WAS THAT?
UH...
AN UPPER-CLASS-MAN AT MY SCHOOL.
HEH.

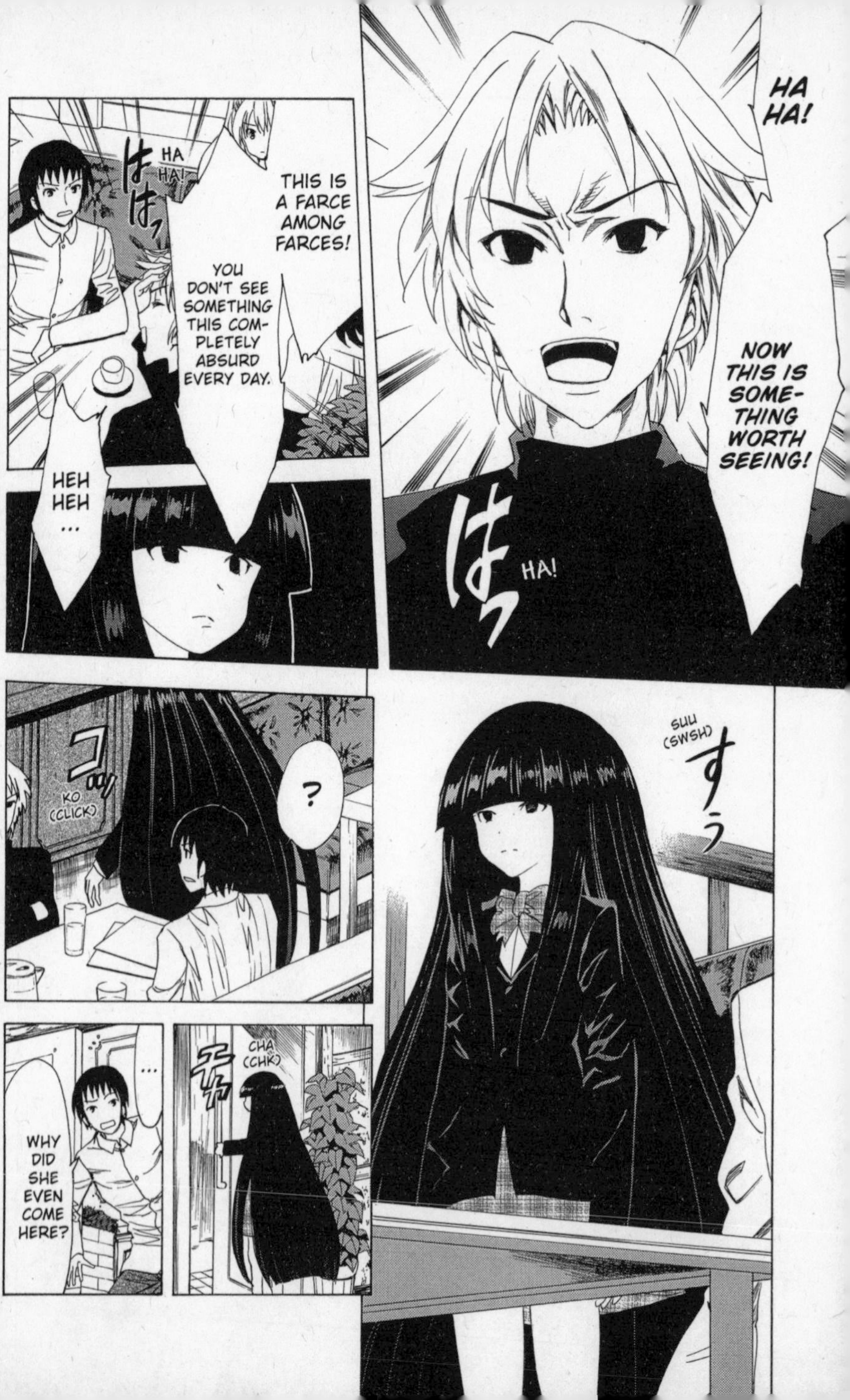
HA HA!
NOW THIS IS SOMETHING WORTH SEEING!
HA!
HA HA!
THIS IS A FARCE AMONG FARCES!
YOU DON'T SEE SOMETHING THIS COMPLETELY ABSURD EVERY DAY.
HEH HEH ...
SUU (SWSH)
?
KO (CLICK)
CHA (CHK)
...
WHY DID SHE EVEN COME HERE?

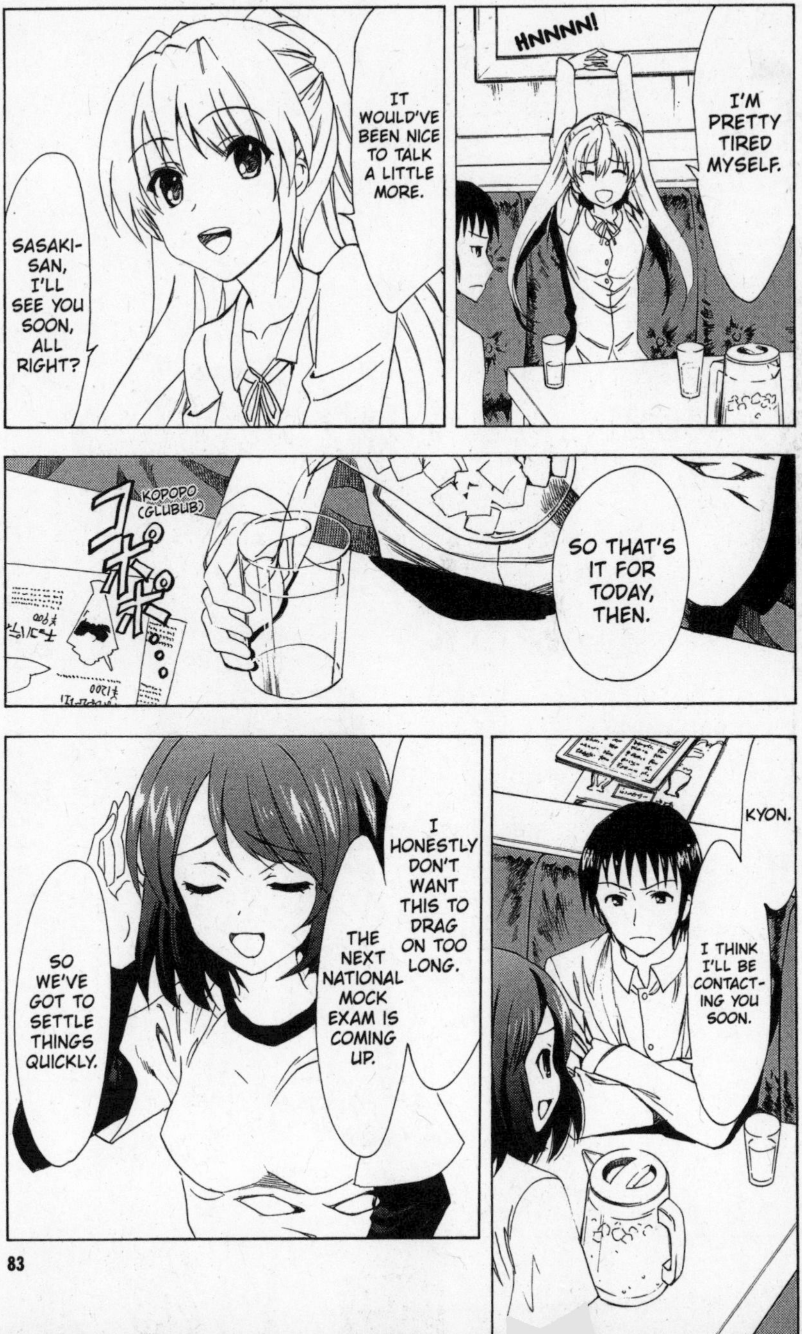
HNNNN!
I'M PRETTY TIRED MYSELF.
IT WOULD'VE BEEN NICE TO TALK A LITTLE MORE.
SASAKI-SAN, I'LL SEE YOU SOON, ALL RIGHT?
SO THAT'S IT FOR TODAY, THEN.
KOPOPO (GLUBUB)
KYON.
I THINK I'LL BE CONTACTING YOU SOON.
I HONESTLY DON'T WANT THIS TO DRAG ON TOO LONG.
THE NEXT NATIONAL MOCK EXAM IS COMING UP.
SO WE'VE GOT TO SETTLE THINGS QUICKLY.

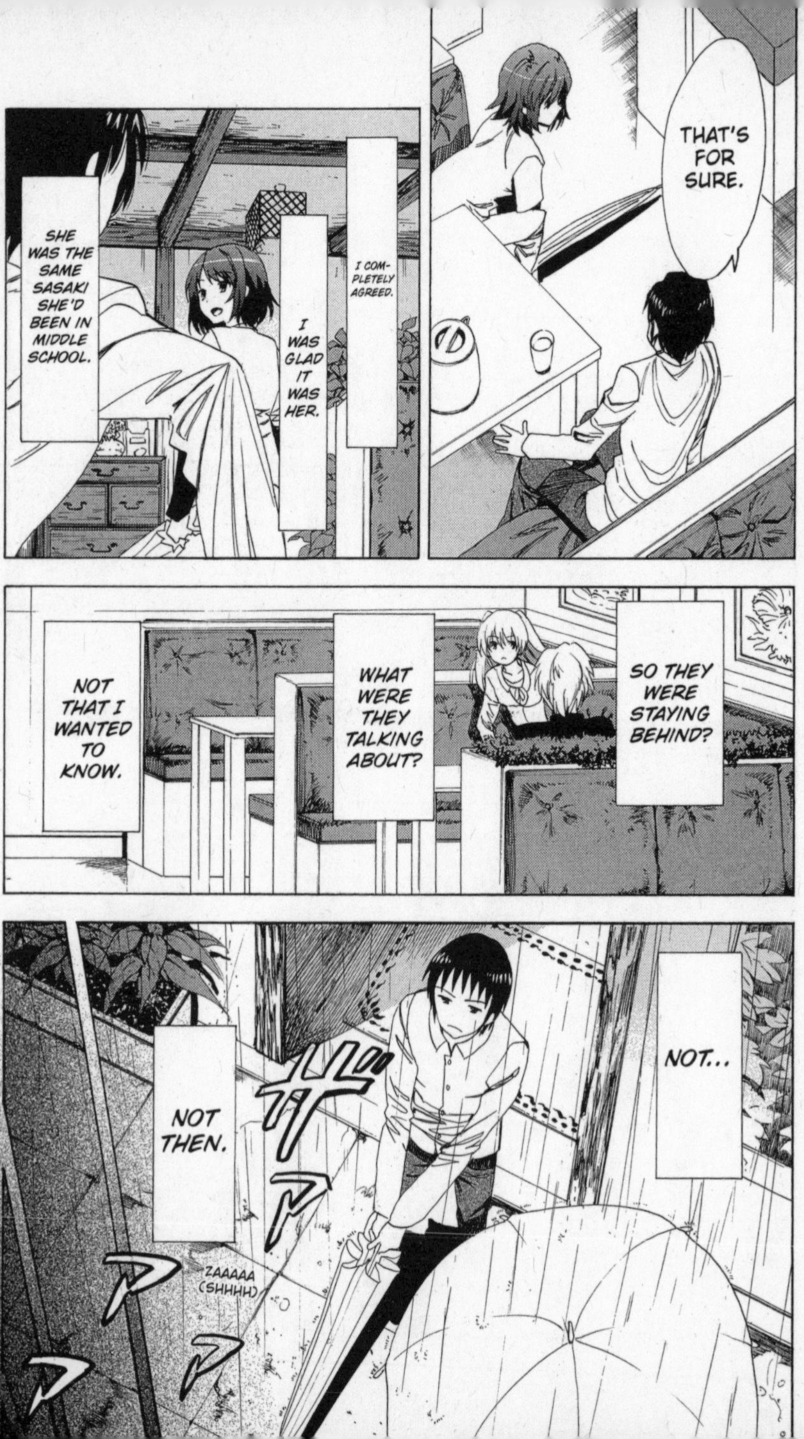
THAT'S FOR SURE.
I COMPLETELY AGREED.
I WAS GLAD IT WAS HER.
SHE WAS THE SAME SASAKI SHE'D BEEN IN MIDDLE SCHOOL.
SO THEY WERE STAYING BEHIND?
WHAT WERE THEY TALKING ABOUT?
NOT THAT I WANTED TO KNOW.
NOT...
NOT THEN.
ZAAAAA (SHHHH)

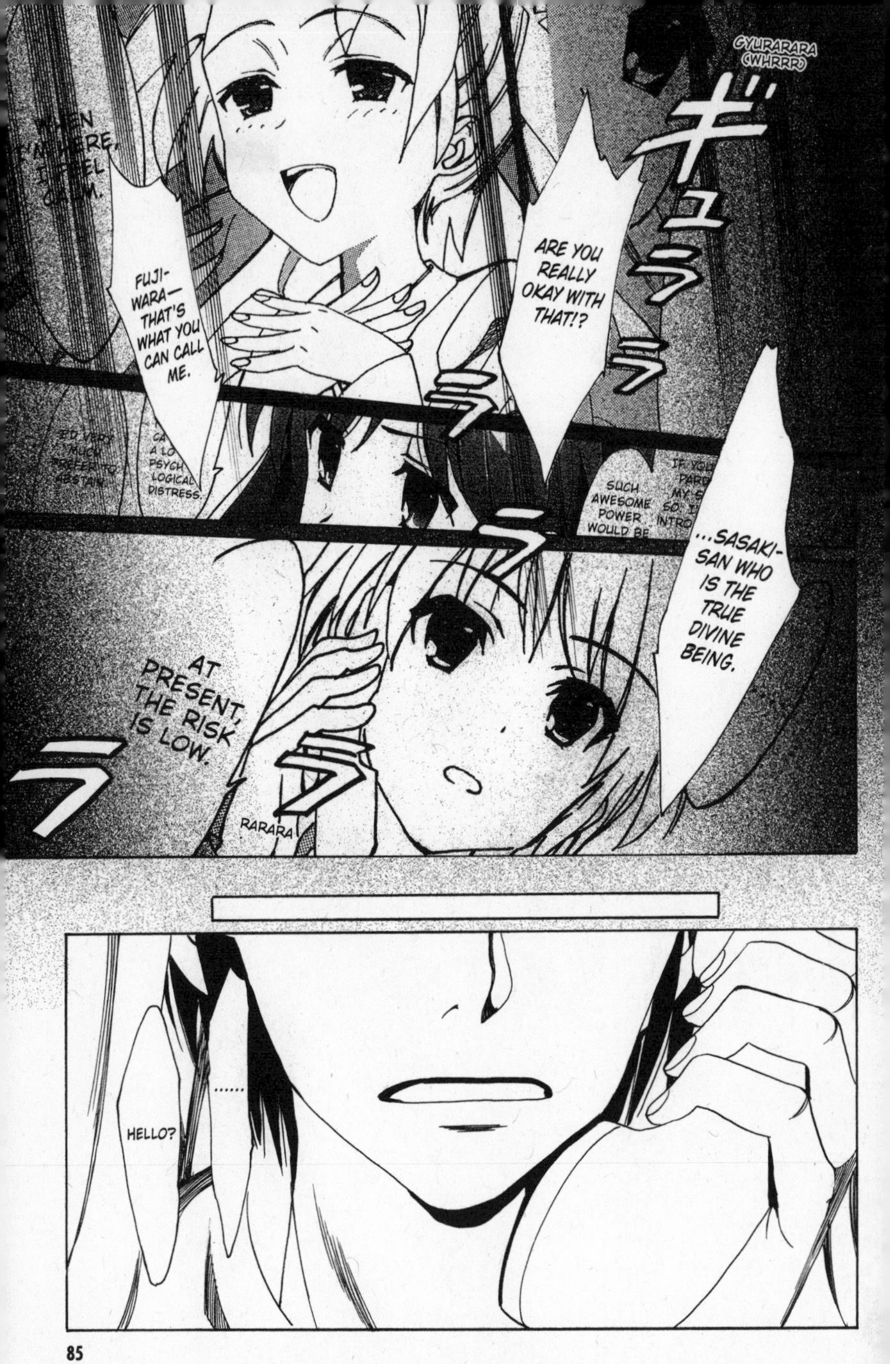
GYURARARA (WHRRR)
ARE YOU REALLY OKAY WITH THAT!?
FUJI-WARA—THAT'S WHAT YOU CAN CALL ME.
WHEN I'M HERE, I FEEL CALM.
SUCH AWESOME POWER WOULD BE
I'D VERY MUCH PREFER TO ABSTAIN.
...SASAKI-SAN WHO IS THE TRUE DIVINE BEING.
AT PRESENT, THE RISK IS LOW.
RARARA
......
HELLO?

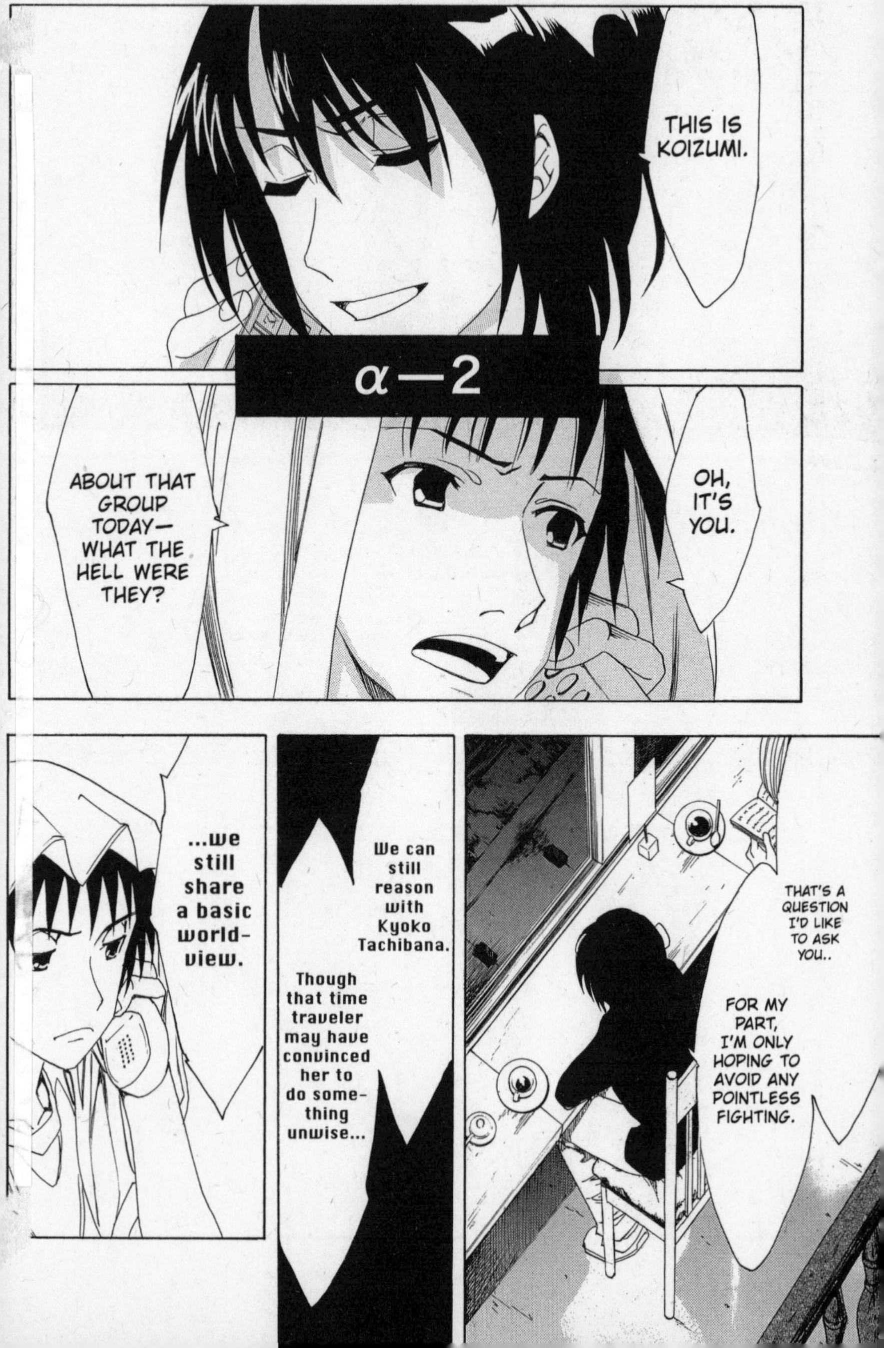
THIS IS KOIZUMI.
α—2
OH, IT'S YOU.
ABOUT THAT GROUP TODAY—WHAT THE HELL WERE THEY?
THAT'S A QUESTION I'D LIKE TO ASK YOU..
FOR MY PART, I'M ONLY HOPING TO AVOID ANY POINTLESS FIGHTING.
We can still reason with Kyoko Tachibana.
Though that time traveler may have convinced her to do something unwise...
...we still share a basic world-view.

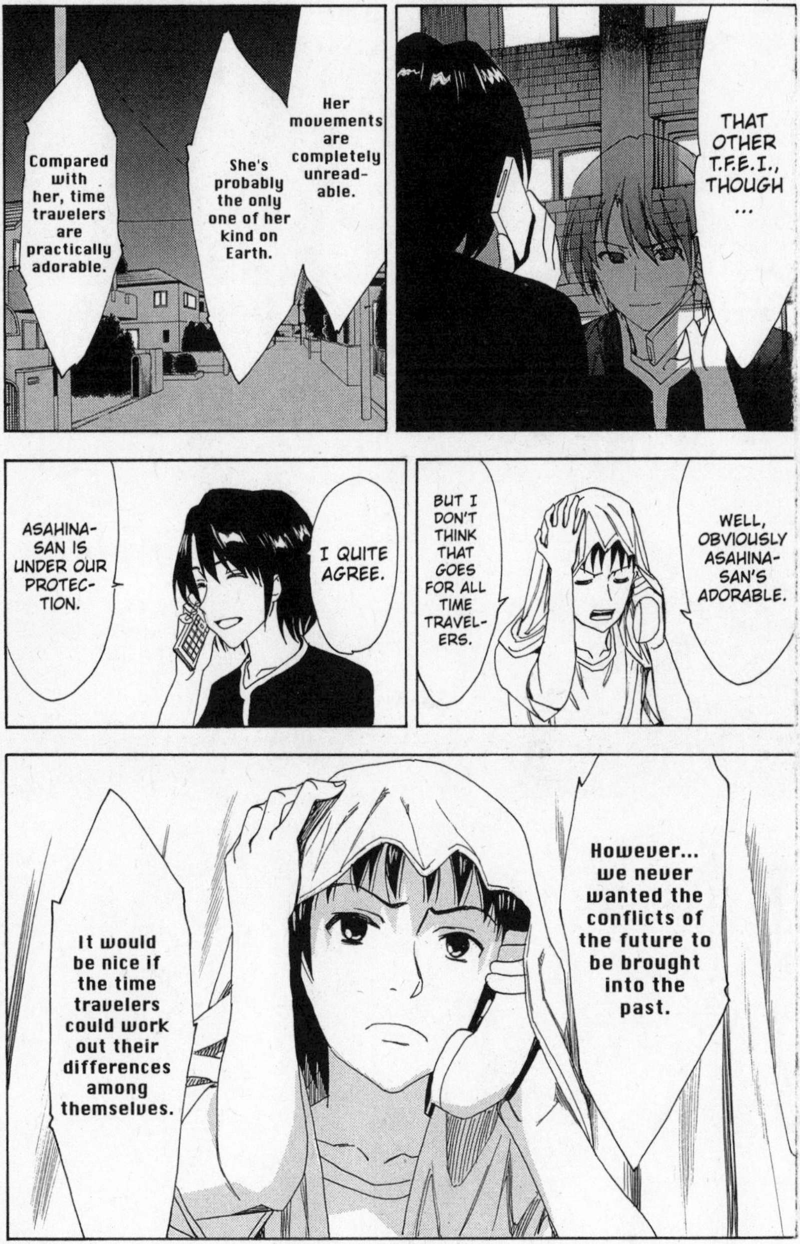
THAT OTHER T.F.E.I., THOUGH ...
Her movements are completely unreadable.
She's probably the only one of her kind on Earth.
Compared with her, time travelers are practically adorable.
WELL, OBVIOUSLY ASAHINA-SAN'S ADORABLE.
BUT I DON'T THINK THAT GOES FOR ALL TIME TRAVELERS.
I QUITE AGREE.
ASAHINA-SAN IS UNDER OUR PROTECTION.
However... we never wanted the conflicts of the future to be brought into the past.
It would be nice if the time travelers could work out their differences among themselves.

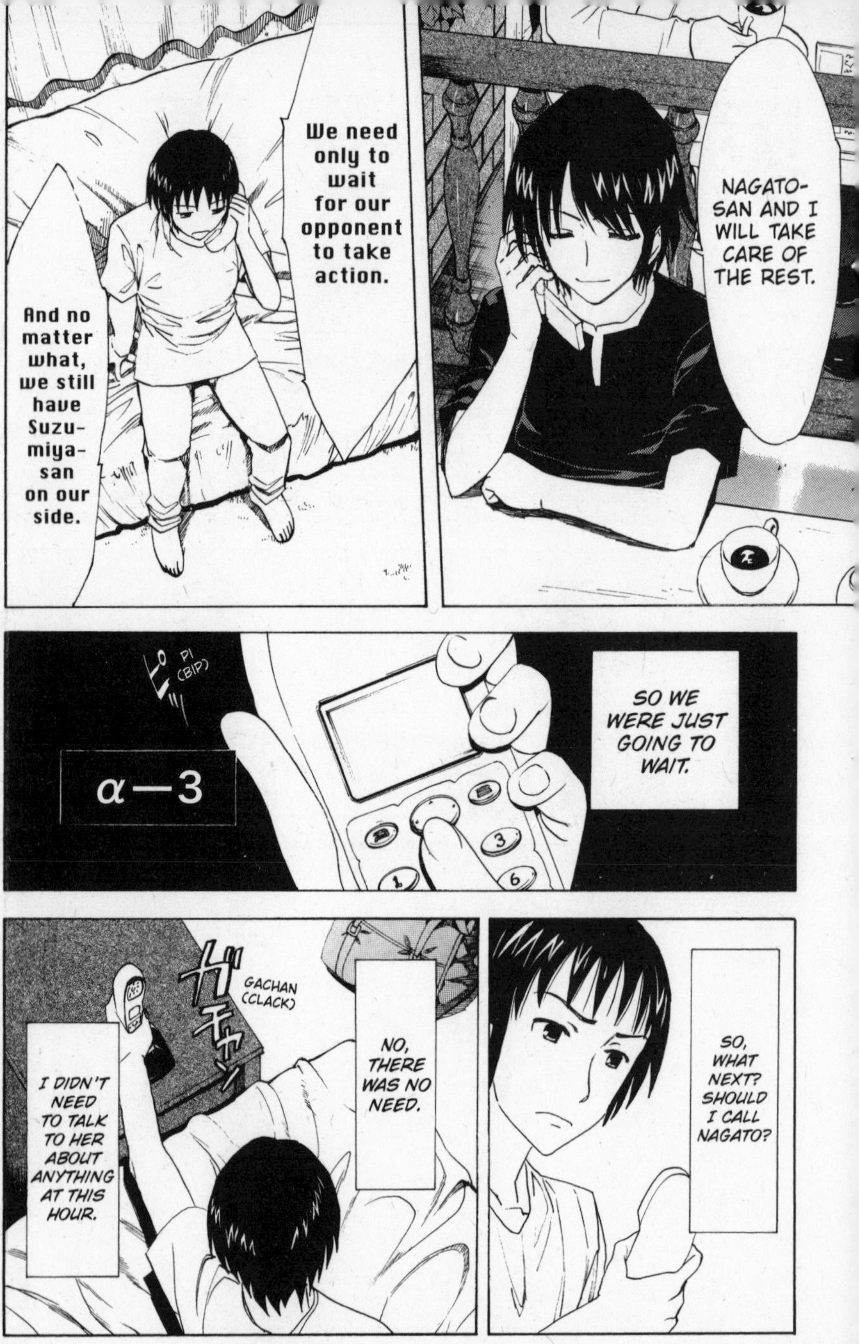
NAGATO-SAN AND I WILL TAKE CARE OF THE REST.
We need only to wait for our opponent to take action.
And no matter what, we still have Suzumiya-san on our side.
SO WE WERE JUST GOING TO WAIT.
PI (BIP)
α—3
SO, WHAT NEXT? SHOULD I CALL NAGATO?
NO, THERE WAS NO NEED.
GACHAN (CLACK)
I DIDN'T NEED TO TALK TO HER ABOUT ANYTHING AT THIS HOUR.

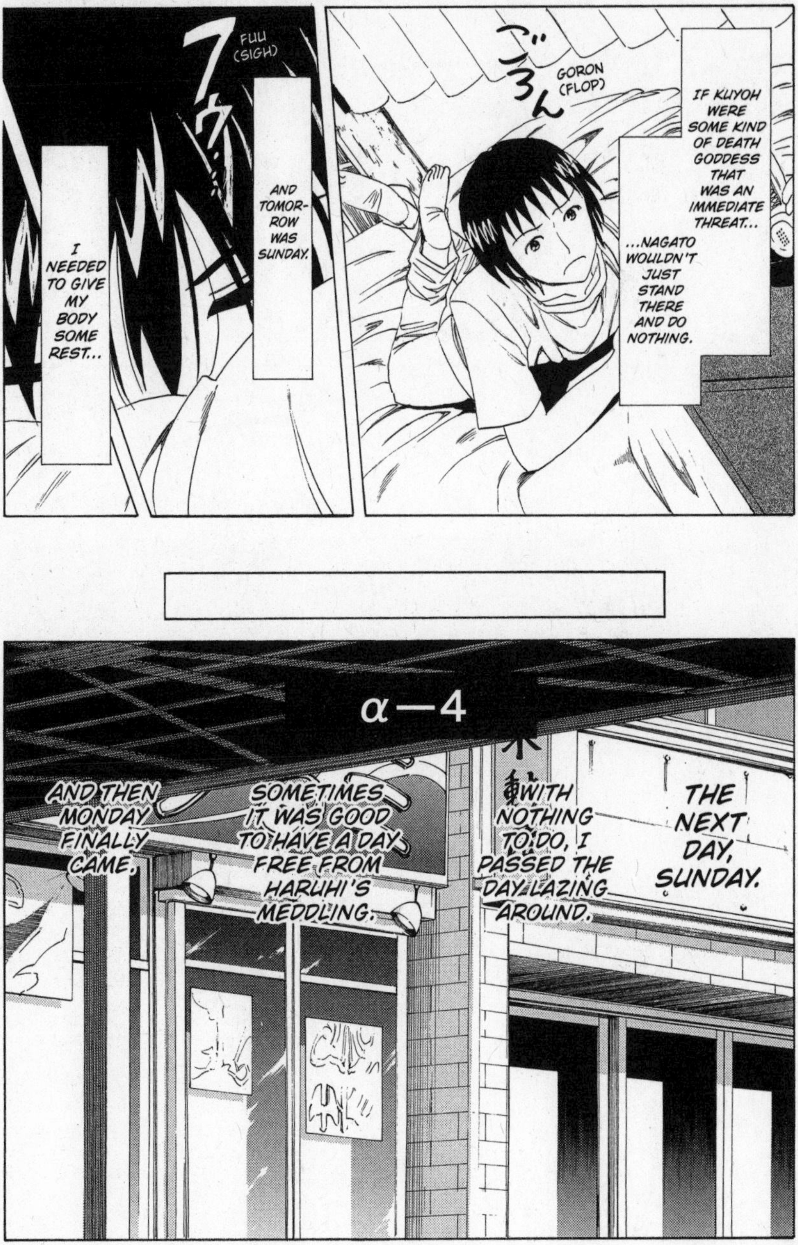
ごろん
GORON (FLOP)
IF KUYOH WERE SOME KIND OF DEATH GODDESS THAT WAS AN IMMEDIATE THREAT...
...NAGATO WOULDN'T JUST STAND THERE AND DO NOTHING.
フゥ…
FUU (SIGH)
AND TOMOR-ROW WAS SUNDAY.
I NEEDED TO GIVE MY BODY SOME REST...
α—4
THE NEXT DAY, SUNDAY.
WITH NOTHING TO DO, I PASSED THE DAY LAZING AROUND.
SOMETIMES IT WAS GOOD TO HAVE A DAY FREE FROM HARUHI'S MEDDLING.
AND THEN MONDAY FINALLY CAME.

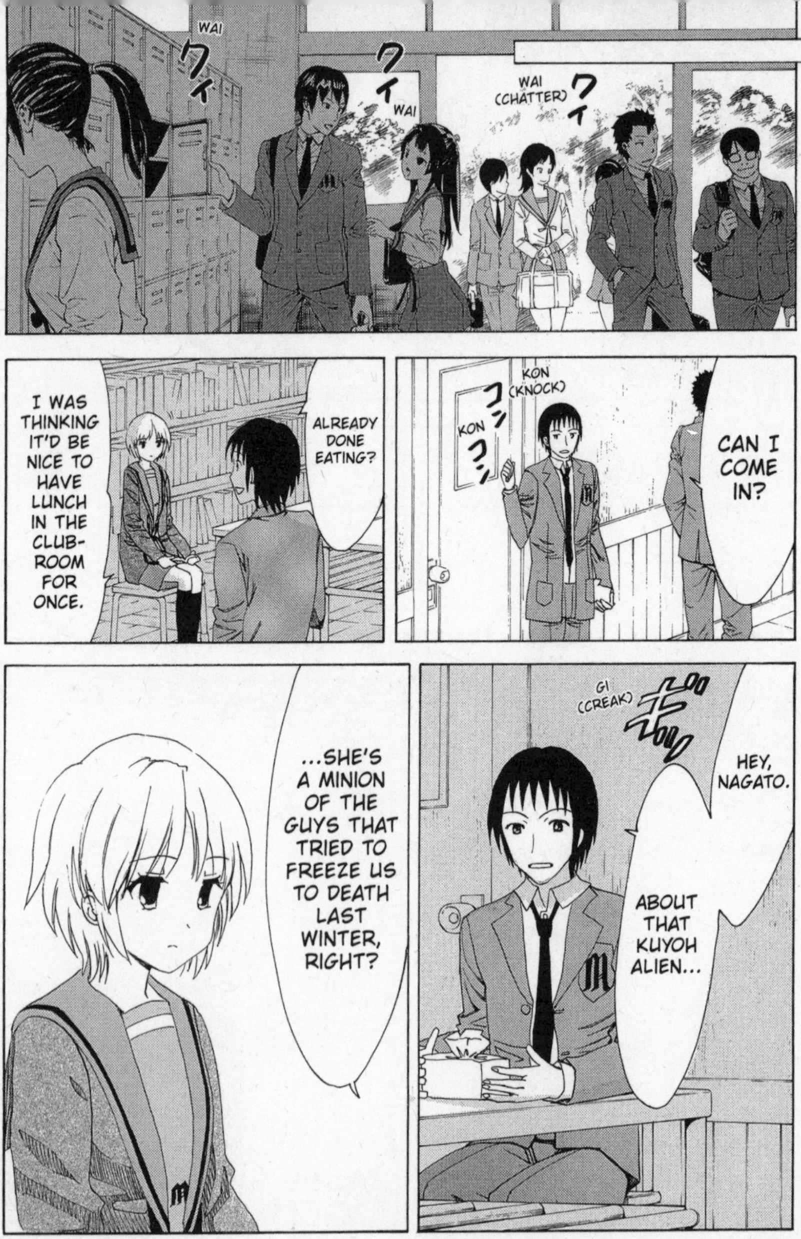
WAI (CHATTER) ワイ
ワイ WAI
WAI ワイ
KON (KNOCK) コン
KON コン
CAN I COME IN?
ALREADY DONE EATING?
I WAS THINKING IT'D BE NICE TO HAVE LUNCH IN THE CLUB-ROOM FOR ONCE.
GI (CREAK) ギィ
HEY, NAGATO.
ABOUT THAT KUYOH ALIEN...
...SHE'S A MINION OF THE GUYS THAT TRIED TO FREEZE US TO DEATH LAST WINTER, RIGHT?

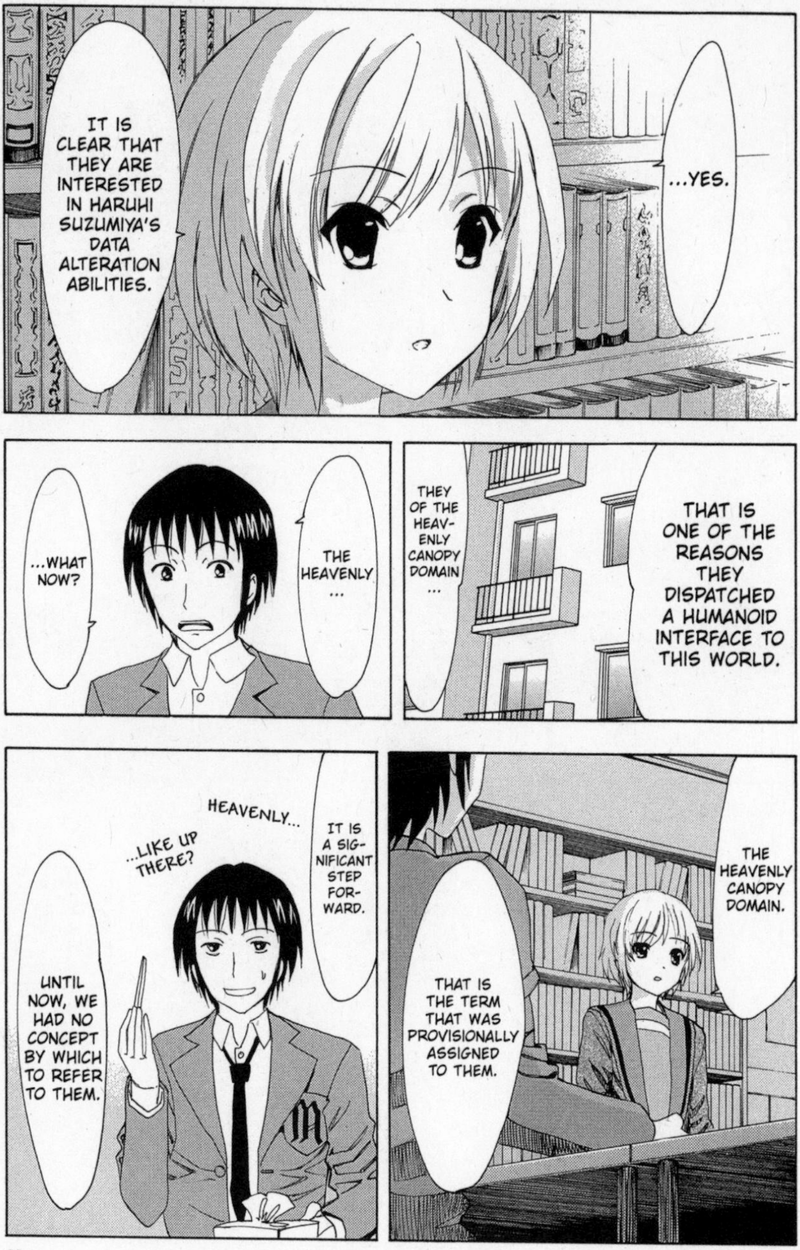
...YES.
IT IS CLEAR THAT THEY ARE INTERESTED IN HARUHI SUZUMIYA'S DATA ALTERATION ABILITIES.
THAT IS ONE OF THE REASONS THEY DISPATCHED A HUMANOID INTERFACE TO THIS WORLD.
THEY OF THE HEAV-ENLY CANOPY DOMAIN ...
THE HEAVENLY ...
...WHAT NOW?
THE HEAVENLY CANOPY DOMAIN.
THAT IS THE TERM THAT WAS PROVISIONALLY ASSIGNED TO THEM.
IT IS A SIG-NIFICANT STEP FOR-WARD.
HEAVENLY...
...LIKE UP THERE?
UNTIL NOW, WE HAD NO CONCEPT BY WHICH TO REFER TO THEM.

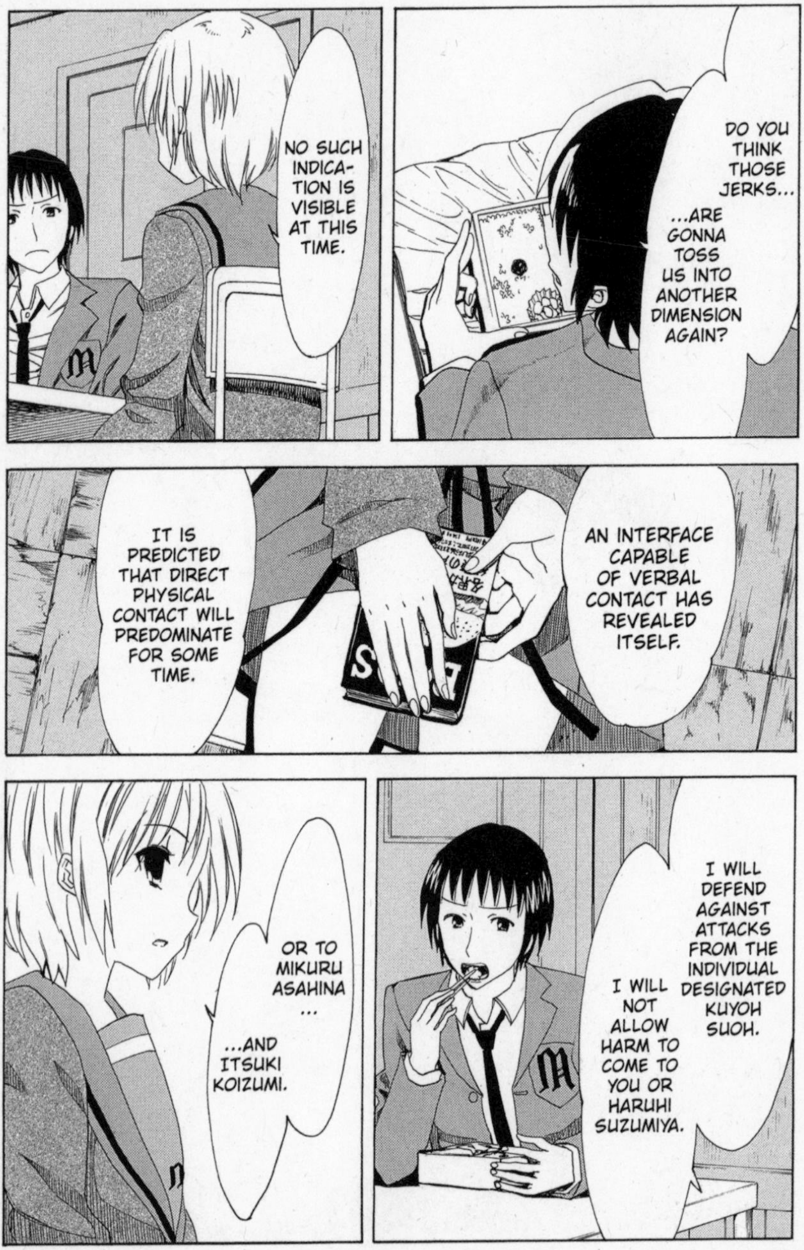
DO YOU THINK THOSE JERKS...
...ARE GONNA TOSS US INTO ANOTHER DIMENSION AGAIN?
NO SUCH INDICATION IS VISIBLE AT THIS TIME.
AN INTERFACE CAPABLE OF VERBAL CONTACT HAS REVEALED ITSELF.
IT IS PREDICTED THAT DIRECT PHYSICAL CONTACT WILL PREDOMINATE FOR SOME TIME.
I WILL DEFEND AGAINST ATTACKS FROM THE INDIVIDUAL DESIGNATED KUYOH SUOH.
I WILL NOT ALLOW HARM TO COME TO YOU OR HARUHI SUZUMIYA.
OR TO MIKURU ASAHINA ...
...AND ITSUKI KOIZUMI.

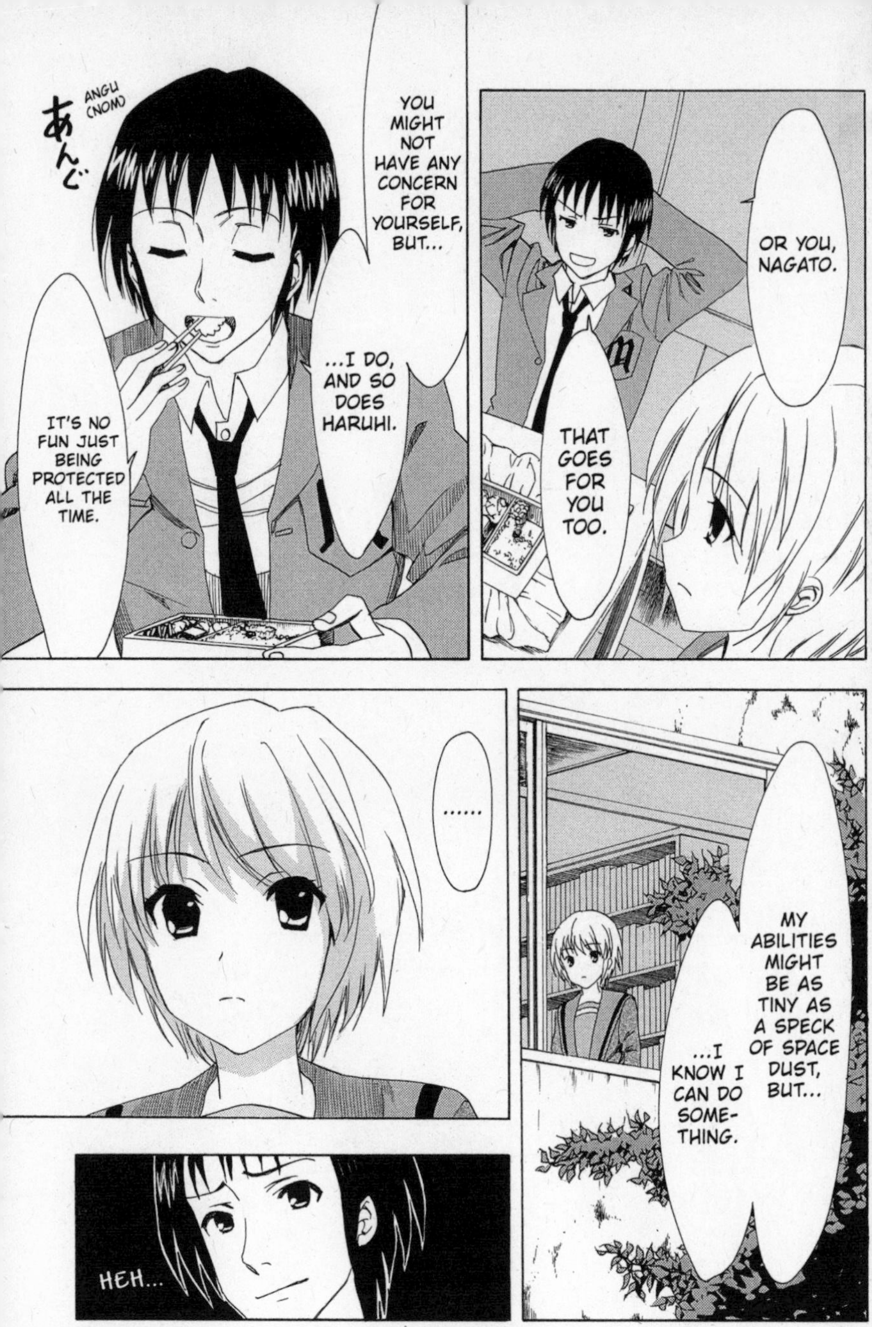
OR YOU, NAGATO.
THAT GOES FOR YOU TOO.
YOU MIGHT NOT HAVE ANY CONCERN FOR YOURSELF, BUT...
...I DO, AND SO DOES HARUHI.
あんぐ
ANGU (NOM)
IT'S NO FUN JUST BEING PROTECTED ALL THE TIME.
MY ABILITIES MIGHT BE AS TINY AS A SPECK OF SPACE DUST, BUT...
...I KNOW I CAN DO SOME-THING.
......
HEH...

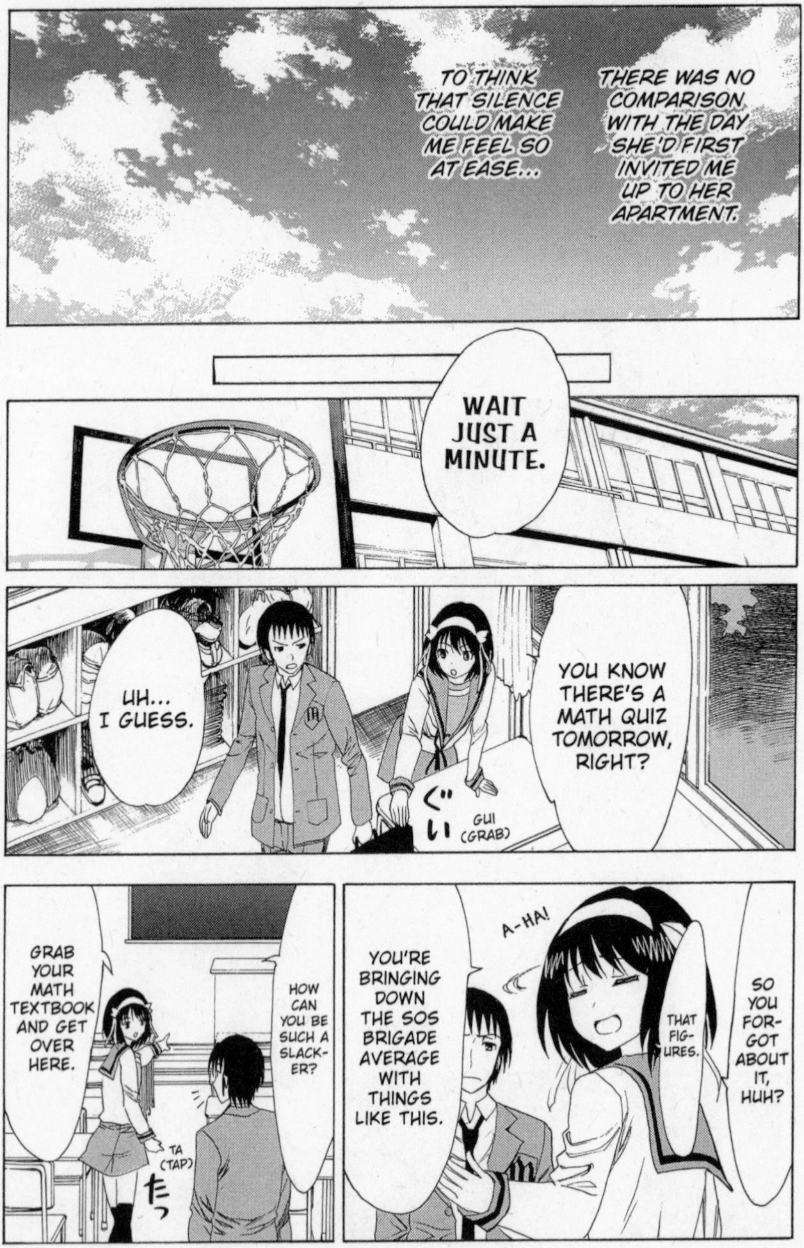
THERE WAS NO COMPARISON WITH THE DAY SHE'D FIRST INVITED ME UP TO HER APARTMENT.
TO THINK THAT SILENCE COULD MAKE ME FEEL SO AT EASE...
WAIT JUST A MINUTE.
YOU KNOW THERE'S A MATH QUIZ TOMORROW, RIGHT?
UH... I GUESS.
ぐい GUI (GRAB)
SO YOU FOR-GOT ABOUT IT, HUH?
THAT FIG-URES.
A-HA!
YOU'RE BRINGING DOWN THE SOS BRIGADE AVERAGE WITH THINGS LIKE THIS.
HOW CAN YOU BE SUCH A SLACK-ER?
GRAB YOUR MATH TEXTBOOK AND GET OVER HERE.
たっ TA (TAP)

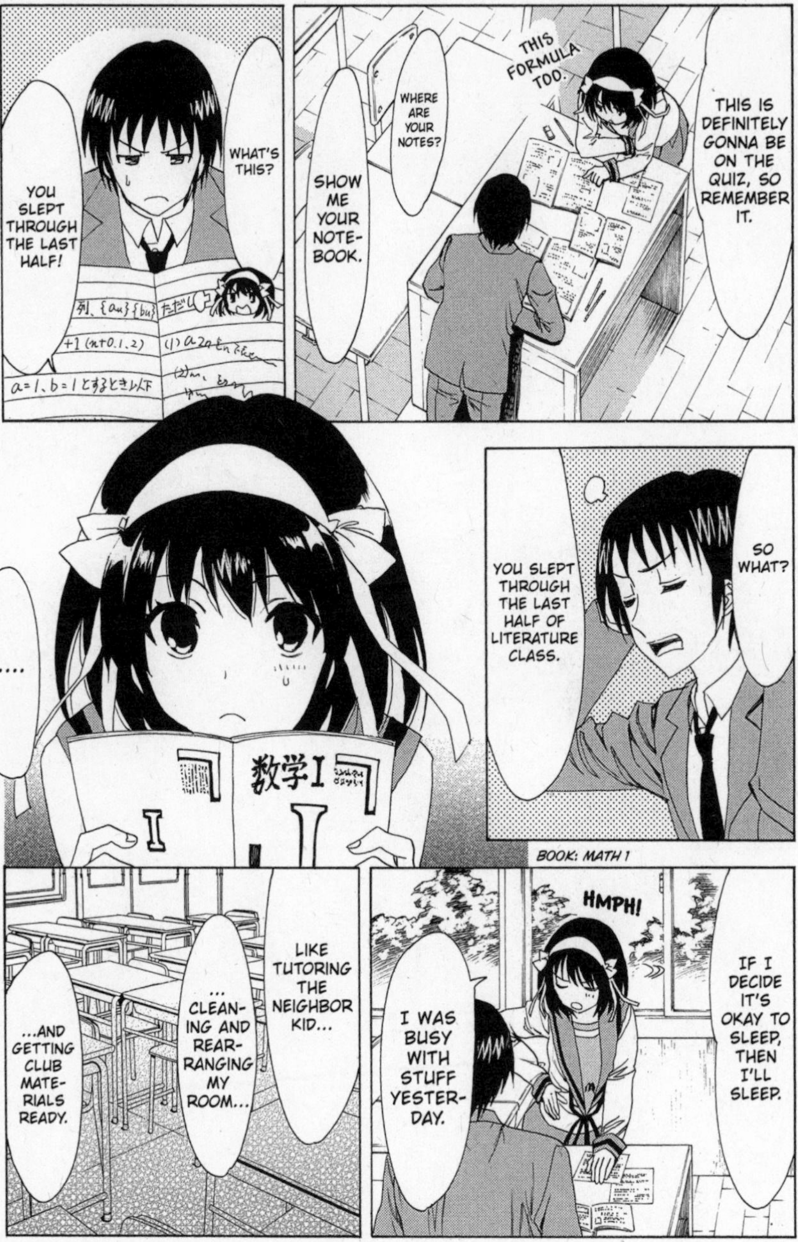
THIS IS DEFINITELY GONNA BE ON THE QUIZ, SO REMEMBER IT.
THIS FORMULA TOO.
WHERE ARE YOUR NOTES?
SHOW ME YOUR NOTE-BOOK.
WHAT'S THIS?
YOU SLEPT THROUGH THE LAST HALF!
SO WHAT?
YOU SLEPT THROUGH THE LAST HALF OF LITERATURE CLASS.
......
数学I
BOOK: MATH 1
IF I DECIDE IT'S OKAY TO SLEEP, THEN I'LL SLEEP.
HMPH!
I WAS BUSY WITH STUFF YESTER-DAY.
LIKE TUTORING THE NEIGHBOR KID...
...CLEAN-ING AND REAR-RANGING MY ROOM...
...AND GETTING CLUB MATE-RIALS READY.

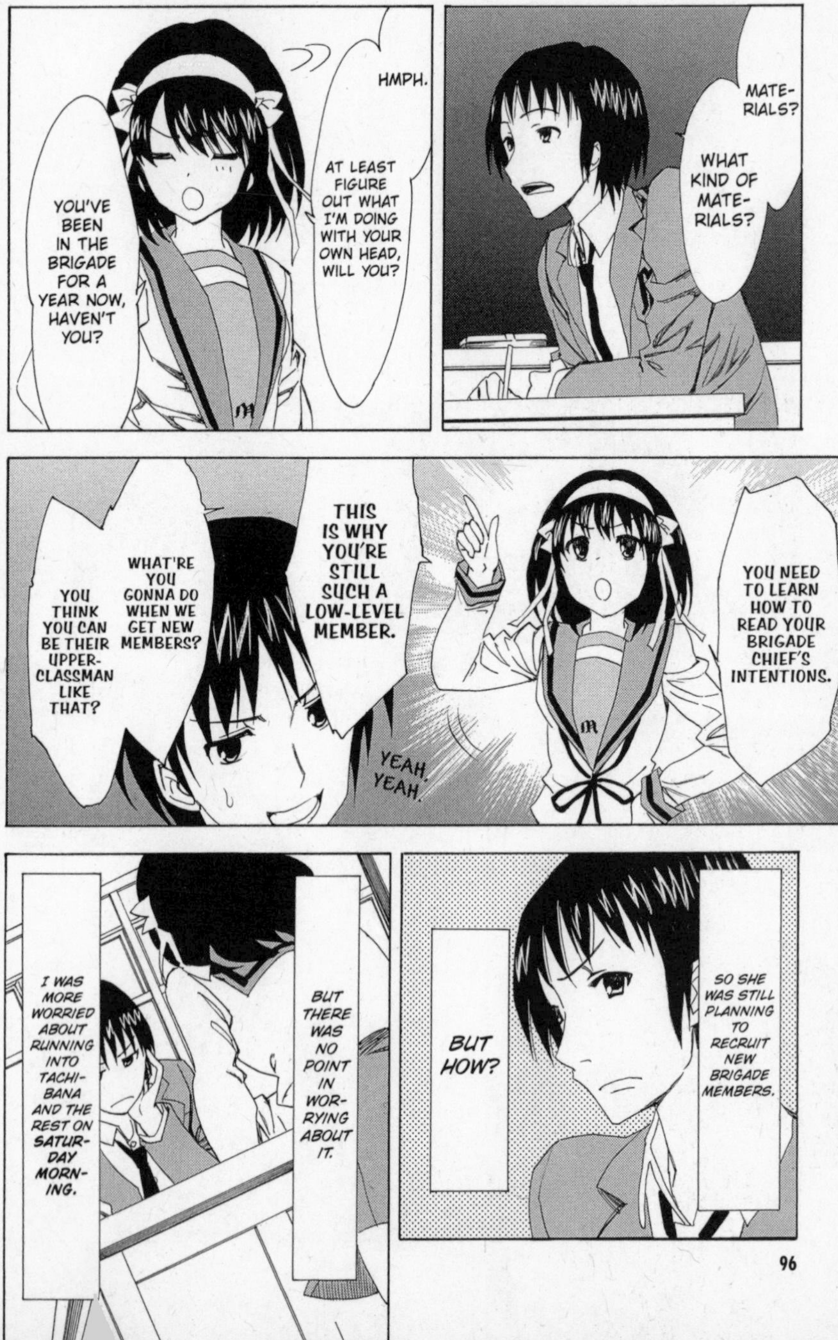
MATERIALS?
WHAT KIND OF MATERIALS?
HMPH.
AT LEAST FIGURE OUT WHAT I'M DOING WITH YOUR OWN HEAD, WILL YOU?
YOU'VE BEEN IN THE BRIGADE FOR A YEAR NOW, HAVEN'T YOU?
YOU NEED TO LEARN HOW TO READ YOUR BRIGADE CHIEF'S INTENTIONS.
THIS IS WHY YOU'RE STILL SUCH A LOW-LEVEL MEMBER.
YEAH, YEAH.
WHAT'RE YOU GONNA DO WHEN WE GET NEW MEMBERS?
YOU THINK YOU CAN BE THEIR UPPERCLASSMAN LIKE THAT?
SO SHE WAS STILL PLANNING TO RECRUIT NEW BRIGADE MEMBERS.
BUT HOW?
BUT THERE WAS NO POINT IN WORRYING ABOUT IT.
I WAS MORE WORRIED ABOUT RUNNING INTO TACHIBANA AND THE REST ON SATURDAY MORNING.

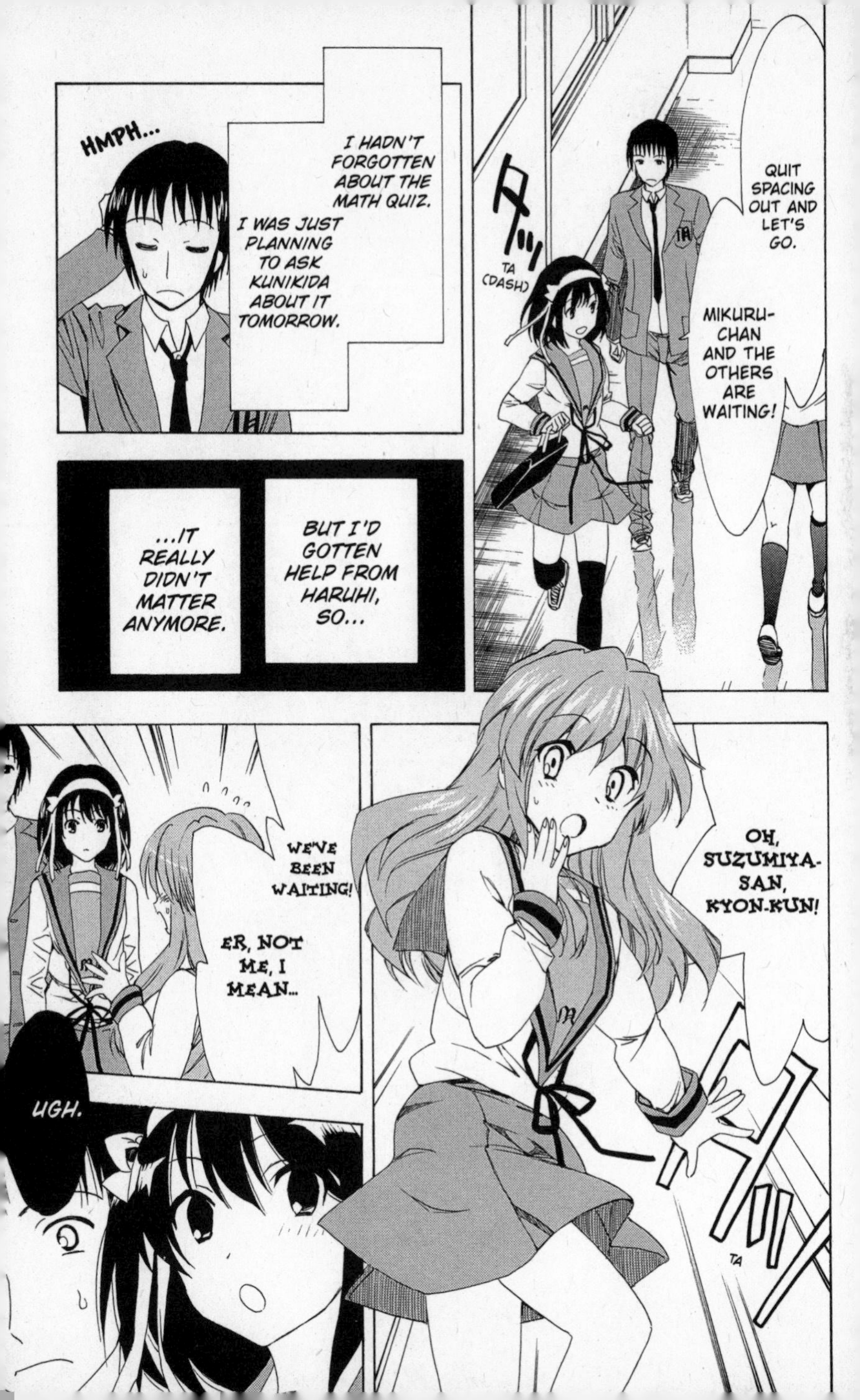
TA (DASH)
QUIT SPACING OUT AND LET'S GO.
MIKURU-CHAN AND THE OTHERS ARE WAITING!
HMPH...
I HADN'T FORGOTTEN ABOUT THE MATH QUIZ.
I WAS JUST PLANNING TO ASK KUNIKIDA ABOUT IT TOMORROW.
BUT I'D GOTTEN HELP FROM HARUHI, SO...
...IT REALLY DIDN'T MATTER ANYMORE.
OH, SUZUMIYA-SAN, KYON-KUN!
TA
WE'VE BEEN WAITING!
ER, NOT ME, I MEAN...
UGH.

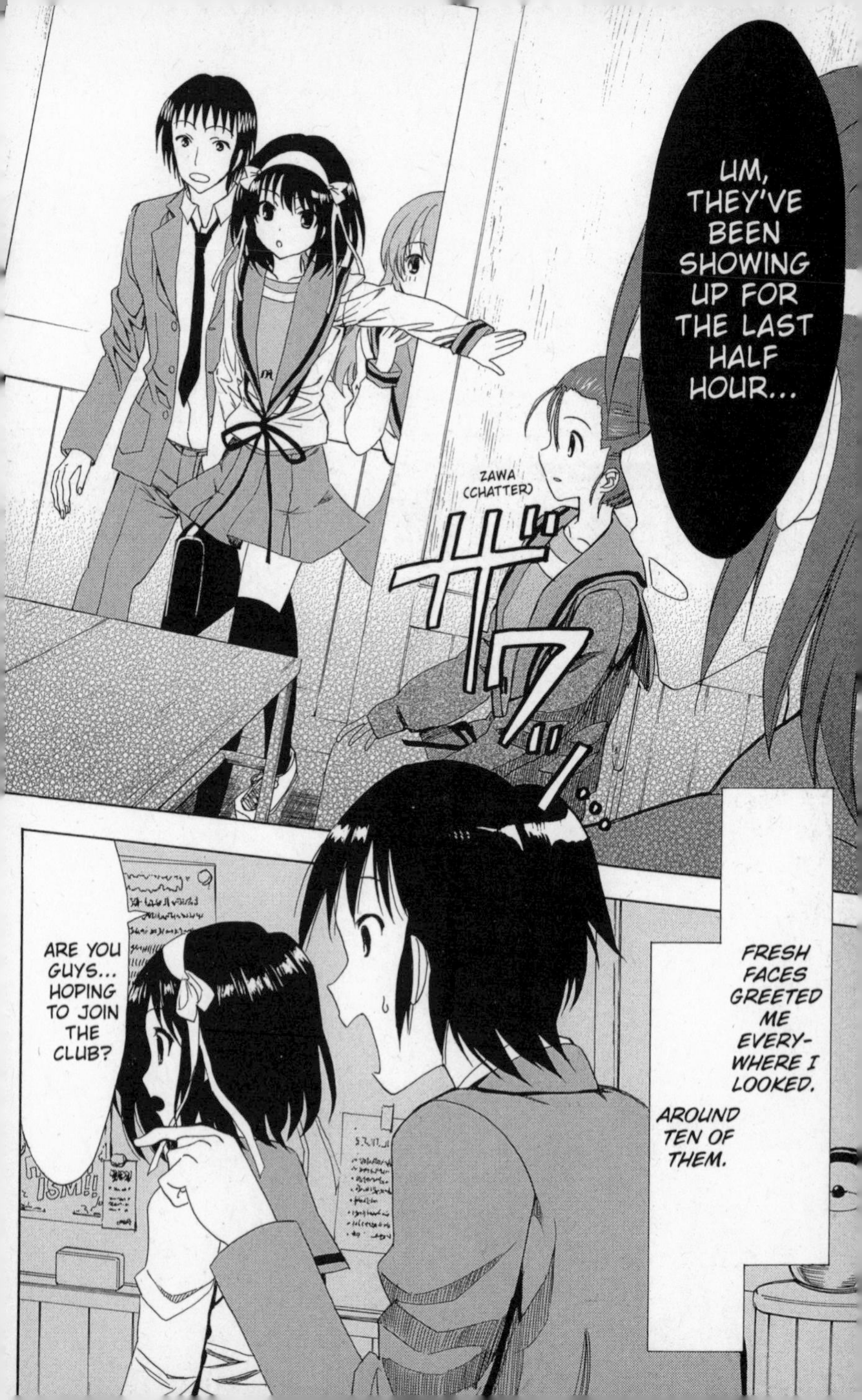
UM, THEY'VE BEEN SHOWING UP FOR THE LAST HALF HOUR...
ZAWA (CHATTER)
FRESH FACES GREETED ME EVERY-WHERE I LOOKED.
AROUND TEN OF THEM.
ARE YOU GUYS... HOPING TO JOIN THE CLUB?

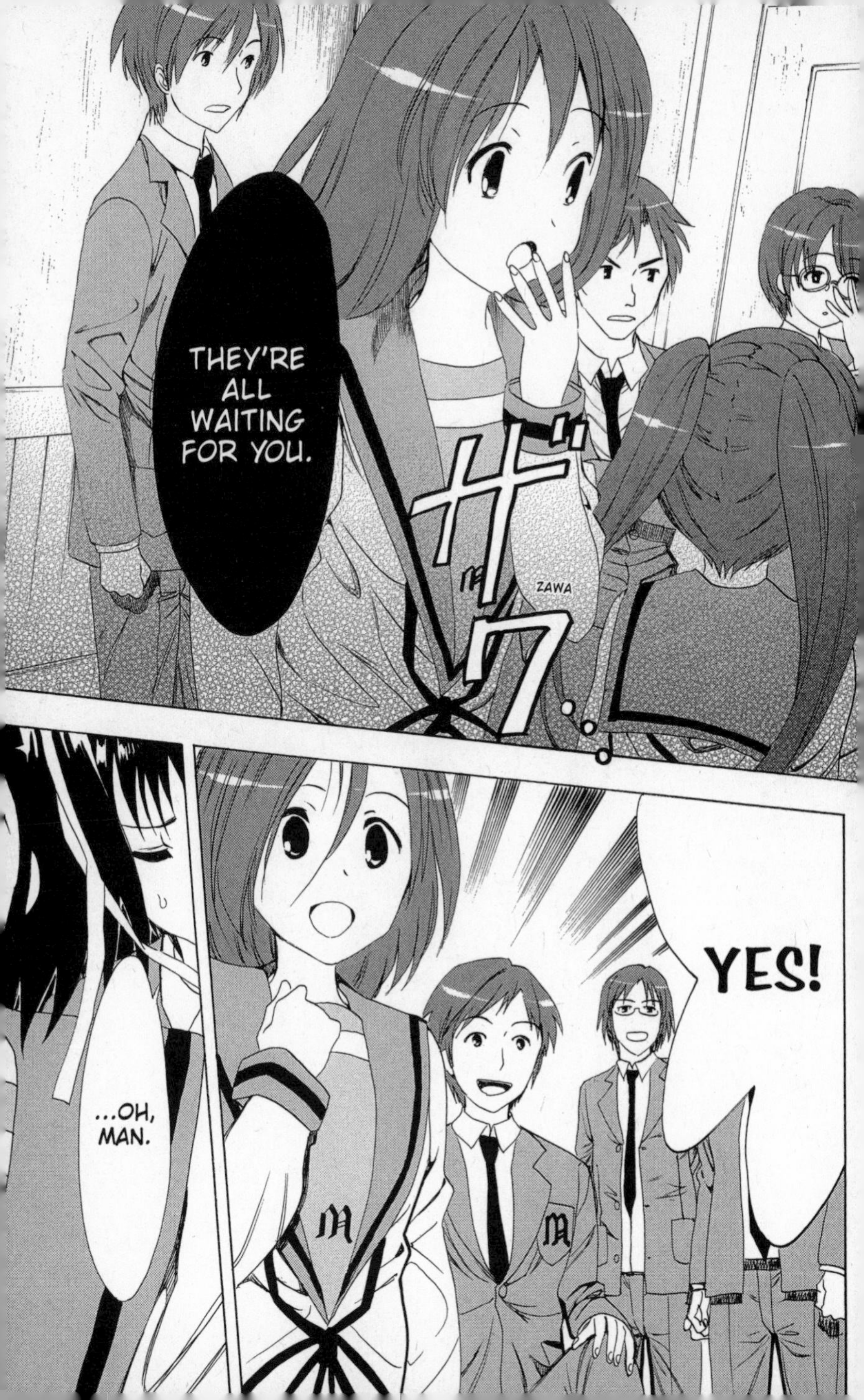
THEY'RE ALL WAITING FOR YOU.
ザワ
ZAWA
YES!
...OH, MAN.

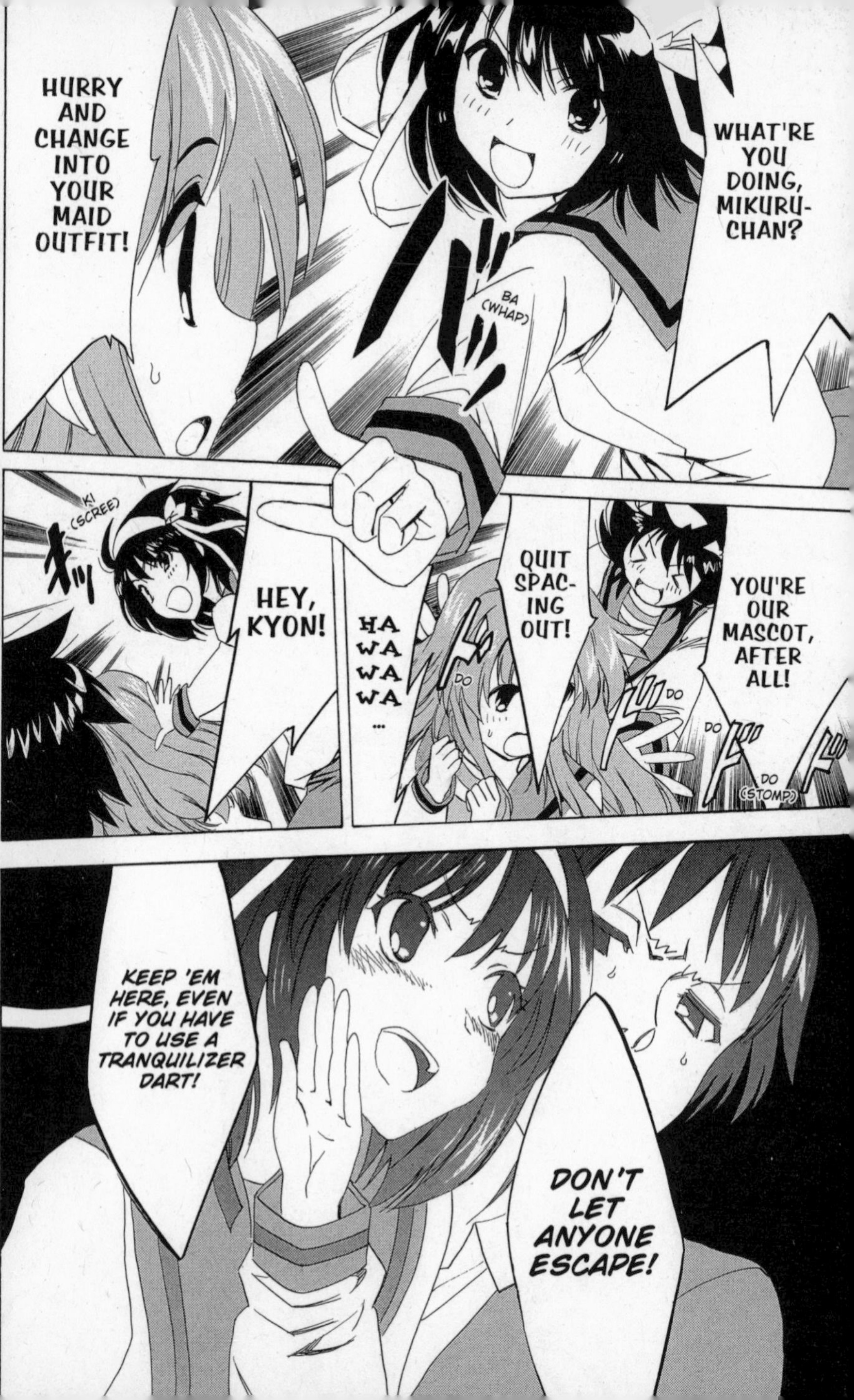
WHAT'RE YOU DOING, MIKURU-CHAN?
BA (WHAP)
HURRY AND CHANGE INTO YOUR MAID OUTFIT!
YOU'RE OUR MASCOT, AFTER ALL!
QUIT SPACING OUT!
DO DO DO DO (STOMP)
HAWAWAWAWA...
HEY, KYON!
KI (SCREE)
DON'T LET ANYONE ESCAPE!
KEEP 'EM HERE, EVEN IF YOU HAVE TO USE A TRANQUILIZER DART!

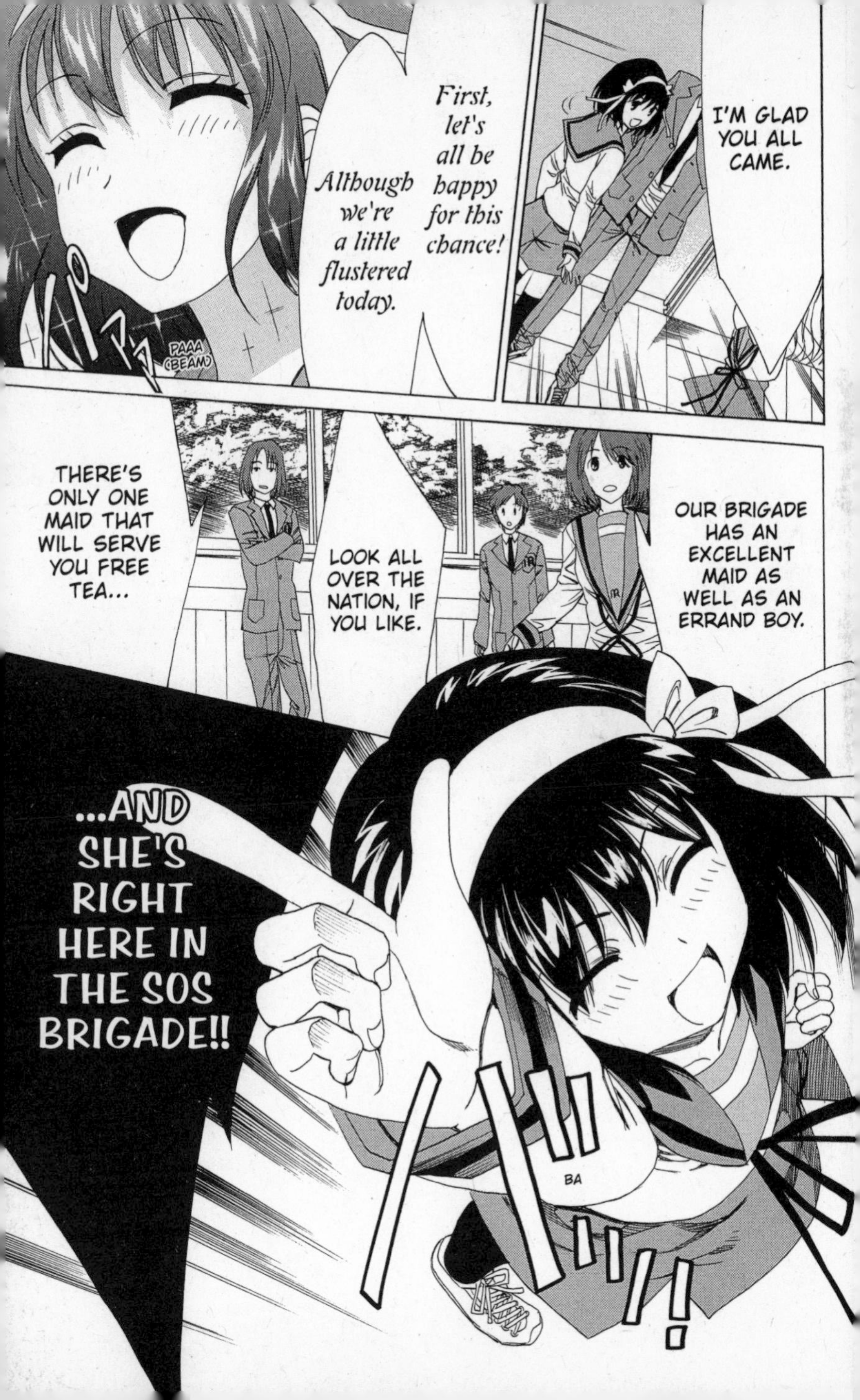
I'M GLAD YOU ALL CAME.
First, let's all be happy for this chance!
Although we're a little flustered today.
PAAA (BEAM)
OUR BRIGADE HAS AN EXCELLENT MAID AS WELL AS AN ERRAND BOY.
LOOK ALL OVER THE NATION, IF YOU LIKE.
THERE'S ONLY ONE MAID THAT WILL SERVE YOU FREE TEA...
...AND SHE'S RIGHT HERE IN THE SOS BRIGADE!!
BA

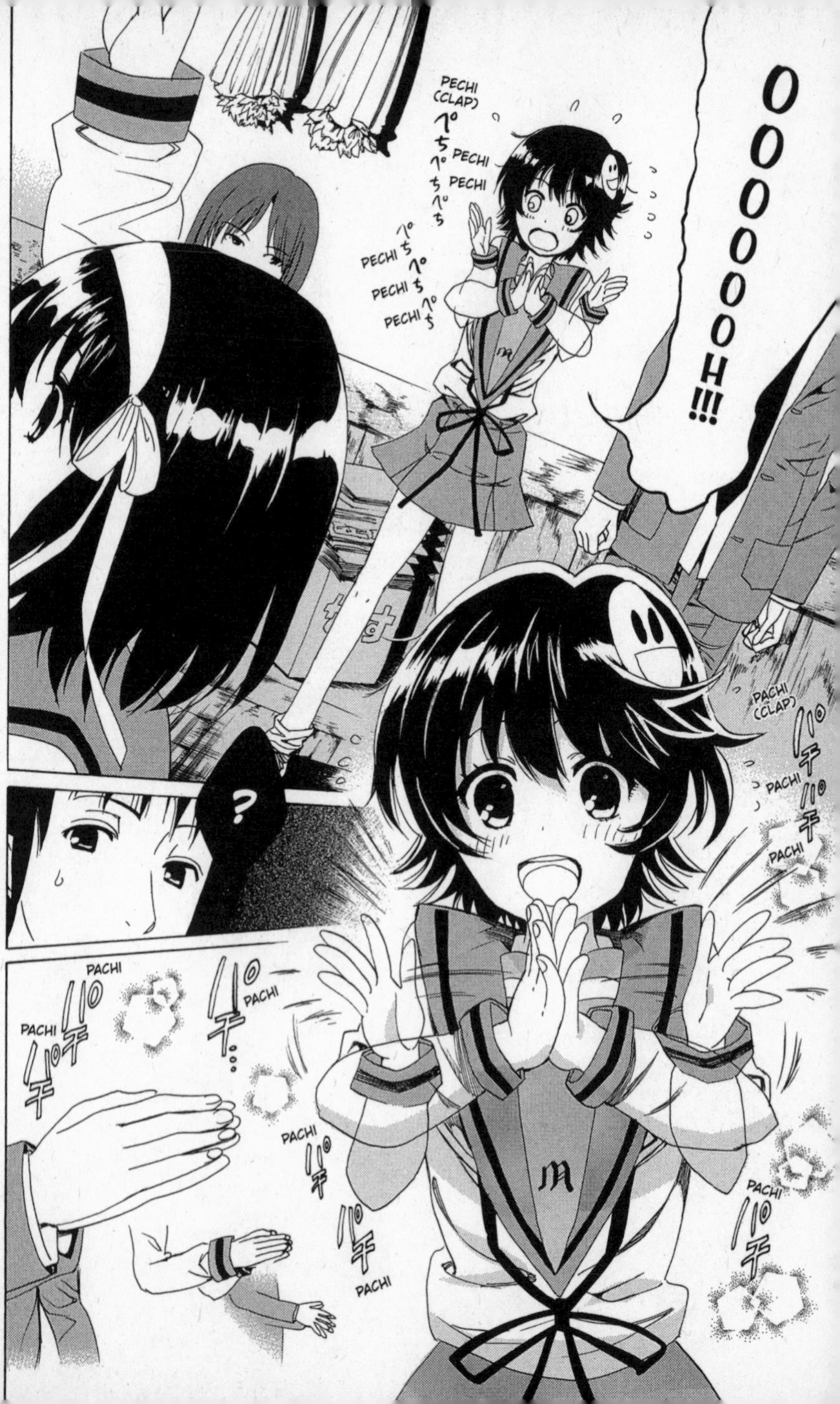
OOOOOOH!!!
PECHI (CLAP)
PECHI
PECHI
PECHI
PECHI
PECHI
PACHI (CLAP)
PACHI
PACHI
?
PACHI
PACHI
PACHI
PACHI
PACHI
PACHI

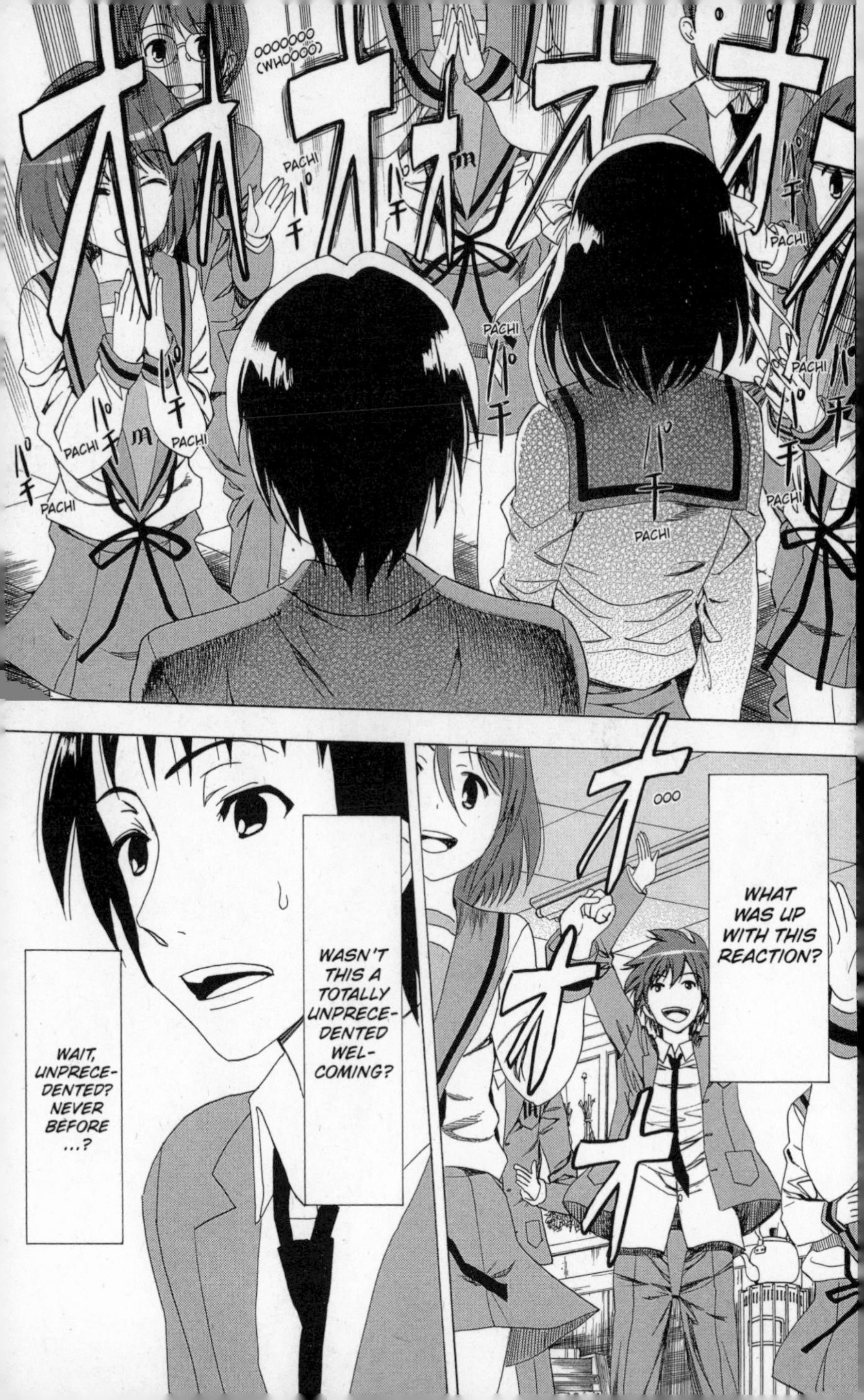
OOOOOOO
(WHOOOO)
PACHI
PACHI
PACHI
PACHI
PACHI
PACHI
PACHI
PACHI
PACHI
OOO
WHAT WAS UP WITH THIS REACTION?
WASN'T THIS A TOTALLY UNPRECE-DENTED WEL-COMING?
WAIT, UNPRECE-DENTED? NEVER BEFORE ...?

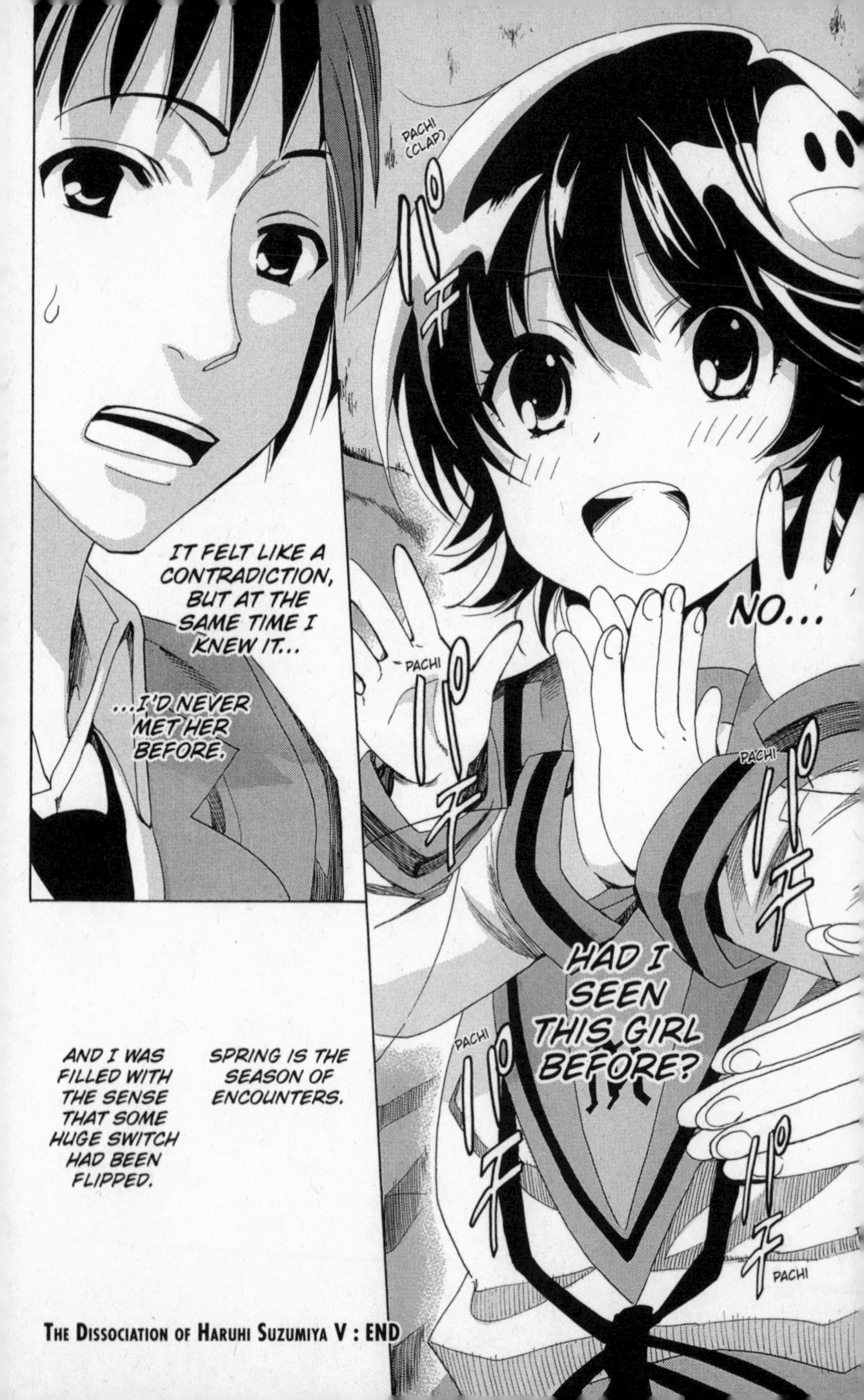
PACHI (CLAP)
NO...
PACHI
PACHI
HAD I SEEN THIS GIRL BEFORE?
PACHI
PACHI
IT FELT LIKE A CONTRADICTION, BUT AT THE SAME TIME I KNEW IT...
...I'D NEVER MET HER BEFORE.
SPRING IS THE SEASON OF ENCOUNTERS.
AND I WAS FILLED WITH THE SENSE THAT SOME HUGE SWITCH HAD BEEN FLIPPED.
THE DISSOCIATION OF HARUHI SUZUMIYA V : END

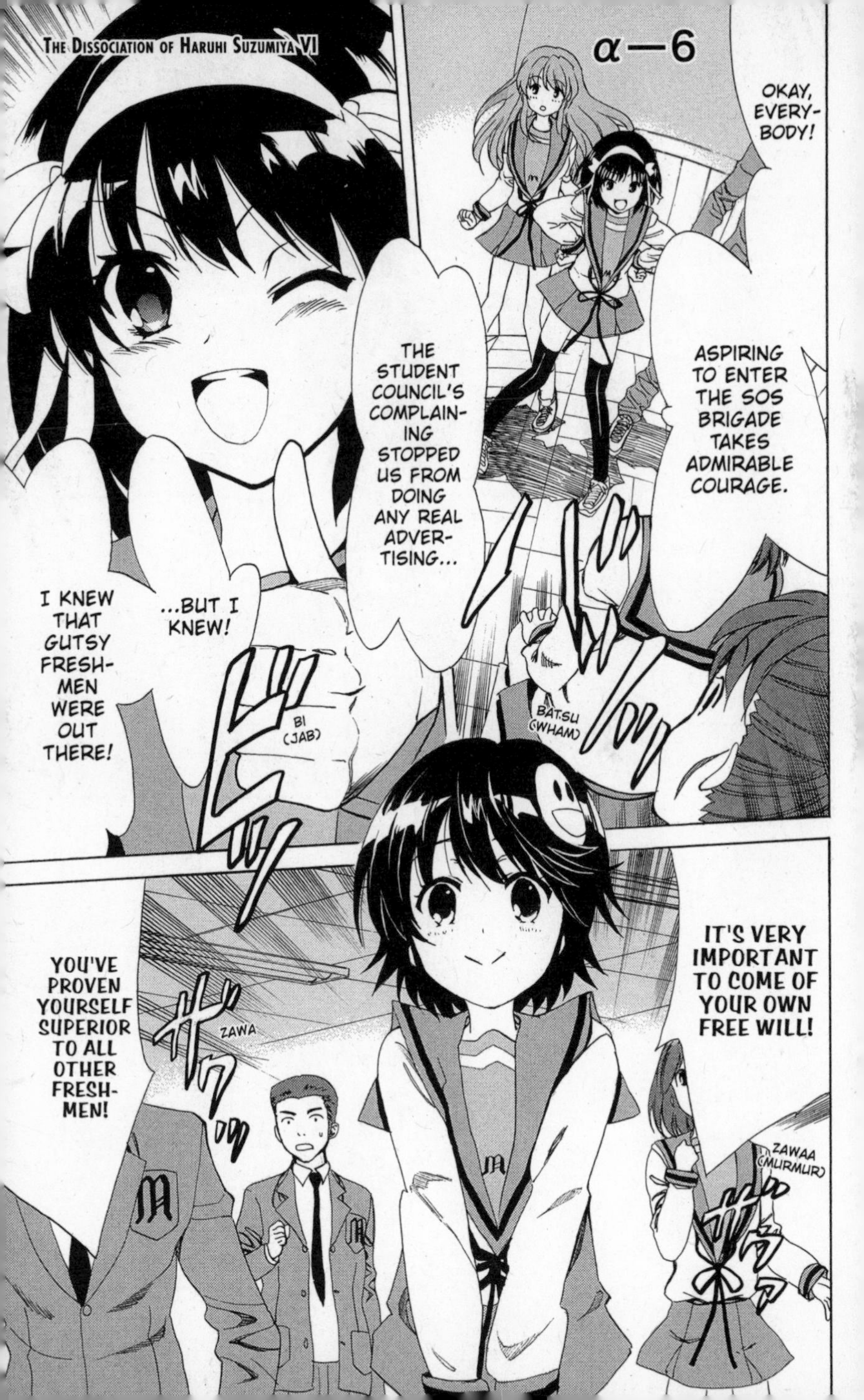
α—6
OKAY, EVERYBODY!
ASPIRING TO ENTER THE SOS BRIGADE TAKES ADMIRABLE COURAGE.
THE STUDENT COUNCIL'S COMPLAINING STOPPED US FROM DOING ANY REAL ADVERTISING...
BATSU (WHAM)
...BUT I KNEW!
I KNEW THAT GUTSY FRESHMEN WERE OUT THERE!
BI (JAB)
IT'S VERY IMPORTANT TO COME OF YOUR OWN FREE WILL!
ZAWAA (MURMUR)
YOU'VE PROVEN YOURSELF SUPERIOR TO ALL OTHER FRESHMEN!
ZAWA

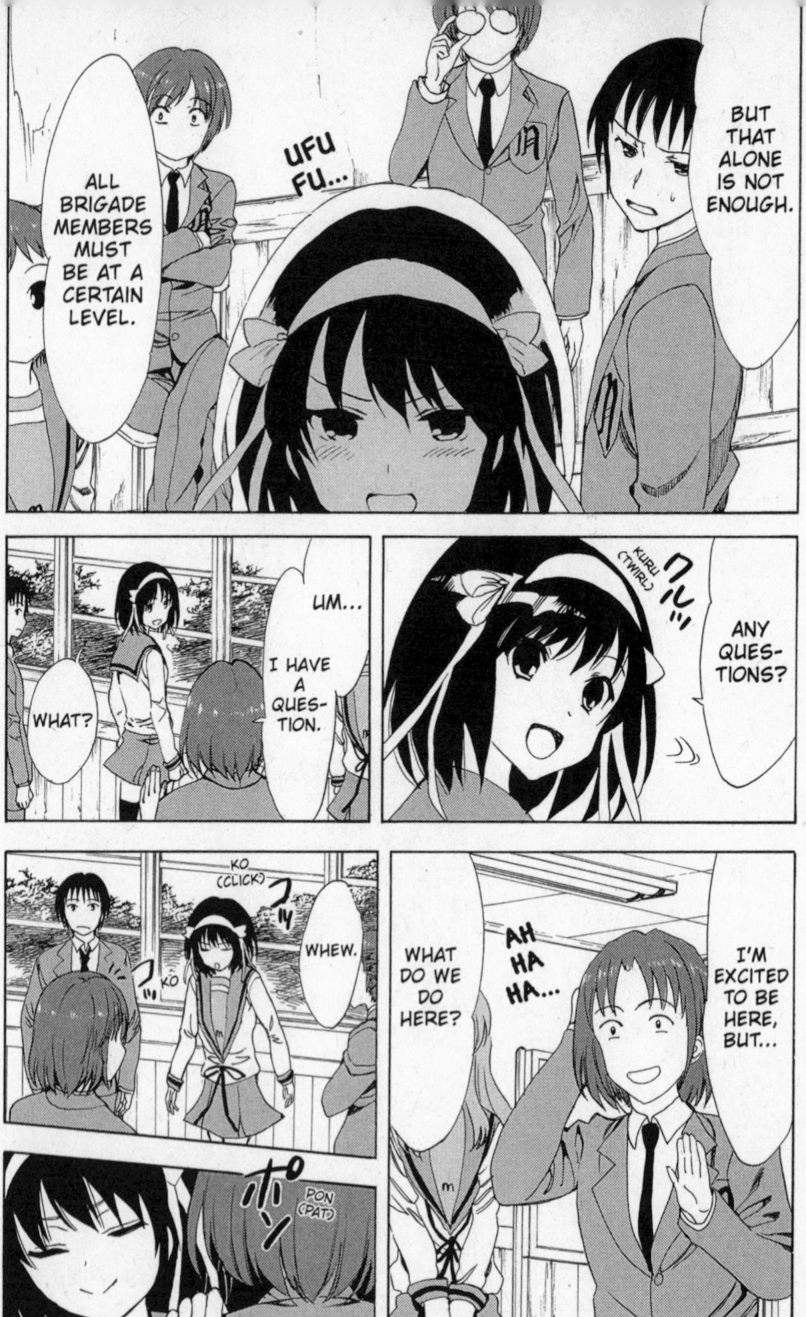
BUT THAT ALONE IS NOT ENOUGH.
UFU FU...
ALL BRIGADE MEMBERS MUST BE AT A CERTAIN LEVEL.
KURU (TWIRL)
ANY QUES-TIONS?
UM...
I HAVE A QUES-TION.
WHAT?
I'M EXCITED TO BE HERE, BUT...
AH HA HA...
WHAT DO WE DO HERE?
KO (CLICK)
WHEW.
KO
PON (PAT)

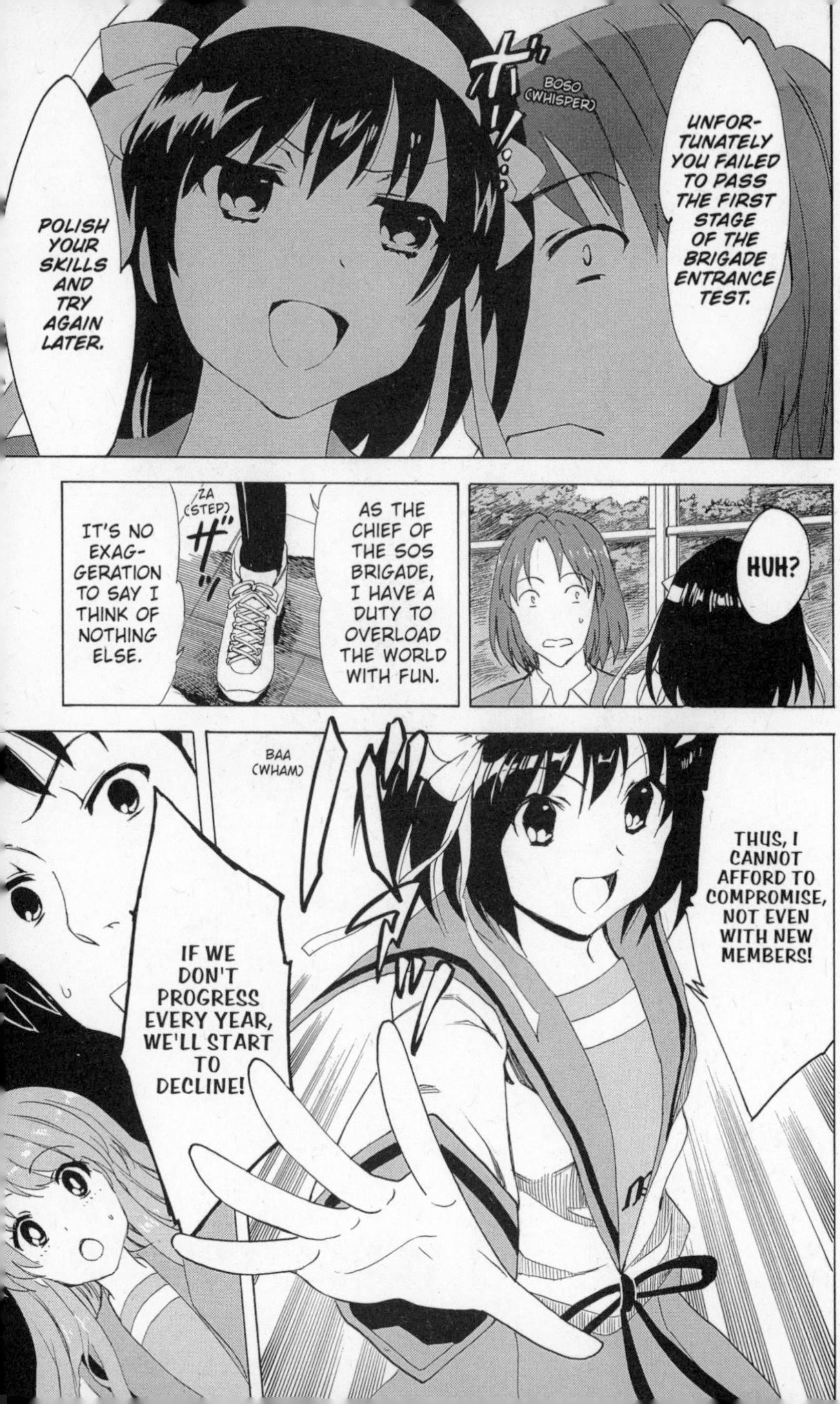
BOSO (WHISPER)
UNFORTUNATELY YOU FAILED TO PASS THE FIRST STAGE OF THE BRIGADE ENTRANCE TEST.
POLISH YOUR SKILLS AND TRY AGAIN LATER.
HUH?
AS THE CHIEF OF THE SOS BRIGADE, I HAVE A DUTY TO OVERLOAD THE WORLD WITH FUN.
ZA (STEP)
IT'S NO EXAGGERATION TO SAY I THINK OF NOTHING ELSE.
THUS, I CANNOT AFFORD TO COMPROMISE, NOT EVEN WITH NEW MEMBERS!
BAA (WHAM)
IF WE DON'T PROGRESS EVERY YEAR, WE'LL START TO DECLINE!

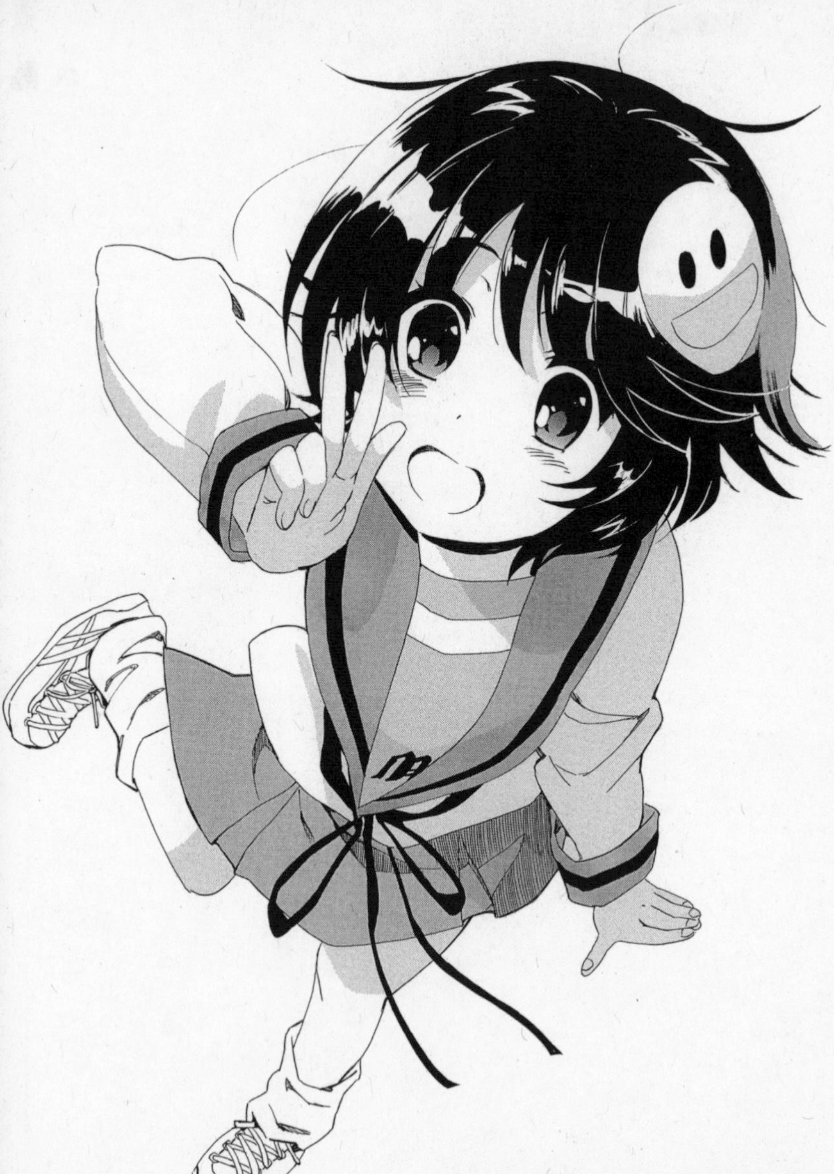

© The Dissociation of Haruhi Suzumiya VI

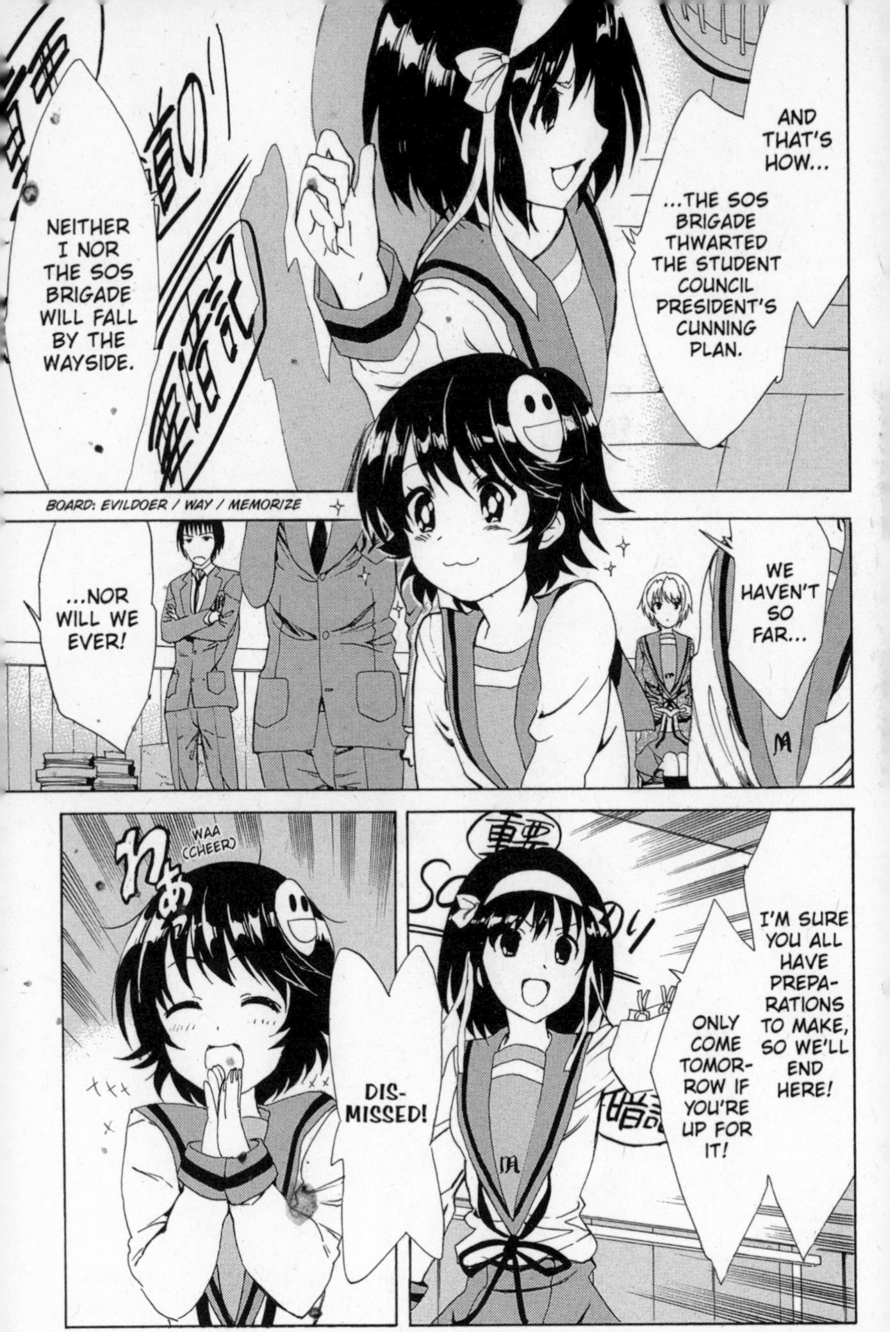
AND THAT'S HOW...
...THE SOS BRIGADE THWARTED THE STUDENT COUNCIL PRESIDENT'S CUNNING PLAN.
NEITHER I NOR THE SOS BRIGADE WILL FALL BY THE WAYSIDE.
BOARD: EVILDOER / WAY / MEMORIZE
WE HAVEN'T SO FAR...
...NOR WILL WE EVER!
I'M SURE YOU ALL HAVE PREPA-RATIONS TO MAKE, SO WE'LL END HERE!
ONLY COME TOMOR-ROW IF YOU'RE UP FOR IT!
WAA (CHEER)
DIS-MISSED!

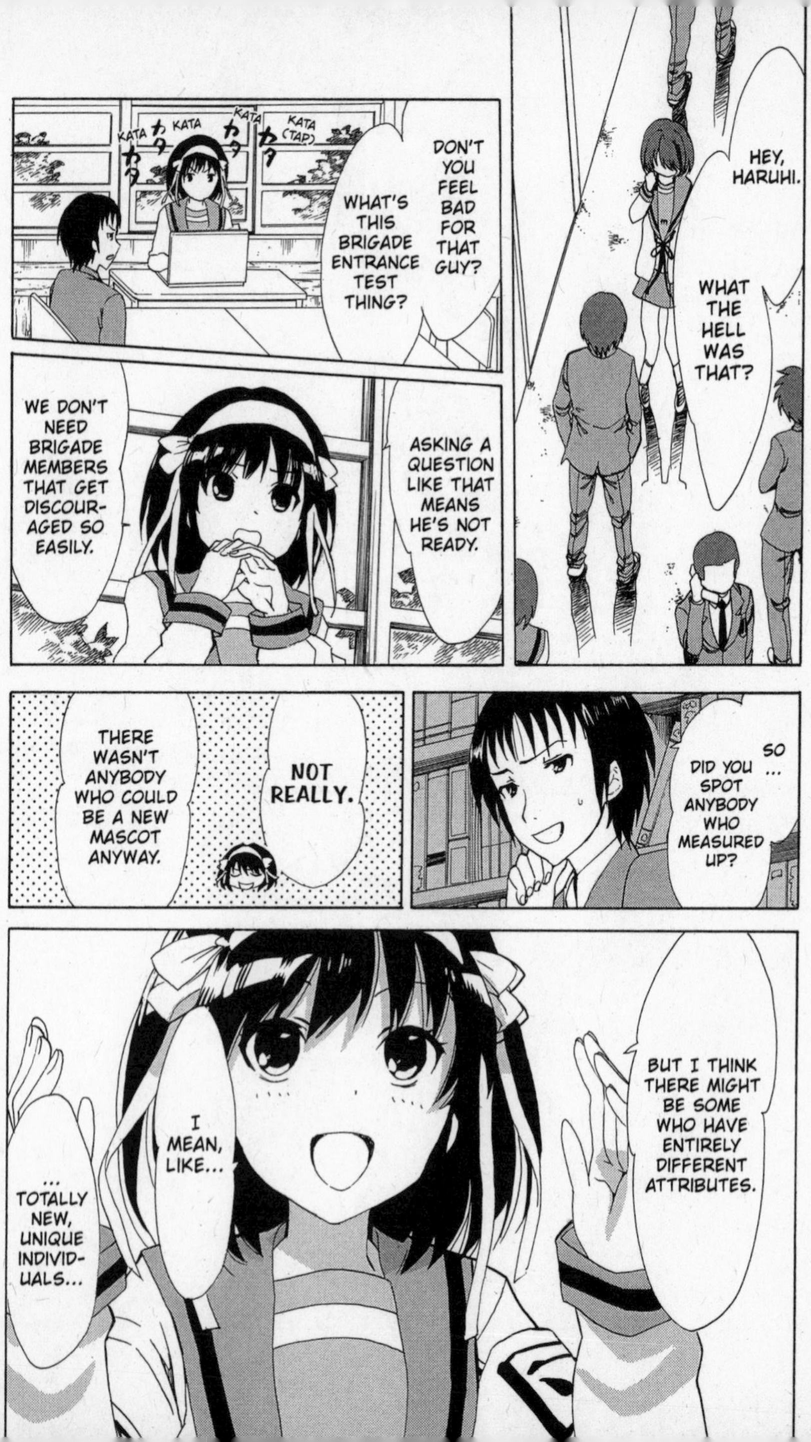
HEY, HARUHI.
WHAT THE HELL WAS THAT?
DON'T YOU FEEL BAD FOR THAT GUY?
WHAT'S THIS BRIGADE ENTRANCE TEST THING?
KATA (TAP)
KATA
KATA
KATA
ASKING A QUESTION LIKE THAT MEANS HE'S NOT READY.
WE DON'T NEED BRIGADE MEMBERS THAT GET DISCOURAGED SO EASILY.
SO ... DID YOU SPOT ANYBODY WHO MEASURED UP?
NOT REALLY.
THERE WASN'T ANYBODY WHO COULD BE A NEW MASCOT ANYWAY.
BUT I THINK THERE MIGHT BE SOME WHO HAVE ENTIRELY DIFFERENT ATTRIBUTES.
I MEAN, LIKE...
... TOTALLY NEW, UNIQUE INDIVIDUALS...

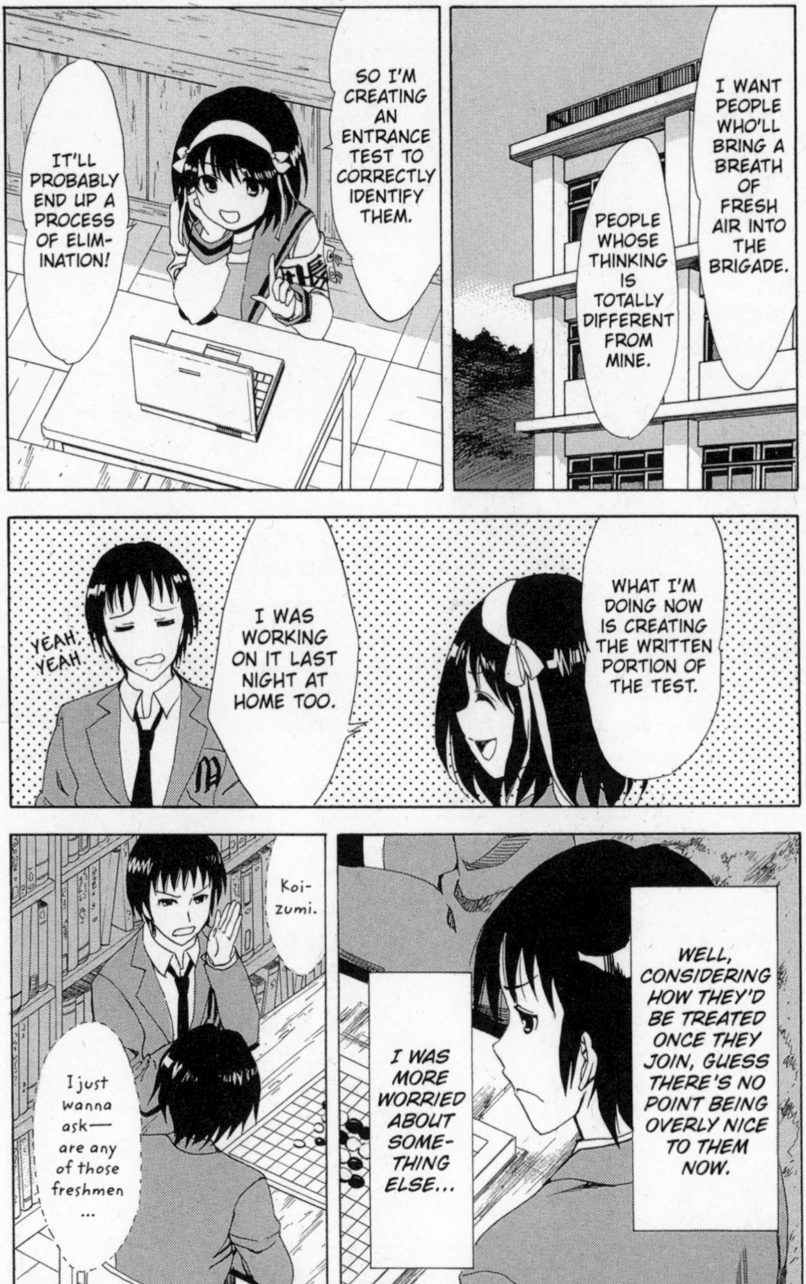
I WANT PEOPLE WHO'LL BRING A BREATH OF FRESH AIR INTO THE BRIGADE.
PEOPLE WHOSE THINKING IS TOTALLY DIFFERENT FROM MINE.
SO I'M CREATING AN ENTRANCE TEST TO CORRECTLY IDENTIFY THEM.
IT'LL PROBABLY END UP A PROCESS OF ELIM-INATION!
WHAT I'M DOING NOW IS CREATING THE WRITTEN PORTION OF THE TEST.
I WAS WORKING ON IT LAST NIGHT AT HOME TOO.
YEAH, YEAH
WELL, CONSIDERING HOW THEY'D BE TREATED ONCE THEY JOIN, GUESS THERE'S NO POINT BEING OVERLY NICE TO THEM NOW.
I WAS MORE WORRIED ABOUT SOME-THING ELSE...
Koi-zumi.
I just wanna ask— are any of those freshmen ...

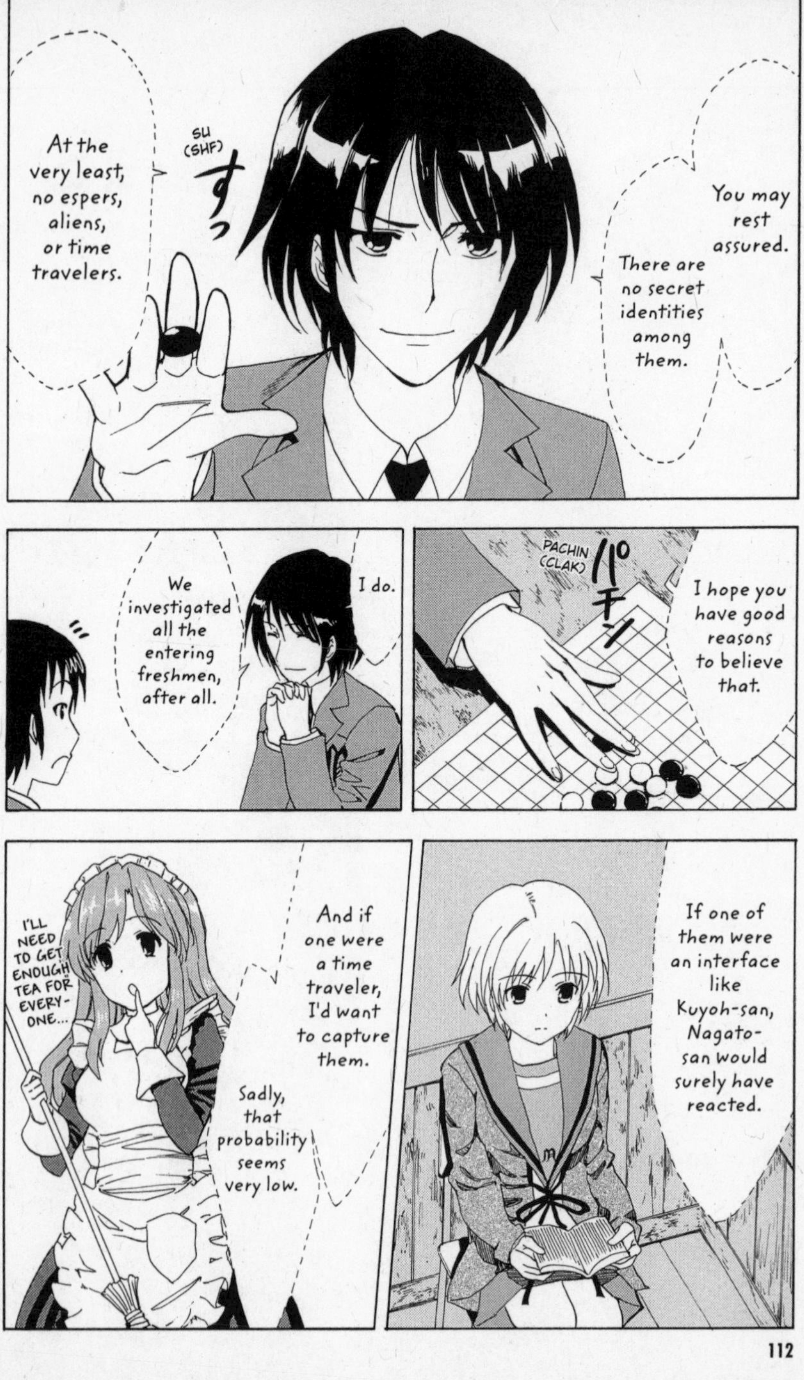
You may rest assured.
There are no secret identities among them.
SU (SHF)
At the very least, no espers, aliens, or time travelers.
PACHIN (CLAK)
I hope you have good reasons to believe that.
I do.
We investigated all the entering freshmen, after all.
If one of them were an interface like Kuyoh-san, Nagato-san would surely have reacted.
And if one were a time traveler, I'd want to capture them.
Sadly, that probability seems very low.
I'LL NEED TO GET ENOUGH TEA FOR EVERY-ONE...

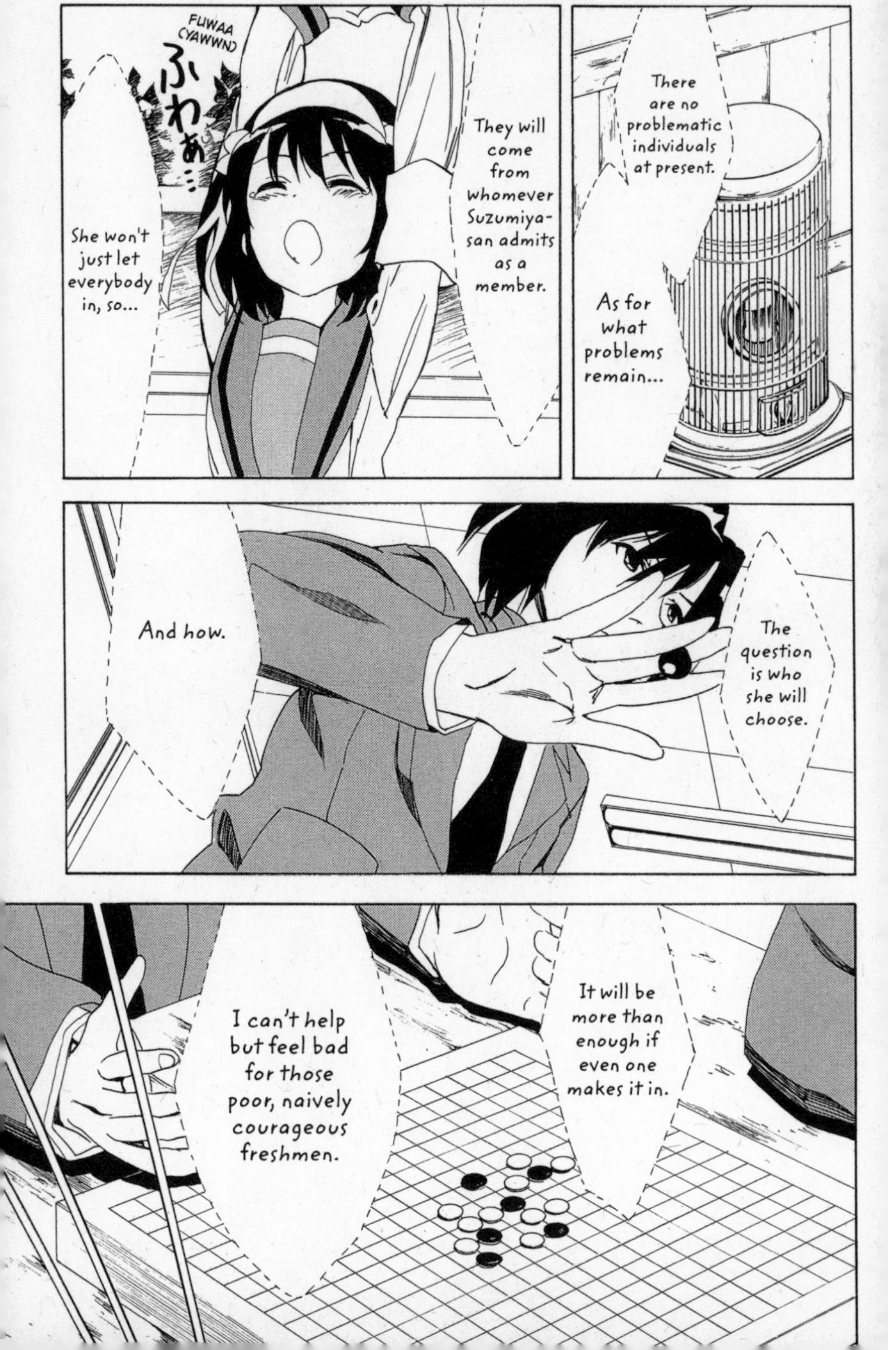
There are no problematic individuals at present.
As for what problems remain...
They will come from whomever Suzumiya-san admits as a member.
FUWAA (YAWWN)
ふわあ
She won't just let everybody in, so...
The question is who she will choose.
And how.
It will be more than enough if even one makes it in.
I can't help but feel bad for those poor, naively courageous freshmen.

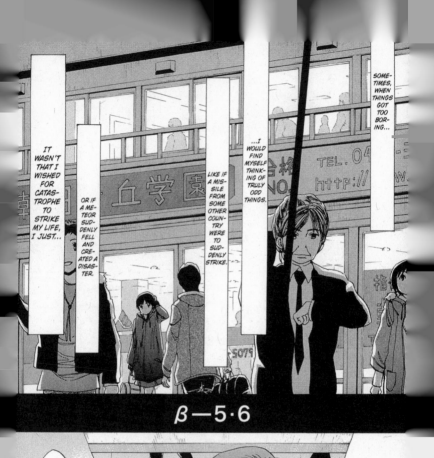

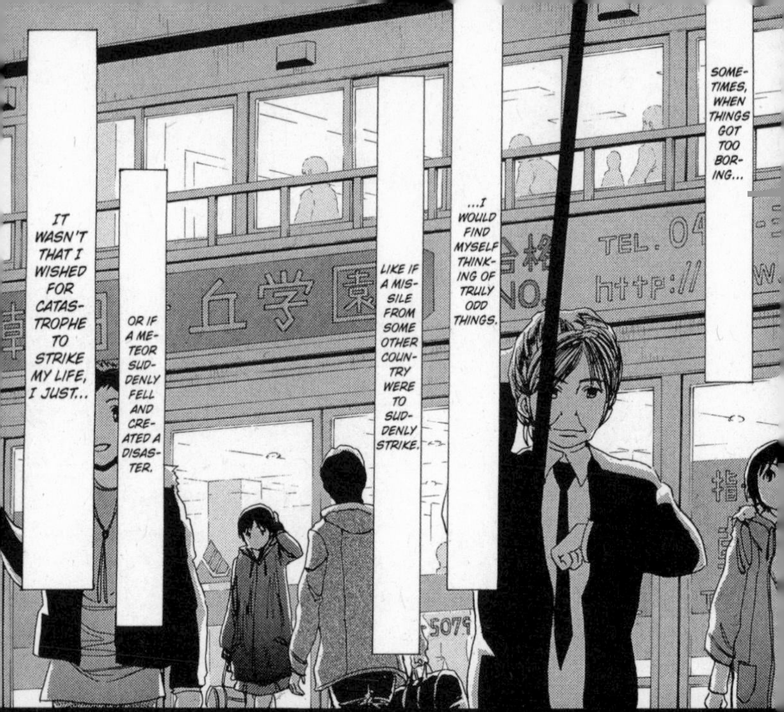
SOMETIMES, WHEN THINGS GOT TOO BORING...
...I WOULD FIND MYSELF THINKING OF TRULY ODD THINGS.
LIKE IF A MISSILE FROM SOME OTHER COUNTRY WERE TO SUDDENLY STRIKE.
OR IF A METEOR SUDDENLY FELL AND CREATED A DISASTER.
IT WASN'T THAT I WISHED FOR CATASTROPHE TO STRIKE MY LIFE, I JUST...

β—5·6

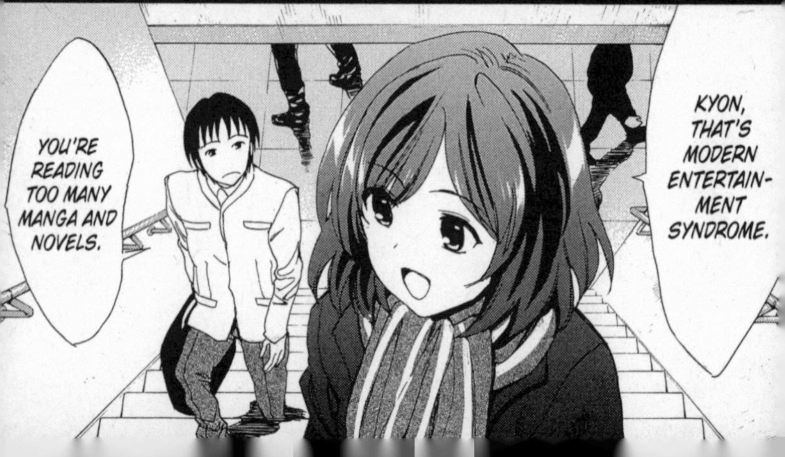
KYON, THAT'S MODERN ENTERTAINMENT SYNDROME.
YOU'RE READING TOO MANY MANGA AND NOVELS.

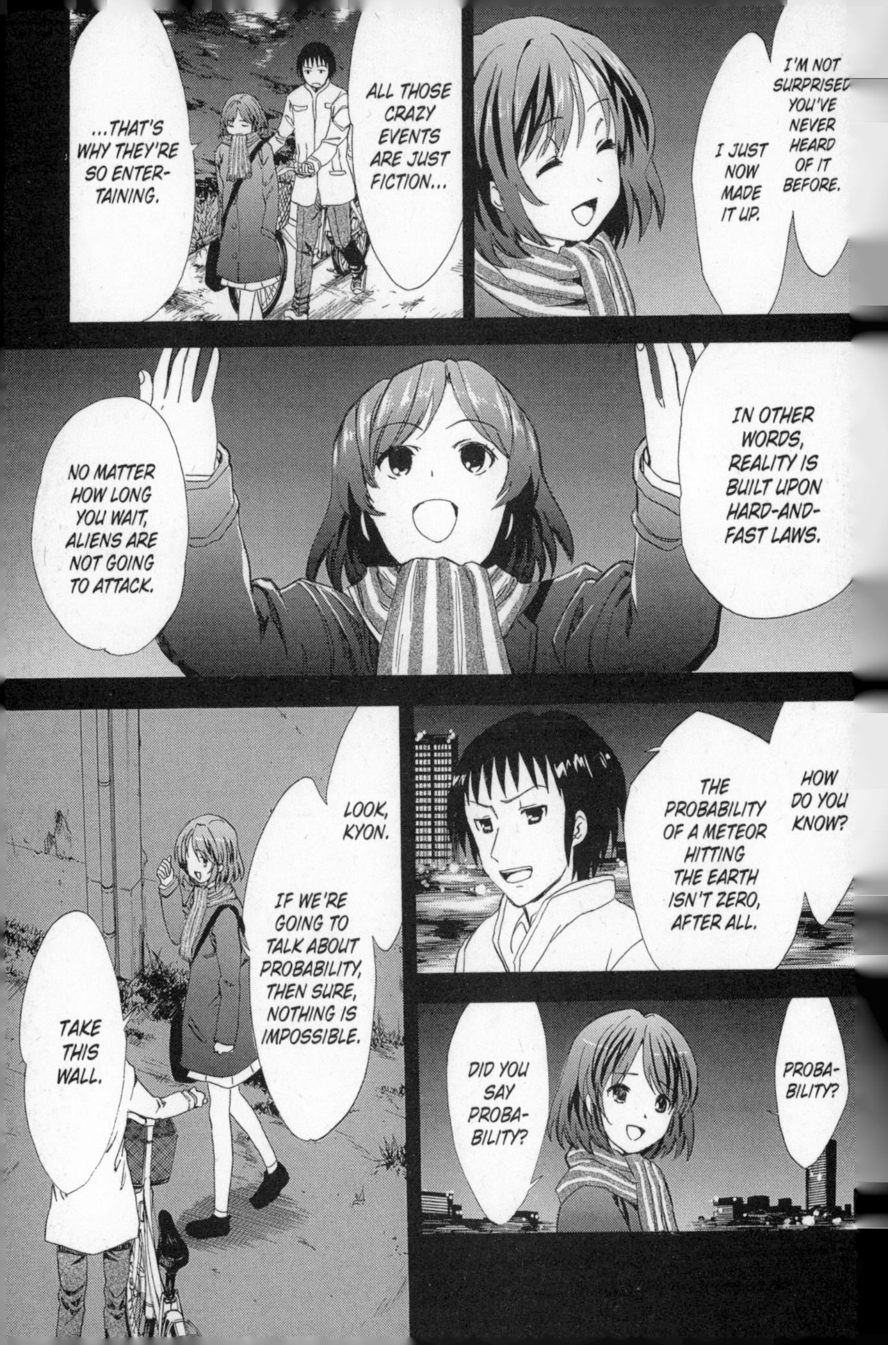
I'M NOT SURPRISED YOU'VE NEVER HEARD OF IT BEFORE.
I JUST NOW MADE IT UP.
ALL THOSE CRAZY EVENTS ARE JUST FICTION...
...THAT'S WHY THEY'RE SO ENTER-TAINING.
IN OTHER WORDS, REALITY IS BUILT UPON HARD-AND-FAST LAWS.
NO MATTER HOW LONG YOU WAIT, ALIENS ARE NOT GOING TO ATTACK.
HOW DO YOU KNOW?
THE PROBABILITY OF A METEOR HITTING THE EARTH ISN'T ZERO, AFTER ALL.
PROBA-BILITY?
DID YOU SAY PROBA-BILITY?
LOOK, KYON.
IF WE'RE GOING TO TALK ABOUT PROBABILITY, THEN SURE, NOTHING IS IMPOSSIBLE.
TAKE THIS WALL.

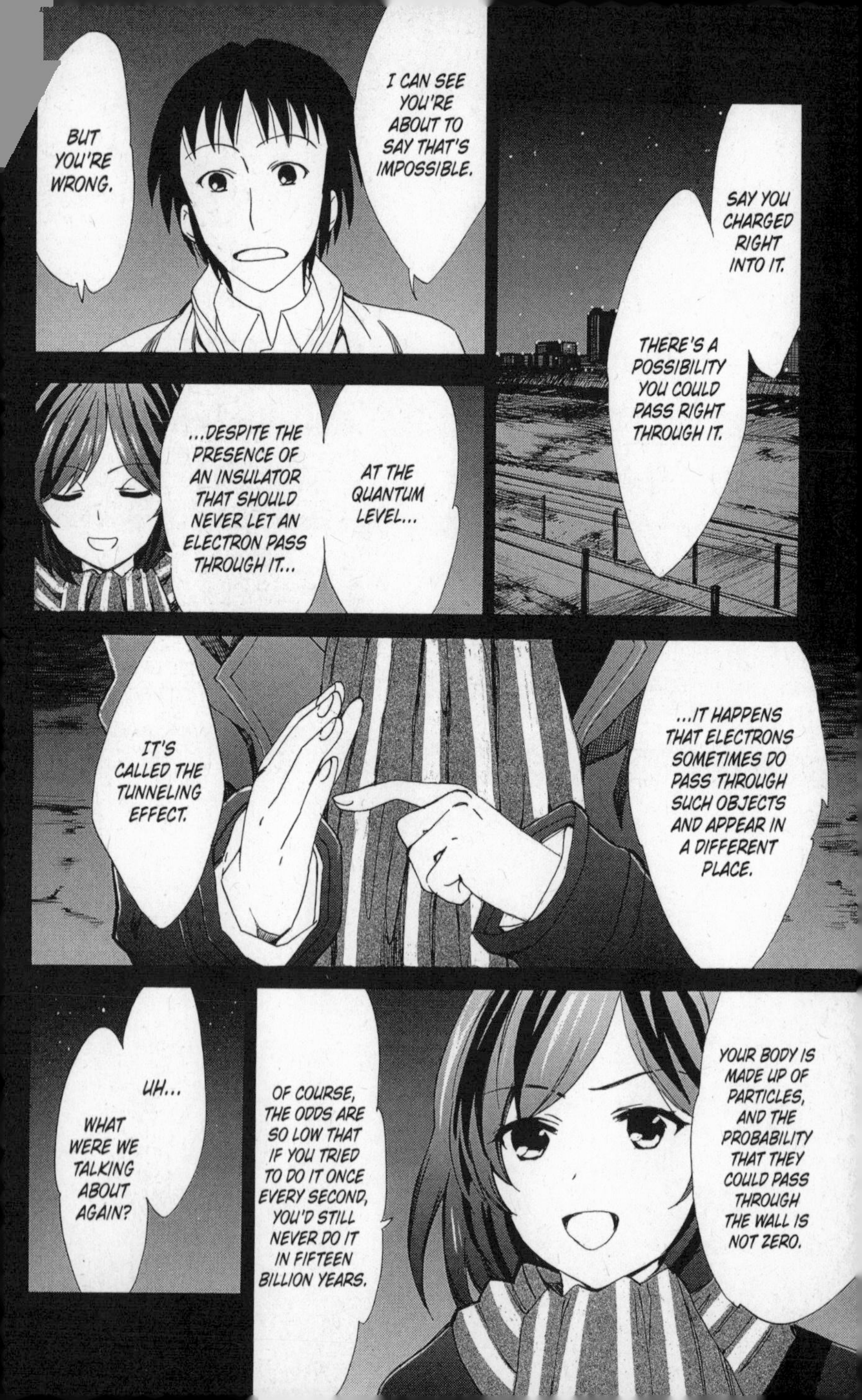
SAY YOU CHARGED RIGHT INTO IT.
THERE'S A POSSIBILITY YOU COULD PASS RIGHT THROUGH IT.
I CAN SEE YOU'RE ABOUT TO SAY THAT'S IMPOSSIBLE.
BUT YOU'RE WRONG.
AT THE QUANTUM LEVEL...
...DESPITE THE PRESENCE OF AN INSULATOR THAT SHOULD NEVER LET AN ELECTRON PASS THROUGH IT...
...IT HAPPENS THAT ELECTRONS SOMETIMES DO PASS THROUGH SUCH OBJECTS AND APPEAR IN A DIFFERENT PLACE.
IT'S CALLED THE TUNNELING EFFECT.
YOUR BODY IS MADE UP OF PARTICLES, AND THE PROBABILITY THAT THEY COULD PASS THROUGH THE WALL IS NOT ZERO.
OF COURSE, THE ODDS ARE SO LOW THAT IF YOU TRIED TO DO IT ONCE EVERY SECOND, YOU'D STILL NEVER DO IT IN FIFTEEN BILLION YEARS.
UH...
WHAT WERE WE TALKING ABOUT AGAIN?

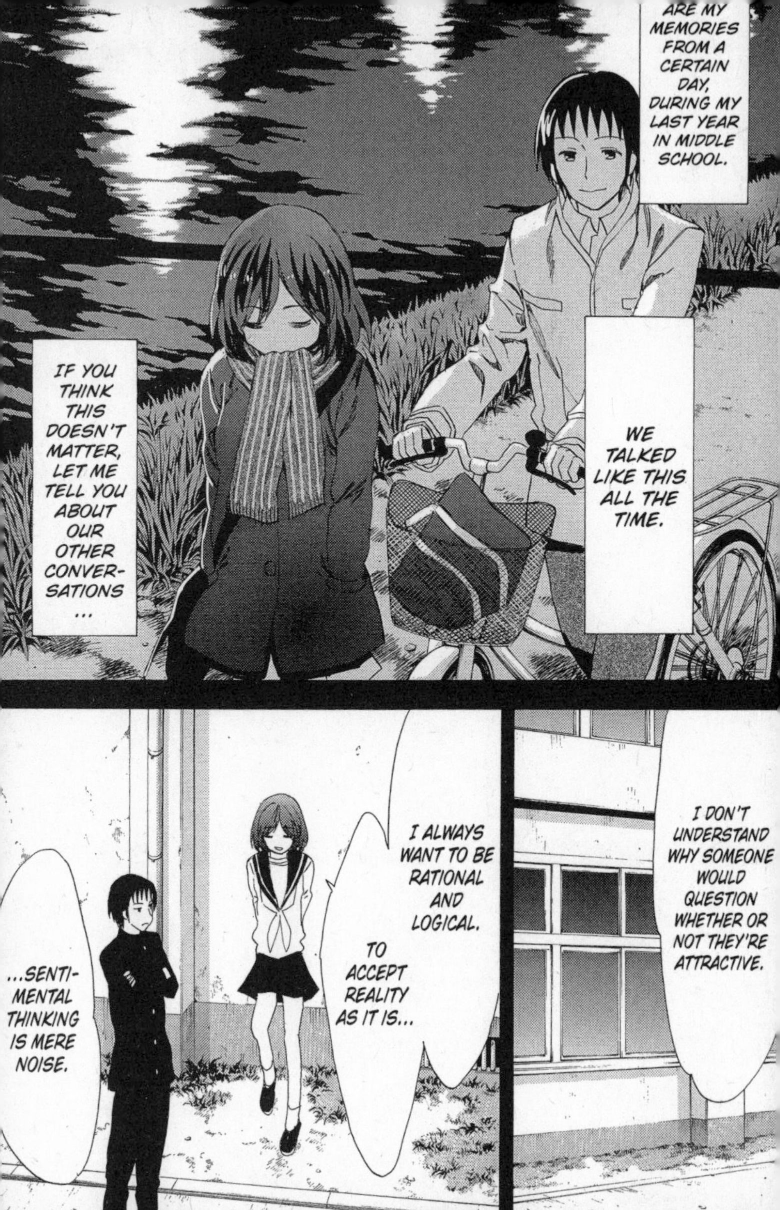
ARE MY MEMORIES FROM A CERTAIN DAY, DURING MY LAST YEAR IN MIDDLE SCHOOL.
WE TALKED LIKE THIS ALL THE TIME.
IF YOU THINK THIS DOESN'T MATTER, LET ME TELL YOU ABOUT OUR OTHER CONVERSATIONS...
I DON'T UNDERSTAND WHY SOMEONE WOULD QUESTION WHETHER OR NOT THEY'RE ATTRACTIVE.
I ALWAYS WANT TO BE RATIONAL AND LOGICAL.
TO ACCEPT REALITY AS IT IS...
...SENTIMENTAL THINKING IS MERE NOISE.

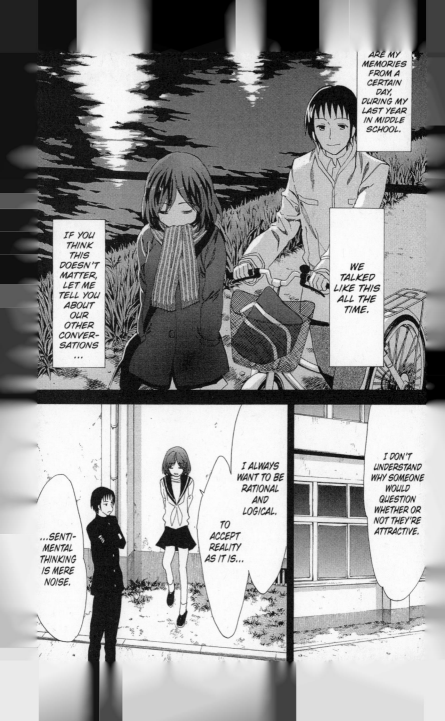

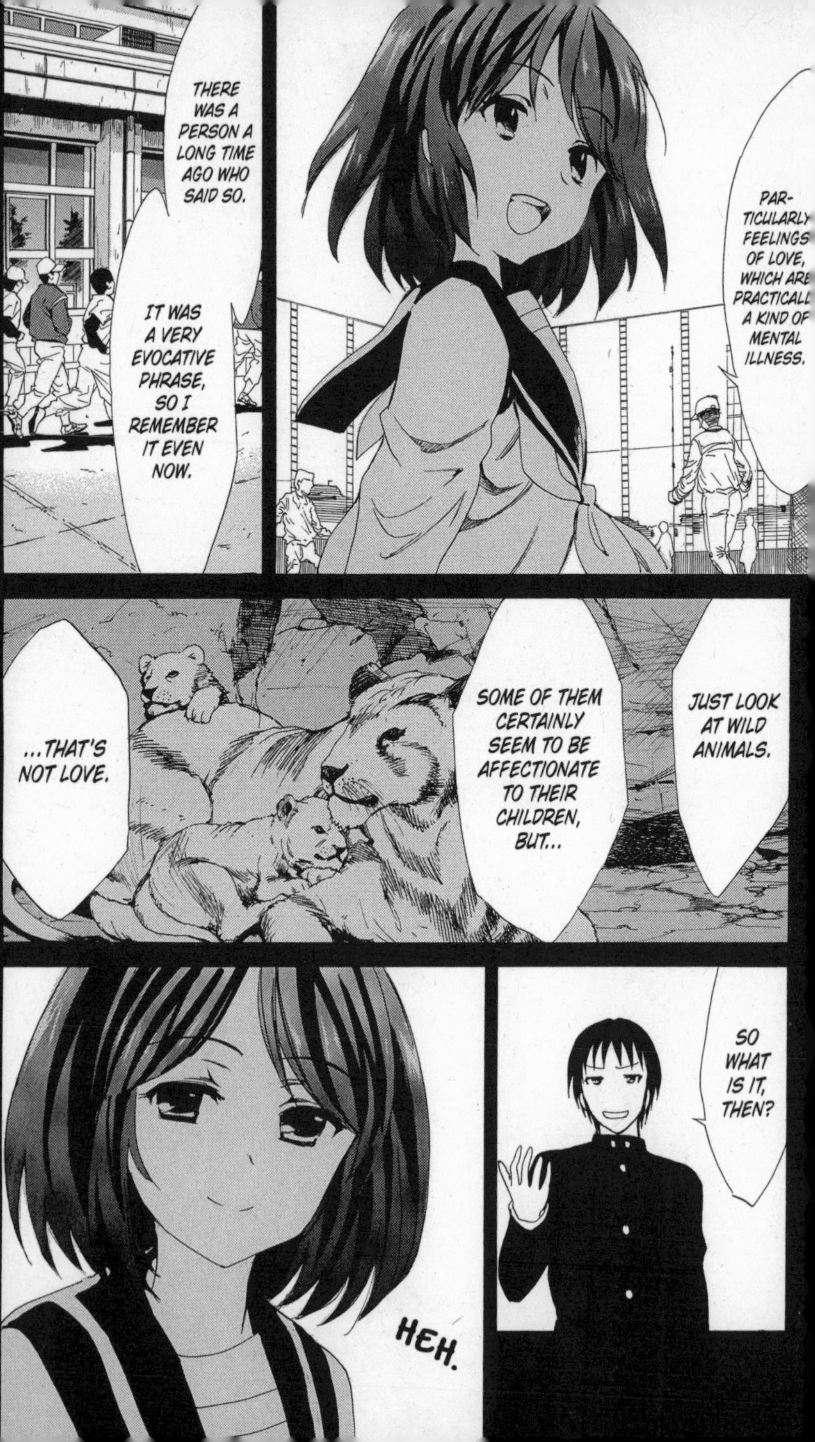
PAR-TICULARLY FEELINGS OF LOVE, WHICH ARE PRACTICALLY A KIND OF MENTAL ILLNESS.
THERE WAS A PERSON A LONG TIME AGO WHO SAID SO.
IT WAS A VERY EVOCATIVE PHRASE, SO I REMEMBER IT EVEN NOW.
JUST LOOK AT WILD ANIMALS.
SOME OF THEM CERTAINLY SEEM TO BE AFFECTIONATE TO THEIR CHILDREN, BUT...
...THAT'S NOT LOVE.
SO WHAT IS IT, THEN?
HEH.

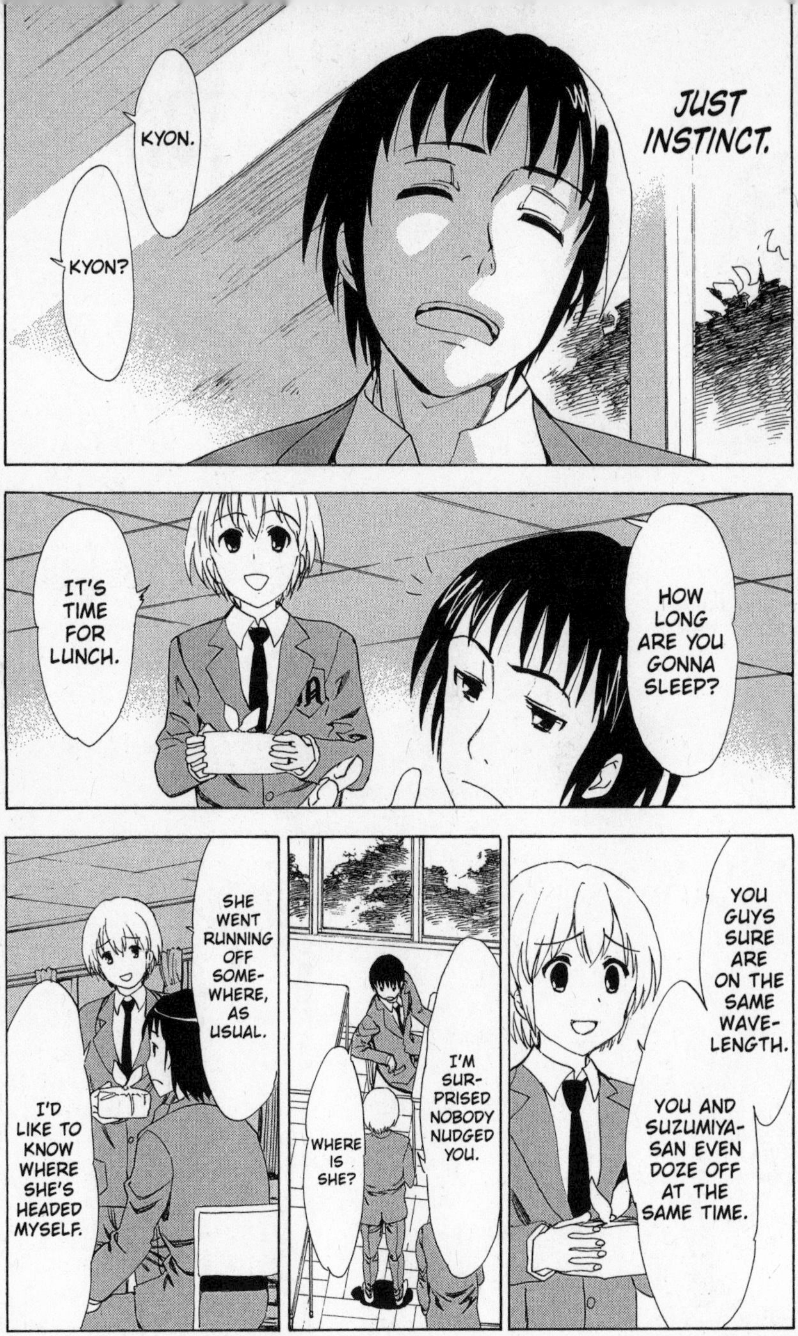
JUST INSTINCT.
KYON.
KYON?
HOW LONG ARE YOU GONNA SLEEP?
IT'S TIME FOR LUNCH.
YOU GUYS SURE ARE ON THE SAME WAVE-LENGTH.
YOU AND SUZUMIYA-SAN EVEN DOZE OFF AT THE SAME TIME.
I'M SUR-PRISED NOBODY NUDGED YOU.
WHERE IS SHE?
SHE WENT RUNNING OFF SOME-WHERE, AS USUAL.
I'D LIKE TO KNOW WHERE SHE'S HEADED MYSELF.

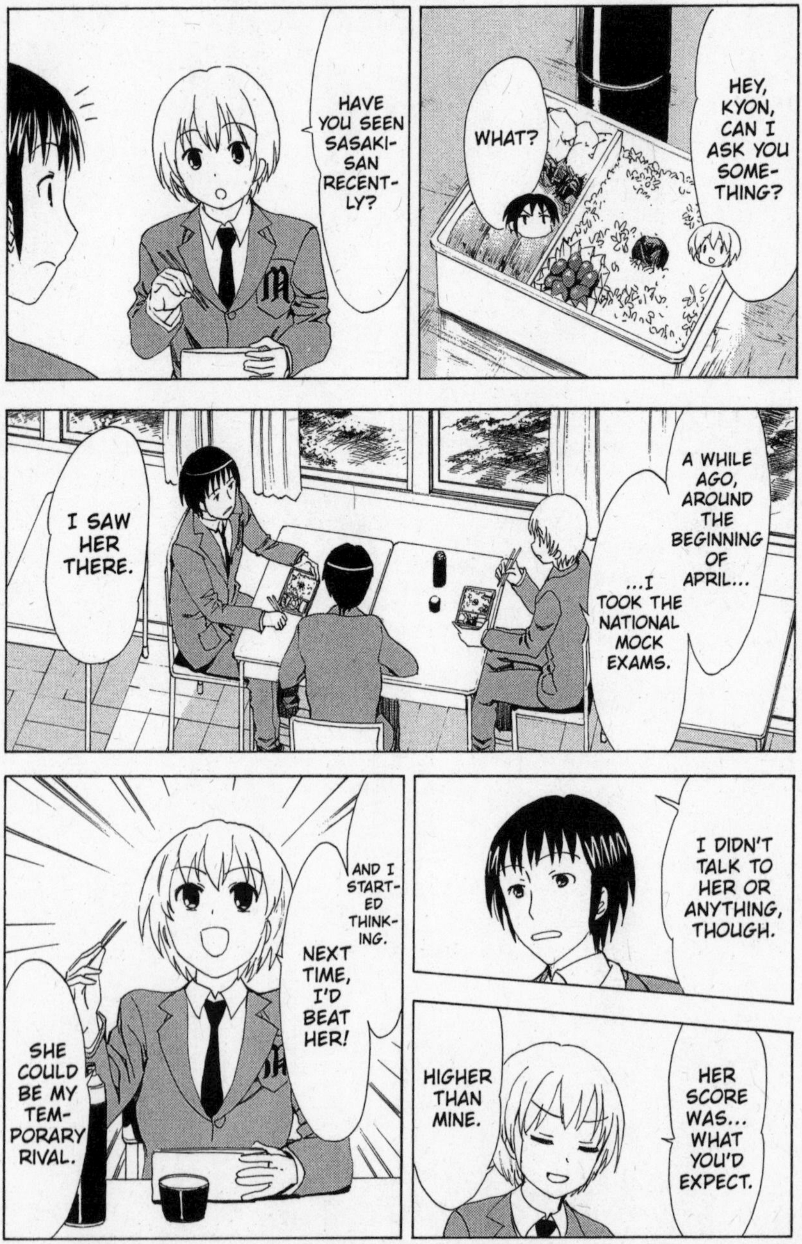
HEY, KYON, CAN I ASK YOU SOME-THING?
WHAT?
HAVE YOU SEEN SASAKI-SAN RECENT-LY?
A WHILE AGO, AROUND THE BEGINNING OF APRIL...
...I TOOK THE NATIONAL MOCK EXAMS.
I SAW HER THERE.
I DIDN'T TALK TO HER OR ANYTHING, THOUGH.
HER SCORE WAS... WHAT YOU'D EXPECT.
HIGHER THAN MINE.
AND I START-ED THINK-ING.
NEXT TIME, I'D BEAT HER!
SHE COULD BE MY TEM-PORARY RIVAL.

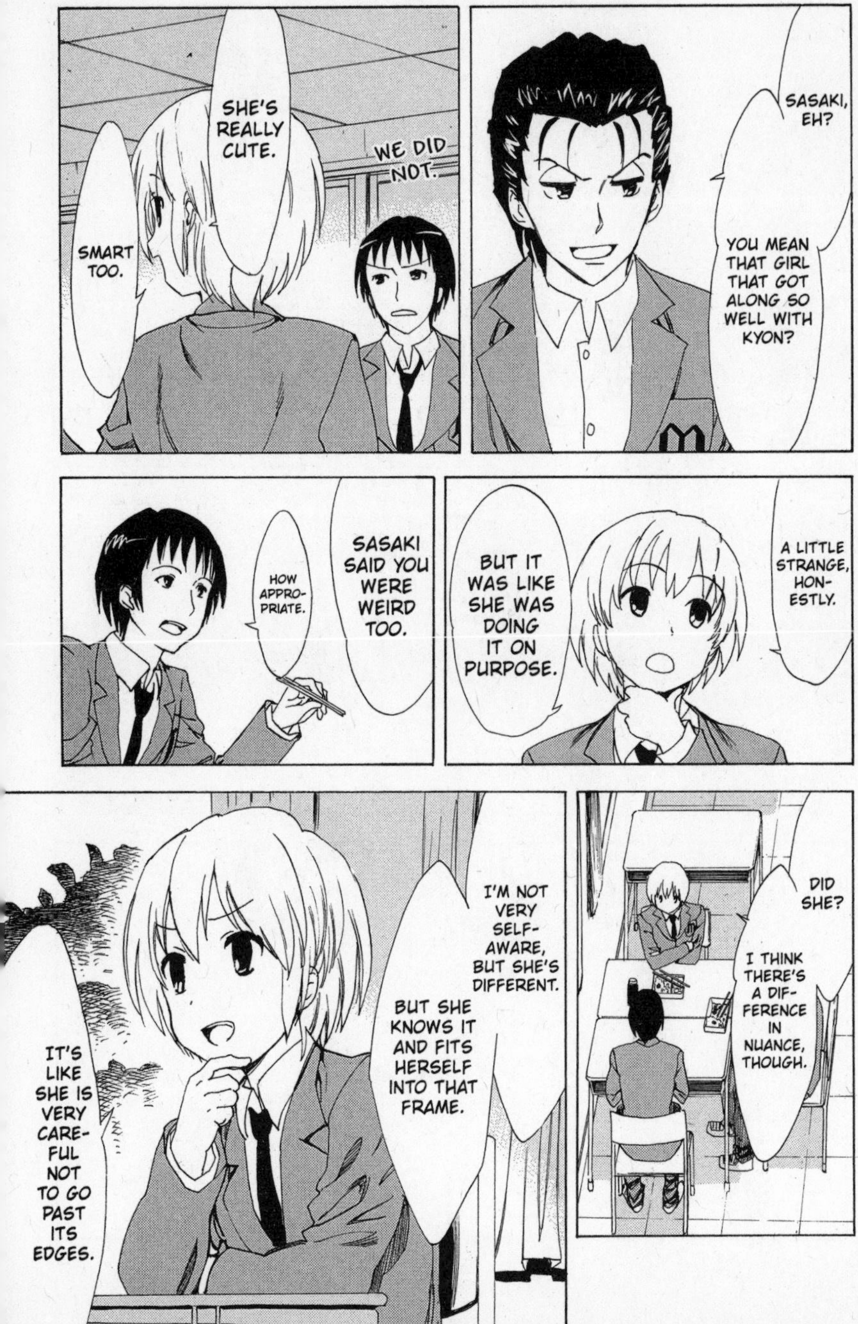
SASAKI, EH?
YOU MEAN THAT GIRL THAT GOT ALONG SO WELL WITH KYON?
WE DID NOT.
SHE'S REALLY CUTE.
SMART TOO.
A LITTLE STRANGE, HON-ESTLY.
BUT IT WAS LIKE SHE WAS DOING IT ON PURPOSE.
SASAKI SAID YOU WERE WEIRD TOO.
HOW APPRO-PRIATE.
DID SHE?
I THINK THERE'S A DIF-FERENCE IN NUANCE, THOUGH.
I'M NOT VERY SELF-AWARE, BUT SHE'S DIFFERENT.
BUT SHE KNOWS IT AND FITS HERSELF INTO THAT FRAME.
IT'S LIKE SHE IS VERY CARE-FUL NOT TO GO PAST ITS EDGES.

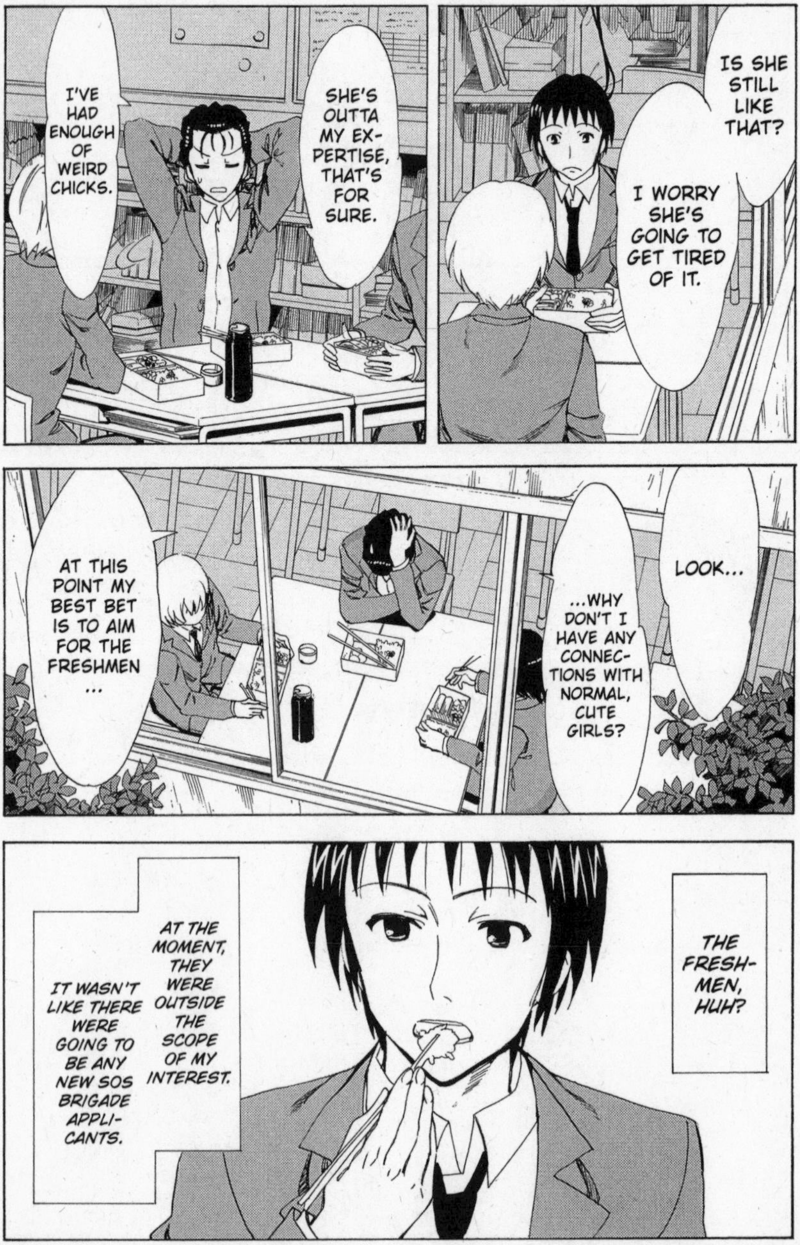
IS SHE STILL LIKE THAT?
I WORRY SHE'S GOING TO GET TIRED OF IT.
SHE'S OUTTA MY EX-PERTISE, THAT'S FOR SURE.
I'VE HAD ENOUGH OF WEIRD CHICKS.
LOOK...
...WHY DON'T I HAVE ANY CONNEC-TIONS WITH NORMAL, CUTE GIRLS?
AT THIS POINT MY BEST BET IS TO AIM FOR THE FRESHMEN...
THE FRESH-MEN, HUH?
AT THE MOMENT, THEY WERE OUTSIDE THE SCOPE OF MY INTEREST.
IT WASN'T LIKE THERE WERE GOING TO BE ANY NEW SOS BRIGADE APPLI-CANTS.

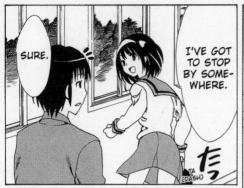

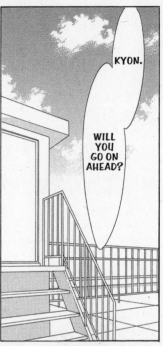

KYON.
WILL YOU GO ON AHEAD?
I'VE GOT TO STOP BY SOMEWHERE.
SURE.
TA (DASH)
I WAS SURE SHE HADN'T SPOTTED AN AAA-RANK FRESHMAN.
GACHA (CLACK)
YEAH, NO WAY...
...NA-GATO?
SHE WASN'T THERE.
WELL, THAT HAP-PENED SOME-TIMES.

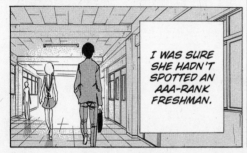

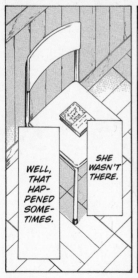

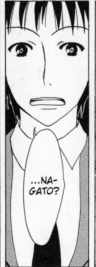

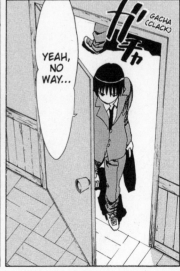

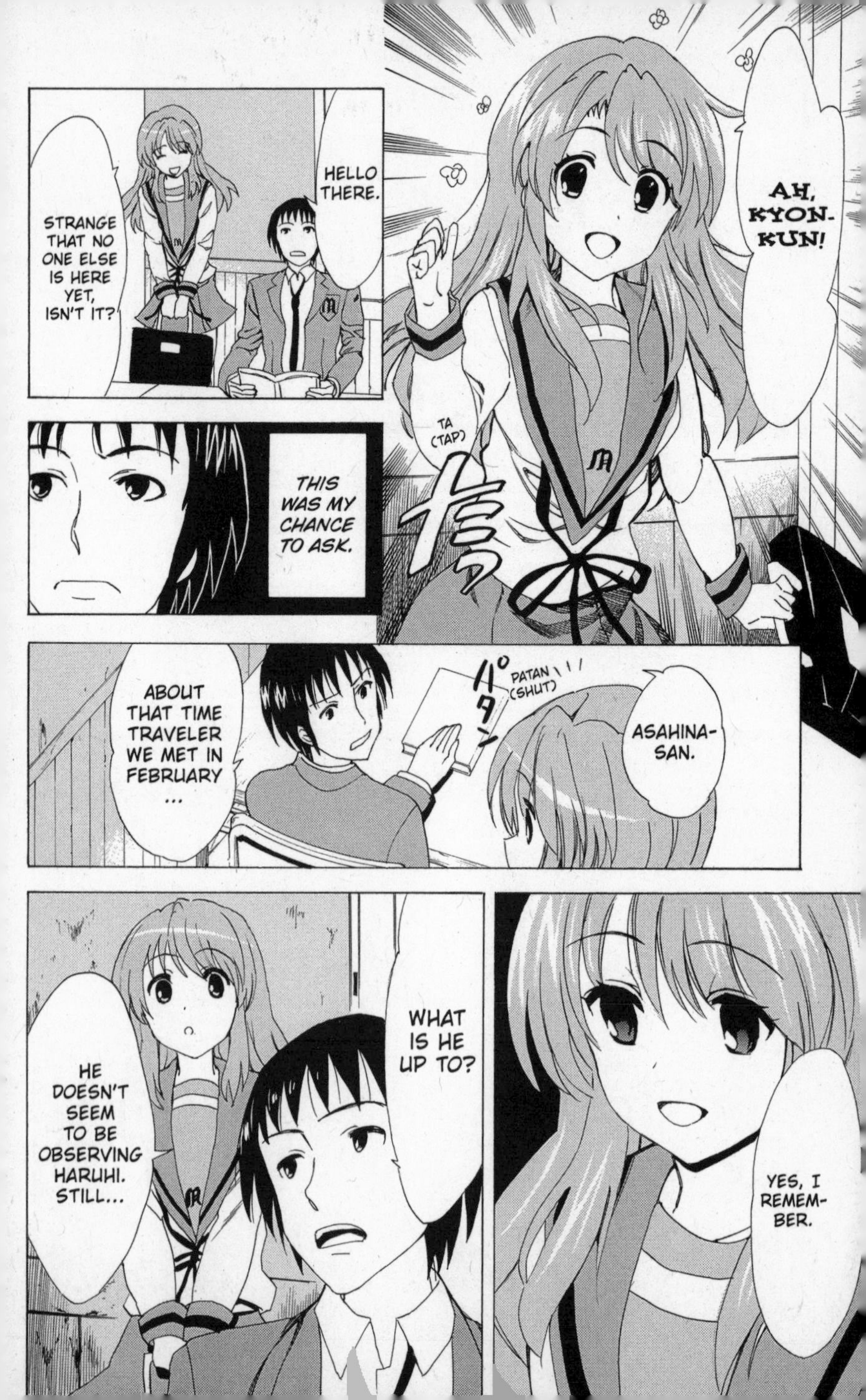
AH, KYON-KUN!
TA (TAP)
HELLO THERE.
STRANGE THAT NO ONE ELSE IS HERE YET, ISN'T IT?
THIS WAS MY CHANCE TO ASK.
ASAHINA-SAN.
PATAN (SHUT)
ABOUT THAT TIME TRAVELER WE MET IN FEBRUARY...
YES, I REMEMBER.
WHAT IS HE UP TO?
HE DOESN'T SEEM TO BE OBSERVING HARUHI. STILL...

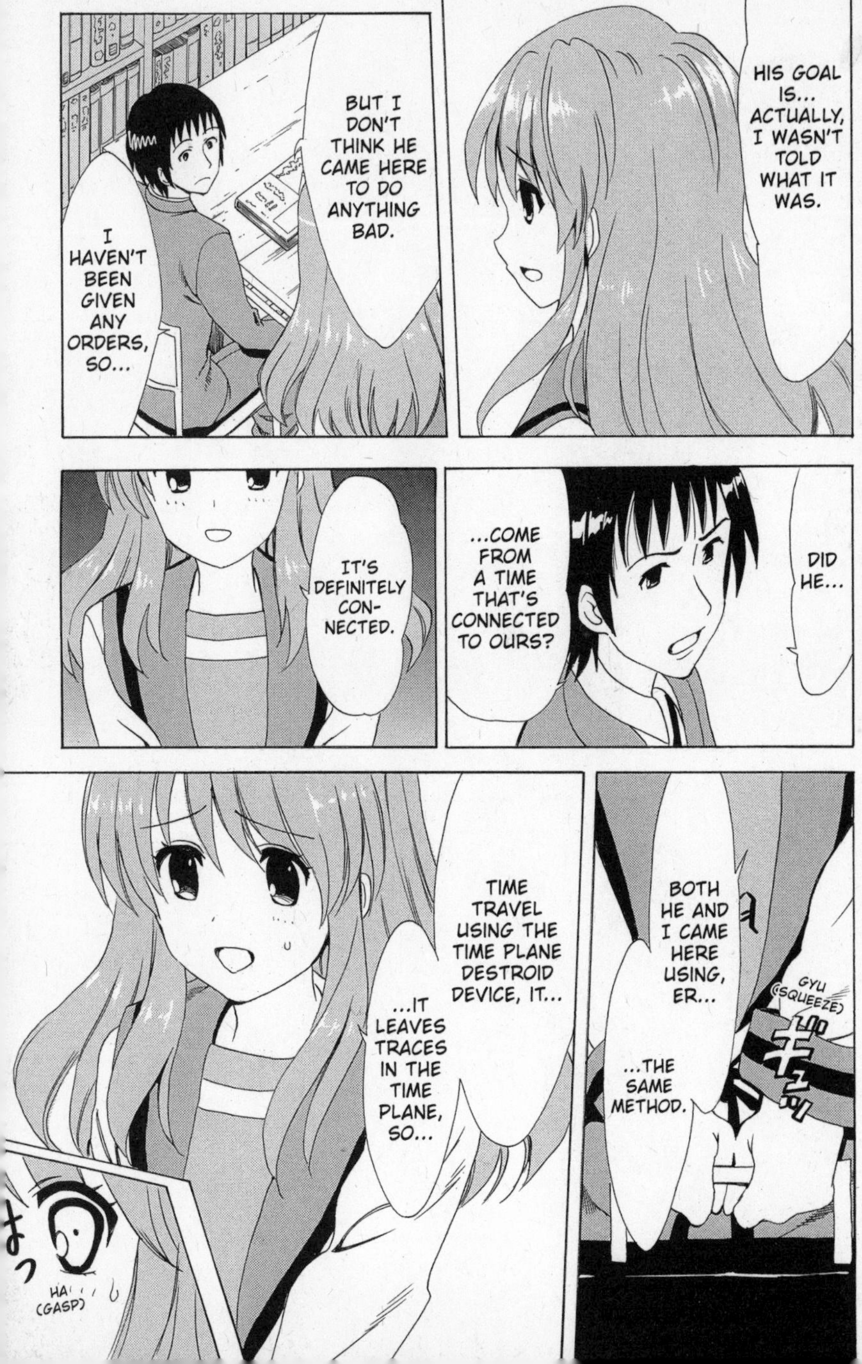
HIS GOAL IS... ACTUALLY, I WASN'T TOLD WHAT IT WAS.
BUT I DON'T THINK HE CAME HERE TO DO ANYTHING BAD.
I HAVEN'T BEEN GIVEN ANY ORDERS, SO...
DID HE...
...COME FROM A TIME THAT'S CONNECTED TO OURS?
IT'S DEFINITELY CON-NECTED.
BOTH HE AND I CAME HERE USING, ER...
...THE SAME METHOD.
GYU (SQUEEZE)
TIME TRAVEL USING THE TIME PLANE DESTROID DEVICE, IT...
...IT LEAVES TRACES IN THE TIME PLANE, SO...
HA (GASP)

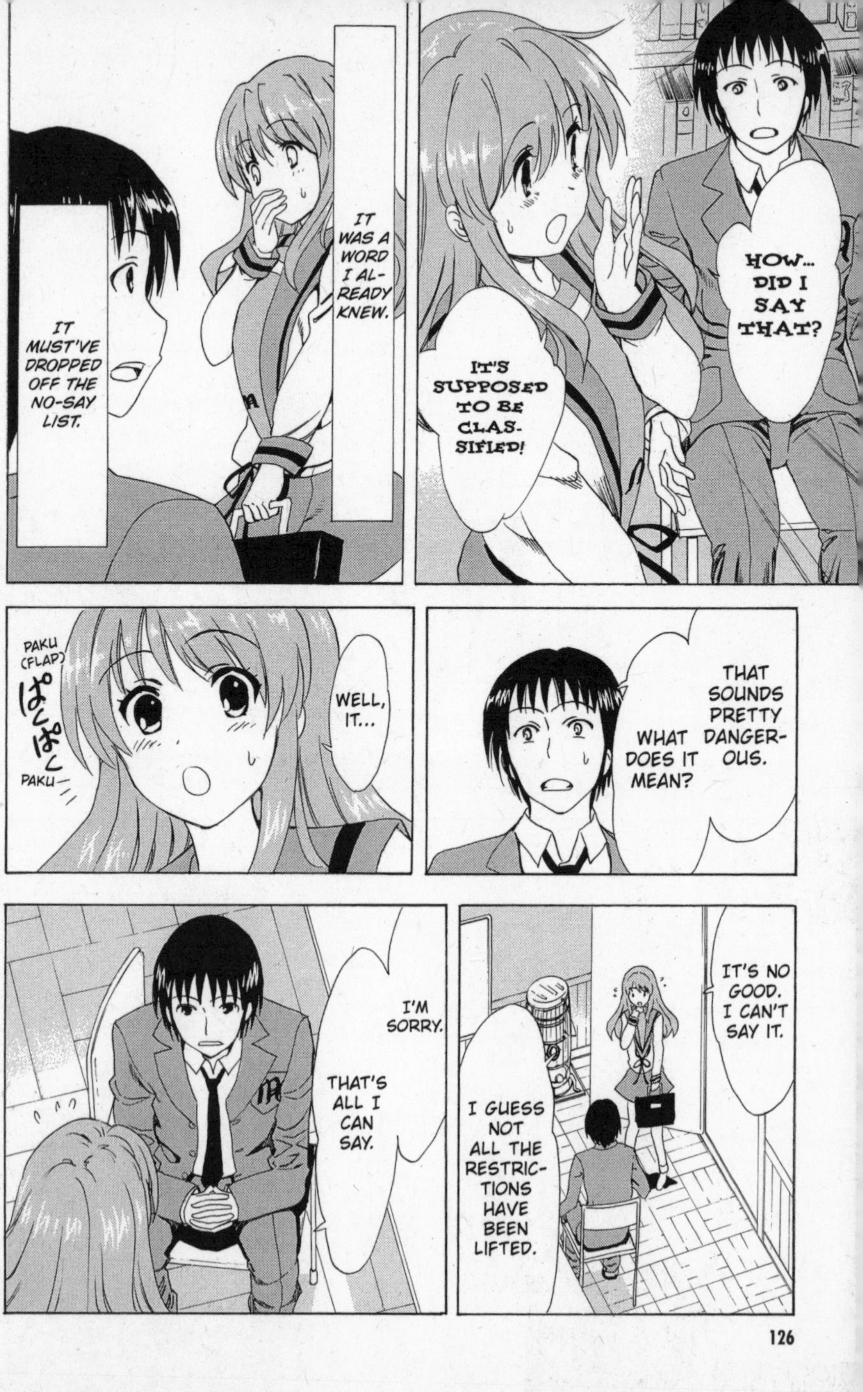
HOW... DID I SAY THAT?
IT'S SUPPOSED TO BE CLAS-SIFIED!
IT WAS A WORD I AL-READY KNEW.
IT MUST'VE DROPPED OFF THE NO-SAY LIST.
THAT SOUNDS PRETTY DANGER-OUS.
WHAT DOES IT MEAN?
WELL, IT...
PAKU (FLAP) ぱくぱく PAKU
IT'S NO GOOD. I CAN'T SAY IT.
I GUESS NOT ALL THE RESTRIC-TIONS HAVE BEEN LIFTED.
I'M SORRY.
THAT'S ALL I CAN SAY.

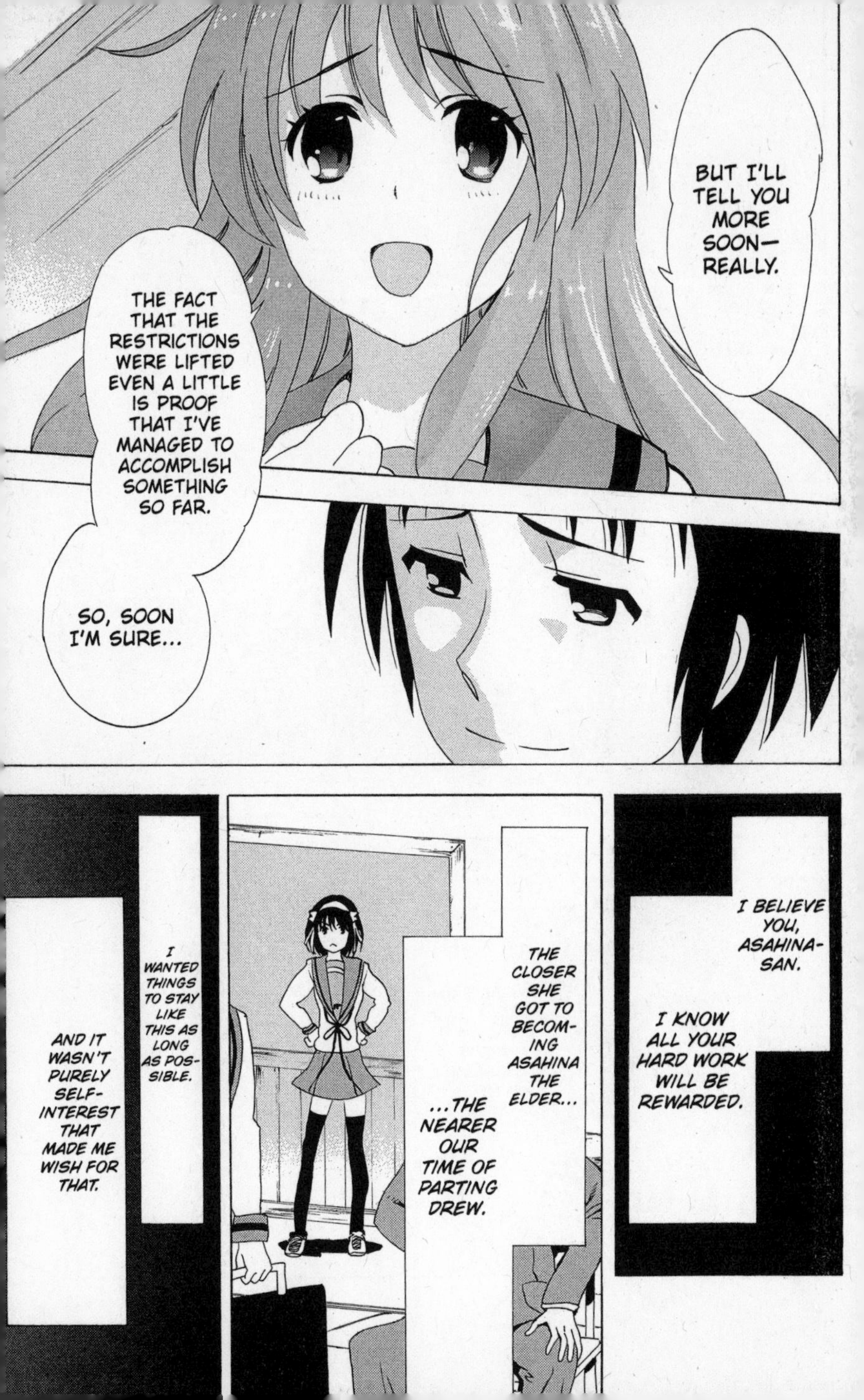
BUT I'LL TELL YOU MORE SOON— REALLY.
THE FACT THAT THE RESTRICTIONS WERE LIFTED EVEN A LITTLE IS PROOF THAT I'VE MANAGED TO ACCOMPLISH SOMETHING SO FAR.
SO, SOON I'M SURE...
I BELIEVE YOU, ASAHINA-SAN.
I KNOW ALL YOUR HARD WORK WILL BE REWARDED.
THE CLOSER SHE GOT TO BECOMING ASAHINA THE ELDER...
...THE NEARER OUR TIME OF PARTING DREW.
I WANTED THINGS TO STAY LIKE THIS AS LONG AS POSSIBLE.
AND IT WASN'T PURELY SELF-INTEREST THAT MADE ME WISH FOR THAT.

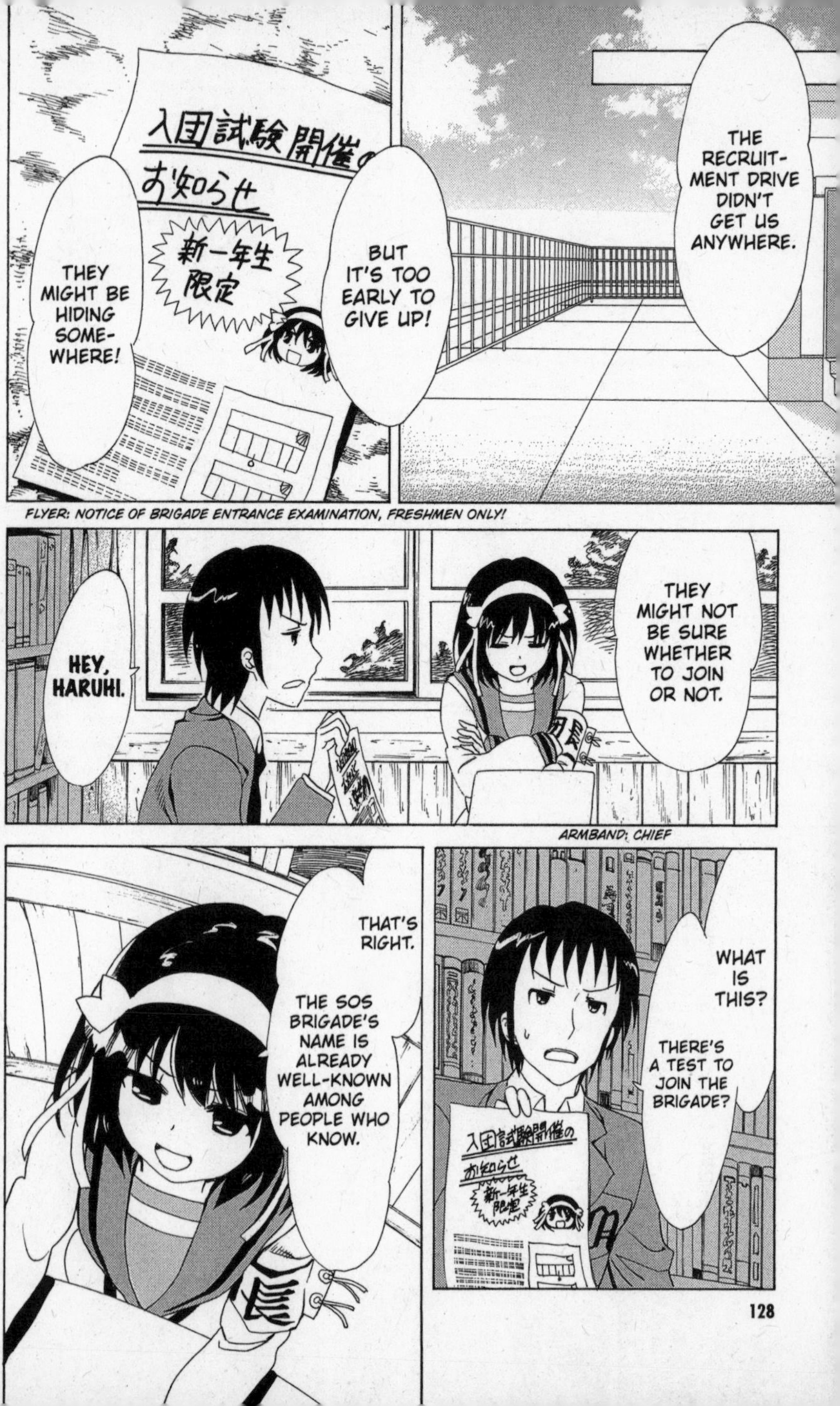
THE RECRUITMENT DRIVE DIDN'T GET US ANYWHERE.
BUT IT'S TOO EARLY TO GIVE UP!
入団試験開催のお知らせ
新一年生限定
THEY MIGHT BE HIDING SOMEWHERE!
FLYER: NOTICE OF BRIGADE ENTRANCE EXAMINATION, FRESHMEN ONLY!
THEY MIGHT NOT BE SURE WHETHER TO JOIN OR NOT.
HEY, HARUHI.
ARMBAND: CHIEF
WHAT IS THIS?
THERE'S A TEST TO JOIN THE BRIGADE?
THAT'S RIGHT.
THE SOS BRIGADE'S NAME IS ALREADY WELL-KNOWN AMONG PEOPLE WHO KNOW.

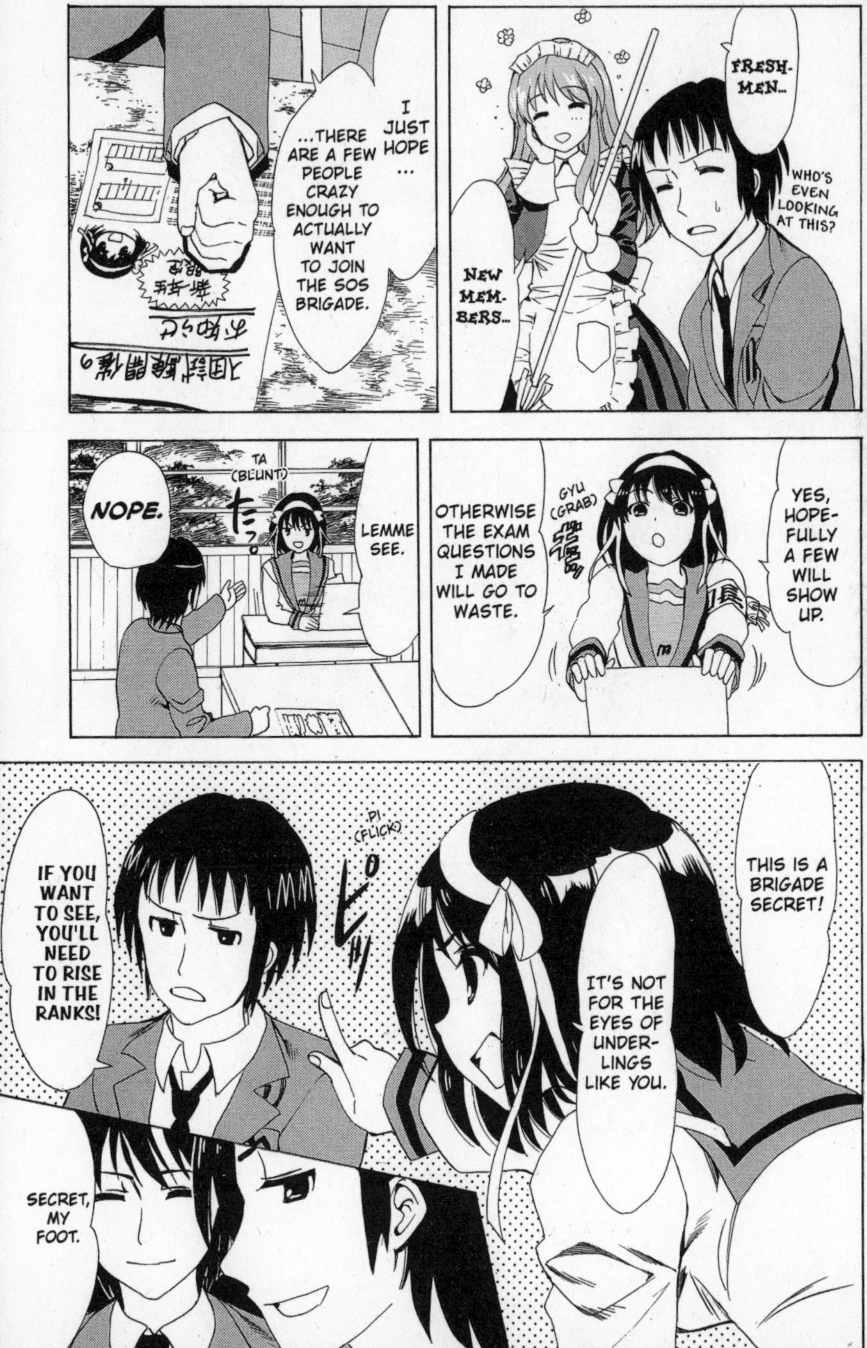
FRESH-MEN...
WHO'S EVEN LOOKING AT THIS?
NEW MEM-BERS...
I JUST HOPE...
...THERE ARE A FEW PEOPLE CRAZY ENOUGH TO ACTUALLY WANT TO JOIN THE SOS BRIGADE.
YES, HOPE-FULLY A FEW WILL SHOW UP.
GYU (GRAB)
OTHERWISE THE EXAM QUESTIONS I MADE WILL GO TO WASTE.
LEMME SEE.
TA (BLUNT)
NOPE.
THIS IS A BRIGADE SECRET!
IT'S NOT FOR THE EYES OF UNDER-LINGS LIKE YOU.
PI (FLICK)
IF YOU WANT TO SEE, YOU'LL NEED TO RISE IN THE RANKS!
SECRET, MY FOOT.

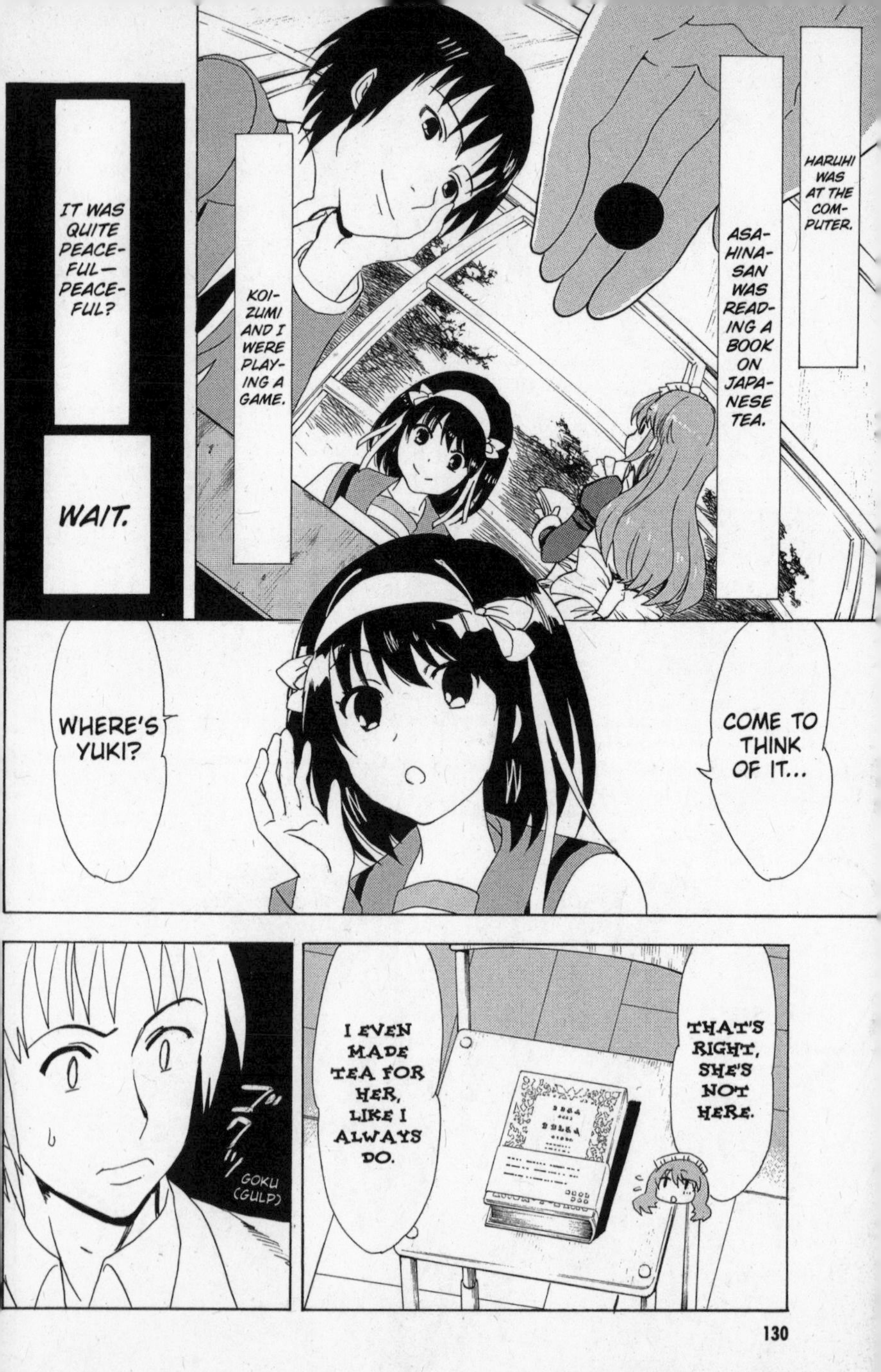
HARUHI WAS AT THE COM-PUTER.
ASA-HINA-SAN WAS READ-ING A BOOK ON JAPA-NESE TEA.
KOI-ZUMI AND I WERE PLAY-ING A GAME.
IT WAS QUITE PEACE-FUL— PEACE-FUL?
WAIT.
COME TO THINK OF IT...
WHERE'S YUKI?
THAT'S RIGHT, SHE'S NOT HERE.
I EVEN MADE TEA FOR HER, LIKE I ALWAYS DO.
GOKU (GULP)

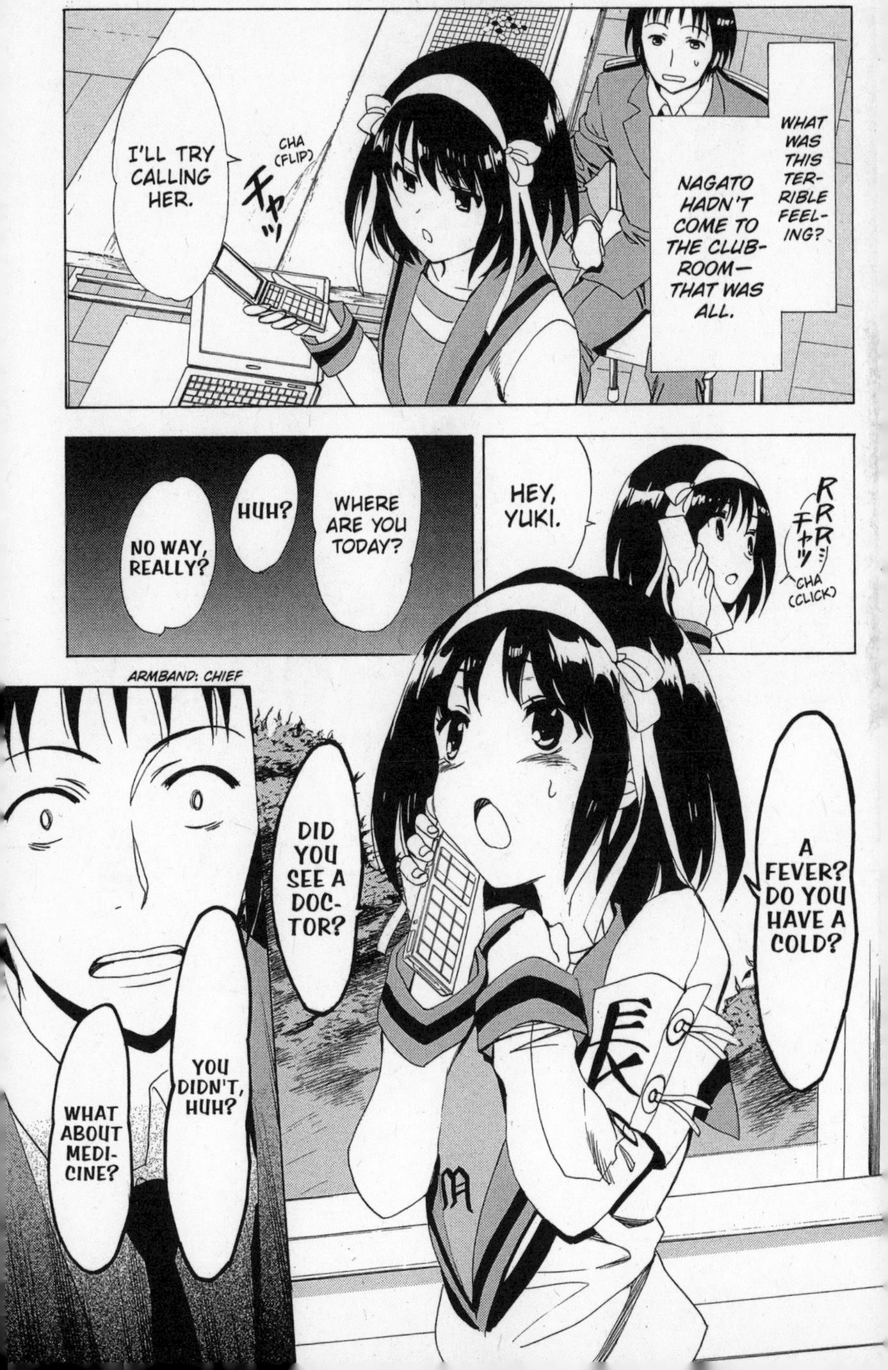
WHAT WAS THIS TERRIBLE FEELING?
NAGATO HADN'T COME TO THE CLUBROOM—THAT WAS ALL.
CHA (FLIP)
チャッ
I'LL TRY CALLING HER.
RRR
チャッ
CHA (CLICK)
HEY, YUKI.
WHERE ARE YOU TODAY?
HUH?
NO WAY, REALLY?
ARMBAND: CHIEF
A FEVER? DO YOU HAVE A COLD?
DID YOU SEE A DOCTOR?
YOU DIDN'T, HUH?
WHAT ABOUT MEDICINE?

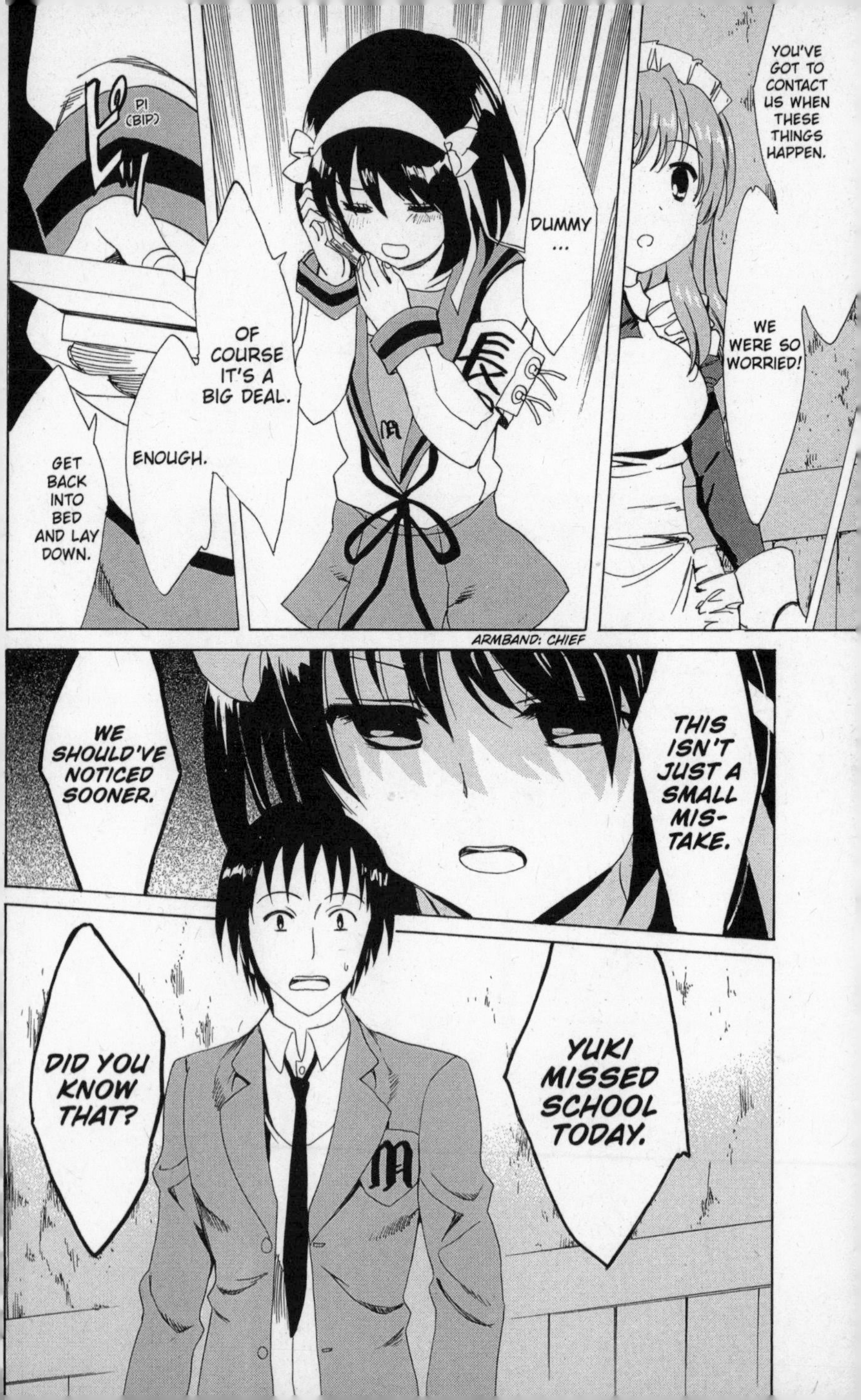
YOU'VE GOT TO CONTACT US WHEN THESE THINGS HAPPEN.
WE WERE SO WORRIED!
DUMMY ...
OF COURSE IT'S A BIG DEAL.
ENOUGH.
GET BACK INTO BED AND LAY DOWN.
PI (BIP)
ARMBAND: CHIEF
THIS ISN'T JUST A SMALL MIS-TAKE.
WE SHOULD'VE NOTICED SOONER.
YUKI MISSED SCHOOL TODAY.
DID YOU KNOW THAT?

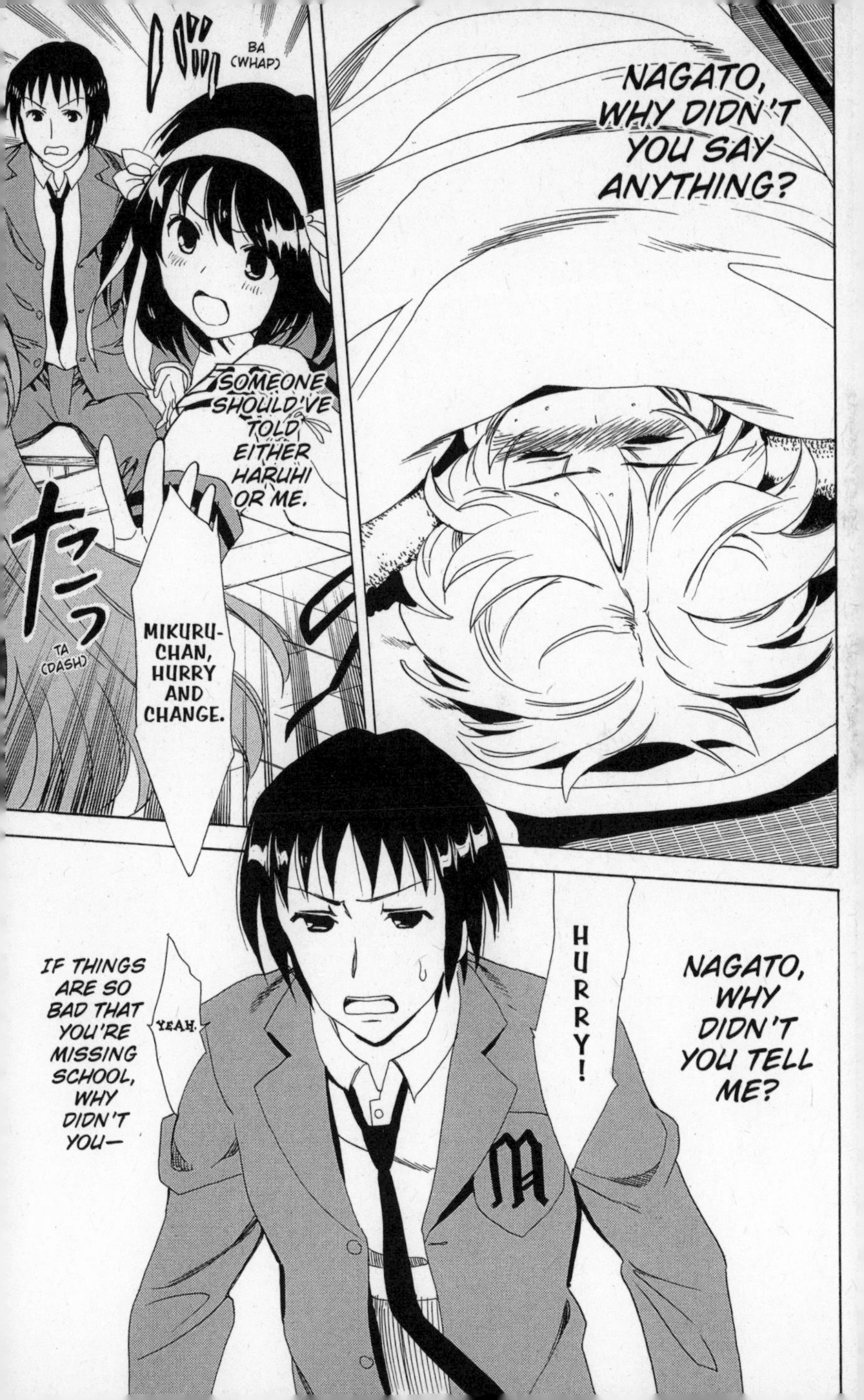
NAGATO, WHY DIDN'T YOU SAY ANYTHING?
BA (WHAP)
SOMEONE SHOULD'VE TOLD EITHER HARUHI OR ME.
MIKURU-CHAN, HURRY AND CHANGE.
TA (DASH)
NAGATO, WHY DIDN'T YOU TELL ME?
HURRY!
YEAH.
IF THINGS ARE SO BAD THAT YOU'RE MISSING SCHOOL, WHY DIDN'T YOU—

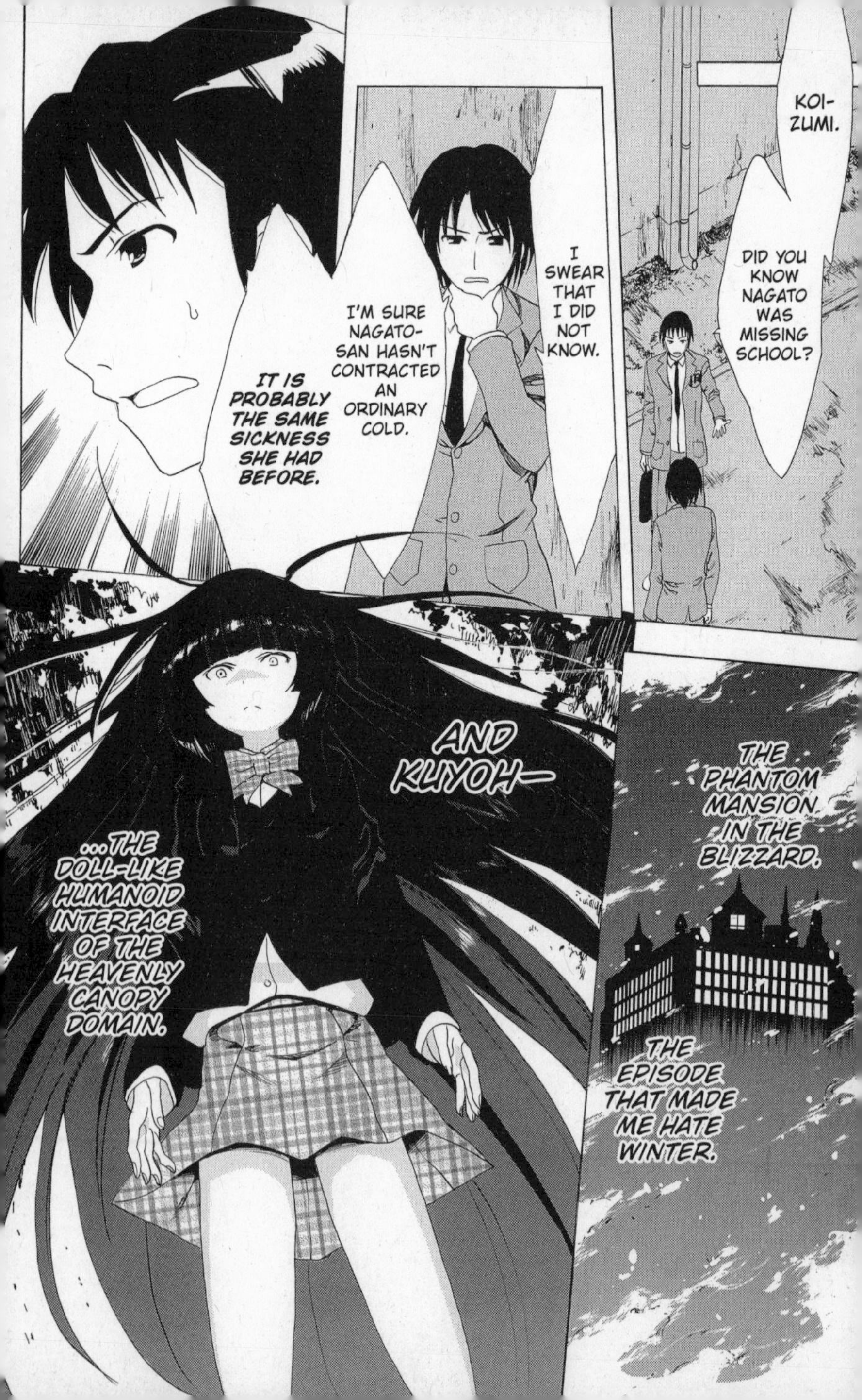
KOI-ZUMI.
DID YOU KNOW NAGATO WAS MISSING SCHOOL?
I SWEAR THAT I DID NOT KNOW.
I'M SURE NAGATO-SAN HASN'T CONTRACTED AN ORDINARY COLD.
IT IS PROBABLY THE SAME SICKNESS SHE HAD BEFORE.
THE PHANTOM MANSION IN THE BLIZZARD.
THE EPISODE THAT MADE ME HATE WINTER.
AND KUYOH—
...THE DOLL-LIKE HUMANOID INTERFACE OF THE HEAVENLY CANOPY DOMAIN.

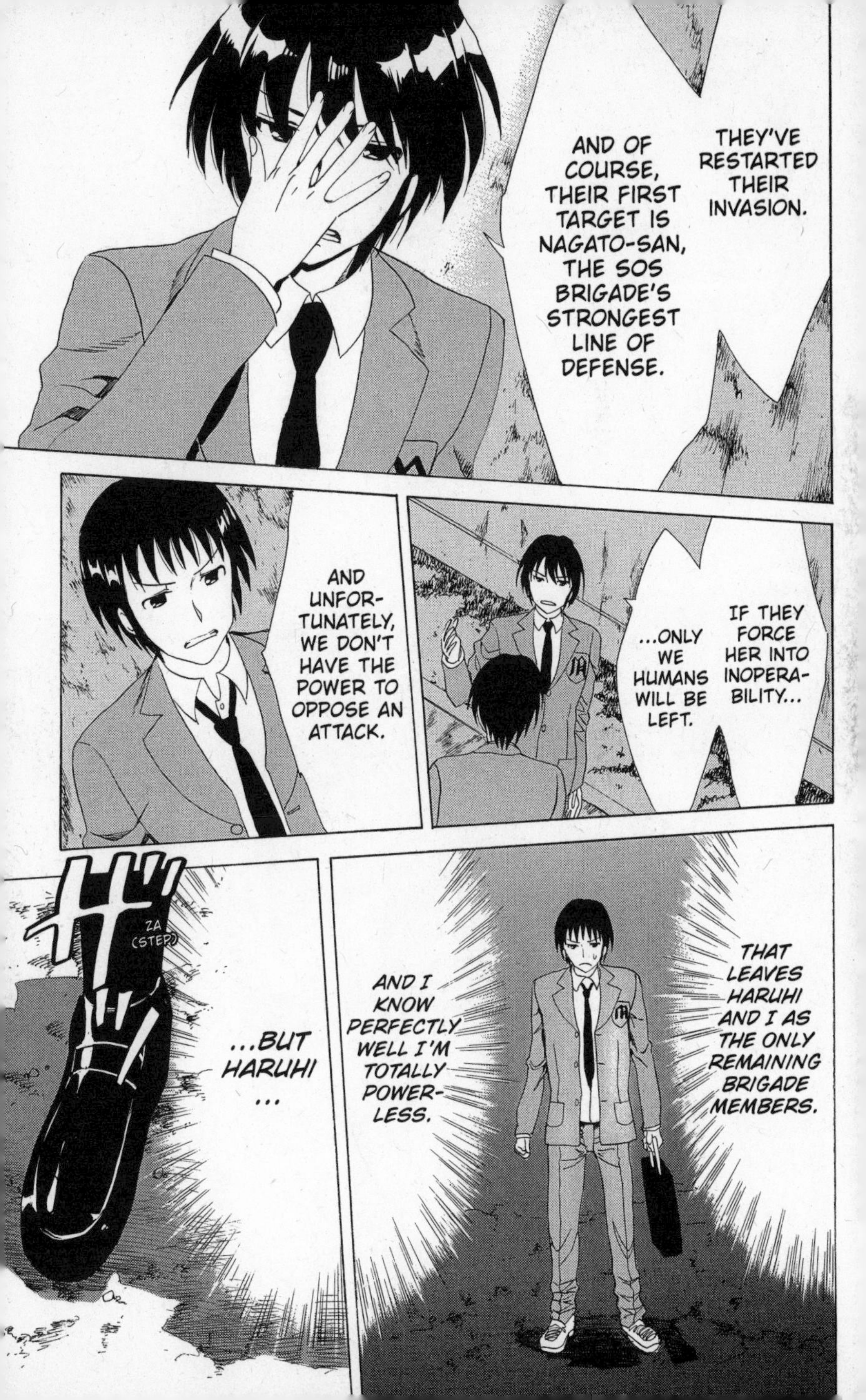
THEY'VE RESTARTED THEIR INVASION.
AND OF COURSE, THEIR FIRST TARGET IS NAGATO-SAN, THE SOS BRIGADE'S STRONGEST LINE OF DEFENSE.
IF THEY FORCE HER INTO INOPERA-BILITY...
...ONLY WE HUMANS WILL BE LEFT.
AND UNFOR-TUNATELY, WE DON'T HAVE THE POWER TO OPPOSE AN ATTACK.
THAT LEAVES HARUHI AND I AS THE ONLY REMAINING BRIGADE MEMBERS.
AND I KNOW PERFECTLY WELL I'M TOTALLY POWER-LESS.
ZA (STEP)
...BUT HARUHI ...

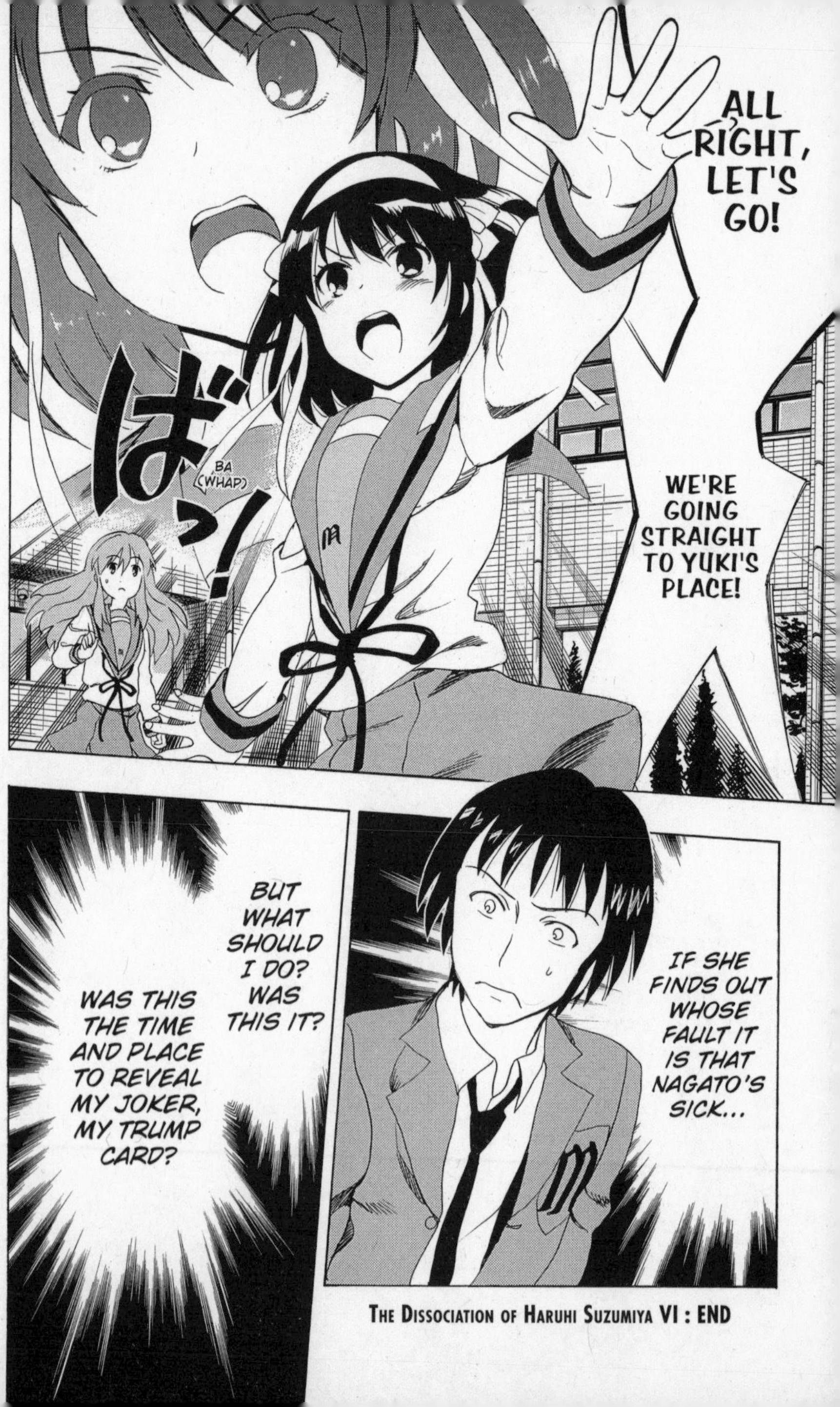
ALL RIGHT, LET'S GO!
WE'RE GOING STRAIGHT TO YUKI'S PLACE!
ばっ！
BA (WHAP)
IF SHE FINDS OUT WHOSE FAULT IT IS THAT NAGATO'S SICK...
BUT WHAT SHOULD I DO? WAS THIS IT?
WAS THIS THE TIME AND PLACE TO REVEAL MY JOKER, MY TRUMP CARD?

THE DISSOCIATION OF HARUHI SUZUMIYA VI : END

THE MELANCHOLY OF HARUHI SUZUMIYA

α—7

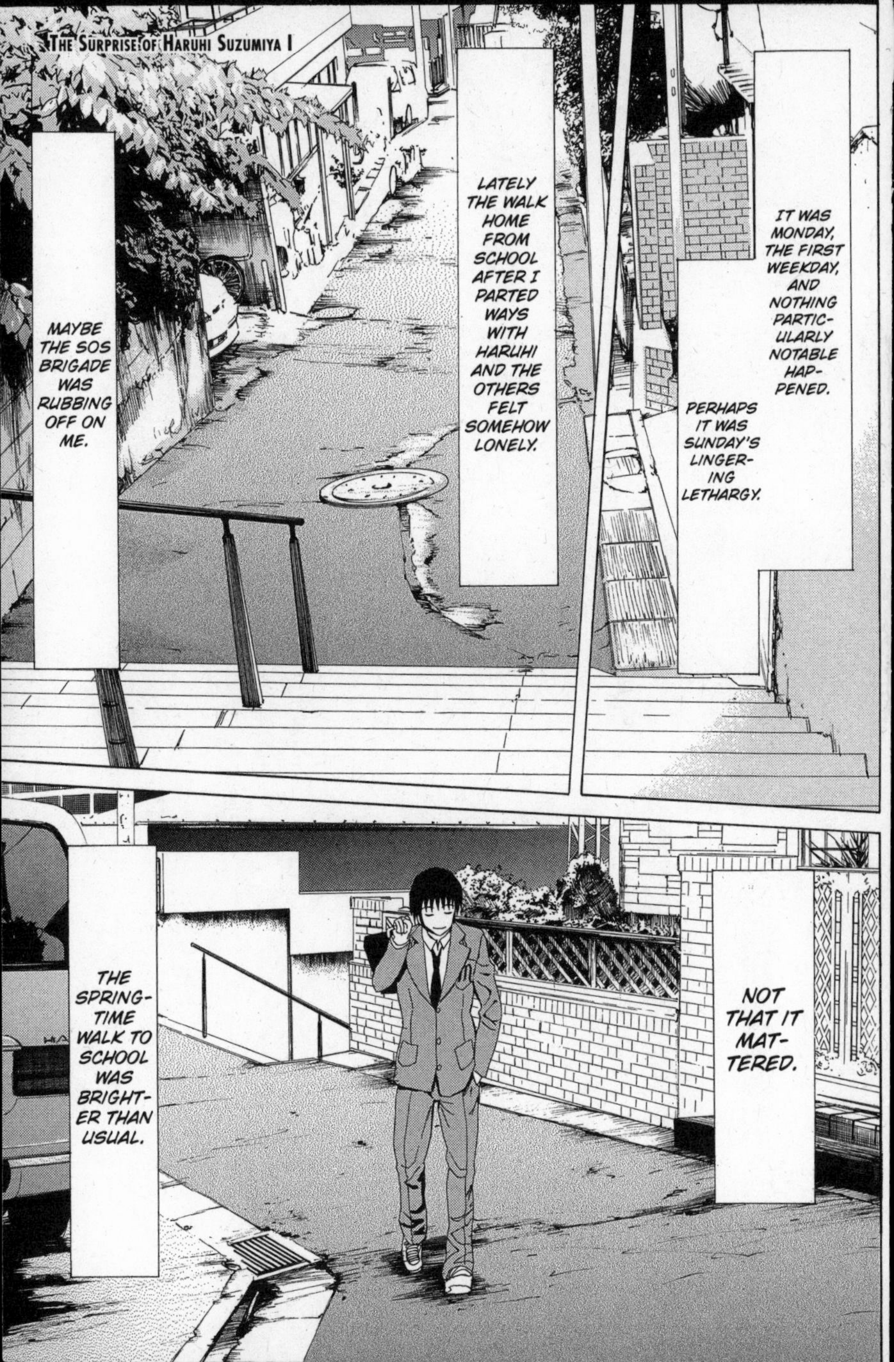
IT WAS MONDAY, THE FIRST WEEKDAY, AND NOTHING PARTIC-ULARLY NOTABLE HAP-PENED.
PERHAPS IT WAS SUNDAY'S LINGER-ING LETHARGY.
LATELY THE WALK HOME FROM SCHOOL AFTER I PARTED WAYS WITH HARUHI AND THE OTHERS FELT SOMEHOW LONELY.
MAYBE THE SOS BRIGADE WAS RUBBING OFF ON ME.
NOT THAT IT MAT-TERED.
THE SPRING-TIME WALK TO SCHOOL WAS BRIGHT-ER THAN USUAL.

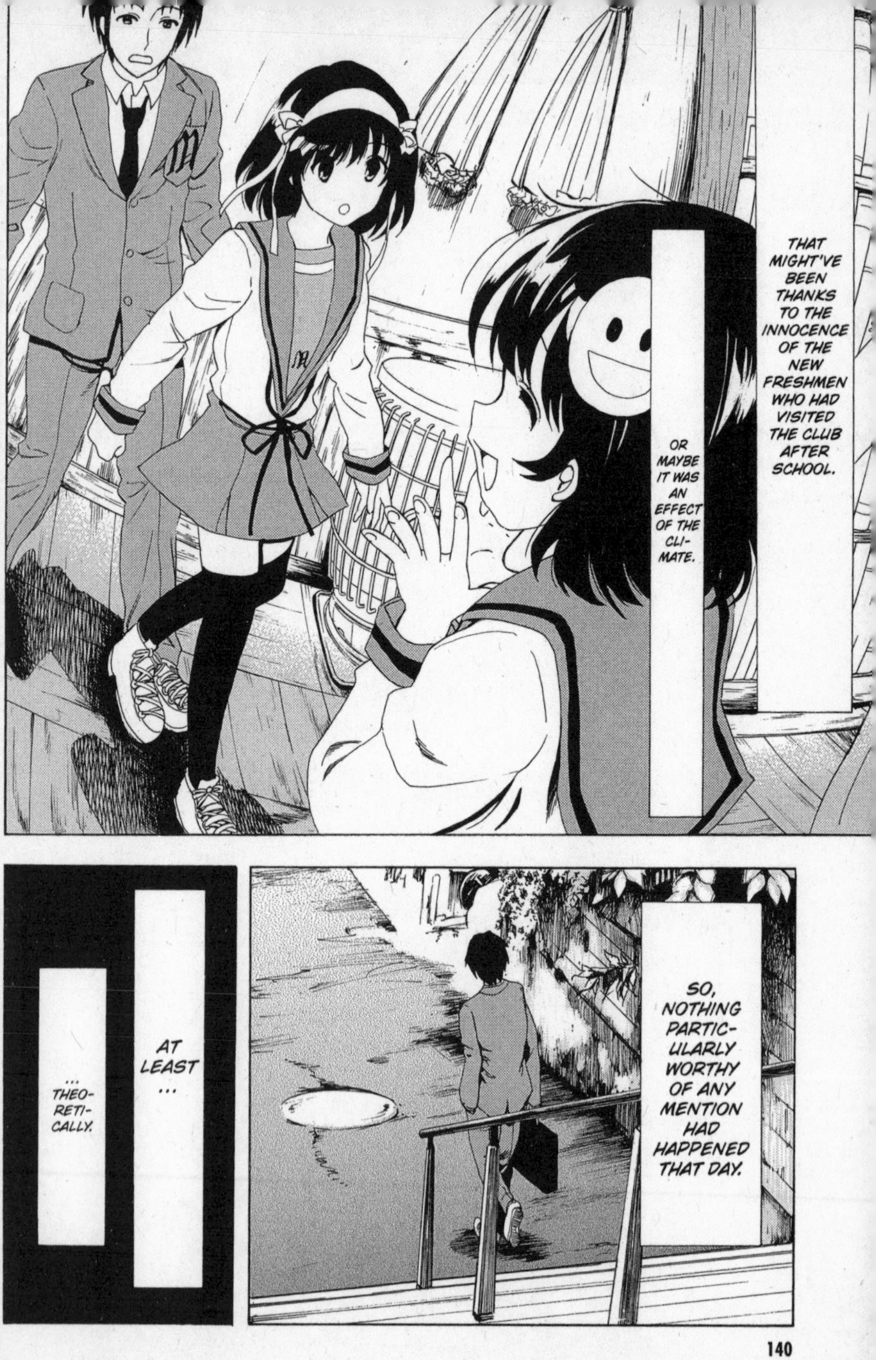
THAT MIGHT'VE BEEN THANKS TO THE INNOCENCE OF THE NEW FRESHMEN WHO HAD VISITED THE CLUB AFTER SCHOOL.
OR MAYBE IT WAS AN EFFECT OF THE CLI-MATE.
SO, NOTHING PARTIC-ULARLY WORTHY OF ANY MENTION HAD HAPPENED THAT DAY.
AT LEAST ...
... THEO-RETI-CALLY.

◎ The Surprise of Haruhi Suzumiya I

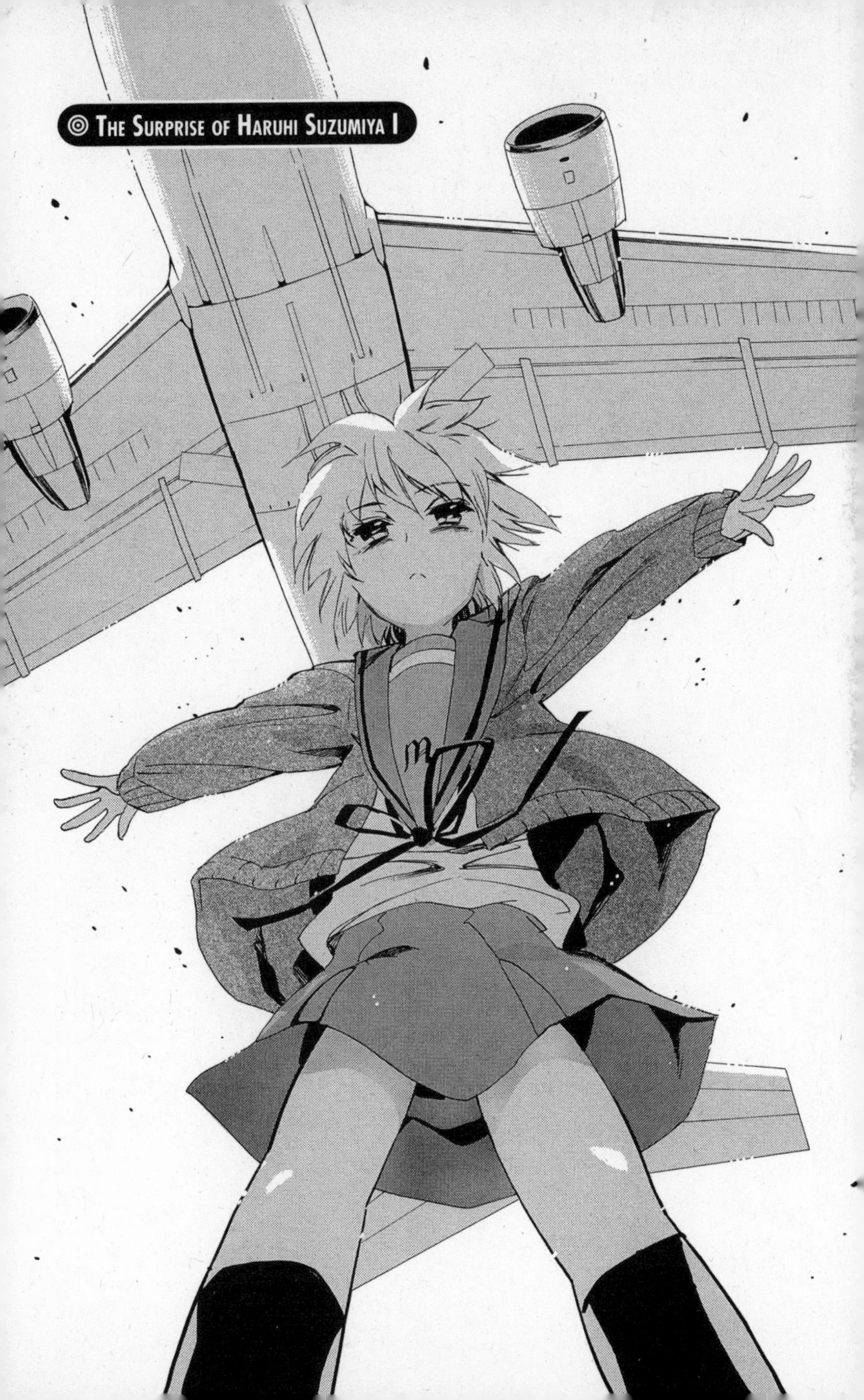

β—6·7

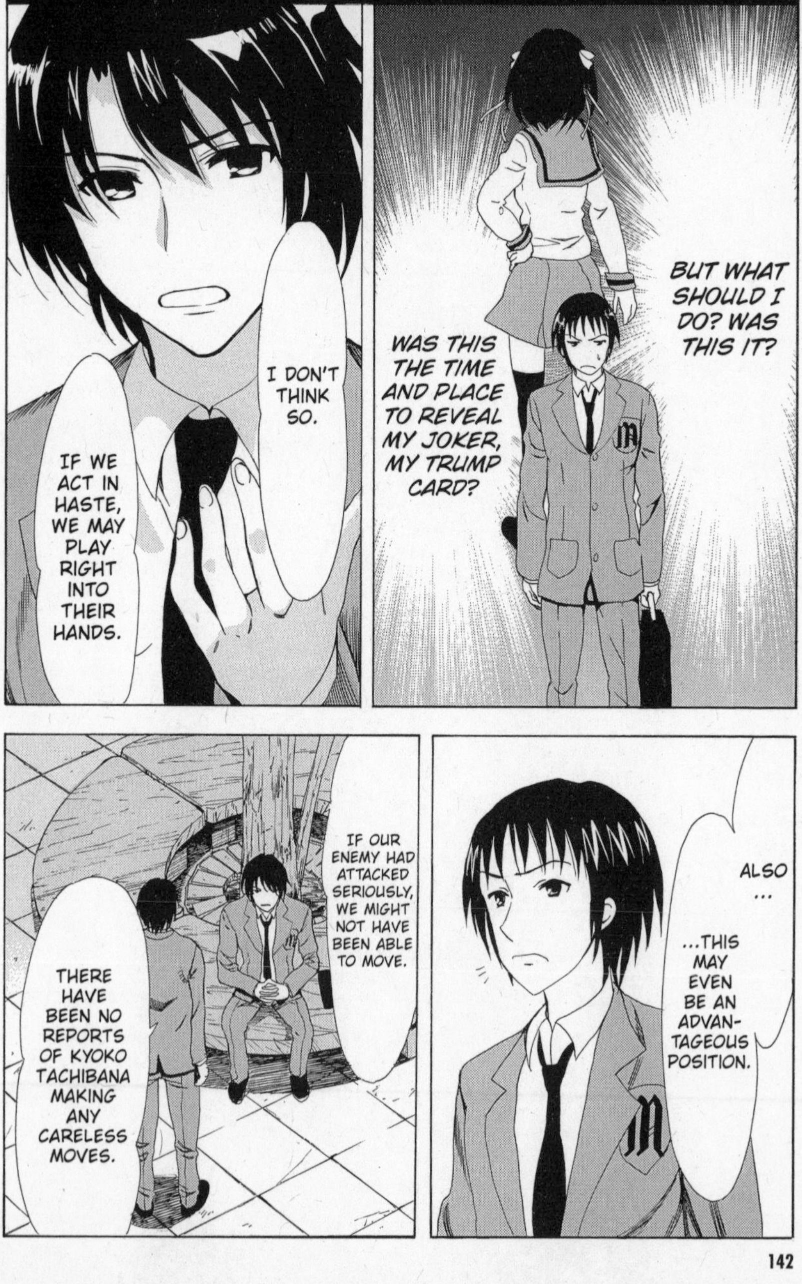
BUT WHAT SHOULD I DO? WAS THIS IT?
WAS THIS THE TIME AND PLACE TO REVEAL MY JOKER, MY TRUMP CARD?
I DON'T THINK SO.
IF WE ACT IN HASTE, WE MAY PLAY RIGHT INTO THEIR HANDS.
ALSO ...
...THIS MAY EVEN BE AN ADVAN-TAGEOUS POSITION.
IF OUR ENEMY HAD ATTACKED SERIOUSLY, WE MIGHT NOT HAVE BEEN ABLE TO MOVE.
THERE HAVE BEEN NO REPORTS OF KYOKO TACHIBANA MAKING ANY CARELESS MOVES.

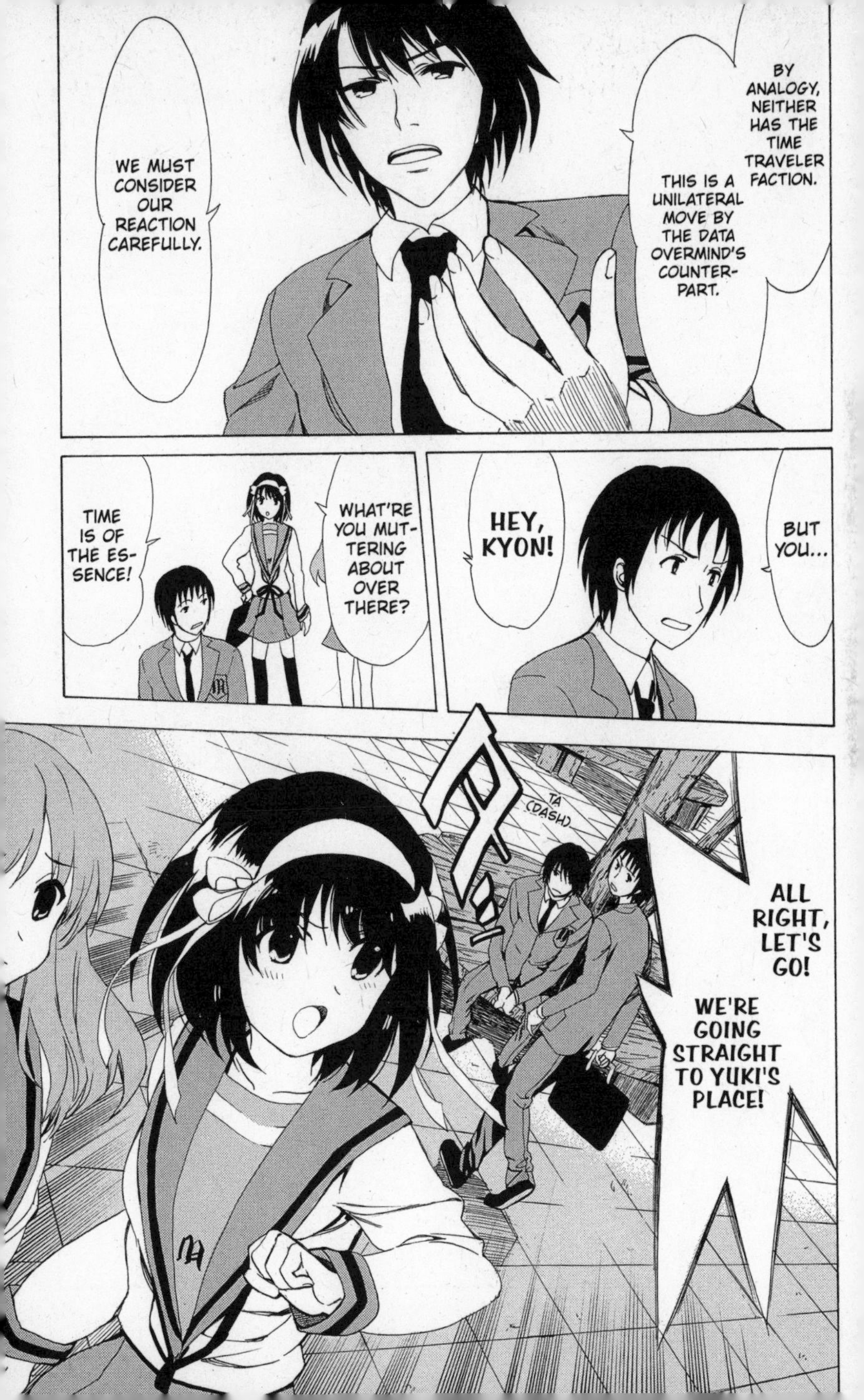
BY ANALOGY, NEITHER HAS THE TIME TRAVELER FACTION.
THIS IS A UNILATERAL MOVE BY THE DATA OVERMIND'S COUNTER-PART.
WE MUST CONSIDER OUR REACTION CAREFULLY.
BUT YOU...
HEY, KYON!
WHAT'RE YOU MUT-TERING ABOUT OVER THERE?
TIME IS OF THE ES-SENCE!
ALL RIGHT, LET'S GO!
WE'RE GOING STRAIGHT TO YUKI'S PLACE!
TA (DASH)

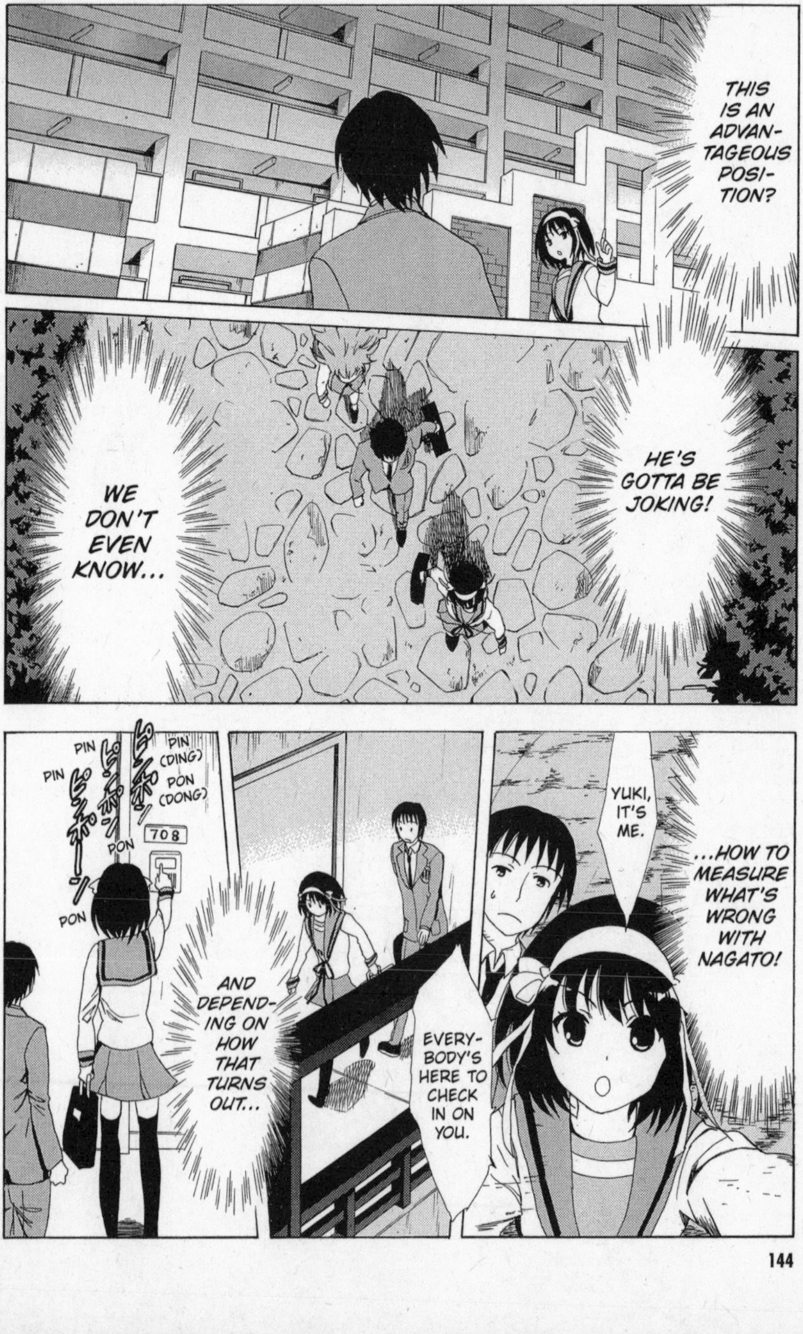
THIS IS AN ADVANTAGEOUS POSITION?
HE'S GOTTA BE JOKING!
WE DON'T EVEN KNOW...
...HOW TO MEASURE WHAT'S WRONG WITH NAGATO!
YUKI, IT'S ME.
EVERYBODY'S HERE TO CHECK IN ON YOU.
PIN (DING)
PON (DONG)
PIN
PIN
PON
PON
AND DEPENDING ON HOW THAT TURNS OUT...
708

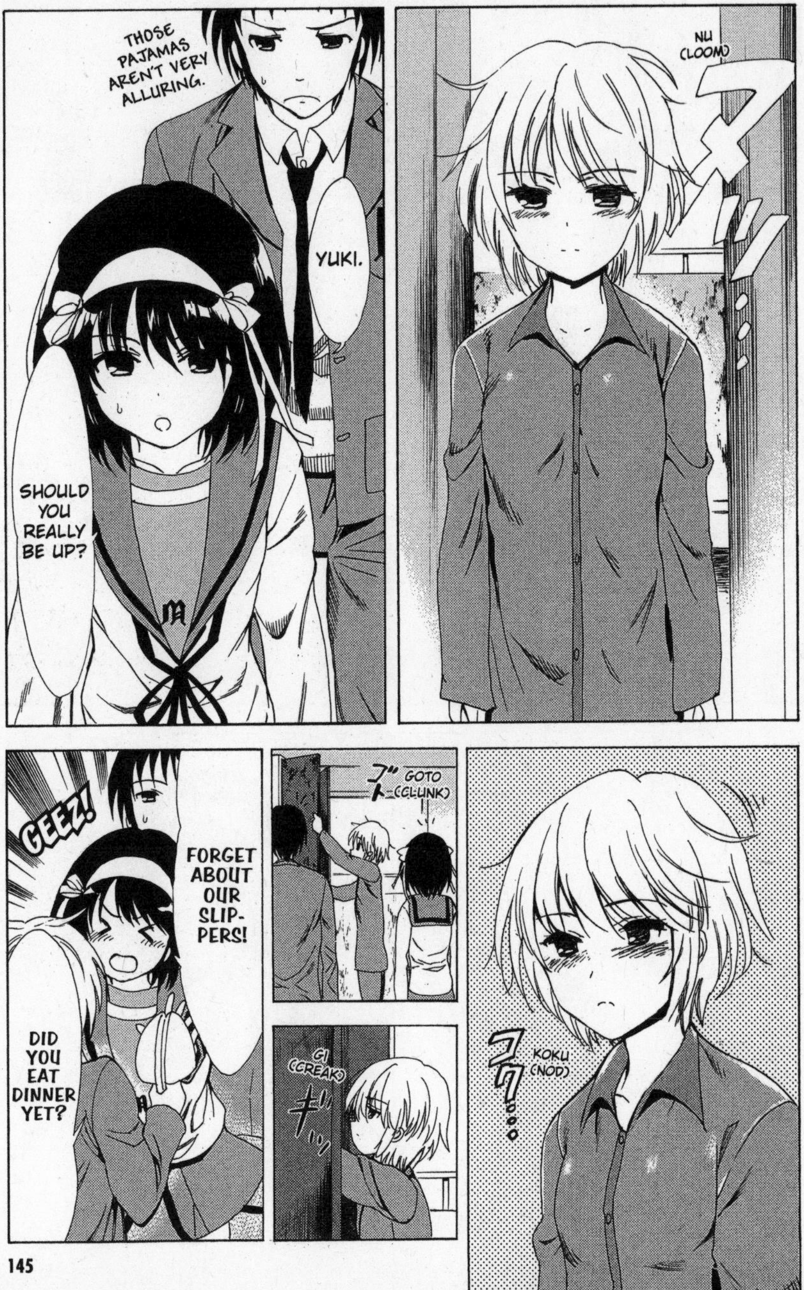
NU (LOOM)
THOSE PAJAMAS AREN'T VERY ALLURING.
YUKI.
SHOULD YOU REALLY BE UP?
KOKU (NOD)
GOTO (CLUNK)
GI (CREAK)
GEEZ!
FORGET ABOUT OUR SLIP-PERS!
DID YOU EAT DINNER YET?

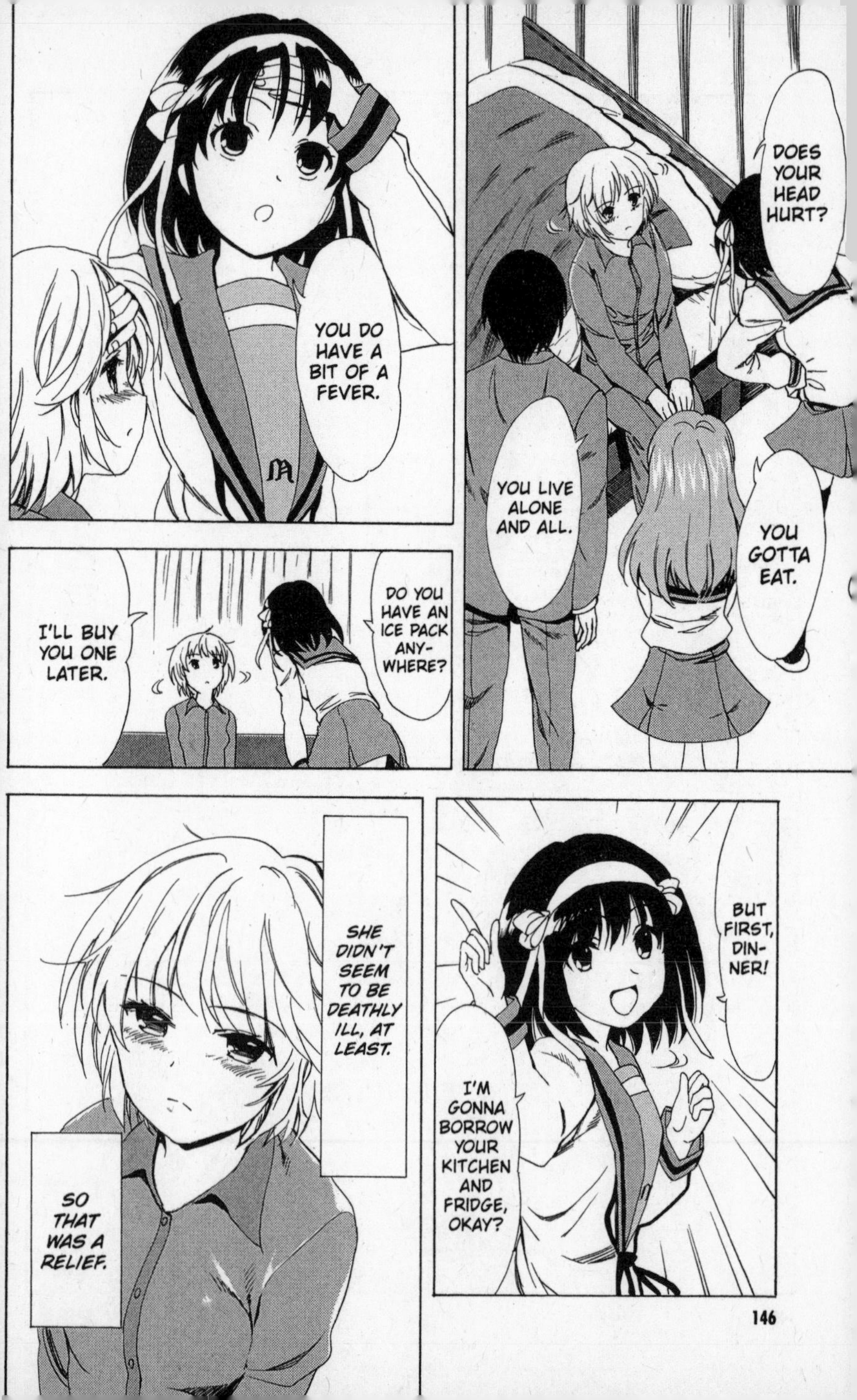
DOES YOUR HEAD HURT?
YOU GOTTA EAT.
YOU LIVE ALONE AND ALL.
YOU DO HAVE A BIT OF A FEVER.
DO YOU HAVE AN ICE PACK ANY-WHERE?
I'LL BUY YOU ONE LATER.
BUT FIRST, DIN-NER!
I'M GONNA BORROW YOUR KITCHEN AND FRIDGE, OKAY?
SHE DIDN'T SEEM TO BE DEATHLY ILL, AT LEAST.
SO THAT WAS A RELIEF.

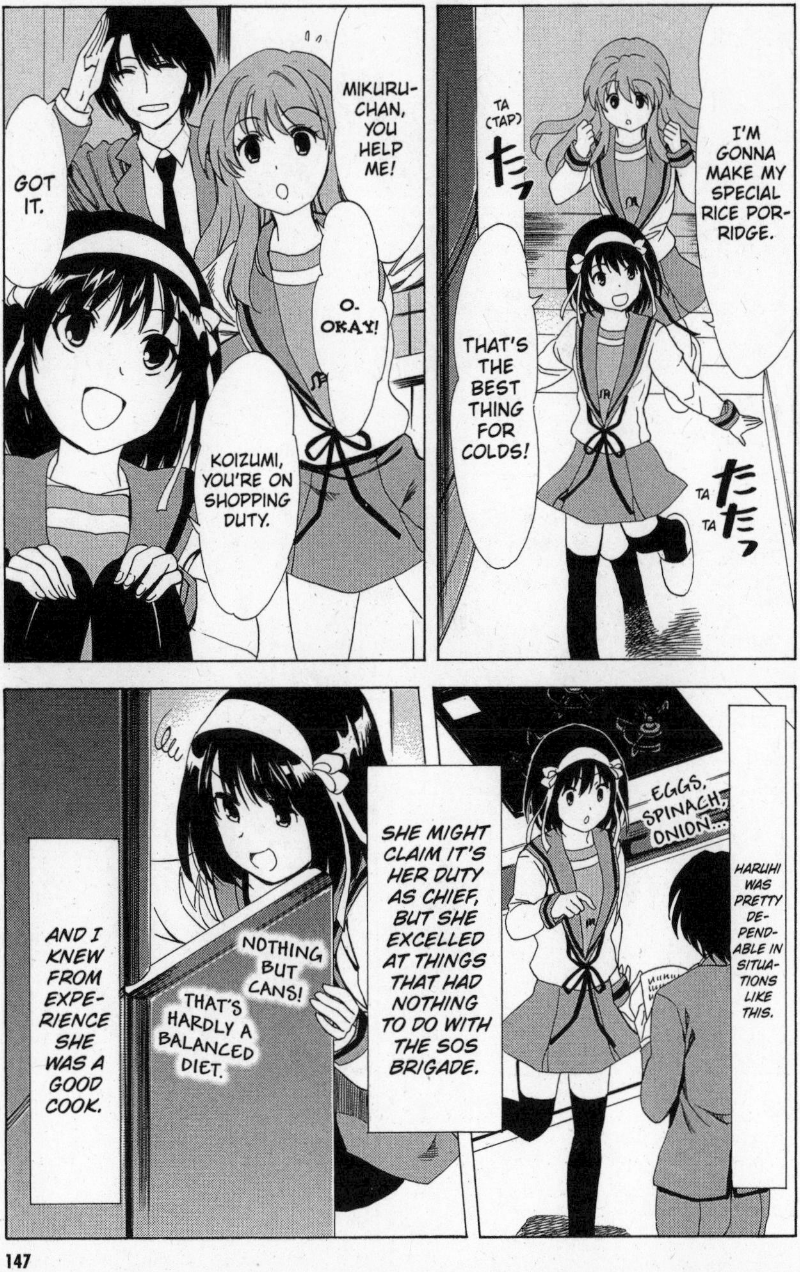
I'M GONNA MAKE MY SPECIAL RICE PORRIDGE.
TA (TAP)
THAT'S THE BEST THING FOR COLDS!
TA TA
MIKURU-CHAN, YOU HELP ME!
O-OKAY!
KOIZUMI, YOU'RE ON SHOPPING DUTY.
GOT IT.
HARUHI WAS PRETTY DEPENDABLE IN SITUATIONS LIKE THIS.
EGGS, SPINACH, ONION...
SHE MIGHT CLAIM IT'S HER DUTY AS CHIEF, BUT SHE EXCELLED AT THINGS THAT HAD NOTHING TO DO WITH THE SOS BRIGADE.
NOTHING BUT CANS!
THAT'S HARDLY A BALANCED DIET.
AND I KNEW FROM EXPERIENCE SHE WAS A GOOD COOK.

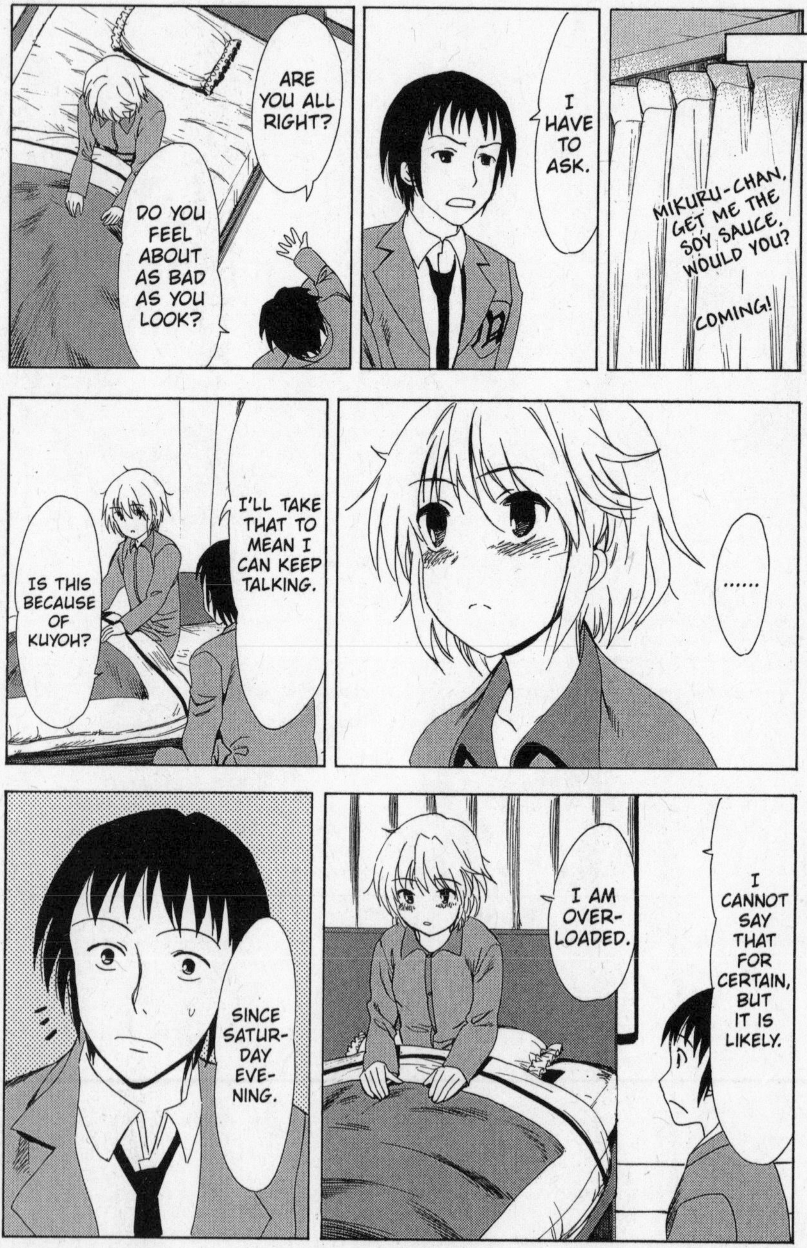
MIKURU-CHAN, GET ME THE SOY SAUCE, WOULD YOU?
COMING!
I HAVE TO ASK.
ARE YOU ALL RIGHT?
DO YOU FEEL ABOUT AS BAD AS YOU LOOK?
......
I'LL TAKE THAT TO MEAN I CAN KEEP TALKING.
IS THIS BECAUSE OF KUYOH?
I CANNOT SAY THAT FOR CERTAIN, BUT IT IS LIKELY.
I AM OVER-LOADED.
SINCE SATUR-DAY EVE-NING.

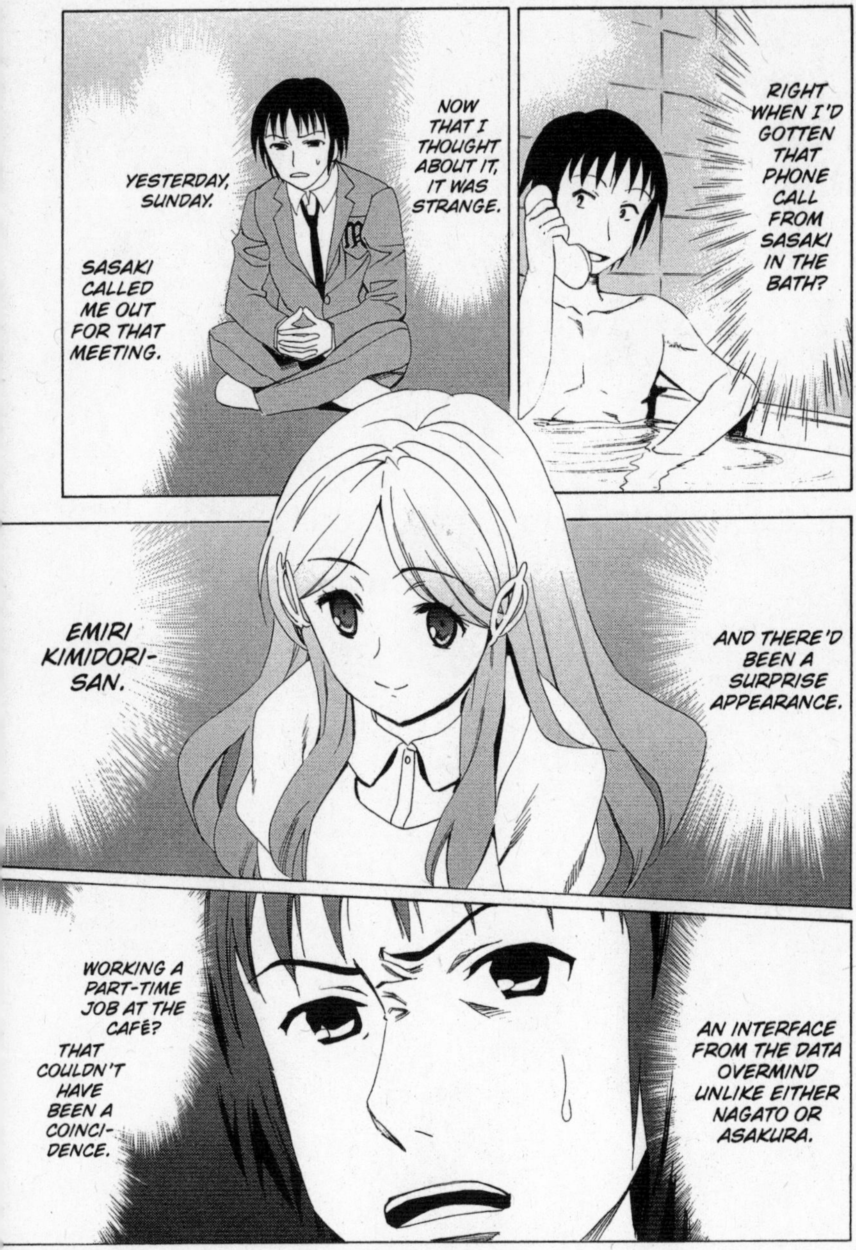
RIGHT WHEN I'D GOTTEN THAT PHONE CALL FROM SASAKI IN THE BATH?
NOW THAT I THOUGHT ABOUT IT, IT WAS STRANGE.
YESTERDAY, SUNDAY.
SASAKI CALLED ME OUT FOR THAT MEETING.
AND THERE'D BEEN A SURPRISE APPEARANCE.
EMIRI KIMIDORI-SAN.
AN INTERFACE FROM THE DATA OVERMIND UNLIKE EITHER NAGATO OR ASAKURA.
WORKING A PART-TIME JOB AT THE CAFÉ?
THAT COULDN'T HAVE BEEN A COINCIDENCE.

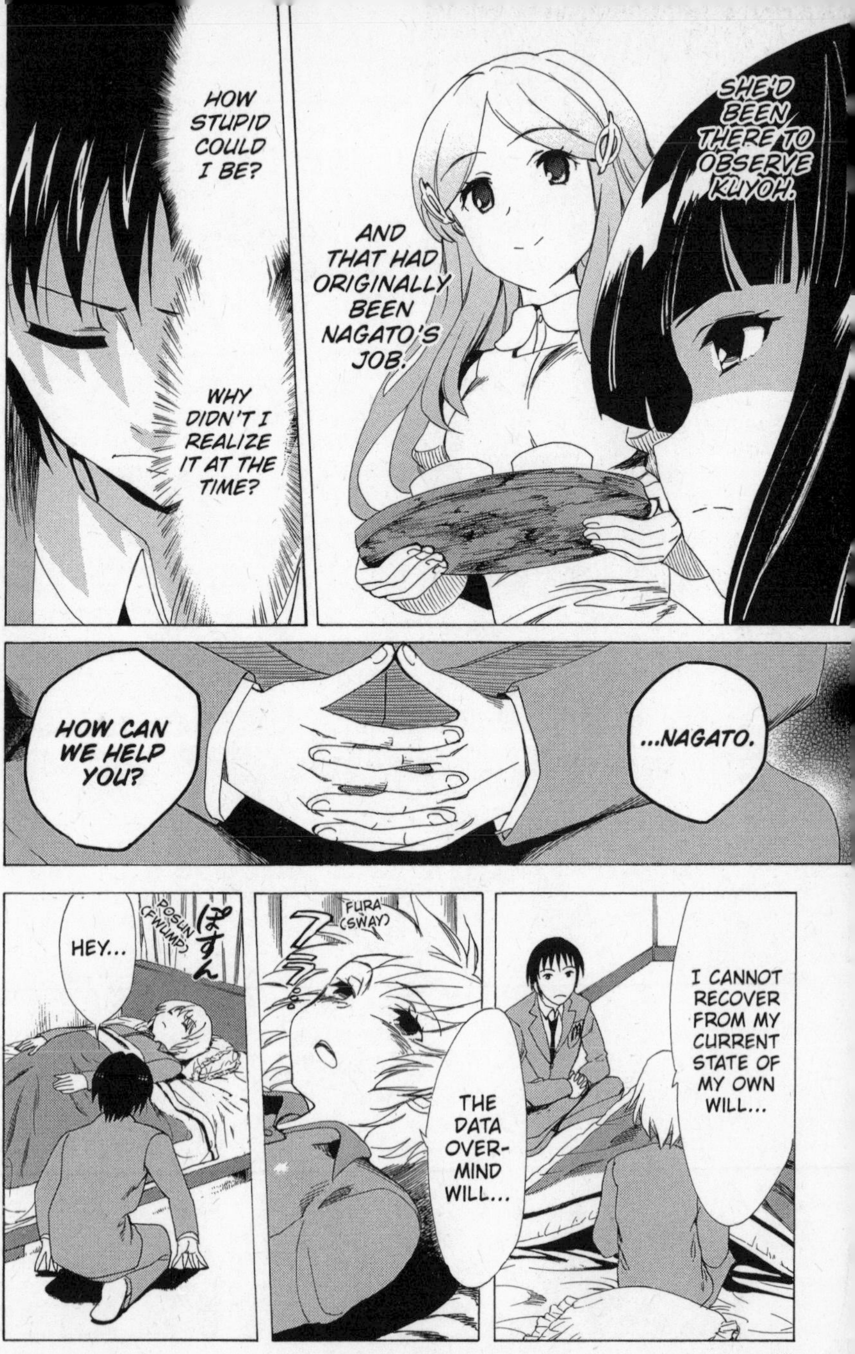
SHE'D BEEN THERE TO OBSERVE KUYOH.
AND THAT HAD ORIGINALLY BEEN NAGATO'S JOB.
HOW STUPID COULD I BE?
WHY DIDN'T I REALIZE IT AT THE TIME?
...NAGATO.
HOW CAN WE HELP YOU?
I CANNOT RECOVER FROM MY CURRENT STATE OF MY OWN WILL...
フラ
FURA (SWAY)
THE DATA OVER-MIND WILL...
ぽすん
POSUN (FWUMP)
HEY...

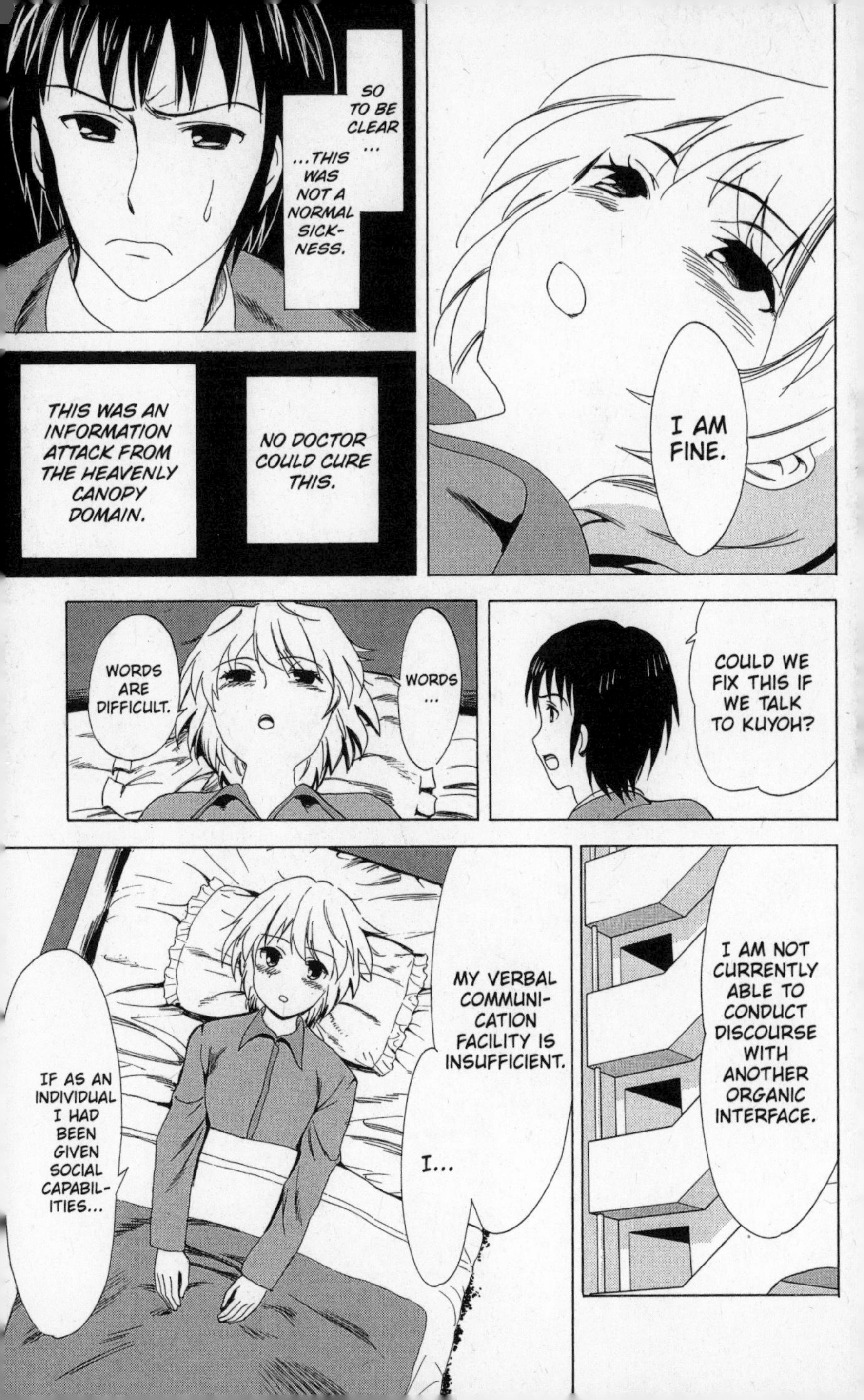
I AM FINE.
SO TO BE CLEAR...
...THIS WAS NOT A NORMAL SICKNESS.
NO DOCTOR COULD CURE THIS.
THIS WAS AN INFORMATION ATTACK FROM THE HEAVENLY CANOPY DOMAIN.
COULD WE FIX THIS IF WE TALK TO KUYOH?
WORDS...
WORDS ARE DIFFICULT.
I AM NOT CURRENTLY ABLE TO CONDUCT DISCOURSE WITH ANOTHER ORGANIC INTERFACE.
MY VERBAL COMMUNICATION FACILITY IS INSUFFICIENT.
I...
IF AS AN INDIVIDUAL I HAD BEEN GIVEN SOCIAL CAPABILITIES...

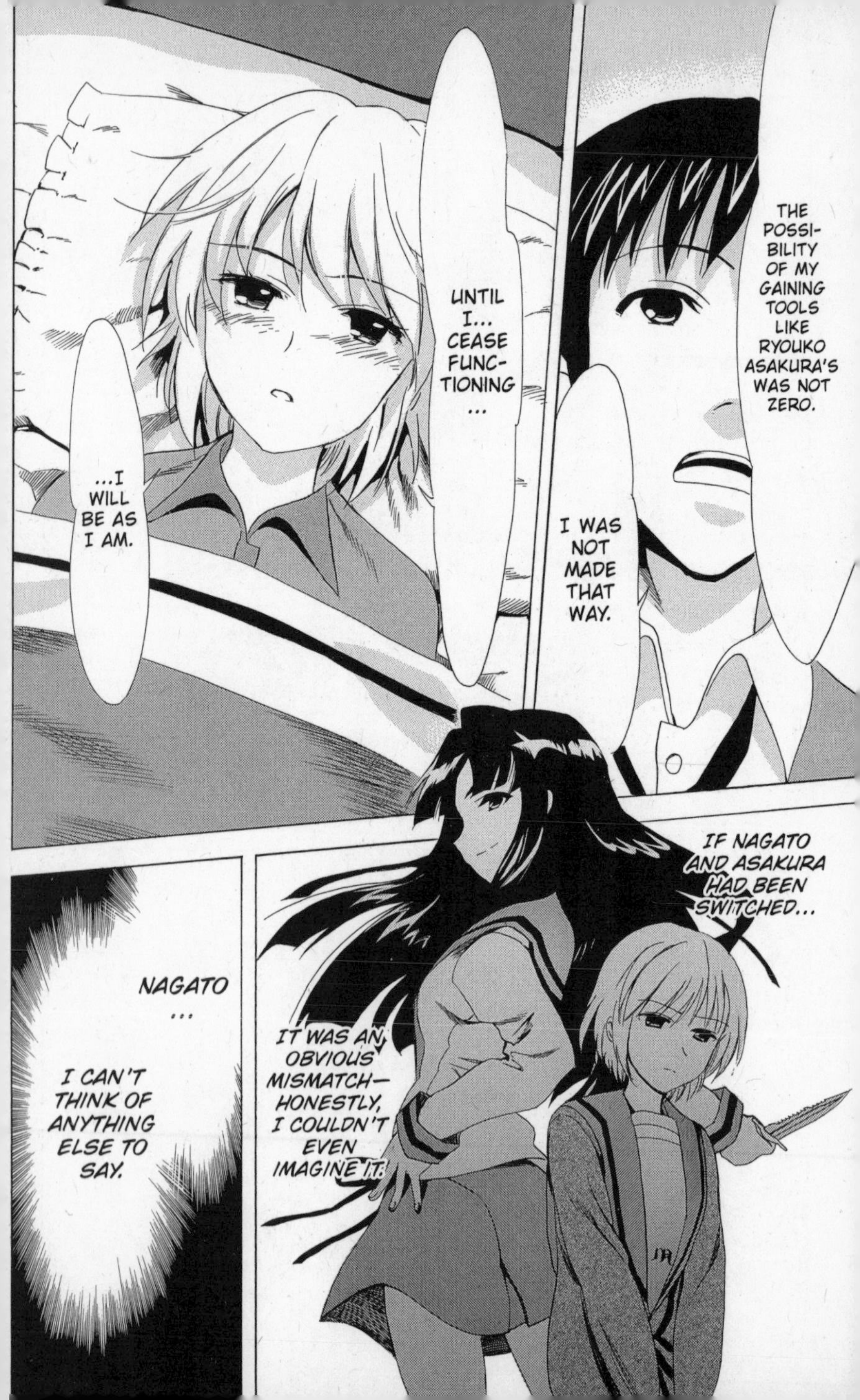
THE POSSIBILITY OF MY GAINING TOOLS LIKE RYOUKO ASAKURA'S WAS NOT ZERO.
I WAS NOT MADE THAT WAY.
UNTIL I... CEASE FUNCTIONING...
...I WILL BE AS I AM.
IF NAGATO AND ASAKURA HAD BEEN SWITCHED...
IT WAS AN OBVIOUS MISMATCH— HONESTLY, I COULDN'T EVEN IMAGINE IT.
NAGATO...
I CAN'T THINK OF ANYTHING ELSE TO SAY.

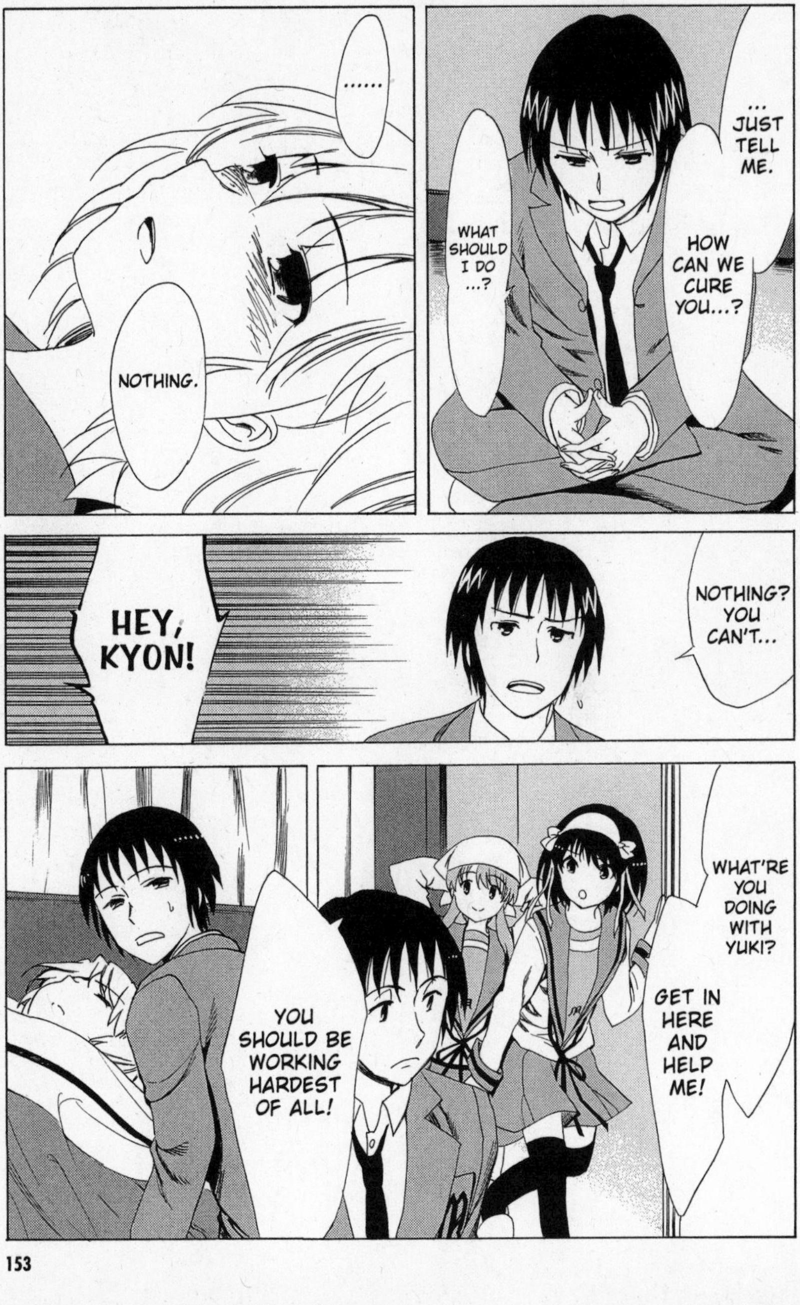
... JUST TELL ME.
HOW CAN WE CURE YOU...?
WHAT SHOULD I DO ...?
......
NOTHING.
NOTHING? YOU CAN'T...
HEY, KYON!
WHAT'RE YOU DOING WITH YUKI?
GET IN HERE AND HELP ME!
YOU SHOULD BE WORKING HARDEST OF ALL!

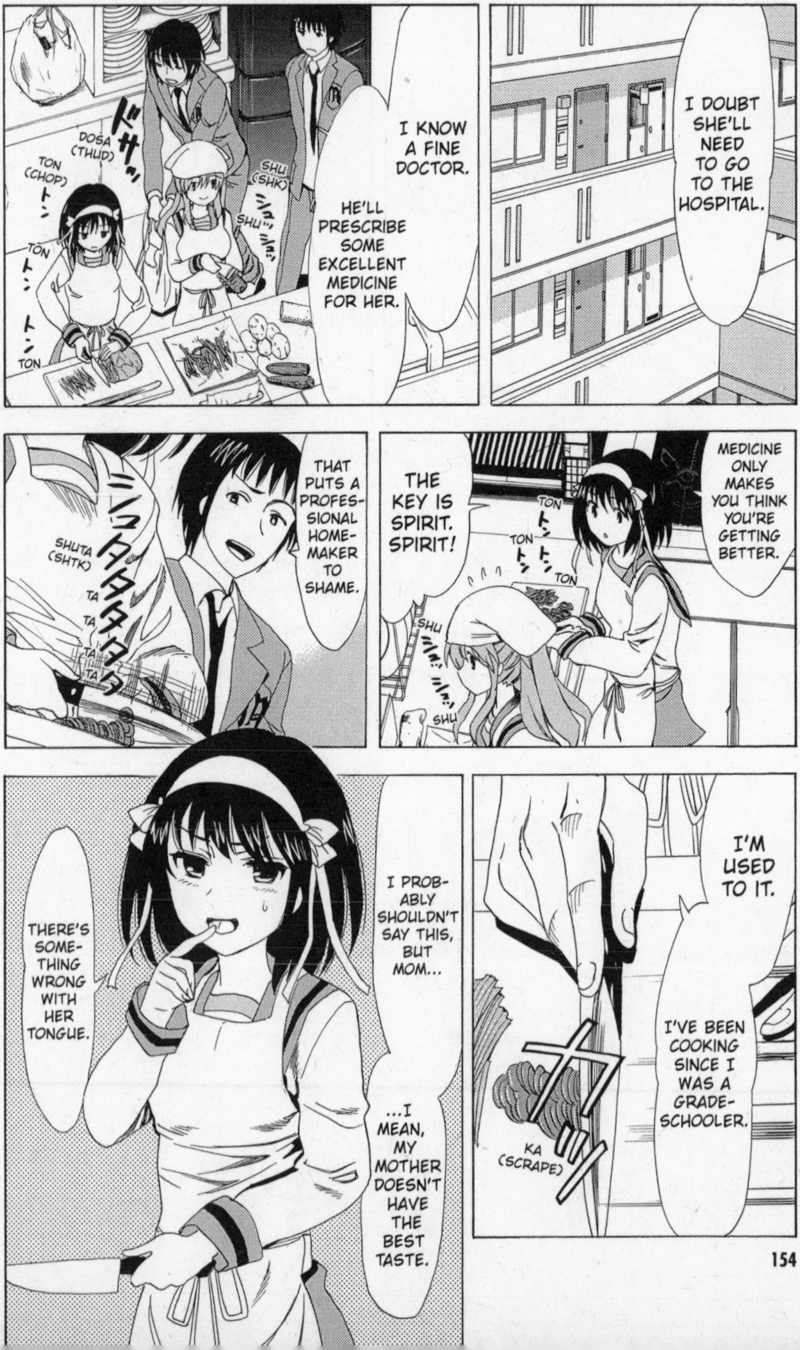
I DOUBT SHE'LL NEED TO GO TO THE HOSPITAL.
I KNOW A FINE DOCTOR.
HE'LL PRESCRIBE SOME EXCELLENT MEDICINE FOR HER.
DOSA (THUD)
SHU (SHK)
SHU
TON (CHOP)
TON
TON
MEDICINE ONLY MAKES YOU THINK YOU'RE GETTING BETTER.
THE KEY IS SPIRIT. SPIRIT!
TON
TON
TON
SHU
SHU
THAT PUTS A PROFES-SIONAL HOME-MAKER TO SHAME.
SHUTA (SHTK)
TA
TA
TA
TA
I'M USED TO IT.
I'VE BEEN COOKING SINCE I WAS A GRADE-SCHOOLER.
KA (SCRAPE)
I PROB-ABLY SHOULDN'T SAY THIS, BUT MOM...
THERE'S SOME-THING WRONG WITH HER TONGUE.
...I MEAN, MY MOTHER DOESN'T HAVE THE BEST TASTE.

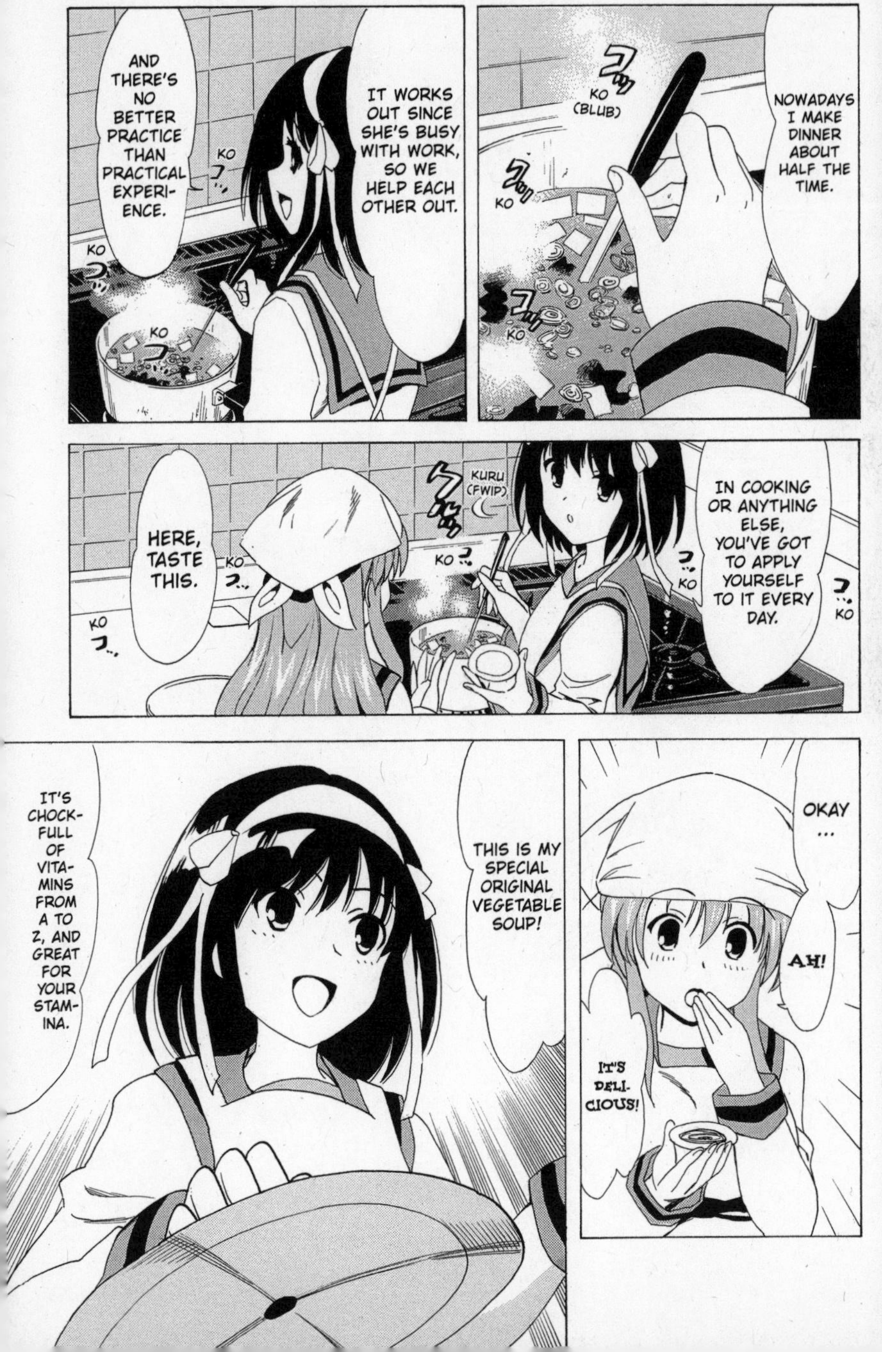
NOWADAYS I MAKE DINNER ABOUT HALF THE TIME.
KO (BLUB)
KO
KO
IT WORKS OUT SINCE SHE'S BUSY WITH WORK, SO WE HELP EACH OTHER OUT.
AND THERE'S NO BETTER PRACTICE THAN PRACTICAL EXPERI-ENCE.
KO
KO
KO
IN COOKING OR ANYTHING ELSE, YOU'VE GOT TO APPLY YOURSELF TO IT EVERY DAY.
KO
KO
KURU (FWIP)
KO
HERE, TASTE THIS.
KO
KO
OKAY...
AH!
IT'S DELI-CIOUS!
THIS IS MY SPECIAL ORIGINAL VEGETABLE SOUP!
IT'S CHOCK-FULL OF VITA-MINS FROM A TO Z, AND GREAT FOR YOUR STAM-INA.

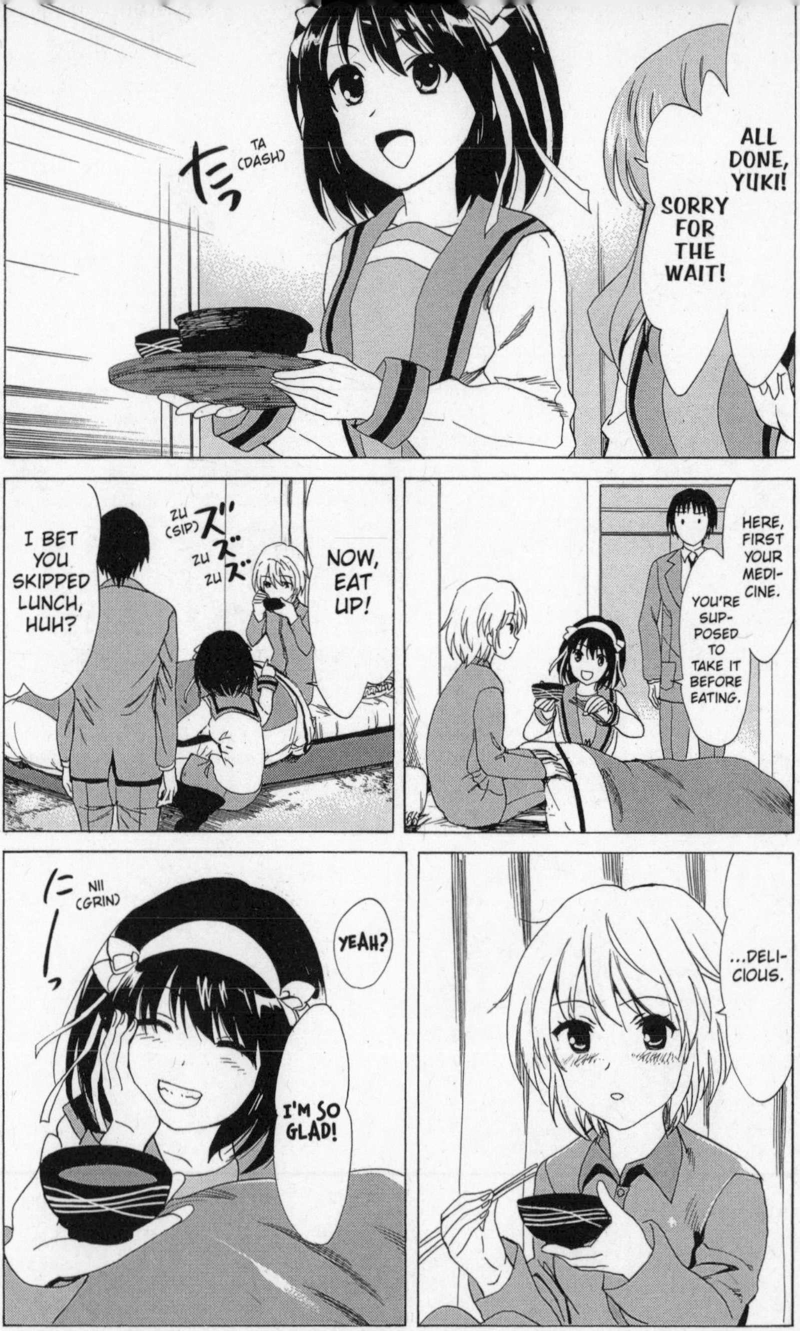
ALL DONE, YUKI!
SORRY FOR THE WAIT!
たっ
TA (DASH)
HERE, FIRST YOUR MEDI-CINE.
YOU'RE SUP-POSED TO TAKE IT BEFORE EATING.
NOW, EAT UP!
ズズズ
ZU (SIP) ZU ZU
I BET YOU SKIPPED LUNCH, HUH?
...DELI-CIOUS.
YEAH?
にーっ
NII (GRIN)
I'M SO GLAD!

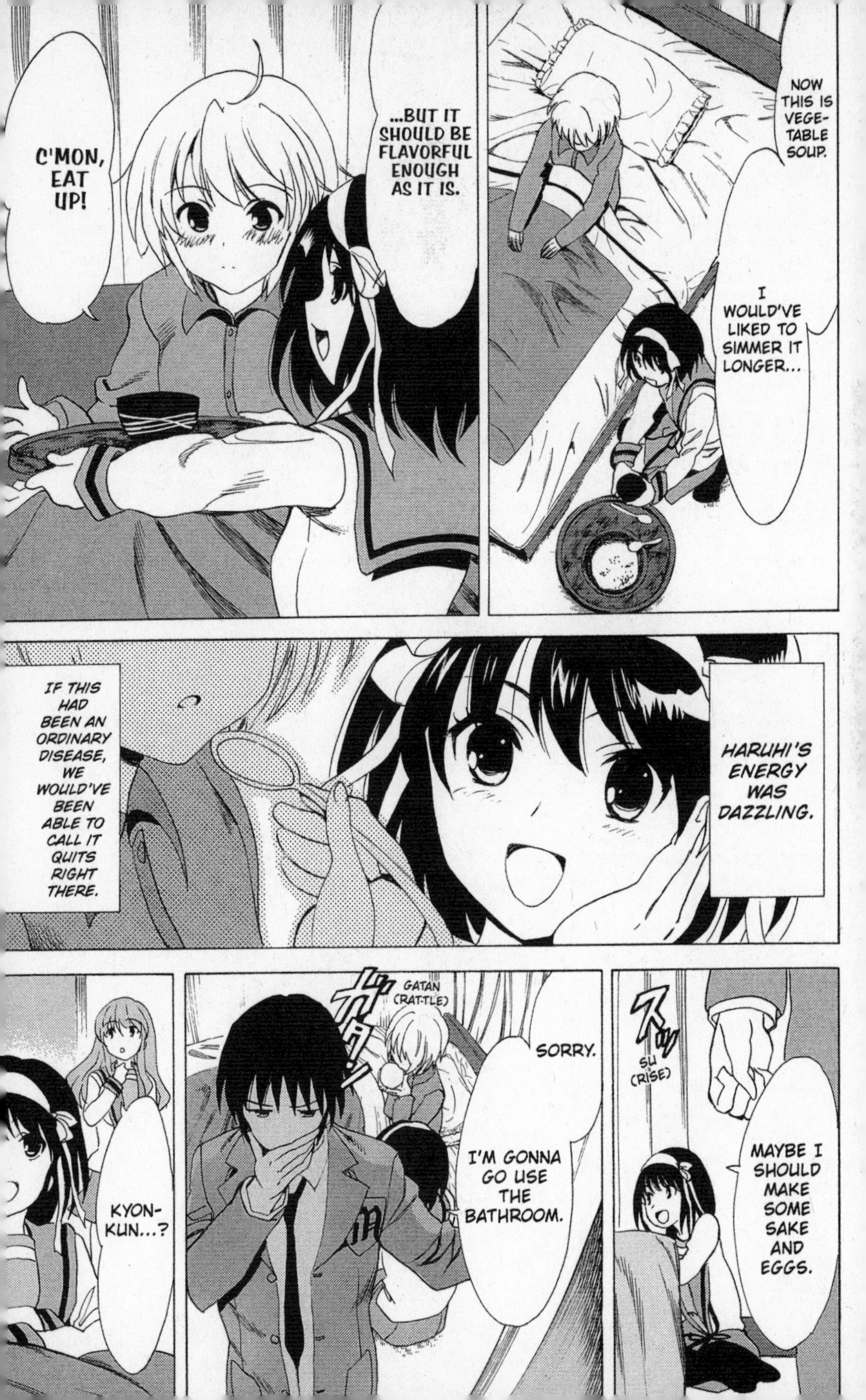
NOW THIS IS VEGE-TABLE SOUP.
I WOULD'VE LIKED TO SIMMER IT LONGER...
...BUT IT SHOULD BE FLAVORFUL ENOUGH AS IT IS.
C'MON, EAT UP!
HARUHI'S ENERGY WAS DAZZLING.
IF THIS HAD BEEN AN ORDINARY DISEASE, WE WOULD'VE BEEN ABLE TO CALL IT QUITS RIGHT THERE.
SU (RISE)
MAYBE I SHOULD MAKE SOME SAKE AND EGGS.
GATAN (RATTLE)
SORRY.
I'M GONNA GO USE THE BATHROOM.
KYON-KUN...?

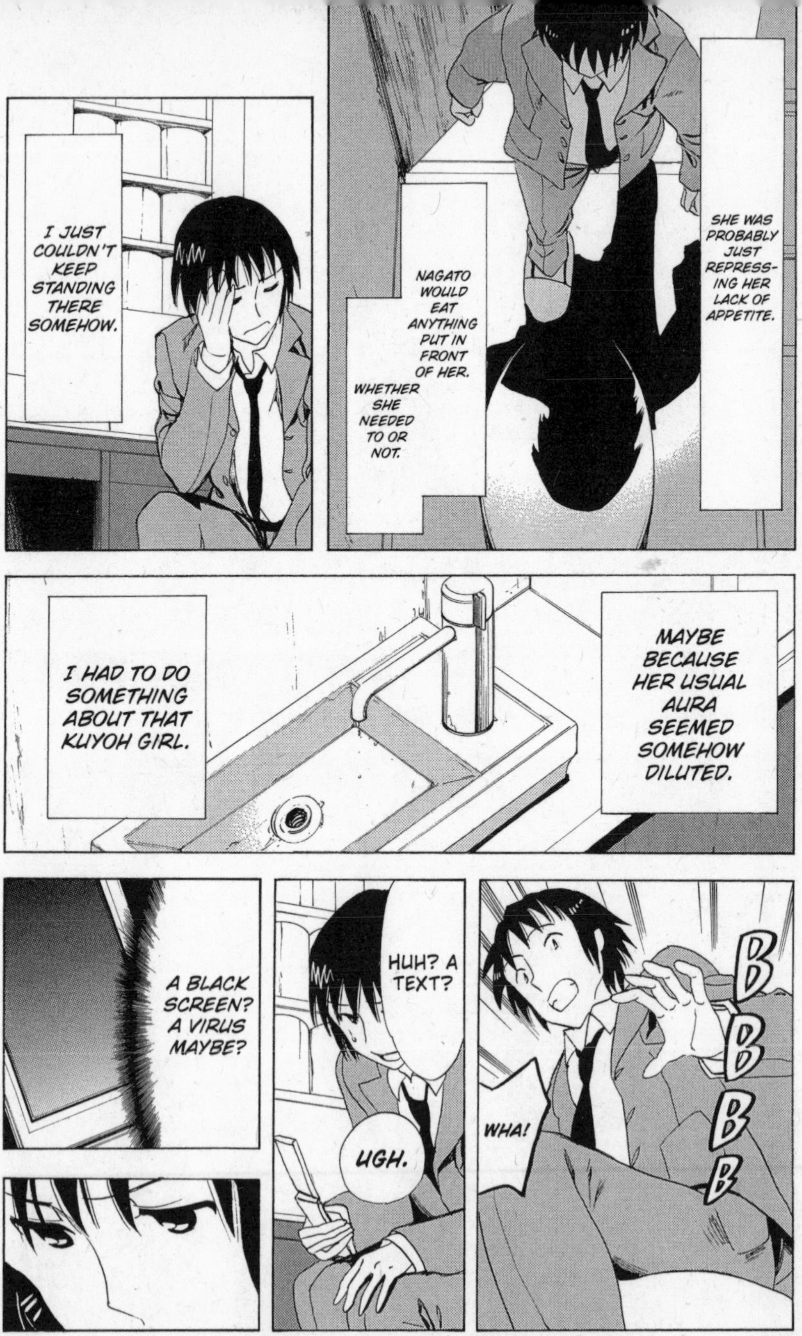
SHE WAS PROBABLY JUST REPRESSING HER LACK OF APPETITE.
NAGATO WOULD EAT ANYTHING PUT IN FRONT OF HER.
WHETHER SHE NEEDED TO OR NOT.
I JUST COULDN'T KEEP STANDING THERE SOMEHOW.
MAYBE BECAUSE HER USUAL AURA SEEMED SOMEHOW DILUTED.
I HAD TO DO SOMETHING ABOUT THAT KUYOH GIRL.
BBBB
WHA!
HUH? A TEXT?
UGH.
A BLACK SCREEN? A VIRUS MAYBE?

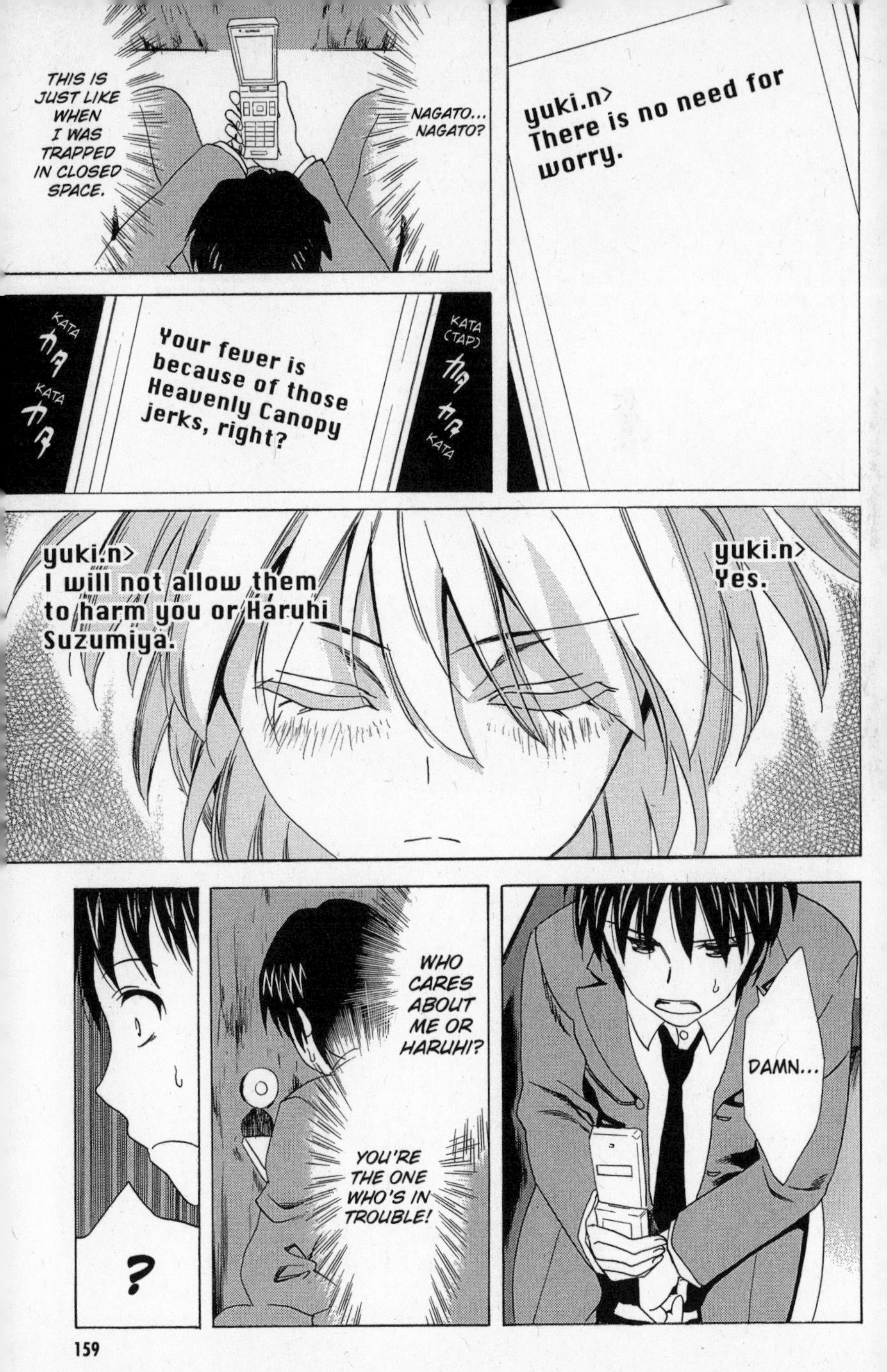
yuki.n>
There is no need for worry.
NAGATO... NAGATO?
THIS IS JUST LIKE WHEN I WAS TRAPPED IN CLOSED SPACE.
KATA (TAP)
KATA
Your fever is because of those Heavenly Canopy jerks, right?
KATA
KATA
yuki.n>
Yes.
yuki.n>
I will not allow them to harm you or Haruhi Suzumiya.
DAMN...
WHO CARES ABOUT ME OR HARUHI?
YOU'RE THE ONE WHO'S IN TROUBLE!
?

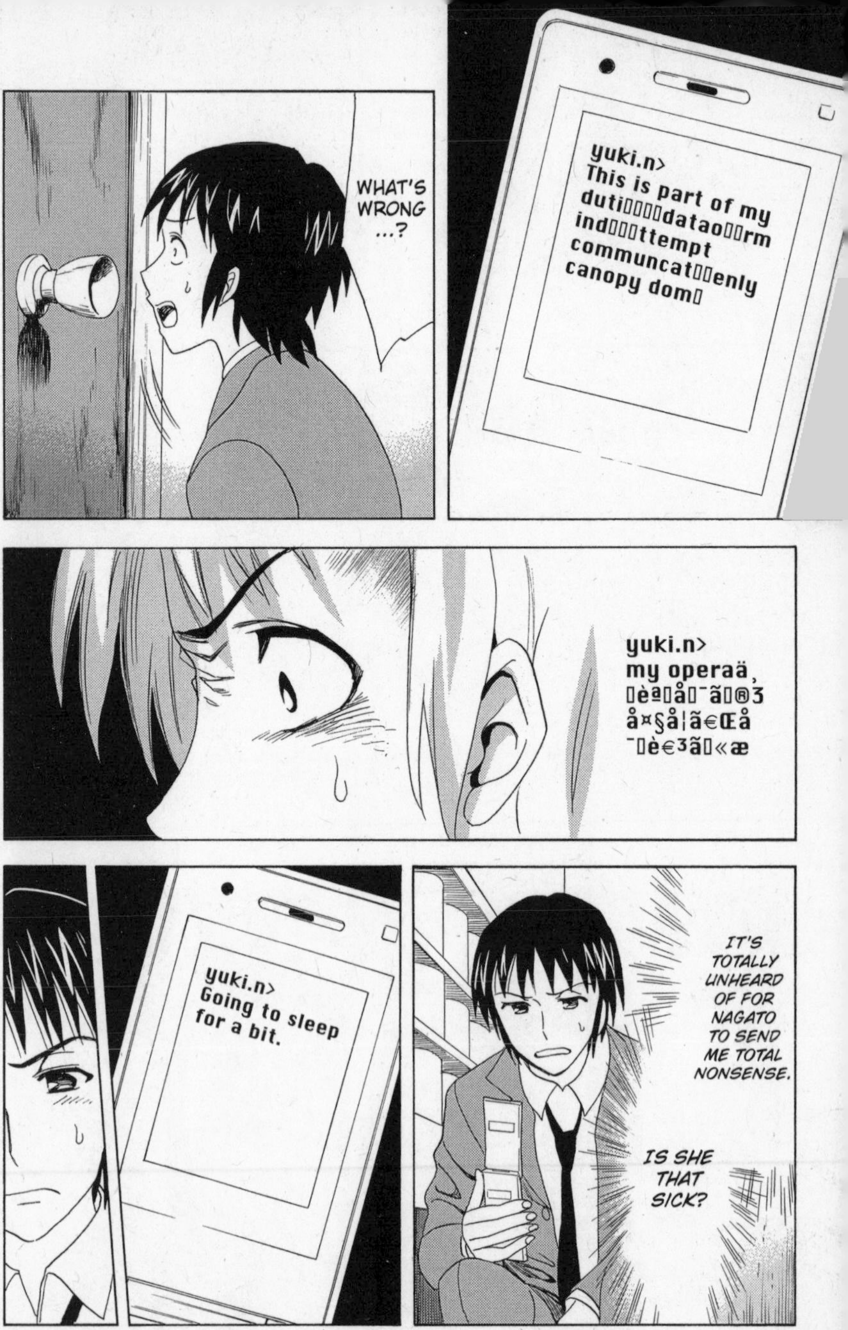
yuki.n>
This is part of my
duti□□□□datao□□rm
ind□□□ttempt
communcat□□enly
canopy dom□
WHAT'S WRONG ...?
yuki.n>
my operaä,
□èª□å□¯ã□®3
å¤§å¦ã€Œå
¯□è€³ã□«æ
IT'S TOTALLY UNHEARD OF FOR NAGATO TO SEND ME TOTAL NONSENSE.
IS SHE THAT SICK?
yuki.n>
Going to sleep
for a bit.

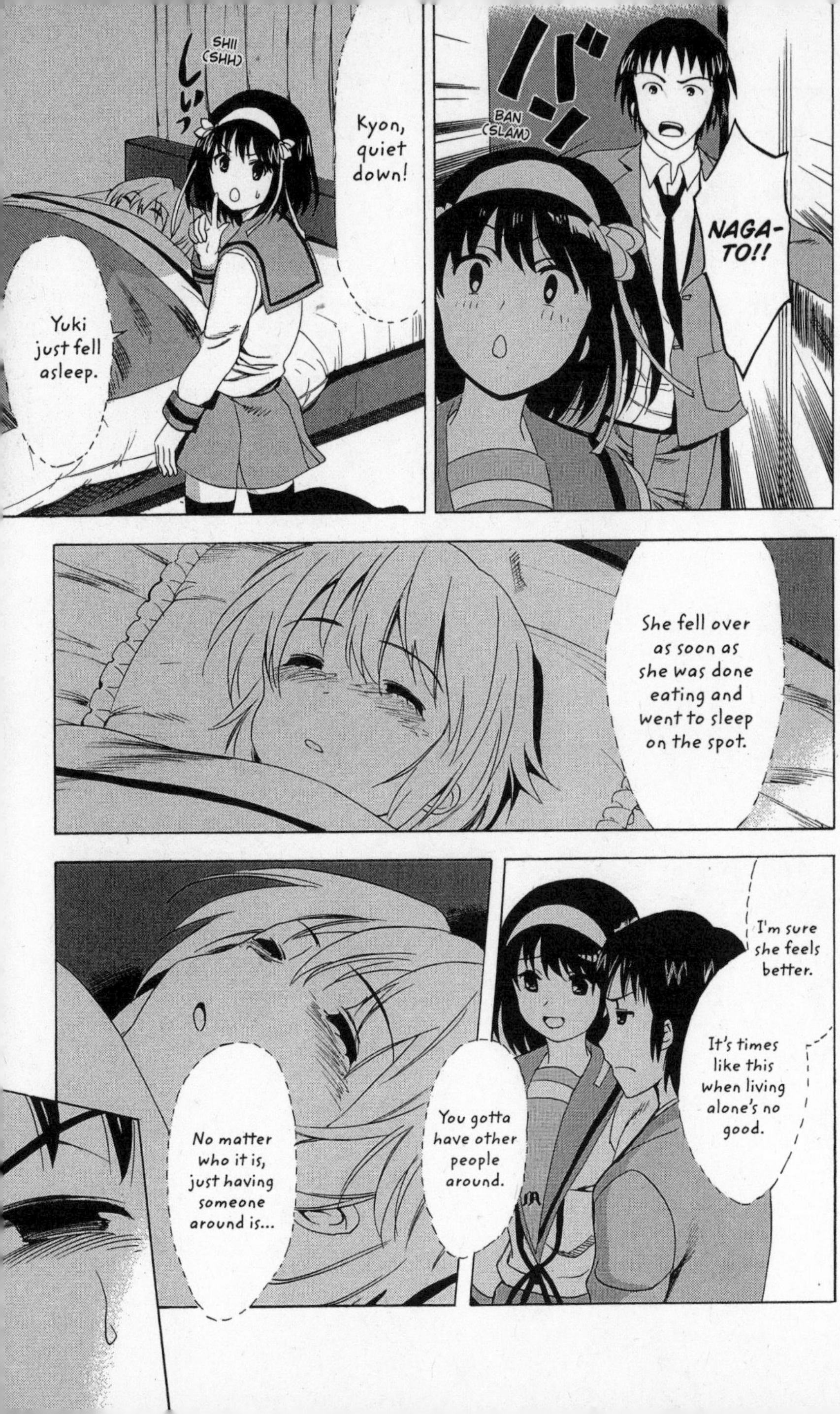
BAN (SLAM)
NAGA-TO!!
SHII (SHH)
Kyon, quiet down!
Yuki just fell asleep.
She fell over as soon as she was done eating and went to sleep on the spot.
I'm sure she feels better.
It's times like this when living alone's no good.
You gotta have other people around.
No matter who it is, just having someone around is...

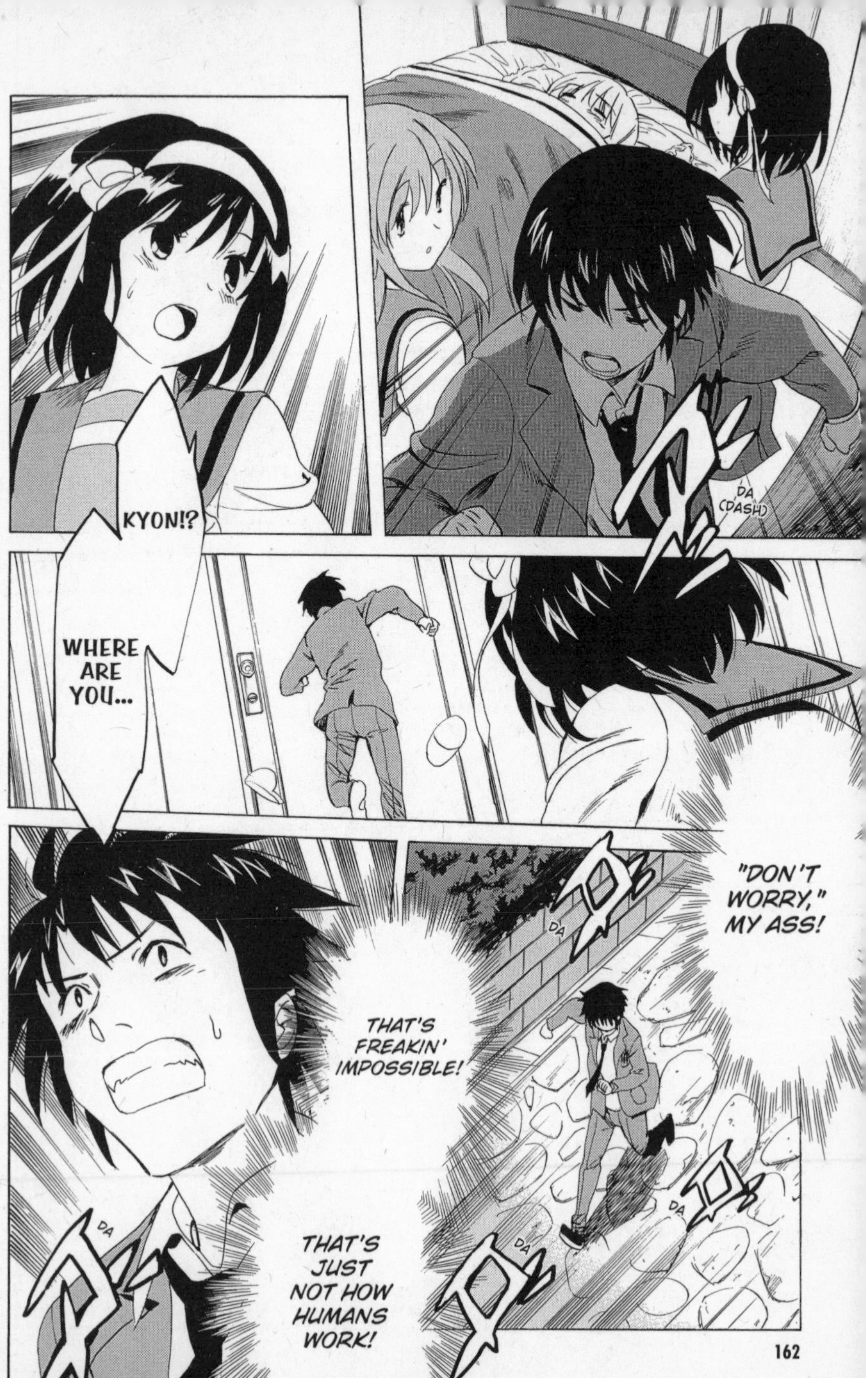
DA (DASH)
KYON!?
WHERE ARE YOU...
"DON'T WORRY," MY ASS!
DA
DA
DA
THAT'S FREAKIN' IMPOSSIBLE!
THAT'S JUST NOT HOW HUMANS WORK!
DA

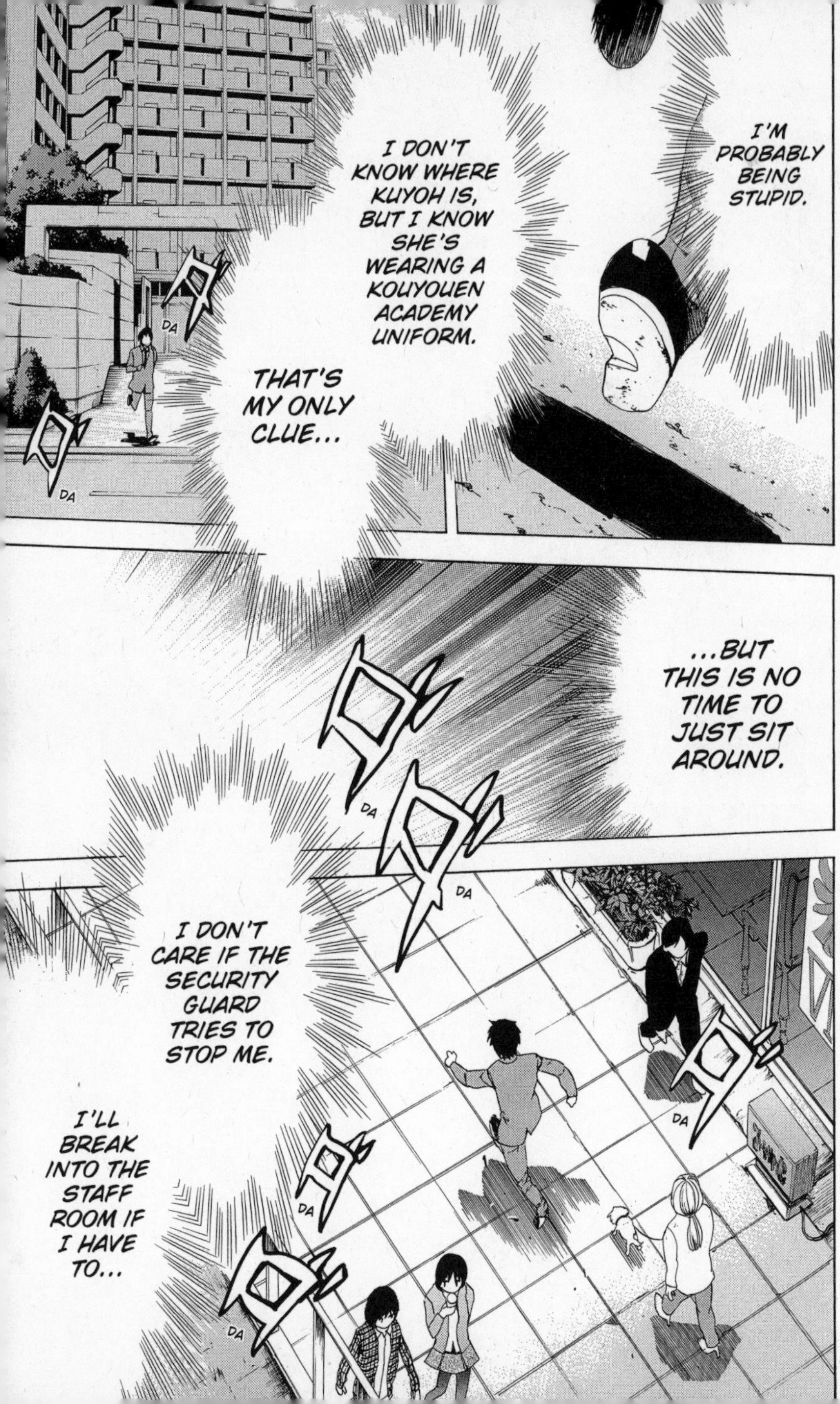
I'M PROBABLY BEING STUPID.
I DON'T KNOW WHERE KUYOH IS, BUT I KNOW SHE'S WEARING A KOUYOUEN ACADEMY UNIFORM.
THAT'S MY ONLY CLUE...
DA
DA
...BUT THIS IS NO TIME TO JUST SIT AROUND.
DA
DA
I DON'T CARE IF THE SECURITY GUARD TRIES TO STOP ME.
DA
I'LL BREAK INTO THE STAFF ROOM IF I HAVE TO...
DA
DA

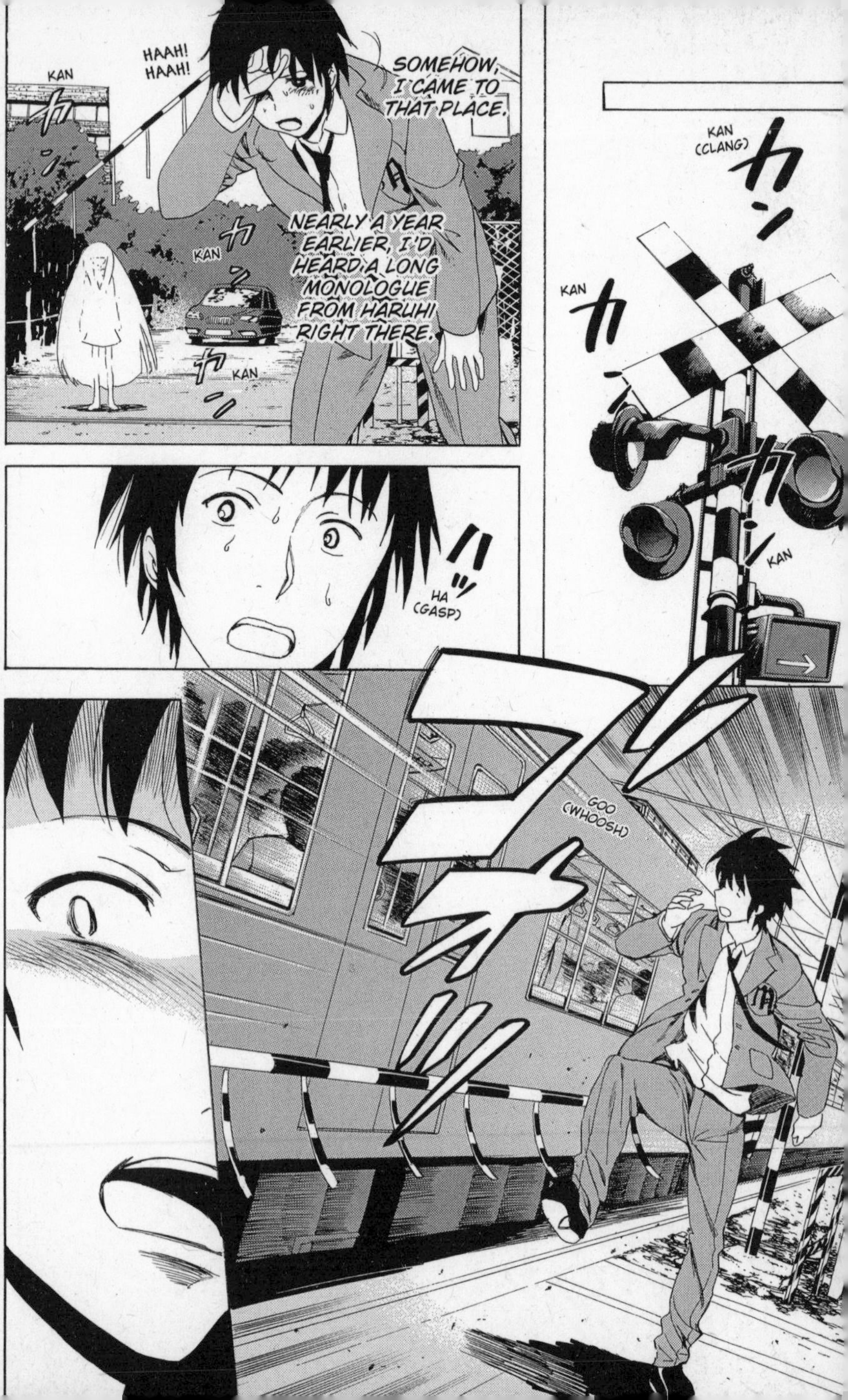
KAN (CLANG)
KAN
KAN
SOMEHOW, I CAME TO THAT PLACE.
HAAH! HAAH!
KAN
NEARLY A YEAR EARLIER, I'D HEARD A LONG MONOLOGUE FROM HARUHI RIGHT THERE.
KAN
KAN
HA (GASP)
GOO (WHOOSH)

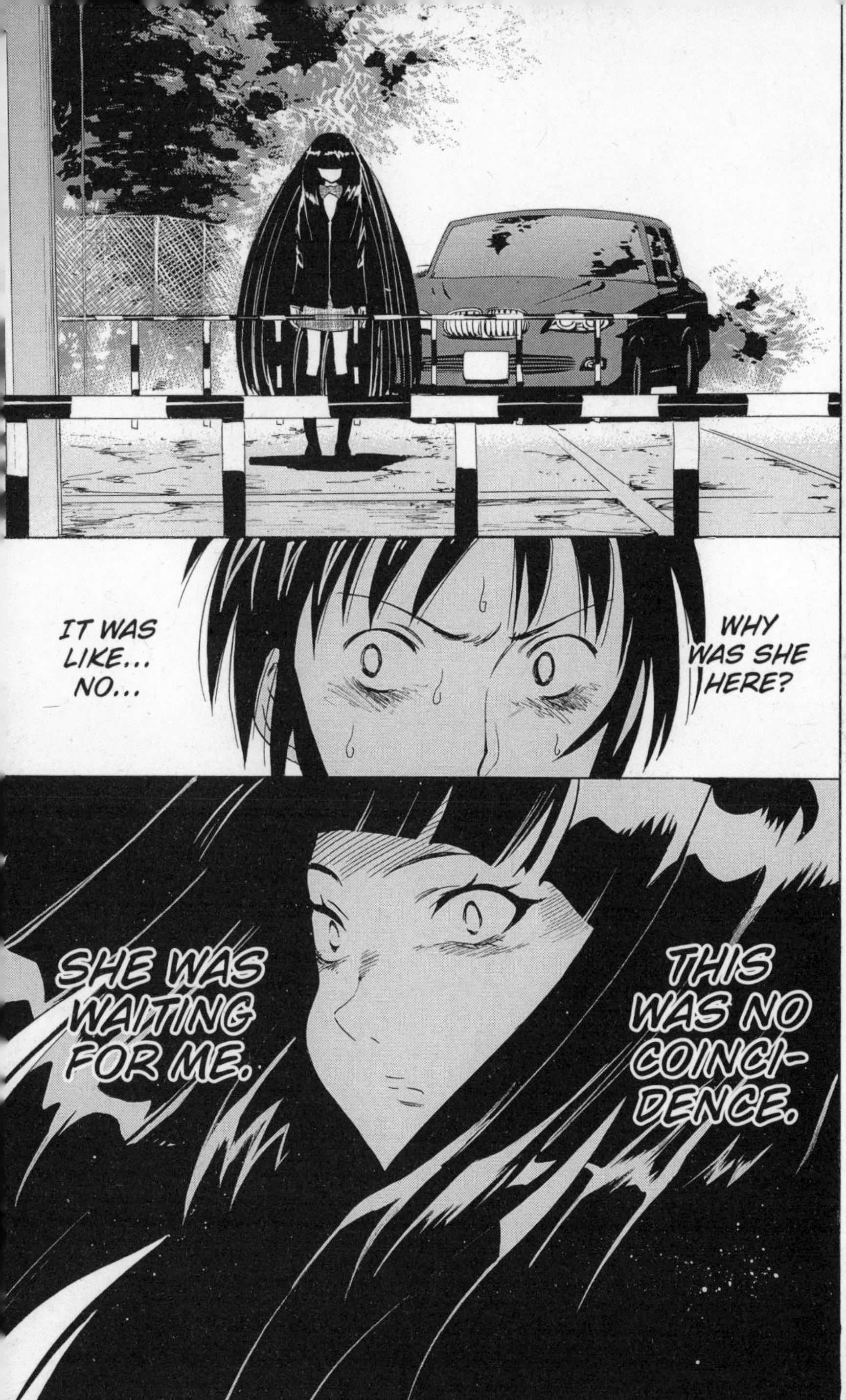
WHY WAS SHE HERE?
IT WAS LIKE... NO...
THIS WAS NO COINCI-DENCE.
SHE WAS WAITING FOR ME.

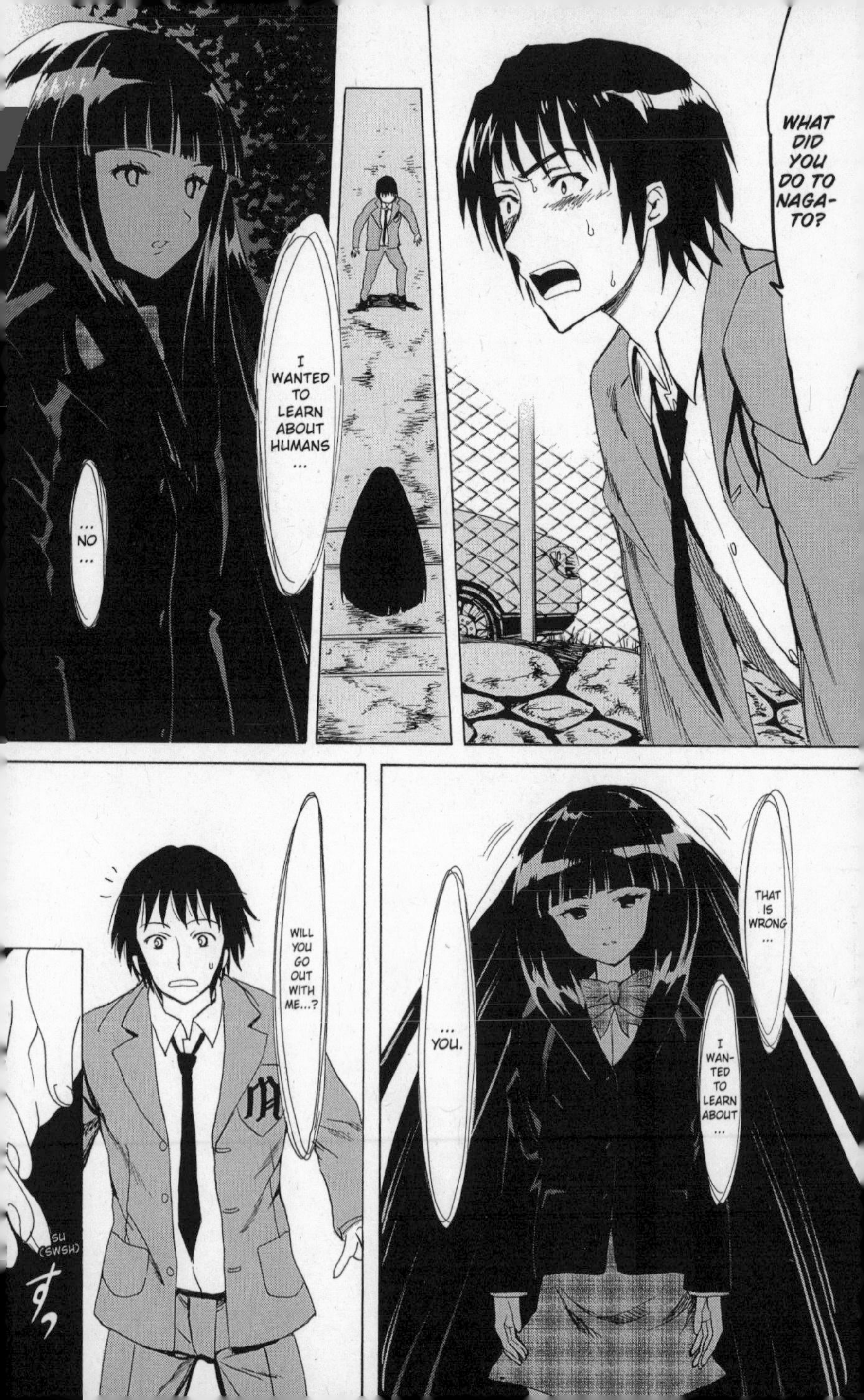
WHAT DID YOU DO TO NAGA-TO?
I WANTED TO LEARN ABOUT HUMANS...
...NO...
THAT IS WRONG...
I WAN-TED TO LEARN ABOUT...
...YOU.
WILL YOU GO OUT WITH ME...?
SU (SWSH)
すっ

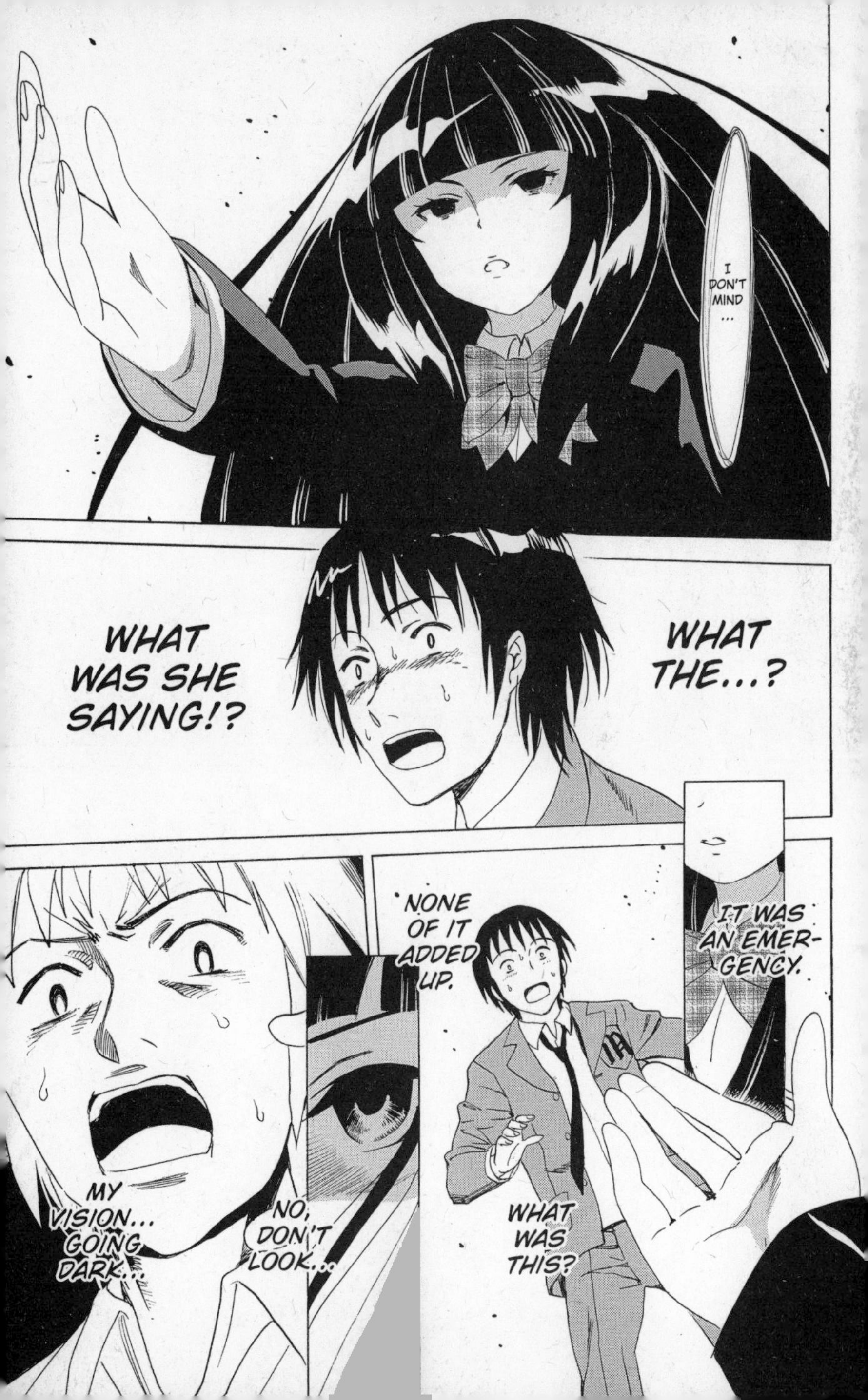
I DON'T MIND...
WHAT THE...?
WHAT WAS SHE SAYING!?
IT WAS AN EMERGENCY.
NONE OF IT ADDED UP.
WHAT WAS THIS?
NO, DON'T LOOK...
MY VISION... GOING DARK...

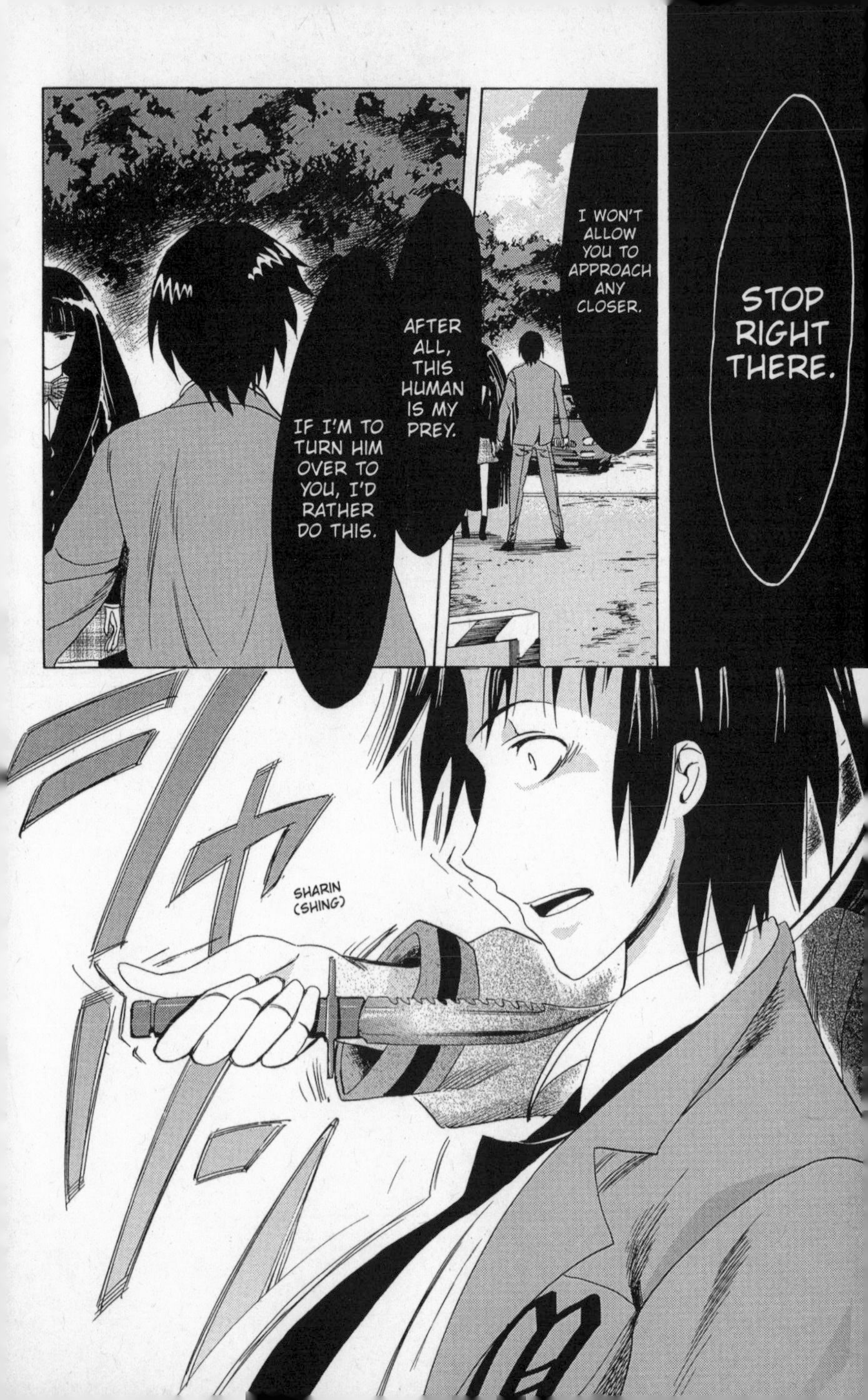
STOP RIGHT THERE.
I WON'T ALLOW YOU TO APPROACH ANY CLOSER.
AFTER ALL, THIS HUMAN IS MY PREY.
IF I'M TO TURN HIM OVER TO YOU, I'D RATHER DO THIS.
SHARIN (SHING)

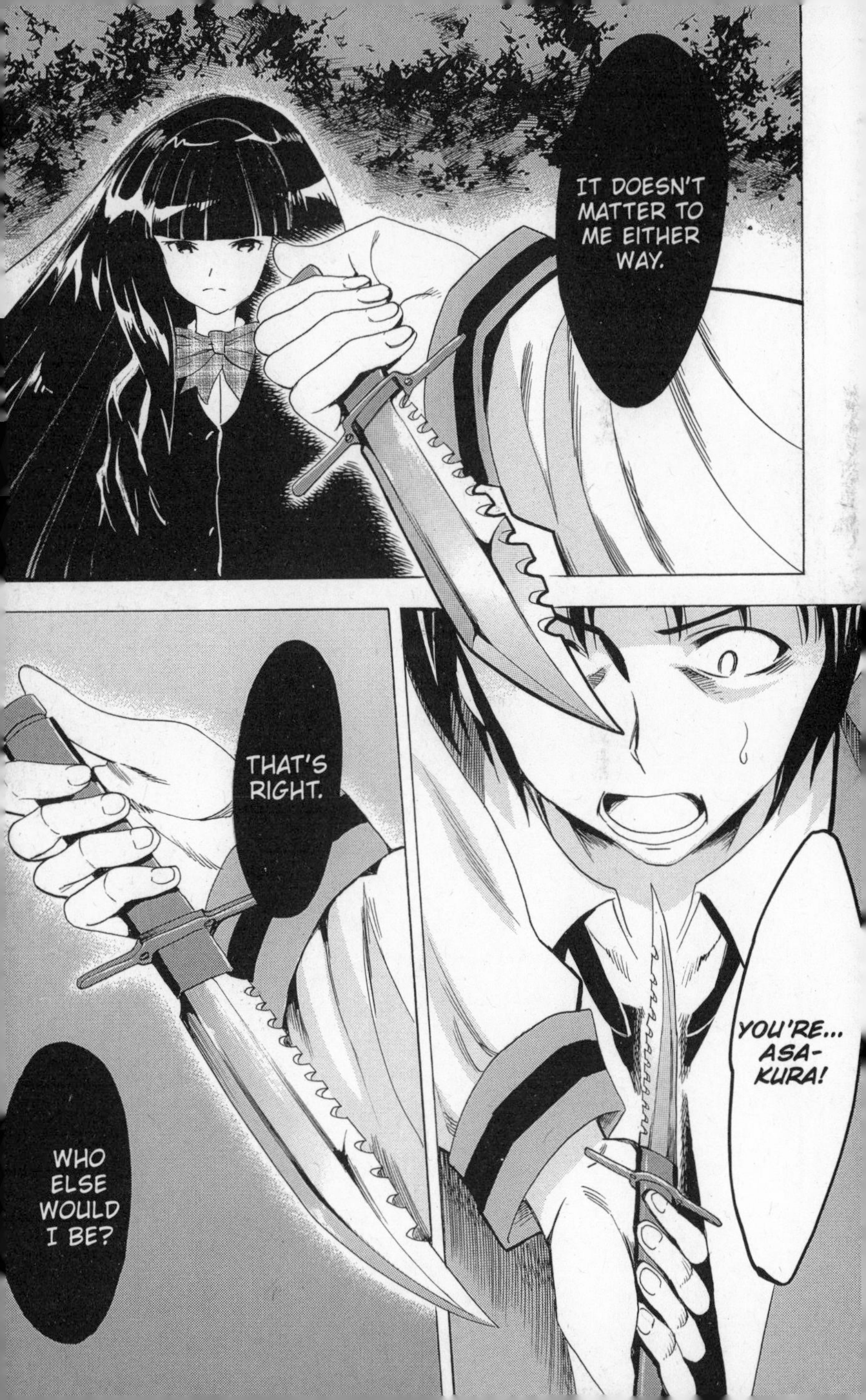
IT DOESN'T MATTER TO ME EITHER WAY.
YOU'RE... ASA-KURA!
THAT'S RIGHT.
WHO ELSE WOULD I BE?

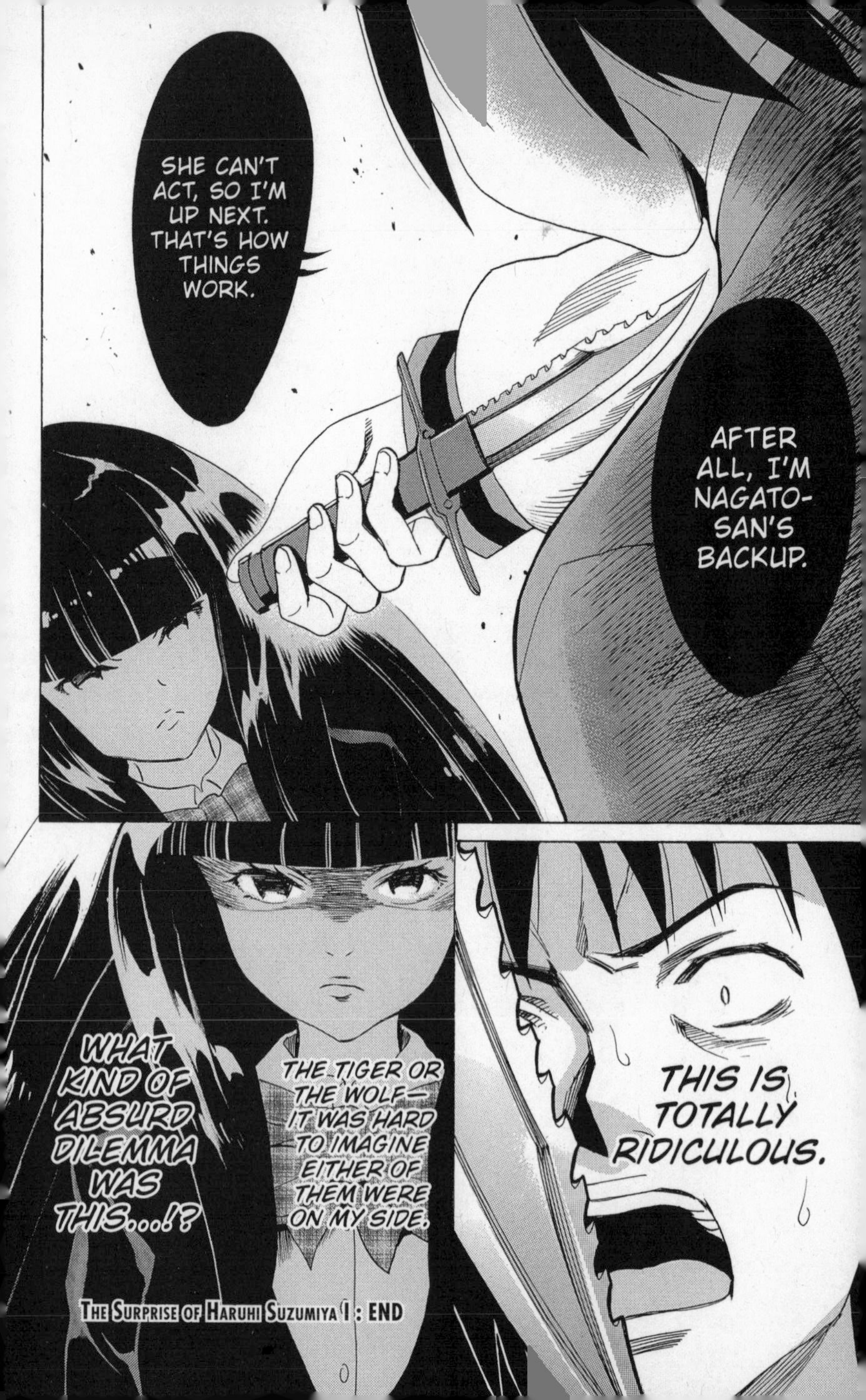

SHE CAN'T ACT, SO I'M UP NEXT. THAT'S HOW THINGS WORK.
AFTER ALL, I'M NAGATO-SAN'S BACKUP.
THIS IS TOTALLY RIDICULOUS.
THE TIGER OR THE WOLF— IT WAS HARD TO IMAGINE EITHER OF THEM WERE ON MY SIDE.
WHAT KIND OF ABSURD DILEMMA WAS THIS...!?
THE SURPRISE OF HARUHI SUZUMIYA I : END

TO BE CONTINUED

JUST HANG IN THERE, NAGATO. WE'LL SAVE YOU!!

THE REVIVED ASAKURA VS. THE EERIE KUYOH! THE INEXPLICABLE SITUATION CONTINUES, AND KYON...!

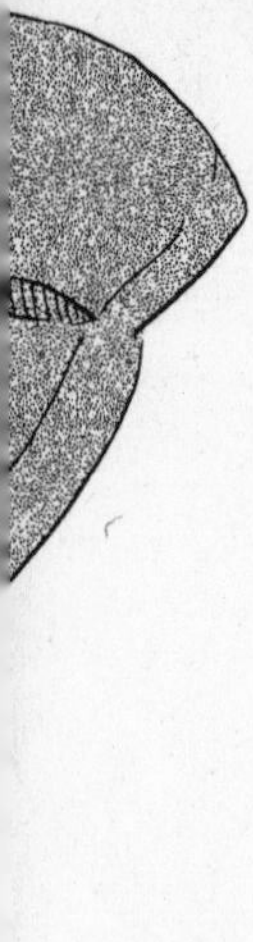

CONFUSION REIGNS AS THE STAKES BECOME HIGHER!

THE SURPRISE ARC CONTINUES IN VOLUME 16!

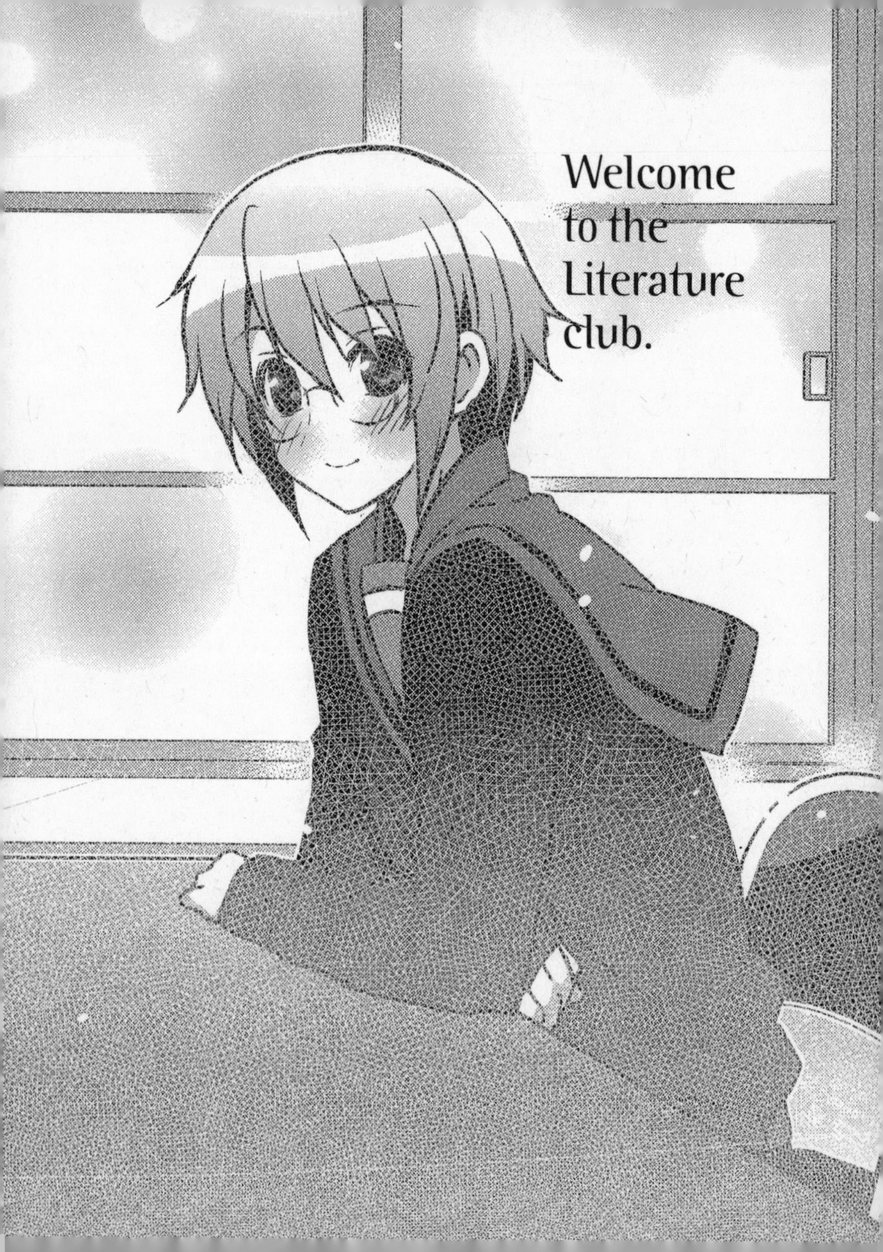
Welcome to the Literature club.

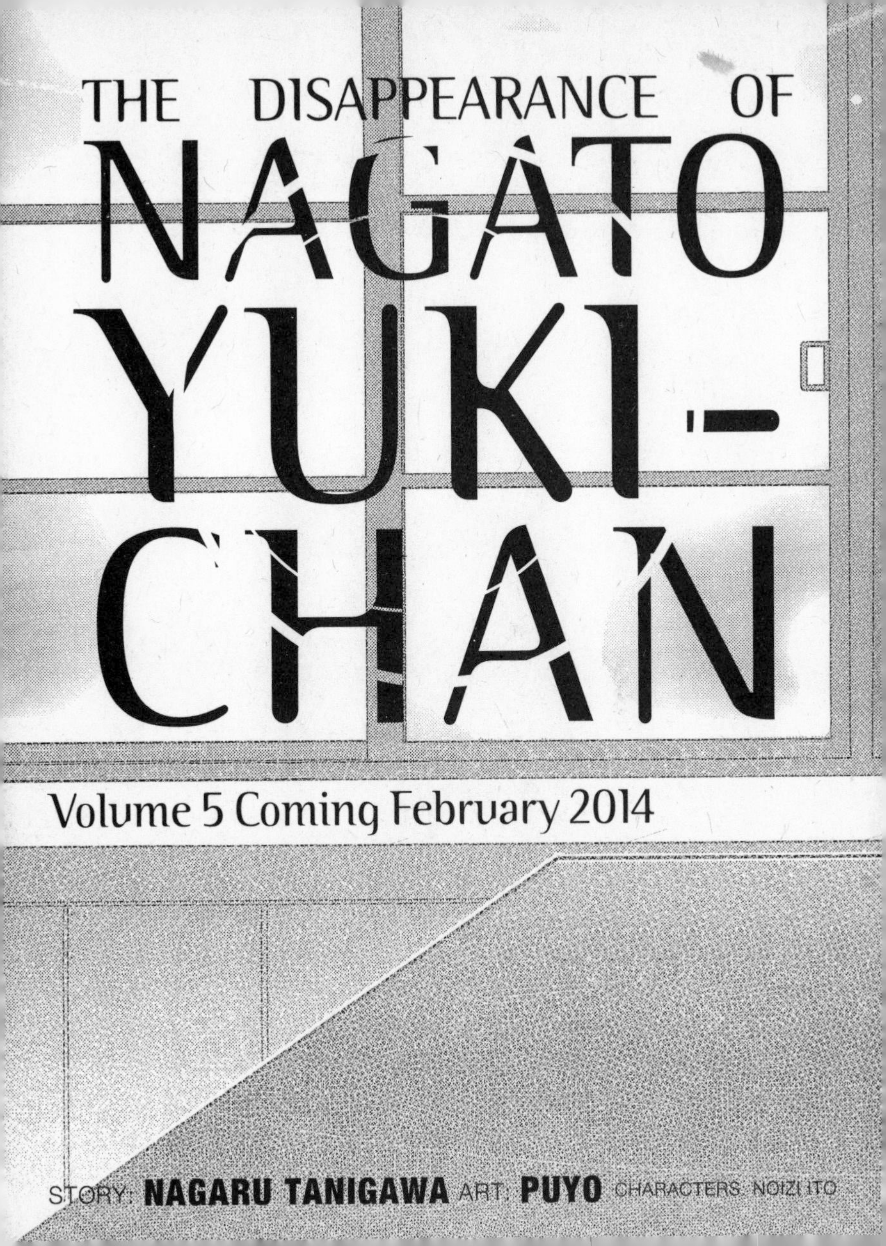
THE DISAPPEARANCE OF
NAGATO YUKI-CHAN
Volume 5 Coming February 2014
STORY: NAGARU TANIGAWA ART: PUYO CHARACTERS: NOIZI ITO

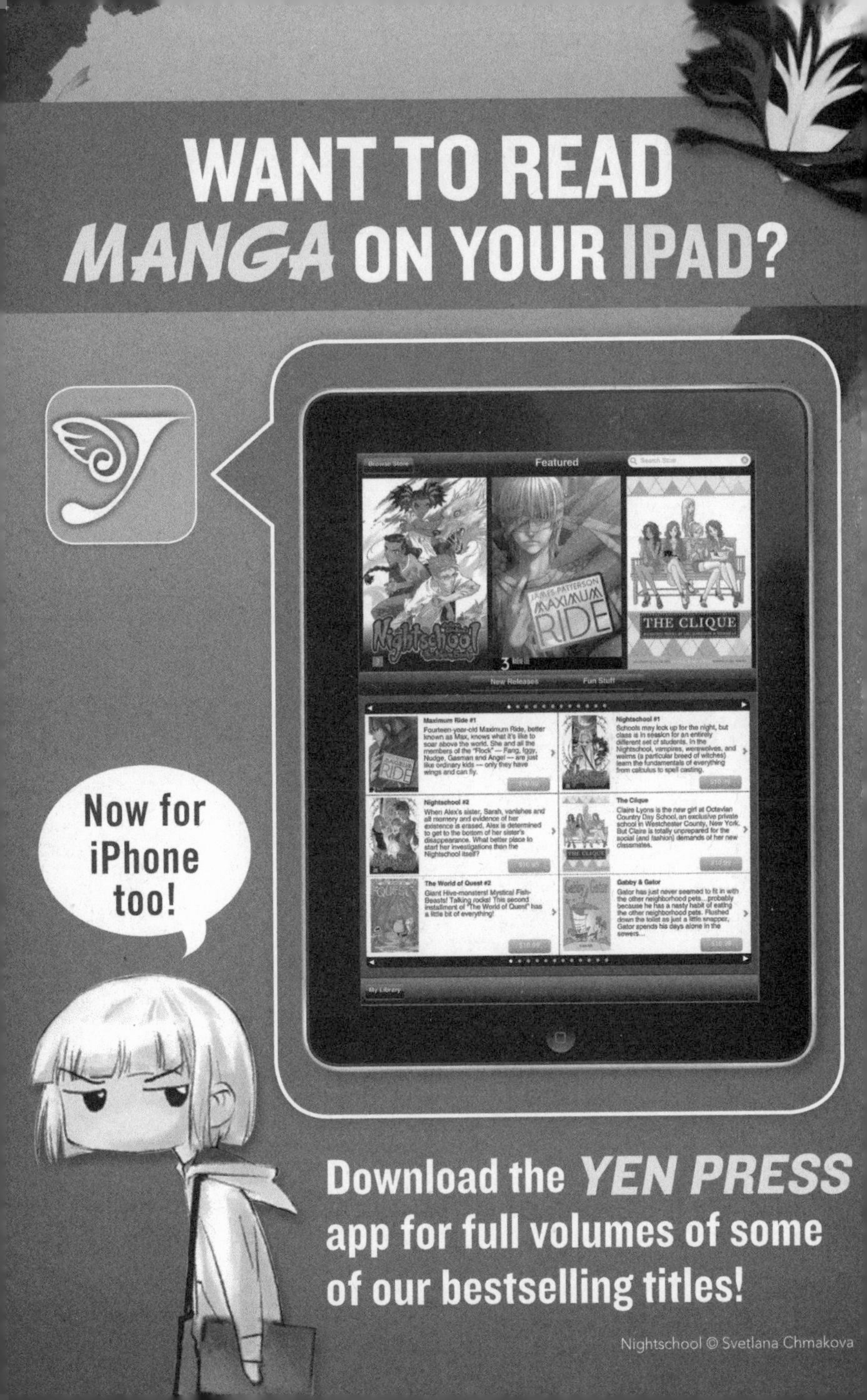
WANT TO READ
MANGA ON YOUR IPAD?
Now for iPhone too!
Download the YEN PRESS app for full volumes of some of our bestselling titles!
Nightschool © Svetlana Chmakova

THE MELANCHOLY OF HARUHI SUZUMIYA

Original Story: Nagaru Tanigawa
Manga: Gaku Tsugano
Character Design: Noizi Ito

Translation: Paul Starr
Lettering: Alexis Eckerman

This book is a work of fiction. Names, characters, places, and incidents are the product of the author's imagination or are used fictitiously. Any resemblance to actual events, locales, or persons, living or dead, is coincidental.

SUZUMIYA HARUHI NO YUUTSU Volume 17 © Nagaru TANIGAWA • Noizi ITO 2012 © Gaku TSUGANO 2012. Edited by KADOKAWA SHOTEN. First published in Japan in 2012 by KADOKAWA CORPORATION, Tokyo. English translation rights arranged with KADOKAWA CORPORATION, Tokyo, through Tuttle-Mori Agency, Inc., Tokyo.

English translation © 2013 by Hachette Book Group, Inc.

Yen Press
Hachette Book Group
237 Park Avenue, New York, NY 10017

www.HachetteBookGroup.com
www.YenPress.com

Yen Press is an imprint of Hachette Book Group, Inc. The Yen Press name and logo are trademarks of Hachette Book Group, Inc.

First Yen Press Edition: December 2013

ISBN: 978-0-316-32234-8

10 9 8 7 6 5 4 3 2 1

BVG

Printed in the United States of America

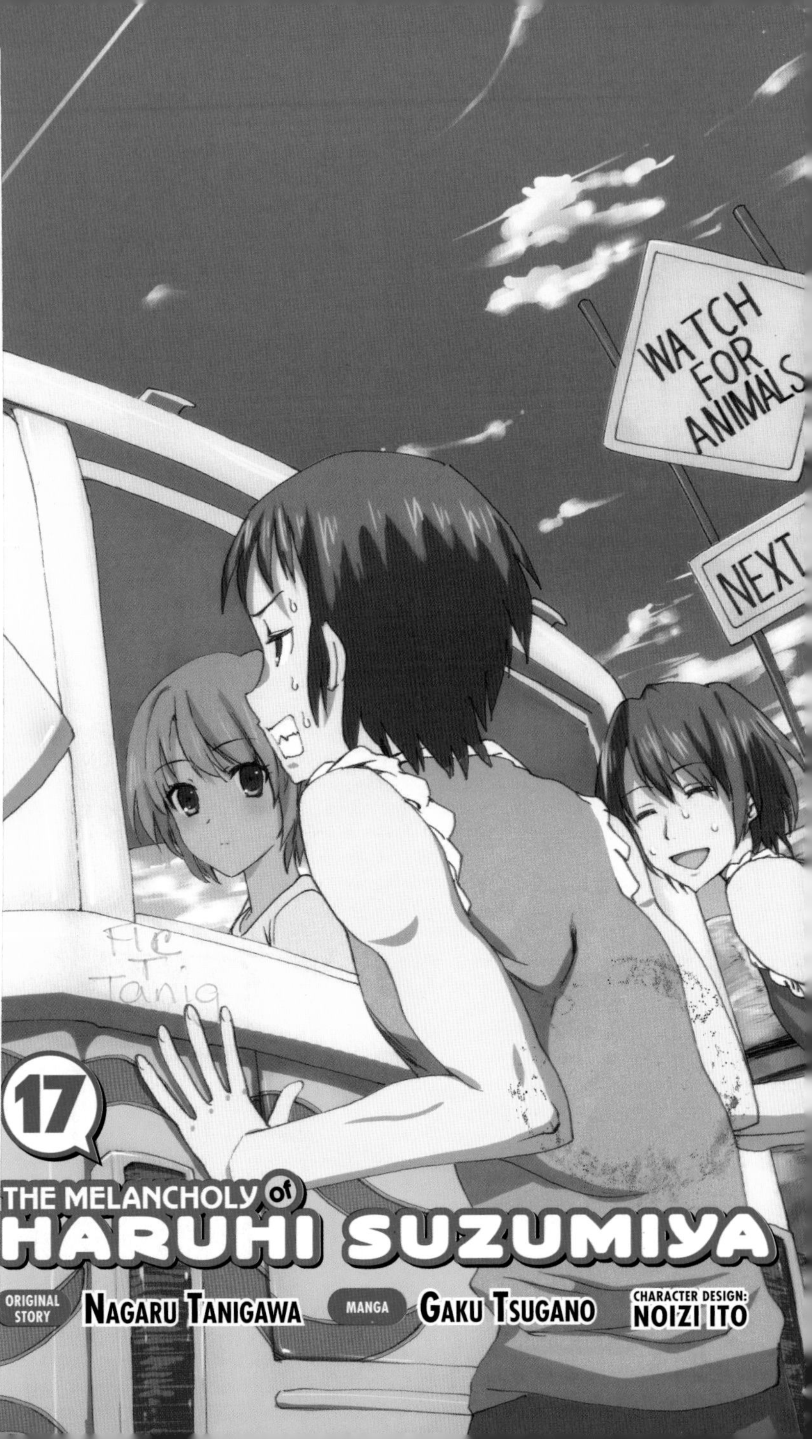
WATCH FOR ANIMALS
NEXT
17
THE MELANCHOLY of HARUHI SUZUMIYA
ORIGINAL STORY NAGARU TANIGAWA
MANGA GAKU TSUGANO
CHARACTER DESIGN: NOIZI ITO

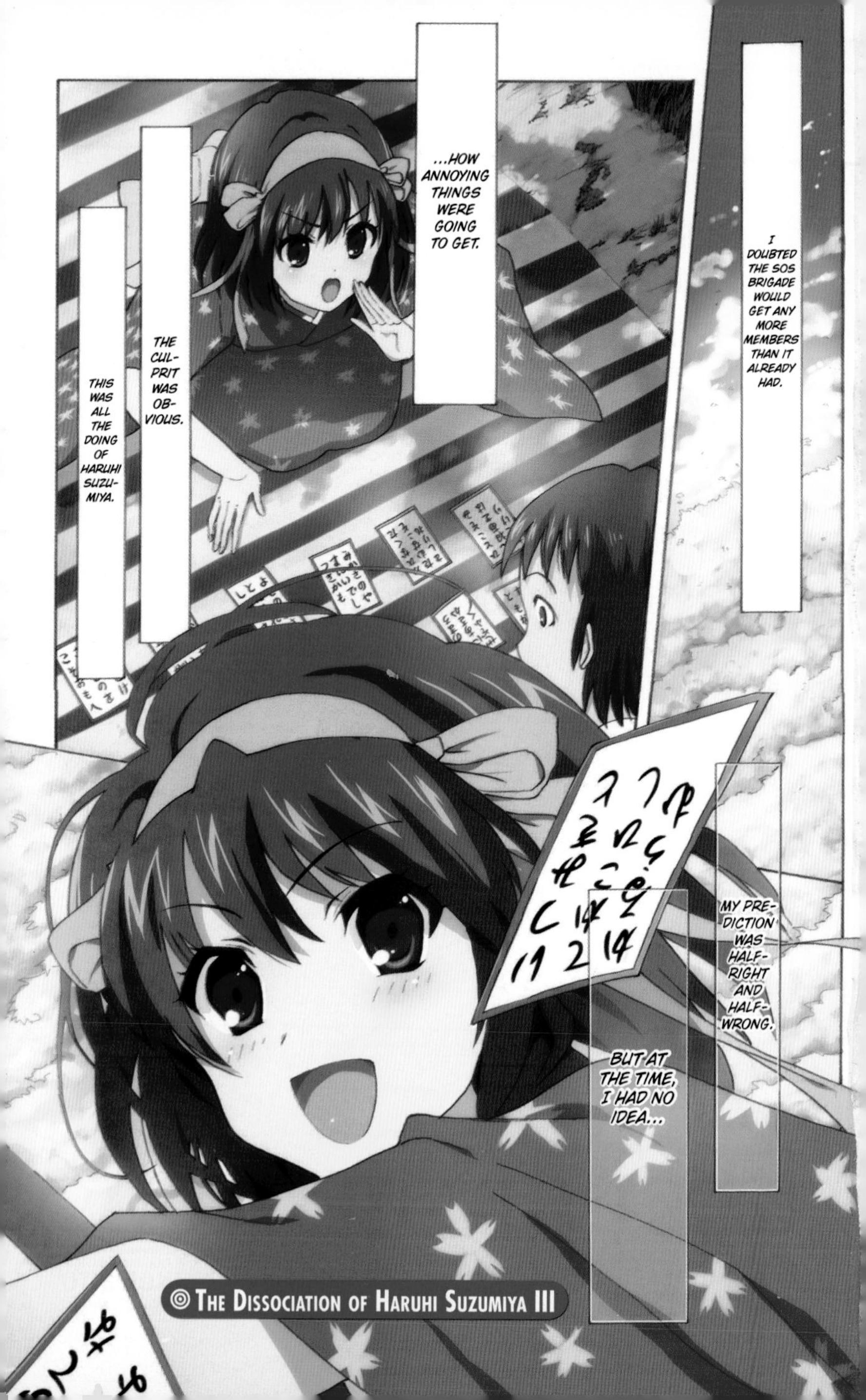
I DOUBTED THE SOS BRIGADE WOULD GET ANY MORE MEMBERS THAN IT ALREADY HAD.
...HOW ANNOYING THINGS WERE GOING TO GET.
THE CULPRIT WAS OBVIOUS.
THIS WAS ALL THE DOING OF HARUHI SUZUMIYA.
MY PREDICTION WAS HALF-RIGHT AND HALF-WRONG.
BUT AT THE TIME, I HAD NO IDEA...
THE DISSOCIATION OF HARUHI SUZUMIYA III